Catalogue presented by:
Rockwell Museum of Western Art

In conjunction with the exhibition

Crafted to Perfection:

The Nancy & Alan Cameros Collection of Southwestern Pottery

November 22, 2007-May 18, 2008

Rockwell Museum of Western Art
Corning, New York

Rockwell Museum of Western Art

Crafted to Perfection:

The Nancy & Alan Cameros Collection of Southwestern Pottery

Foreword by:
Dwight Lanmon

Written by:
Sheila K. Hoffman

Edited by:
Bryce T. Hoffman

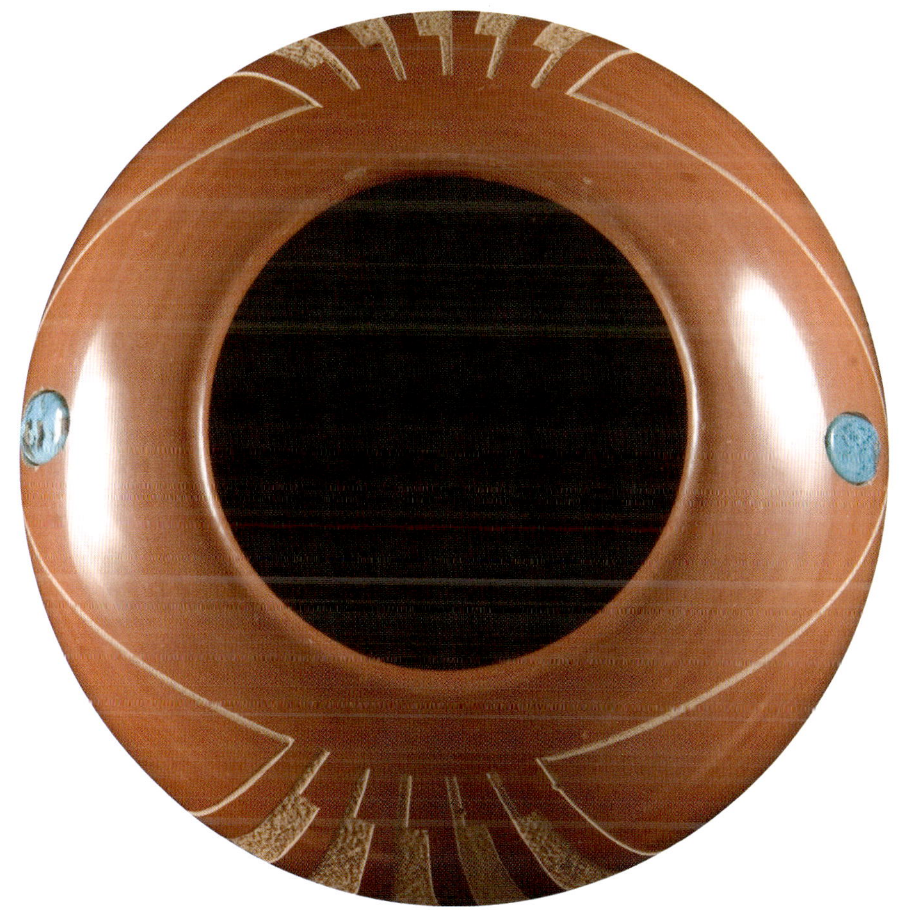

Staff

Gigi Alvaré
Director of Education

Andrew Braman
Controller

Patty Campbell
Executive Secretary

Lisa Combs
Admissions Coordinator

Sheila K. Hoffman
Curator of Collections

Dan Hoffmann
Registrar

Stafford Lyons
Museum Educator

Beth Manwaring
Marketing & Communications Specialist

Andrea Nichols
Administrative Assistant

Rita Reed
Accounting Assistant

Robert F. Rockwell, III
Preparator

Lori Rajsky
Education Coordinator

Kristin A. Swain
Executive Director

Cindy Weakland
Director of Public Programs & Visitor Services

ISBN: 9780976991915

Library of Congress Control Number: 2007931975

Produced by the Rockwell Museum of Western Art
In association with Nancy and Alan Cameros

Production and design by: osp catalogs
Photography by: Amy Cave, Earl Kage, and Maria Strinni Gill
Frontispiece: *Tony Da (San Ildefonso), redware jar with sgraffito and turquoise inlay, c. 1970.*

Contents

Steve Lucas, polychrome jar (detail), 2003.

Foreword

At first, it might seem a bit strange that a significant collection of 20th-century Southwestern Indian pottery is being shown at the Rockwell Museum of Western Art in Corning, New York—2,000 miles from its place of origin. How did this come to be? A partial answer may be found in the widespread appeal of the potter's art, but I think it relates primarily to the lives of three prolific art collectors and how their shared passion somehow converged in this small-but-cosmopolitan place.

The outstanding collection of Southwestern pottery that this catalogue records is the accomplishment of two collectors—Nancy and Alan Cameros of Rochester, New York. They amassed a very nice collection of glass art through the years, but during annual holidays in Taos, New Mexico, they also became aware of the artistry of contemporary pueblo potters, who have infused ancient techniques with new creativity and artistic power. The exhibition of the Cameros Collection at the Rockwell Museum demonstrates the enthusiasm and admiration that they have developed for the products of many of the most talented and respected Southwestern potters of the past 125 years.

The Rockwell Museum is the product of another prolific collector, Bob Rockwell, whose interest in the art and culture of the American West was awakened in childhood. He grew up on the western slope of the Rocky Mountains in Colorado, where he was surrounded by artifacts of the "Wild West." He could walk the fields and find arrowheads and other artifacts of cultures that had nearly disappeared from the landscape, but there were undoubtedly many around him who recalled when Indians lived there. These experiences sparked in him a fascination with objects of the West: Artifacts of the Indians and the cowboys and pictures and sculptures that evoked the not-so-distant past.

Family connections eventually brought Bob Rockwell east to New York, but he did not leave the West behind. When he assumed ownership of his uncle's department store in downtown Corning, he began to fill it with treasures ranging from petrified dinosaur dung to paintings by Remington and Russell. It was a cabinet of curiosities (in the Renaissance sense of collected things—natural and man-made—that evoke wonder), and it became a magnet for visitors from across the country. Beginning in 1976, the new Rockwell Museum began exhibiting many of those objects. Today, they continue to enthrall visitors from around the world in an expanded setting dedicated to Bob's love for Western art.

Like Bob Rockwell and the Cameros family, I feel a shared connection to Upstate New York, to the art of the American West, and to pueblo pottery. I grew up in Denver, and my family's collections included a box of Indian arrowheads, axes, and pottery. Of the stories that I heard from my grandparents and mother, many were about Indians. My grandparents, who also lived for a time on Colorado's western slope, recalled seeing the famous Utes, Chief Ouray and his wife, Chipeta, and they told me of the ancient dwellings at Mesa Verde and Chaco Canyon. These experiences awakened in me the interests that Bob Rockwell, the Cameroses, and I share today.

My wife and I moved to Corning in 1973, where I was associated with the Corning Museum of Glass and the Rockwell Museum. Before long, we began traveling to Santa Fe nearly every summer. We fell under the spell of the dramatic landscape, intense sun, brilliant turquoise sky, great food, stunning opera house, and ancient pueblo villages and cultures nearby. My boyhood disease of collecting, long dormant, went into full relapse as we began to acquire and study pueblo pottery. We retired to Santa Fe in 1999, and since that time we have become increasingly focused on studying pueblo pottery. Three books and several articles have resulted, with more on the way.

This brings me back to my original question: "Why would a collection of this nature end up on display in Corning, New York?" Some of the answers are obvious: family connections, family histories, and careers that are unrelated to collecting interests. But it is impossible to dismiss the unusual qualities and character of this small community. Corning may be somewhat physically isolated, but its residents are worldly in their ambitions and outlook. Corning is, in some ways, similar to Santa Fe. Interesting and interested people are drawn to them, both as visitors and as residents, and that is what keeps both places so vibrant, exciting, and satisfying. In other words, it is an ideal setting for the Cameros Collection of Southwestern pottery to find its audience, which in this case is not defined geographically but instead by a concentration of people who share an appreciation of artistry, craftsmanship, and an interest in what ancient traditions can tell us about the past and about life today. By displaying a collection that is so rich and diverse, the Rockwell Museum of Western Art contributes to the cultural enrichment of Corning's residents and its visitors. Southwestern pottery, as an art form, also benefits when it is treated as the Rockwell Museum treats it—as high art that merits serious attention anywhere in the world. Finally, by staging special exhibitions such as *Crafted to Perfection: The Nancy & Alan Cameros Collection of Southwestern Pottery*, the museum complements its own collections and enhances the quality of life in an amazing city that my wife and I enjoyed for 19 years and today remember fondly.

Dwight P. Lanmon
Retired Director, Corning Museum of Glass
Former President, Board of Trustees, Rockwell Museum

"Creation" (detail) by Lawrence Namoki, incised polychrome, 2005.

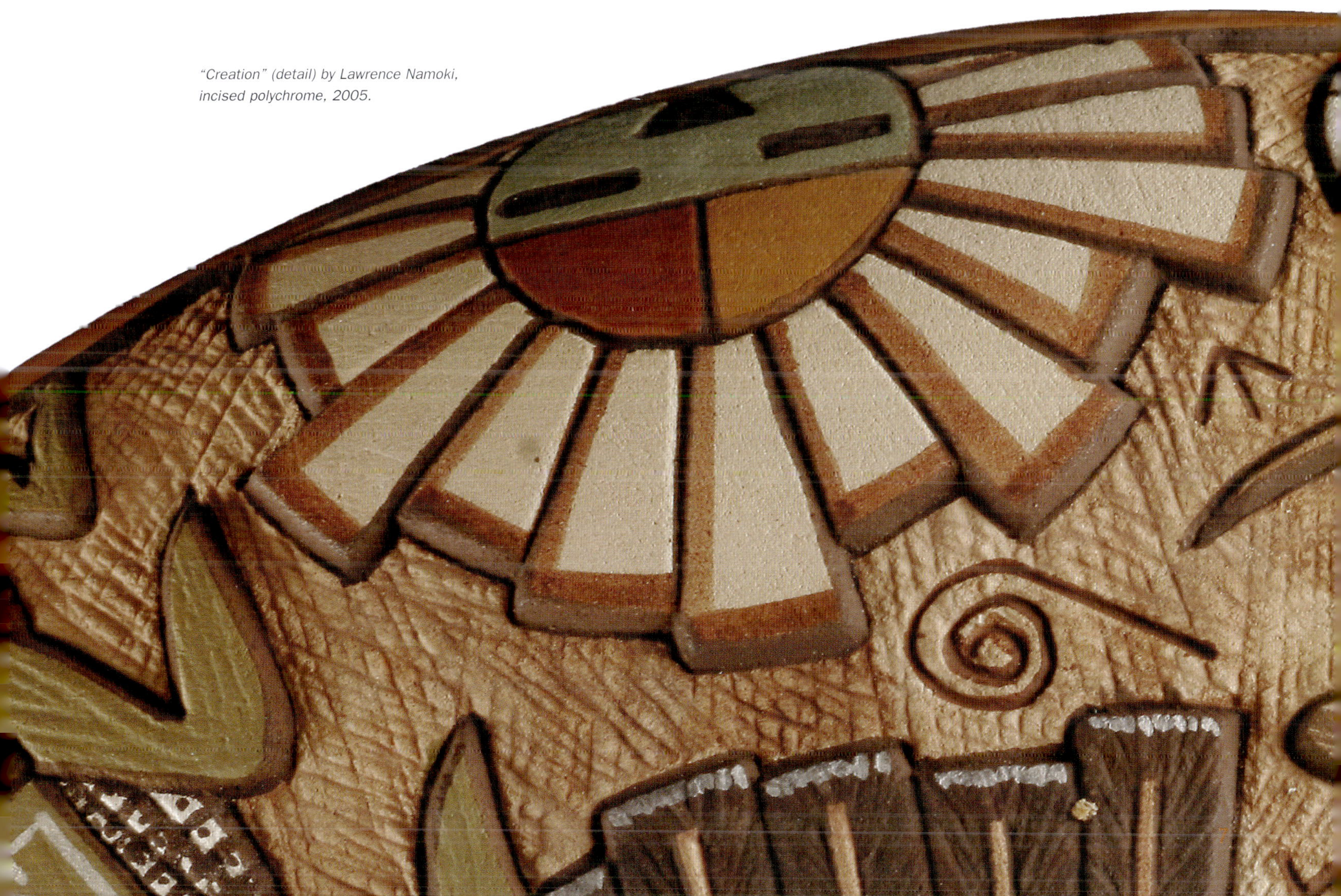

Director's Acknowledgements

For more than 30 years, the Rockwell Museum of Western Art has preserved, interpreted, and enhanced its collections while engaging countless local residents, visitors, students, scholars, and collectors in special exhibitions, which awaken insight and deepen understanding of the rich cultures and traditions of the American West.

With the exhibition *Crafted to Perfection: The Nancy & Alan Cameros Collection of Southwestern Pottery*, the Rockwell Museum hones its mission and expands its scope to include the medium of clay. We are pleased to present some 100 pieces of Native American pottery from the remarkable collection of Nancy and Alan Cameros of Rochester, New York. The Cameroses have collected Southwestern pottery with a passion that is reflected in the diversity of pieces they have generously loaned to the Rockwell. Crafted by artists often related by clan, the form, function, and finishes of the pottery are varied and replete with ancient symbols, geometric designs, and innovative approaches to customary subjects. Produced through a wealth of traditional and nontraditional techniques, the work has the capacity to connect the viewer to relational themes of family, time, space, and our place in the outer environment. While visually dissimilar in many instances, the vessels share a unifying spirit of creative awareness, expressing multiple perceptions of what it means to connect also with the inner landscape, thus potentially linking us to universal threads in the human experience.

With *Crafted to Perfection*, the Rockwell Museum offers a vibrant and enlightening opportunity to individuals in the region. An important focus for the Board of Trustees and staff of the Museum, however, is connecting also with the world beyond the Chemung Valley. Dwight Lanmon makes the point eloquently in his Foreword to this catalogue. It, indeed, is about connection on several levels. And, sometimes, it is about connecting instances of seeming serendipity, and then recognizing when a golden chance emerges to expand the arts experience for audiences from near and far, today and tomorrow.

My gratitude goes out to several people who made this exhibition and catalogue possible. Most important, I want to thank Nancy and Alan Cameros for their interest in the Rockwell Museum, for their passion for learning about the art and history of Southwestern pottery, and for their unwavering persistence and enthusiasm for making this project a reality. To Dwight Lanmon, I extend a heartfelt thank you, not only for his contribution to this catalogue but also for his continuing interest in the Rockwell Museum and for his scholarship and guidance on the exploration of Native American craftsmanship.

And, to Sheila Hoffman, Curator of Collections, I extend special recognition for her development of the exhibition and its accompanying catalogue. Sheila has worked tirelessly in collaboration with the Cameroses. Her leadership, attention to detail, and enthusiasm have made an important contribution to the history and study of Southwestern pottery.

I invite you, now, to discover the collection that Nancy and Alan Cameros began more than 25 years ago, and to explore their connections with an extraordinary group of Southwestern craftswomen, craftsmen, and the objects of their artistry. As did Bob Rockwell before them, the Cameroses have created an outstanding collection that is characterized by depth and discernment, and I thank them for the privilege of presenting some of their treasures to the varied audiences of the Museum. Finally, I thank you, the reader, for continuing on the Rockwell Museum's journey, and I hope that a few discoveries await you as well!

Kristin A. Swain
Executive Director
Rockwell Museum of Western Art

Author's Note

Shortly after joining the Rockwell Museum of Western Art in 2004, I was introduced to Nancy and Alan Cameros and their incredible collection of Southwestern pottery. Though my art historical expertise lay elsewhere, it was easy to recognize the significance of this collection, which had never been shown publicly. It was obvious that the collectors wanted to find just the right venue to share their passion for pottery with a larger audience. I am pleased that they placed their faith in the Rockwell Museum and me.

As with all projects of this magnitude, little could have been accomplished without the enthusiasm and support of many. First, I am grateful to the Native American artists past and present who are responsible for these exceptional works of art and who are the latter day stewards of an ancient tradition. I am especially appreciative of the potters who allowed me to interview them in the course of my research: Autumn Borts-Medlock, Preston Duwyenie, Tammy Garcia, Greg Lonewolf, Rosemary Lonewolf, Jody Naranjo, Les Namingha, Virgil Ortiz, Al Qöyawayma, Susan Romero, Richard Zane Smith, Lonnie Vigil, Nancy Youngblood, and Nathan Youngblood.

Several galleries and scholars made themselves indispensable by fielding my never-ending questions. Among them are Blue Rain Gallery and Leroy Garcia, Wright's Indian Art Gallery and Judith Bennet, and Martha Hopkins-Struever.

For their extraordinary hospitality during my travels for this project, a quick but heartfelt thank you goes to Joe and Lisa McCutcheon, innkeepers at Casa Europa in Taos, New Mexico.

I am grateful to Dwight Lanmon for letting me persuade him to write the Foreword to this catalogue. His contribution—as a past president of the Rockwell Museum, and as a pottery scholar—is a valuable addition to this catalogue and exhibition.

I owe a great deal to my reviewers, most of whom sought no credit for poring over page after page and providing timely feedback. You know who you are; please also know the extent of my gratitude. Among these, special thanks go to G. Peter Jemison, Historic Site Manager, Ganondagan State Historic Site, who served as a sounding board for my ideas and a guide to cultural sensitivities. A friend to the collectors and to this museum, he continues to be one of my most valuable resources.

To Charles King, I am simply indebted forever. After being initially inspired by an article of his, I continued to seek his counsel as the catalogue progressed. Charles responded with amazing generosity, ultimately reading and vetting most aspects of this catalogue. The passion and knowledge he has for Southwestern pottery is immense and invaluable. The catalogue has benefited from his insight and opinions, and is an unquestionably superior product because of him.

This project would not have been possible without the personal and professional encouragement of my husband and editor, Bryce T. Hoffman. His expertise honed the text of this volume, while his love and support made it possible to complete this catalogue during my developing pregnancy.

Finally, it has been a pleasure and honor to work with Nancy and Alan Cameros. They have acted not only as lenders and sponsors but also as readers and resources. They have placed extraordinary trust in me and provided unflagging encouragement. Their passion for Southwestern art has found a new disciple in me. I only hope that my efforts herein do it justice.

Sheila K. Hoffman
Curator of Collections
Rockwell Museum of Western Art

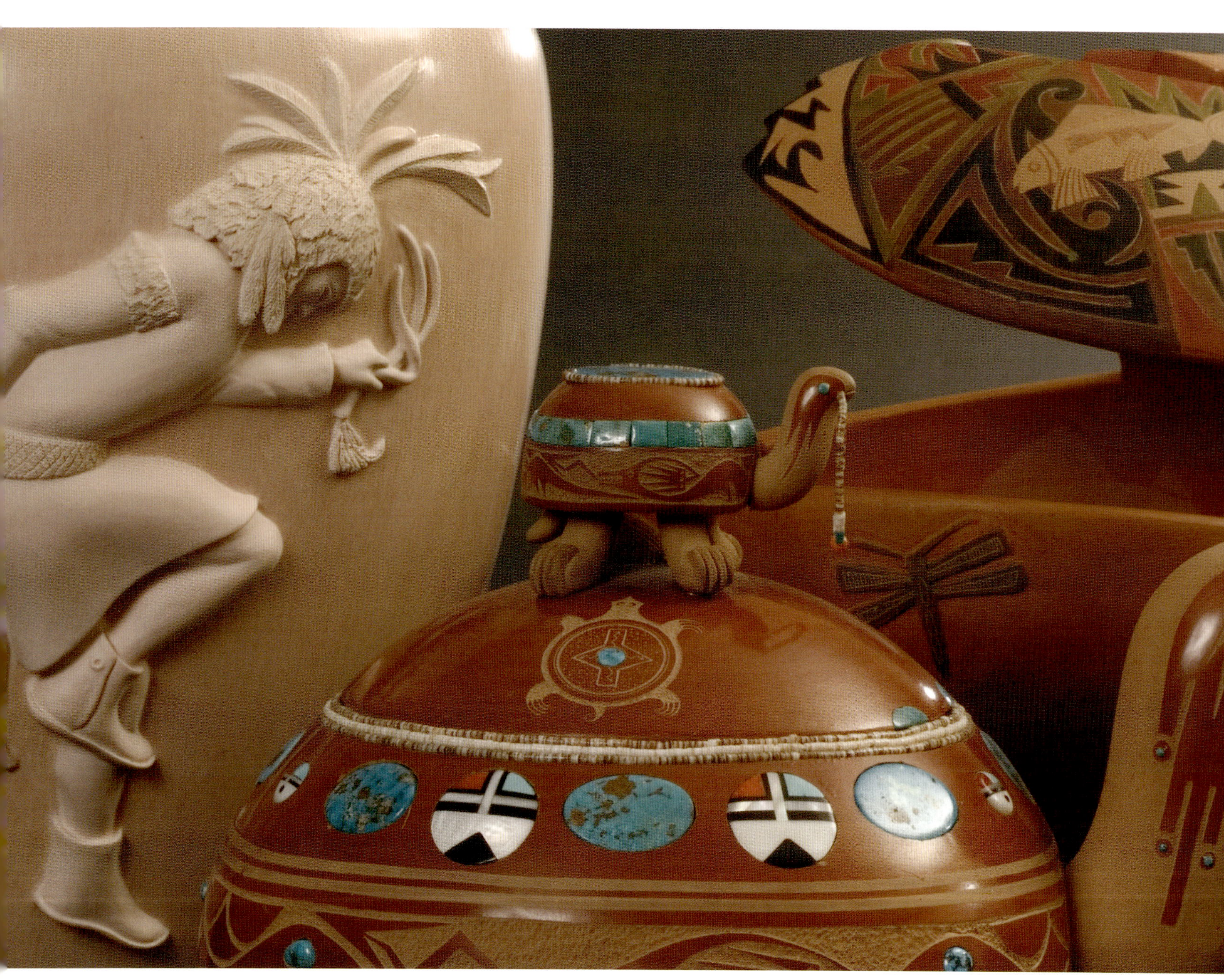

A few of the Cameros's favorite pieces within their collection (L-R)
Al Qöyawayma, buffware vase with Buffalo Dancer, 1991.
Tony Da, sculpted redware turtle, c. 1975.
Grace Medicine Flower, redware cut out with polychrome, 2005.

Crafted to Perfection:

The Nancy & Alan Cameros Collection of Southwestern Pottery

Introduction to the Collection

"Be careful with her. She's a sweet old lady, and she doesn't like to be moved," Nancy Cameros cautions her husband with nearly suspended breath, as if the slightest puff of air might jeopardize the operation at hand. It is easy to see why. Nancy's husband, Alan, has just picked up a small, ancient pot from one of the many display cases that surround their living room. Pottery, from the large and colorful to the dainty and delicate, covers these shelves. The pot that Alan cups in his hands is one of the oldest and most fragile, and has the added distinction of being attributed to one of the great matriarchs of the Southwestern pottery tradition, Nampeyo of Hano.

For a curator, it is touching to hear collectors speak of their treasures as people; perhaps even more so to see an influential businessman cradle an old piece of clay as if it were a baby bird fallen from its nest. Collectors are always motivated by personal interest, and many by passion; but it is investment value that typically dictates purchase. Cost is understood to reflect intrinsic value, and justifiably so. But it is always exciting to come upon those who share such an enormous respect for art that the dollar value someone else has placed on a work becomes merely a factor of acquisition, not the reason for it.

Nancy and Alan Cameros are just such collectors. In a quarter century, these lifelong Rochester residents have amassed a collection of more than 200 pieces of Southwestern pottery—not just any pieces, but museum-quality examples of some of the finest Native American potters of the past 125 years. And while this catalogue and the Rockwell Museum of Western Art exhibition, *Crafted to Perfection: The Nancy & Alan Cameros Collection of Southwestern Pottery*, pay homage to the intrinsic value of this collection, the Cameroses never collected with the intent of boasting. Instead,

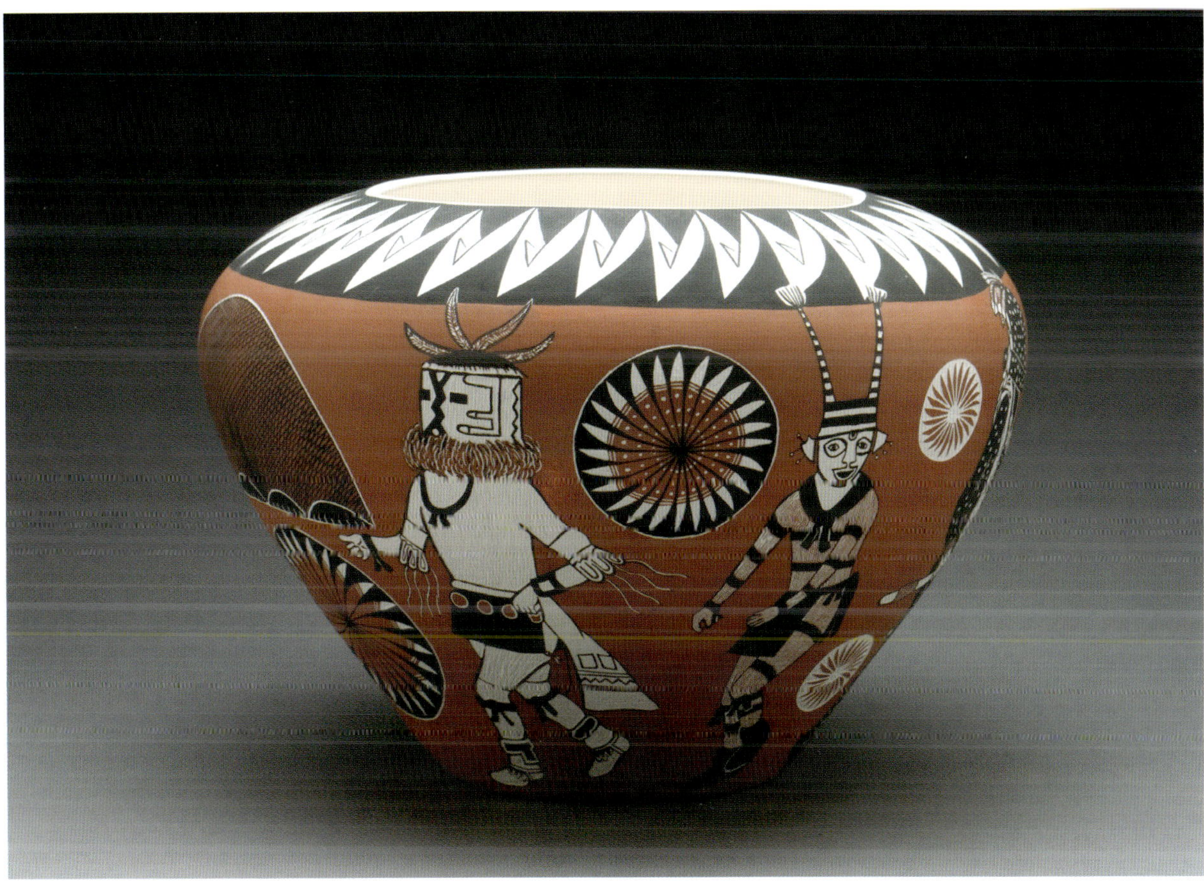

The first piece of pottery purchased by Nancy and Alan Cameros. Souvenir greenware.

they have always collected from a place of interest-turned-passion; along the way, they have developed a keen eye for it.

The Cameroses began collecting in the early 1980s when Alan's position as chairman of the Museum Trustee Association took him to Santa Fe to scout the location for the association's annual meeting. Ten years earlier, Alan qualified to become a docent for the Memorial Art Gallery in Rochester and was soon after appointed to the Board of Directors, giving him eligibility to join the Museum

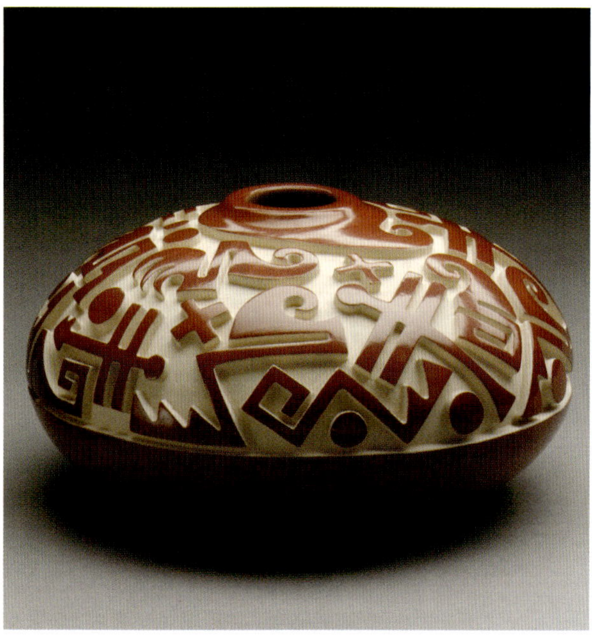

The first piece of Tammy Garcia's pottery acquired for the Cameros Collection. Redware with white slip and dragonfly motif, 1994.

Trustee Association. Around this time, Nancy and Alan also became members of the Corning Museum of Glass and began collecting glass art.

During this first trip to the Southwest, they purchased what Nancy calls "a pretty souvenir"—a large piece of greenware pottery from the Acoma Pueblo. They paid $250. Greenware is essentially unfired clay pottery that is usually cast-formed and mass-produced. These "blanks" are then quickly painted and sold to tourists.

Every collector has to start somewhere, and Nancy and Alan soon learned the difference between that first purchase and the exceptional art that exemplifies the best of Southwestern pottery. From that year forward, the Cameroses have made an annual trip to the Santa Fe and Taos areas—budget and wish list in hand. Early on they met Leroy Garcia, founder of Blue Rain Gallery and husband of Tammy Garcia, an award-winning potter from the Santa Clara Pueblo.

With his help, Nancy and Alan gained a quick appreciation for what constituted quality in pottery, and they began to collect seriously. Pottery from Santa Clara was an obvious starting point. Tammy Garcia is well known for a style descended from one of the great matriarchs of Santa Clara, Sara Fina Tafoya—a style of high polish and precision carving. In many ways, it exemplified what Nancy and Alan appreciated about glass art. By examining exceptional Santa Clara pottery, the Cameroses learned to identify subtle differences in shapes, skillful carving, and excellent polishing. They also became aware of the importance of the potter and his or her individual contribution to a style. From then on, the product of an individual's talent would trump a mass-produced piece.

This in mind, Nancy and Alan began to form relationships with potters. Through these interactions, they began to more fully understand the distinct pottery styles from different pueblos and reservations. Their method of collecting began to take shape: They prefer to identify emerging talent and to establish lasting relationships within the current generation of potters, though they stay alert for pieces by famous potters of the past.

Friend of the collectors and Scottsdale gallery owner Charles King calls Nancy and Alan "risk takers" who have a gift for recognizing burgeoning talent in young potters. The Cameroses are more modest. "We're just having fun!" Nancy says. "Yes, we look for standard bearers, but we want pieces that speak to us personally, something that catches our eyes." Alan admits that it is Nancy who has the eye for craftsmanship, something she inherited from her many family members who have worked in the glass industry. He relates a story that exemplifies Nancy's ability.

While visiting the Antique Indian Art Show in Santa Fe, Nancy spotted an unlabled redware pot with a *sgraffito* (shallow surface scratch) feather pattern and turquoise

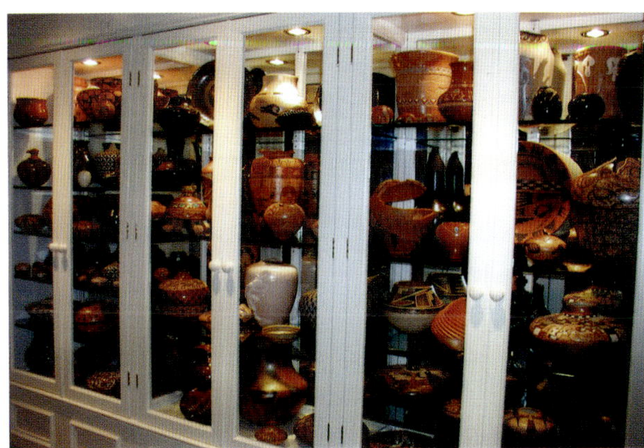

Some of the Cameros Collection on display in their living room.

inlay. She immediately felt sure that it was a quintessential pot by Tony Da, grandson of Maria Martinez, matriarch of the San Ildefonso pottery tradition. Da's grandfather, Julian Martinez, is said to have revived the feather pattern from ancient pueblo ware. Da's father, Popovi Da, was among the first to experiment with both *sgraffito* and turquoise inlay—techniques Tony Da later perfected. The person tending the booth seemed unaware of the importance of this pot among the many others for sale and quoted an attractive purchase price. When the owner returned, he agreed to complete the sale in good-natured esteem of Nancy's ability to recognize exceptional work. The pot was later found to have been pictured in a book by Richard Spivey, "The Legacy of Maria Poveka Martinez"—a quintessential Tony Da indeed. (See frontispiece.)

For reasons such as these, the Cameros Collection is perhaps a more intimate reflection of the owners than other private collections. This becomes obvious upon seeing the collection *in situ* in their Rochester home. Almost the entire collection is on display in their living room. Yet, this is not as ostentatious as it might sound. Their living room is a modest space, not the large gallery one might expect, and space for new pottery is limited. Excellence abounds in their collection because there is no room for mediocrity. For this reason, the Cameroses not only have to make the difficult decision of what to acquire, but at this point they sometimes have to determine what they are willing to part with—a process they term "deaccessioning."

This term is accurate and appropriate, but mostly it is impressive that they use the term at all. "Deaccessioning" is museum language. It refers to the organized procedure by which a museum will formally remove an object from its permanent collection after much research and debate. It is not merely a matter of getting rid of a work of art. The process is always difficult and sensitive. So it is, in a way, comforting that these collectors use the term. It underscores the significant level of consideration with which they undertake any object removal, and it demonstrates the primacy given to the emotional value of every piece they have acquired. As "risk-takers," they understand that some risks disappoint. Sometimes Nancy & Alan have to admit that an artist did not grow in his or her abilities, as they once thought he or she would. So they will deaccession a technically excellent piece in favor of an artist who shows equal ability but more promise.

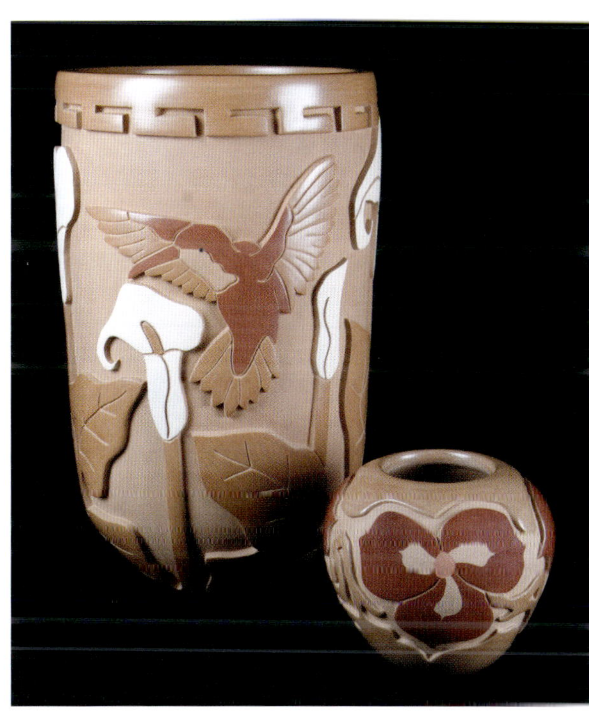

Pieces by Autumn Borts-Medlock in the Cameros Collection. (L-R) polychrome redware "Hummingbird" vase, 2001; polychrome redware "flower" jar, 1995.

They cite two examples where crucial collecting decisions have been made because of a potter's maturing ability. They currently own three pieces by Autumn Borts-Medlock, another Santa Clara potter they admire and sister of Tammy Garcia. They have come very close to owning several pots by Autumn at different times, but they feel strongly that the pots in their collection today best represent her style and ability. Nancy and Alan spent a great deal of time determining which of her pieces to purchase, and on one occasion Alan camped out in line all night before the famous annual Indian Market to obtain one of Autumn's works. Likewise, they have not purchased other of her pieces that became available to them when they believed that an evolving style was not exemplified therein. In another instance, a few years ago, they acquired a piece by a potter of Hopi descent, Lawrence Namoki. At the time of purchase, during a visit to Namoki's native home on the First Mesa, the piece

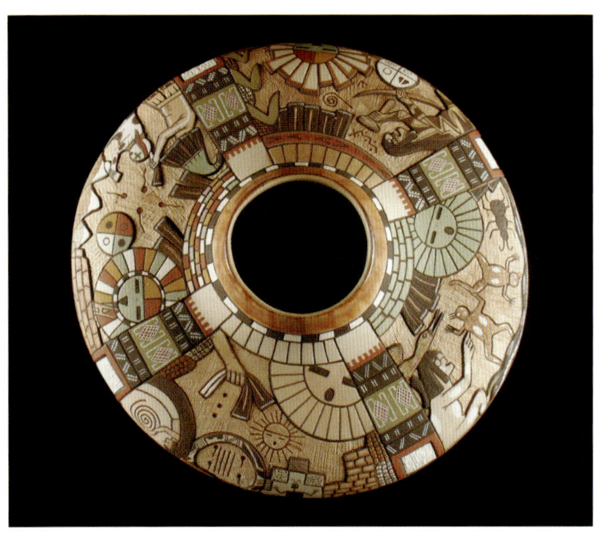

"Creation" by Lawrence Namoki, incised polychrome, 2005.

was only a concept in the artist's mind. After Namoki described a pot representing the cycle of Creation, Nancy and Alan agreed to purchase the work so that he could undertake his design. That "Creation" pot was the prototype for what has become one of his most sought-after designs.

A collection of quality, not quantity, is clearly Nancy and Alan's ultimate goal, which bodes well for a collection that already exceeds 200 pieces. At the same time, they are trying to balance works that are unique with those that exemplify a style. Whereas they used to arrive early at Indian Market, queuing with hundreds of other collectors to try to buy that special piece, they now rely more on their relationships with gallery owners and the reach of the Internet to locate works to add to their collection. They acknowledge that the Internet does, in some ways, make collecting harder rather than easier. "It's like being a kid in a candy store," laughs Alan. And they freely admit to "blowing their budget" when they covet an outstanding piece. At least they almost always agree on what to purchase. They have also entered that next echelon of collectors who commission unique works rather than wait to chance upon them.

It is fitting that their current commission is with Tammy Garcia, whose work they have adored from the beginning. Once completed, the commissioned pot will be the largest in their collection, surpassing both the greenware pot they first purchased as well as a rare storage jar created by Sara Fina Tafoya, Garcia's great-great-grandmother and matriarch of the Santa Clara pottery tradition. In addition, the commissioned pot will illustrate *koshari* (pueblo clowns) carved in a narrative around the vessel. The Cameros's 2-year old grandson served as inspiration for including these clowns. Yet, subconsciously or not, and for all their acquired knowledge, the same taste that inspired their first purchase is guiding this commission, for *koshari* are the same figures that appear on their greenware.

"When we tell acquaintances that we collect pottery, most people seem to think that we collect some sort of kitchen crockery," quips Nancy. This is not surprising, considering how close the couple lives to Corning, New York, formerly the epicenter of the kitchenware industry. Apparently this is a more natural conclusion to reach than that anyone would amass a collection of Southwestern pottery in the Northeastern United States. It is not so different from the Rockwell Museum of Western Art's founding collector, Bob Rockwell, who established in Upstate New York an enormous and excellent collection of art inspired by the American West. Like Bob Rockwell, the Cameroses collect what *they* like. They are not misguided or unschooled, and they are not put off by the seeming oddness of feeling an affinity for things foreign to their immediate surroundings.

Also similar to Bob Rockwell, they do not particularly care what others think of their collecting practices. Alan sees

Southwestern pottery as an under-recognized art form in the East, and Nancy hopes that, through their collection, people will gain an appreciation for the vessels they find so inspiring. "We're no pottery scholars," she admits. "This is a personal collection, collected for personal reasons." Which is why sometimes, late at night, Nancy and Alan will go into the living room to sit with the pieces, admiring the craftsmanship of each pot. Pottery scholars may or may not agree, but for the Cameroses, their collection continues to be crafted to perfection.

Sheila K. Hoffman
Curator of Collections
Rockwell Museum of Western Art

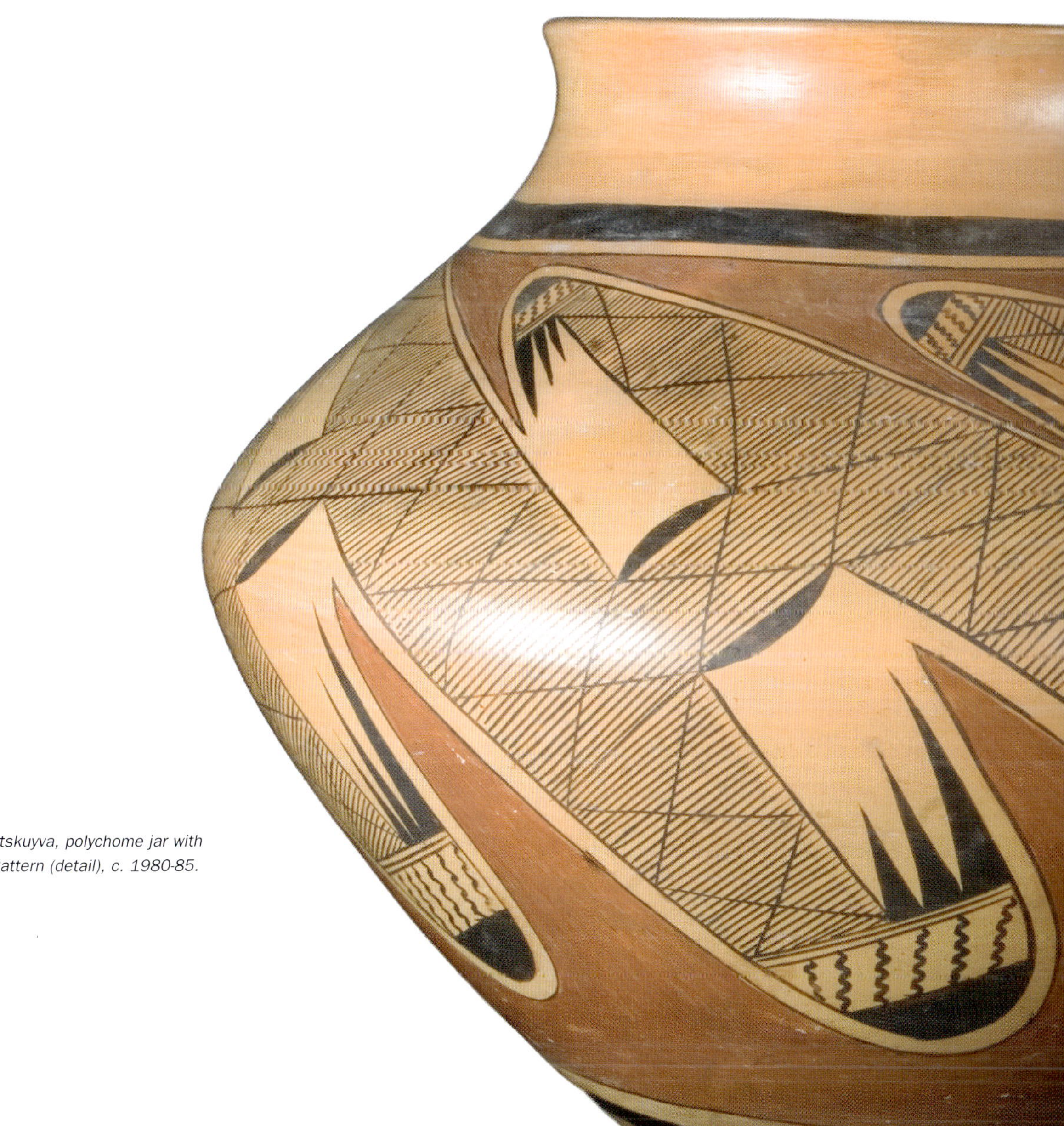

Dextra Quotskuyva, polychome jar with Migration Pattern (detail), c. 1980-85.

Preface

Southwestern pottery is at the forefront of art historical recognition and has been written about exhaustively by scholars as well as amateurs. Pottery catalogues abound, and they address subtopics of the field too numerous to mention. This volume attempts to contribute value to this wider discussion by accounting for one of the significant private collections in this field. Moreover, it is hoped that the organizational structure of the book itself might challenge long-held assumptions about how Native pottery is considered and classified.

One thing that books about Southwestern pottery tend to share is a particular structure, one that organizes works according to either the potters' matriarchal lineages, or their ancestral geographic homes (i.e. their pueblo or tribal reservation). Such categories are remnants of an era when Euro-American archeologists and anthropologists studied Southwestern pottery as artifacts of "primitive" cultures and peoples. These scholars coldly recorded the physical appearance of these vessels and their locus of discovery, speculating about their significance. The artistry was of secondary concern, if it was noticed at all.

Today, we are somewhat removed from the prejudice of that era. We no longer dismiss traditional art forms from indigenous cultures as mere craft. Southwestern pottery is regarded as equal if not superior to the finest European and Asian ceramics. Yet, we still tend to classify these works of art in an archaic manner, relying on the familiar-but-flawed taxonomy of early anthropologists to inform our views of art. Pueblo, tribe, matriarchal lineage...these attributions have their uses, but they inhibit both novice and expert from appreciating the individual and collective artistry of Southwestern pottery. Furthermore, such rigid codification chafes when applied to the potters of today, whose Native lineage is often mixed and whose styles frequently represent cross-influence at its finest.

So, in devising the structure of this catalogue, it became apparent that it must reflect the tastes of the collectors, the collection itself, and the artists' works within. The accepted method of objective, academic organization was poorly suited to illuminating a subjectively composed private collection. A new method was needed. Charles King, of the King Galleries of Scottsdale, Arizona, deserves credit for inspiring the structure that became a solution for this book. His article in the winter 2005 *American Indian Art Magazine*, "Pueblo Pottery: From Folk Art to Fine Art" divided contemporary potters (those producing in the past 30 years) into three groups: The Foundation, Contemporary Traditionalists, and Contemporary Innovators. After a discussion with Charles King, he generously gave permission to use his ideas as a springboard.

For the purposes of this catalogue, which comprises work from more than 100 years of Southwestern pottery, Charles King's categories needed to be expanded and altered. It seemed clear that this catalogue should begin with the great matriarchs who revived or created traditions in their respective pueblos or reservations. From there, it seemed initially obvious that some potters since that time became known for either preserving tradition (traditionalists, if you will) or expanding upon it (innovators).

However, these latter categories are inherently problematic, making the process of separating the majority of artists between them challenging. First, the meanings of the words "traditional" and "innovative" have become depreciated and stereotyped through overuse. Second, arguments could be made that many "traditionalists" experimented while many "innovators" were bound by tradition, further muddying the waters. Finally, at the crux of all of this is that, in an effort to compensate for past ignorance toward Native culture, non-Natives are hesitant to be critical. Would a potter be angry at being labeled traditional? Is it more politically correct to call contemporary work innovative? Upon reflection of these issues, this catalogue presents the Cameros Collection in the following manner:

The Great Mothers:
Though the body of this catalogue begins with the founders and revivers of the current tradition, it is not intended to hold a linear or chronological progression from thenceforth. These founders, the matriarchs, are termed "The Great Mothers" and are honored separately, providing historic information intended to inform the novice reader as to the beginnings of the current iterations of this art form.

However, the entirety of the Cameros Collection, including all the pieces by the matriarchs, could not be accommodated in the exhibition. An appendix to this catalogue provides a complete visual listing of the collection. Since it is admittedly simple to reference artists geographically, the appendix follows the more accepted methods of categorization—divided first by pueblo or reservation, then by family relations if such is well represented within the collection.

Artists Without Reservation:
After "The Great Mothers," the reader proceeds to a section on innovative potters within the collection. This grouping had to be harshly defined as well as relabeled. There is a superfluity of the term "innovator" as used to describe Southwestern potters. Indeed, it is a covetable characterization, for it automatically conveys an air of distinction among the throngs of potters in the Southwest. But its use has proliferated to a point where it no longer expresses true merit or meaning.

This desire to be known as innovative is relatively new among Southwestern potters. For decades, there existed a preference for tradition because pueblos and reservations benefited directly from an art market that favored traditional styles. Such demand-based markets encourage repetition, not experimentation. The pueblos and reservations likewise discouraged variation for fear of losing market share. Thus, in order to escape such stylistic constraints, an artist who wishes to truly innovate must be either successful enough to withstand the possible financial loss or daring enough to defy both market and community.

For this reason, this last section is titled "Artists Without Reservation." The potters assigned to this section are not constrained by manmade boundaries, be they geographical or philosophical. These potters are blending traditional styles from one region to another, and some are even adapting influences from other continents. Not all of these artists are contemporary (meaning "of this current generation"). People tend to conflate the term "contemporary" with a stylistic judgment, implying "innovative." However many current potters adhere strictly to traditional styles, while even "The Great Mothers" were innovators. Rather, our "Artists Without Reservation" are recognized as the vanguard of things to come no matter their generation.

Keepers of Tradition:
Finally, the last chapter is dedicated to the "Keepers of Tradition." Though the group name has been changed from "traditionalists," this is no attempt to beguile the reader (or pacify the potter) through word-smithing. Rather, it is an effort to replace the insinuation of stagnancy or mimicry with an association of honor and reverence for one's past. These "Keepers of Tradition" should be seen as mediums for the same spirit that guided their ancestors. These potters have become the means for perfecting methods of the past, continuing to fill their vessels with the ether of creativity, skill, and culture that is tradition.

Within the "Keepers of Tradition" grouping, the objects are arranged stylistically. This format is intended to promote a visual comprehension of the stylistic trends both within and among families and pueblos reservations. It should help the novice gain a better understanding of technique, and the expert a more encompassing view of the collection.

In a collection that is based on excellence, division into categories such as the ones proposed here cannot mean hierarchy—merely distinction. Both excellence and risk-taking are characteristics of the Cameros Collection on the whole, and perhaps these terms apply both to our "traditionalists," who exemplify excellence in established methods, and to our "innovators," who take risks in extension of these traditions. And yet, in defiance of any category, there is no status more significant than being admitted into a collection of quality. Nancy and Alan Cameros have decided which works merit their respect. It is now up to the reader to discover why.

Sandra Victorino, whiteware with swirled fine line pattern (detail), 2000.

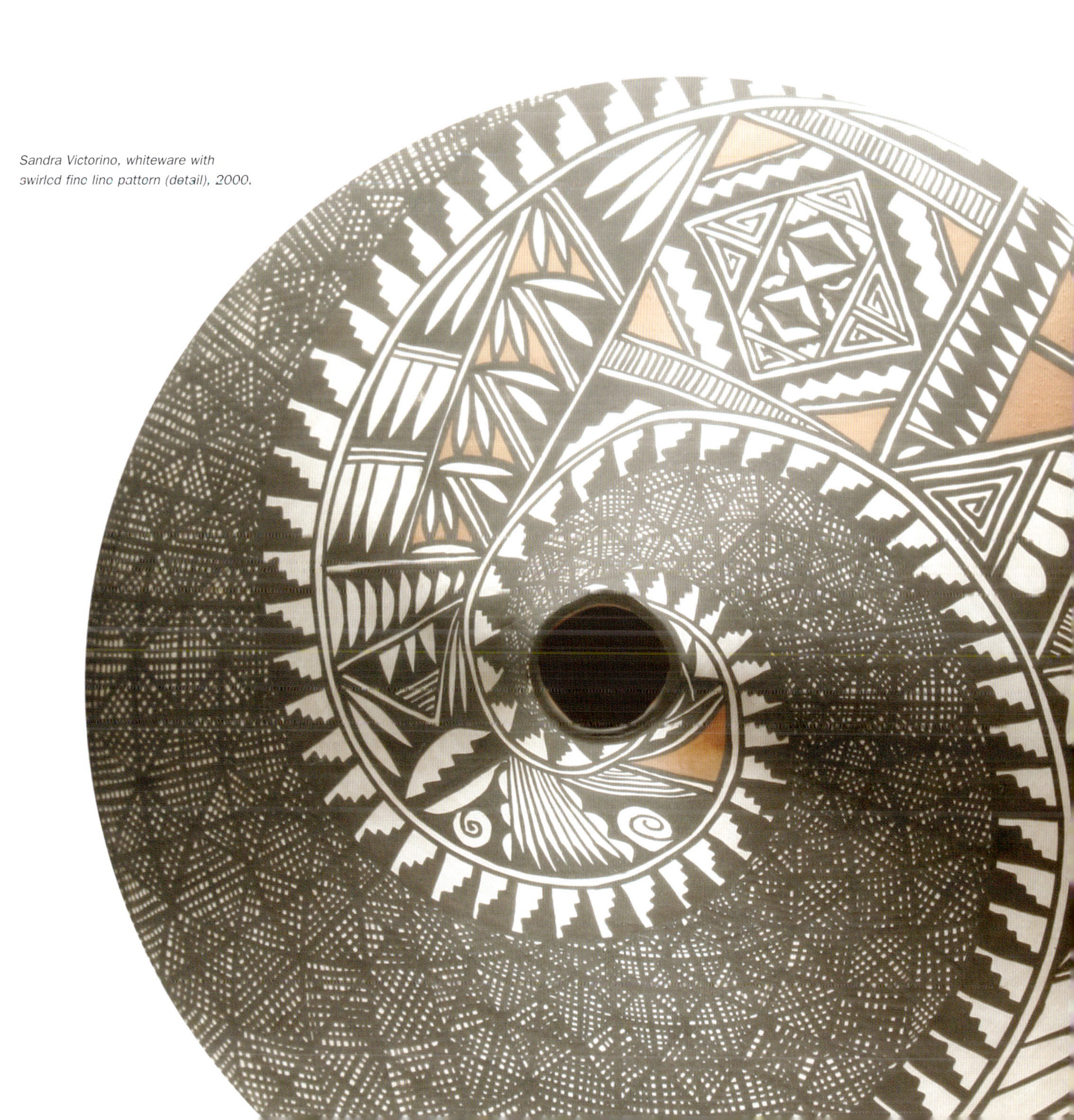

(Clockwise from top) Maria Martinez & Popovi Da, black-on-blackware feather plate, June 1960; Nampeyo of Hano (attributed to) polychrome cylinder jar, c 1915-20; Lucy Lewis, fineline jar, 1953; Maria Martinez and Popovi Da, polychrome jar, 1959; Margaret Tafoya, polished redware with impressed bear paw, c. 1980s.

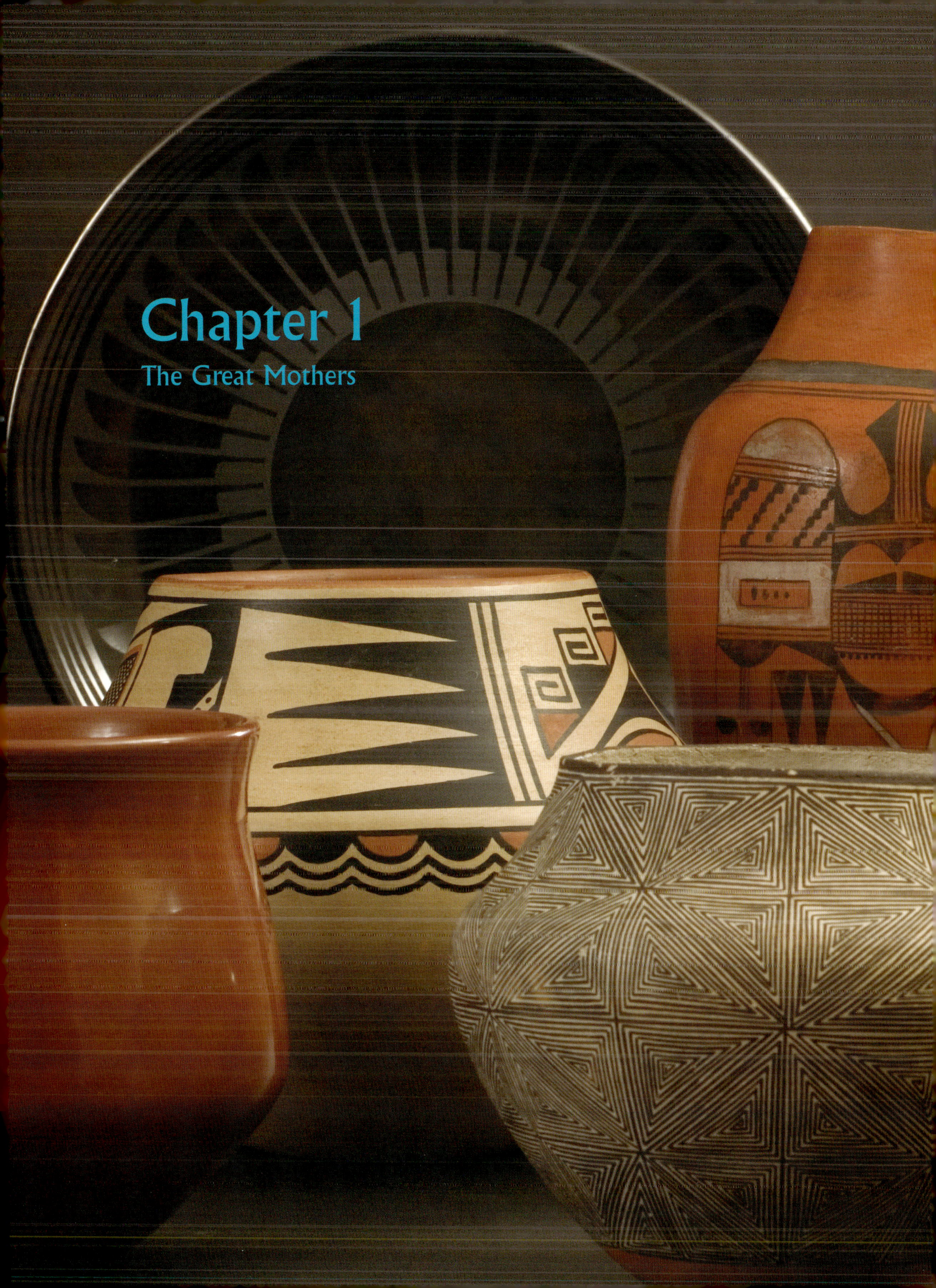

Chapter 1

The Great Mothers

Chapter 1: The Great Mothers

It is fitting that when we speak of the *renaissance*, or perhaps better yet of the *naissance*, of an art form, we couch it in terms of matriarchy or maternal lineage. It is commonly said that Southwestern pottery was reborn through the genius of several matriarchs, Nampeyo, a Hopi-Tewa of the Hano village; Maria Martinez of the San Ildefonso Pueblo; Sara Fina Tafoya and her daughter, Margaret, of the Santa Clara Pueblo; and Lucy Lewis of the Acoma Pueblo. Prior to these women's individual contributions and the collective influence of their era, the pottery of the Southwest had declined in quality and artistry, betraying the many centuries of tradition and craftsmanship that preceded it.

Though pottery had been continuously produced in the Southwest for at least 2,000 years, protracted periods of economic hardship and political strife had diminished artistic expression and cultural tradition. As with most cultures that experience dark times, it is not the ability to craft that is lost but the luxury of time and the tools necessary to create fine examples. In times of hardship, only the bare essentials are required. Thus, practice and mastery of many art forms is abandoned and sometimes lost.

When a group of individuals has the talent, time, and inclination to foster the revival of a tradition, it is appropriate to credit them with its rebirth. Each of these Great Mothers accomplished more than mere rediscovery and application of ancient techniques. Each learned and adapted tradition, begetting a new style that contemporaries could only imitate and future generations sought to advance and adapt for themselves—true art historical indicators of significance.

In discussing his Great Mother archetype, psychologist Carl Jung calls her earthly manifestations, “accidental carrier[s] of that great experience.”[i] Perhaps it is true that these innovators are only accidentally women. Many Southwest tribes are matrilineal by tradition and women the traditional pottery makers. Some of these great matriarchs relied on the assistance of male counterparts (husbands and sons) in the creation of the wares. Furthermore, it is probably no accident, but rather a confluence of events that yielded the right environment for artistic revivals to occur. Nevertheless, it is these women who seized upon the opportune moment, providing the creative impetus that would give new life to an ancient tradition and conceive new traditions as well. Indeed the last century has been a fertile one for Southwestern pottery, and for that the mothers of this art merit the honorific, “Great.”

Nampeyo of Hano (c. 1859 - 1942) / Hopi-Tewa

Before all the other recognized matriarchs of various pottery traditions, there was an exceptionally talented young potter named Nampeyo. She was born to a Tewa mother of the Corn Clan, a matrilineal society where custom dictated that she live in her mother's village of Hano on the so-called First Mesa of the Hopi Reservation. Nampeyo's father was a Hopi farmer of the Snake Clan, and so Nampeyo was given a name, meaning "Snake that does not bite" to honor her father's lineage as well.[ii]

The Hopi and Tewa peoples had coexisted peacefully since the Spanish invasions of the late 17th century. When Nampeyo was born, drought and plague had forced both Hopi and Tewa to flee to their Zuni neighbors. What little we know about this exodus is recorded in the changes in pottery of the time. When the Hopi returned to their abandoned lands, they brought with them Zuni pottery shapes, techniques, and designs that were substantially different from the Hopi wares of the past.

This is where Nampeyo makes her mark on history. She is often credited with single-handedly bringing about the "Sikyatki Revival," a late 19th-century resurrection of ancient Hopi pottery styles. But Nampeyo was not alone in looking to the past for inspiration, nor did she merely copy the local, prehistoric Sikyatki pottery. Rather, she employed her unique talent to construct a new vocabulary of forms and designs. So, she is more correctly credited with the birth of contemporary Hopi pottery.

Pervasive legend has it that Nampeyo became aware of Sikyatki designs when her husband Lesou (also Lesso) worked for J. Walter Fewkes at his 1895 excavation of a prehistoric ruin. While it is true that Fewkes's dig unearthed vast quantities of whole Sikyatki pottery, the rest of the apocryphal story has been attributed to a glory-seeking Fewkes, who portrayed himself as an altruistic foreigner who inspired Nampeyo to revive the ancient styles he found. In truth, Lesou never worked for Fewkes, and Nampeyo's fame was well established before Fewkes ever visited the Southwest.[iii]

Other stories contend that a trading post operator, Thomas Keam, encouraged Nampeyo and other potters to make historic-style pottery for trade[iv]—a likely occurrence. But such a story once again seeks to redistribute credit unfairly. No matter who originally conceived of incorporating ancient designs into current pottery, it was indisputably Nampeyo who used her unique talent to combine various elements of form and design. In doing so, she created something so qualitatively superior to anything else produced at the time that she could only have successors and imitators, not rivals.

In addition to excelling at form and design, Nampeyo abandoned the gritty clay commonly used in pottery at the time, which greatly impacted the final quality of a vessel. Prior to this improvement, Mesa potters applied a finer clay slip to the surface of each pot to compensate for the inferior clay beneath. However, the slip and the base clay had different expansion characteristics. During the firing process, the slip would crack, marring the painted designs. The finer quality clay that Nampeyo employed fired to a smooth surface, making the use of a slip unnecessary and allowing for finished designs unscathed by cracks.

Around the 1880s, through a confluence of events, the West became both more open and more intriguing to outsiders. In 1880, Buffalo Bill's Wild West Show brought much attention to Western and Native American culture, priming the Eastern public to travel on the Santa Fe Railroad when it was completed in 1881. In 1884, Geronimo was conquered, ending open warfare with Native tribes, and Teddy Roosevelt began a series of articles and books on his exploits in the West. In addition, the Smithsonian's Bureau of Ethnology began to collect Native objects zealously, spurring on many imitators both public and private.

In the midst of all this, Nampeyo became an icon of the Southwest, and the fame of her pottery spread internationally. Yet she remained a humble village woman, teaching others her craft even as she grew blind in the 1920s. Even then, she continued to form her wares by feel. Her husband and her children, many of whom became highly respected potters in their own rights, helped her to paint her designs. Indeed, the descendants of Nampeyo still profess ownership of designs that Nampeyo originated, continuing to adapt and interpret them. Among these are the Eagle Feather (or Eagle Tail) Design and the Migration Pattern.

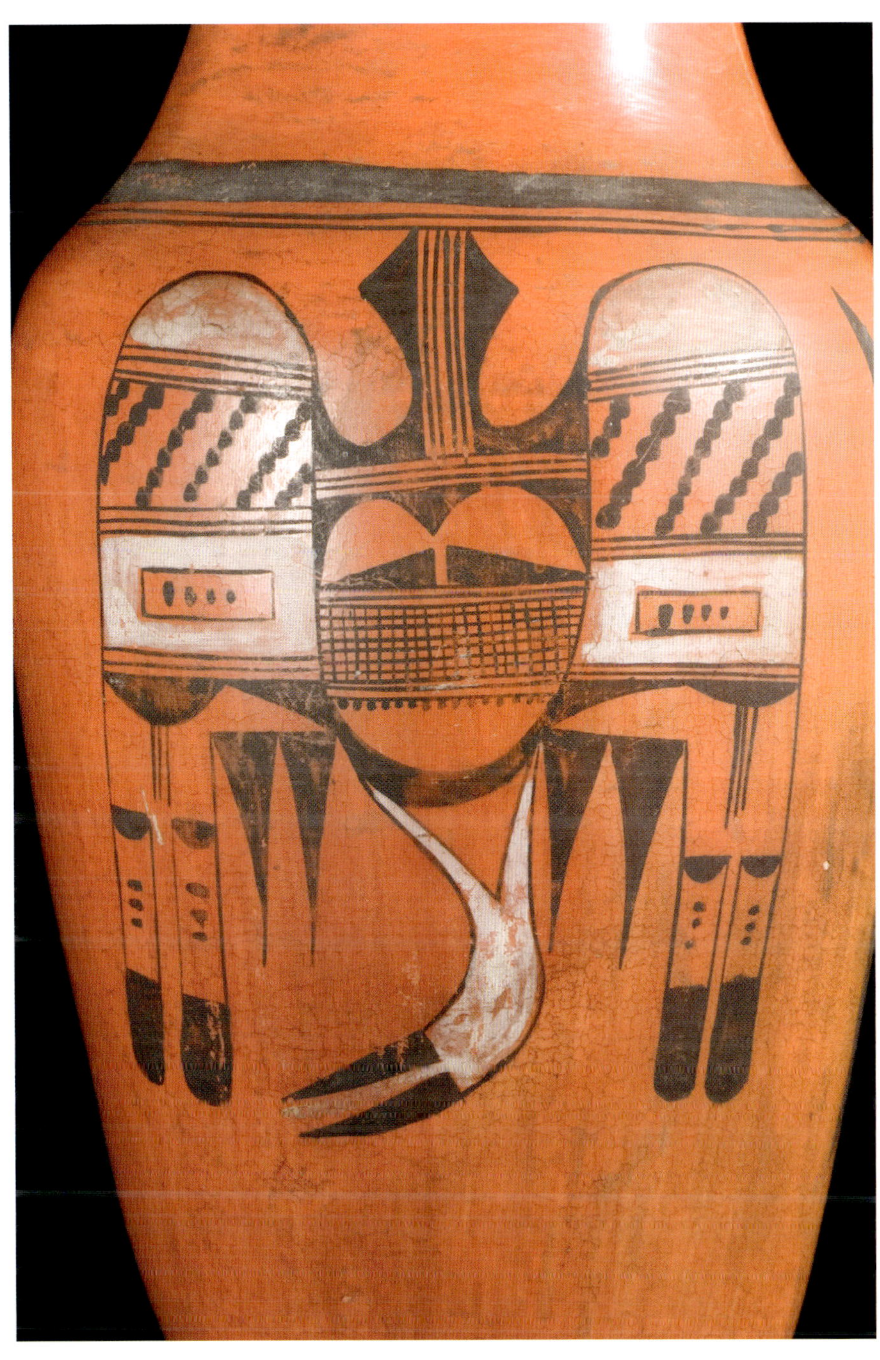

Nampeyo of Hano (attributed to) polychrome cylinder vase (detail).

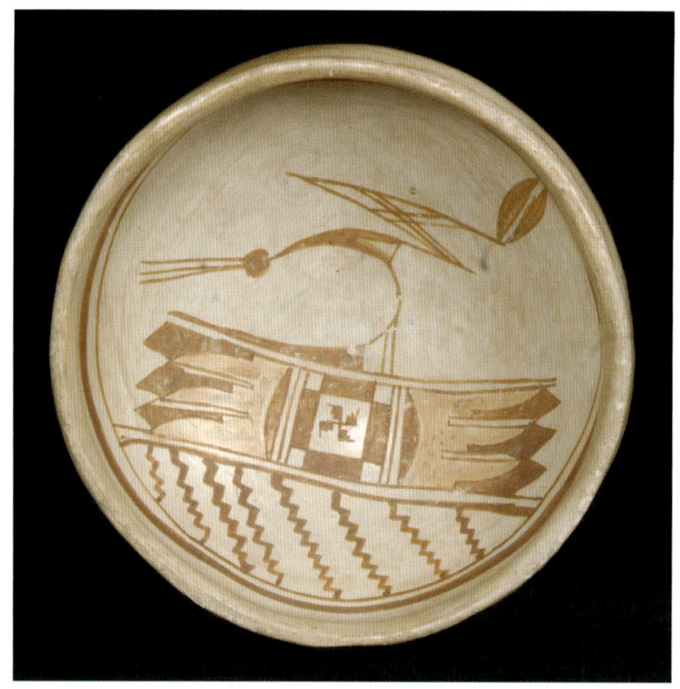

Nampeyo of Hano (attributed to) polychrome bowl, c. 1915-20.

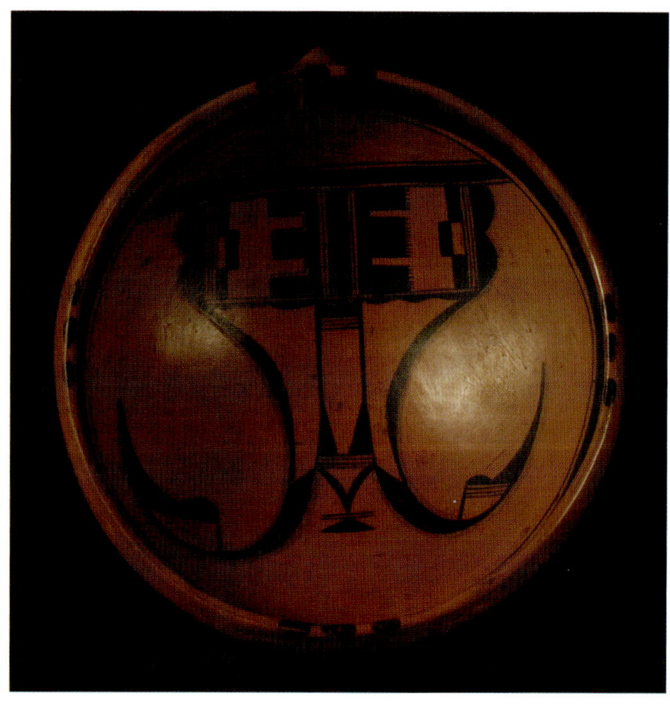

Nampeyo of Hano (attributed to) polycrome bowl, c. 1905.

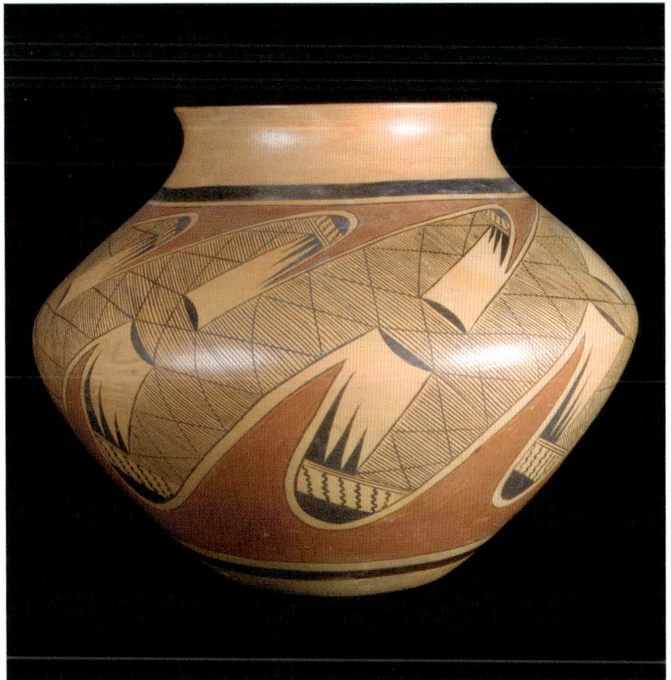

An example of the Migration Pattern.
Dextra Quotskuyva, polychrome jar, c. 1980-85.

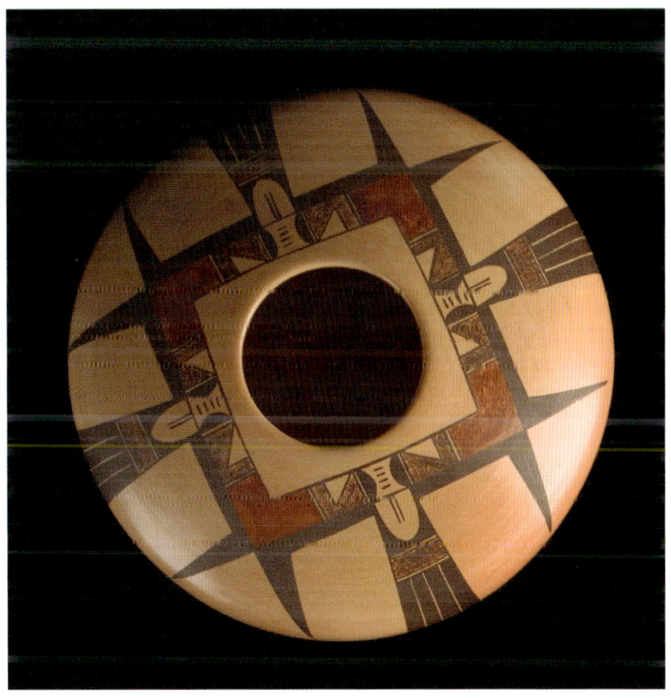

An example of the Eagle Feather Design. Dolly Joe "White Swan" Navasie, polychrome jar, c. 2004.

Maria Martinez (1887-1980) / San Ildefonso

Even to those uninitiated in the passion that is Southwestern pottery, the name "Maria" is nearly synonymous with the art. Few artists in any medium ever earn as much worldwide acclaim as Maria Martinez. For reasons of merit and circumstance, her fame surpassed those in her craft who preceded her, and it remains uneclipsed by those who follow.

Maria is best known for the black-on-blackware she and her husband, Julian, pioneered in 1919. It is erroneous to say that she and Julian invented blackware pottery—a style using iron-rich clay slip that turns black when fired in an oxygen-poor environment. In fact, the nearby Santa Clara Pueblo and Maria's native San Ildefonso Pueblo had produced blackware for many years. Rather, through experimentation, Maria and Julian invented a technique that allowed for both glossy and matte areas of finish on blackware pottery.

Like many young pueblo girls, Maria learned her craft from female relatives. She was always considered an accomplished potter; her special talent was the speed with which she could form the clay. But in her youth, pottery was not a valuable commodity. Inexpensive Spanish tinware and Anglo enamelware had replaced the need for handmade cooking and storage pottery. In the increasingly cash-based economy that arrived with the completion of the Santa Fe Railroad around 1880, Native families found other means of subsisting. In 1908, early in their marriage, Maria and Julian took jobs with one o00 f the archaeological excavations that were proliferating near the pueblos. Julian worked as a laborer and Maria as a cook. The leader of that excavation, Dr. Edgar Lee Hewitt, asked Maria to replicate some prehistoric polychrome pottery styles that had been unearthed, but Maria's talent was not in painting. To satisfy Hewitt's request and produce the colorful pottery, Julian taught himself to paint pots that Maria had formed. It was not long before Maria and Julian were creating their own polychrome pottery and designs. Maria herself has stated that it was Dr. Hewitt who first showed her a prehistoric style of black-on-blackware, thus prompting her and Julian's investigations into recreating this style.[v]

Though it is Maria who garners more attention, Julian deserves much of the credit for reinstituting prehistoric designs such as the *avanyu* (horned water serpents) and eagle feathers now featured regularly on contemporary pottery. Maria's surpassing fame may be a product of her lifespan. She outlived her husband by nearly 40 years and continued to perfect the product of their legacy. After Julian's death in 1943, Maria began working with her daughter-in-law, Santana, and later with her son, Popovi Da, both of whom continued Julian's decorative efforts. Popovi also became adept at public speaking and promotions, and helped market Maria's work across the country.[vi]

Maria was one of the first Native American potters to sign her work, and her success encouraged others to do the same. This simple act simultaneously forced the quality of pueblo pottery to improve by setting standards, and it led to the recognition of each piece of pottery as a unique work of art by an individual, not an ethnographic curiosity made by "a people." Because of this, and in addition to her striking, innovative work, her pioneered techniques, and her establishment of a new tradition, Maria Martinez's greatest contribution is elevating pottery from craft to art.

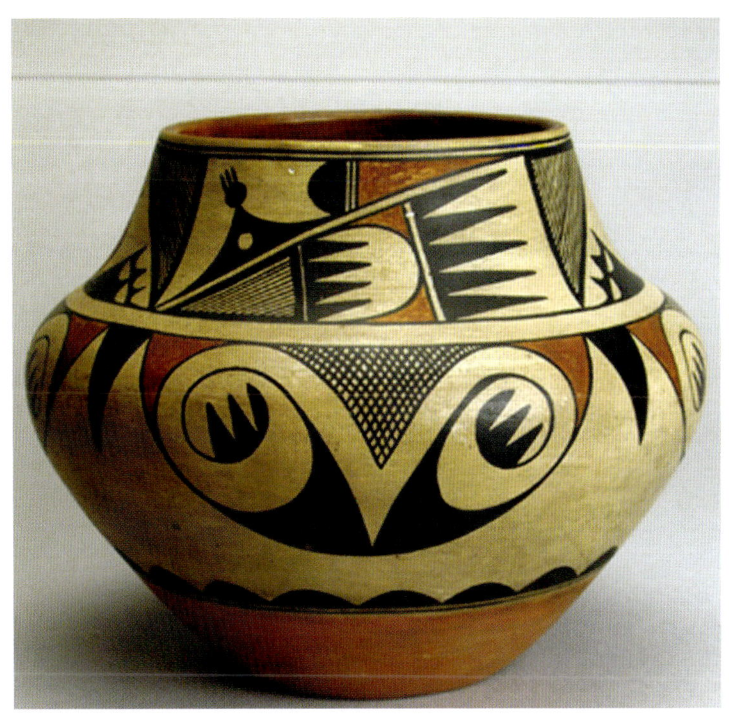

Maria and Julian Martinez, polychrome jar, c. 1920.

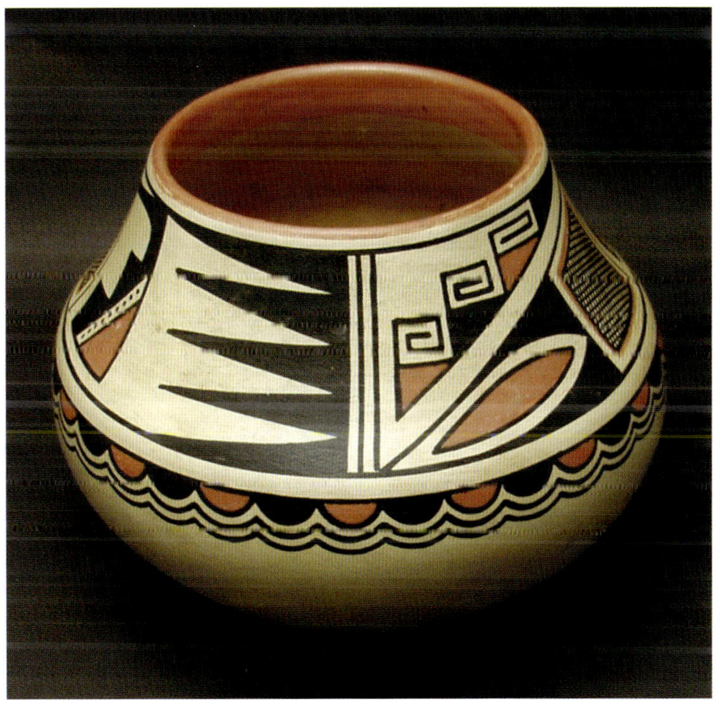

Maria Martinez and Popovi Da, polychrome jar, 1959.

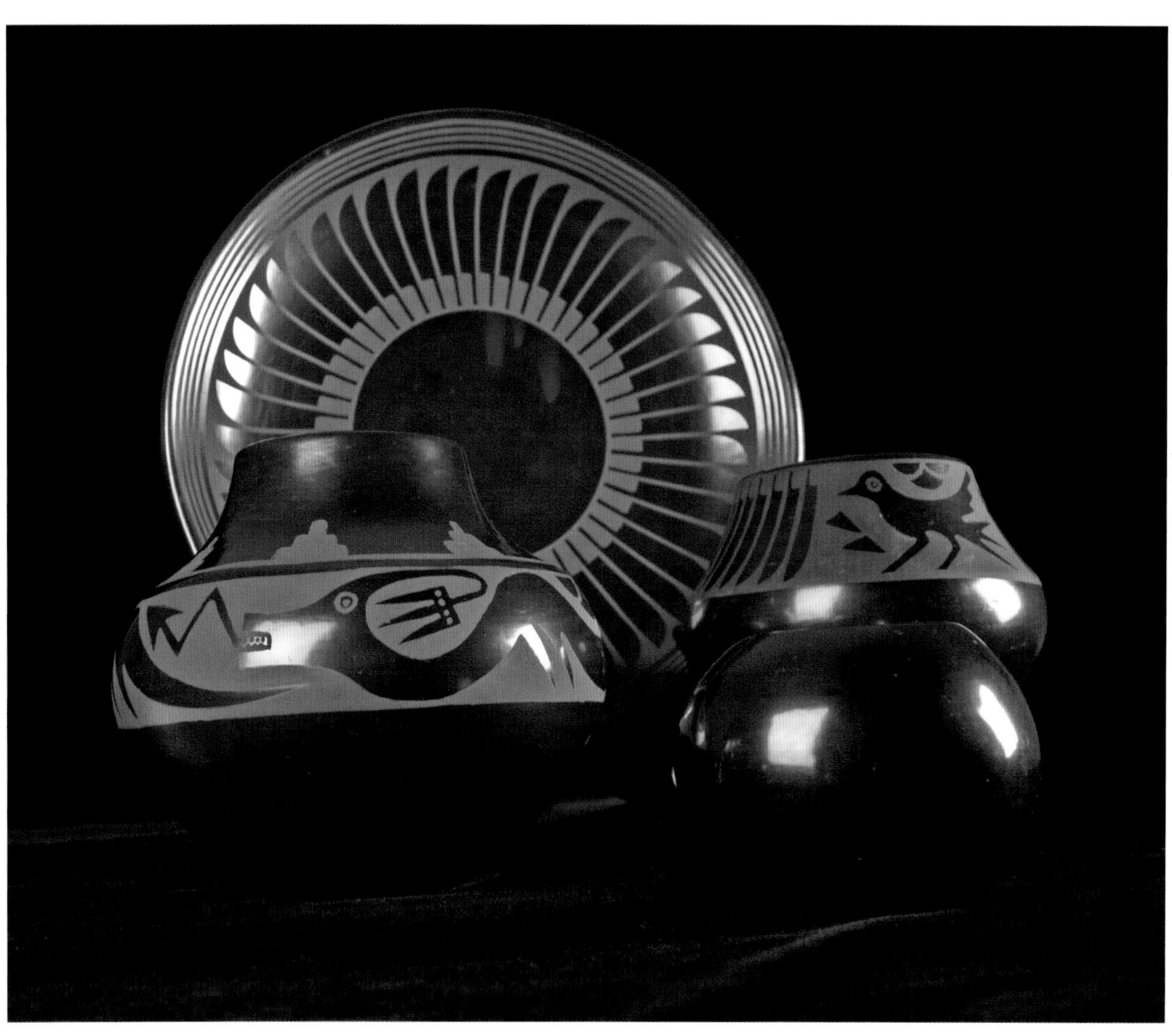

(Clockwise from top) Maria Martinez and Popovi Da, black-on-blackware feather plate, June 1960; Maria and Santana Martinez, black-on-blackware jar, c. 1950s; Maria Martinez, blackware bowl, c. 1950s; Adam and Santana Martinez, black-on-blackware avanyu *jar, 1988.*

Sara Fina (1863-1949) & Margaret Tafoya (1904-2001) / Santa Clara

Like the other Great Mothers of Southwestern pottery tradition, Sara Fina Tafoya, along with her daughter Margaret Tafoya, not only revived ancient pottery practices but also transformed what had become purely utilitarian forms into fine art. Around 1883, partly in response to the just-burgeoning tourist market and partly by internal impetus, a newly married Sara Fina began to create high-quality storage jars that combined visual appeal and functionality.

Credited with developing the Santa Clara style of simple, high-polish, monochrome red or blackware vessels, it is Sara Fina among all the pueblo and reservation potters who is also said to have been the first to carve or impress design elements into her pottery.[vii] Like the innovations of San Ildefonso (black-on-black designs) and the Hopi (finer clay and slips to improve surface appearance), Sara Fina's innovation did not improve the functionality of the vessel. However, it did add an element of artistry and creativity that set her wares apart and, over time, brought global fame.

All of the matriarchs of Southwestern pottery traditions fervently pursued excellence in their craft. But in the case of Sara Fina Tafoya, this becomes exceedingly evident. Not only do the scale and polish of her vessels surpass others produced at the time, but the extraordinary amount of time needed to achieve these characteristics is an added accomplishment. Sara Fina's daughter, Margaret, would perfect and expand her mother's techniques—making the Tafoya name still more famous and becoming a matriarch of the tradition in her own right.

Margaret was the youngest of Sara Fina's eight children and, like most of the family, took to making pottery as way to supplement the family's income. Even after she married in 1924, pottery was not a primary employment for Margaret.[viii] At that time, she was trading her wares for whatever the family needed in terms of clothes and food. Her granddaughter, Susan Roller Whittington, said in her grandmother's eulogy that Margaret used to say, "I clothed my children with clay."[ix] It was not until the 1960s that Margaret found herself recognized for her art, though she had been selling it for years.

Sara Fina taught Margaret to adhere strictly to traditional techniques: scraping with cracked gourds, polishing with corncobs, and giving thanks to Mother Clay during the process. Indeed, Margaret became known for the special attention she seemed to devote to each pot, polishing it to a high sheen even as she enlarged her repertoire of forms to include the enormous storage jars for which she is best known. Though she expanded on her mother's first use of impressed designs by carving increasingly complicated elements, her repeated use of the simple bear paw became nearly synonymous with her name, though its use is not unique to her family.

It has been said that the Tafoya clan is more numerous and produces more pottery than any other family of the Southwestern pottery tradition.[x] True or not, through Sara Fina, the Tafoya clan does encompass numerous exceptional potters such as the Youngbloods and Tafoyas descended from Margaret; the Lonewolfs and Grace Medicine Flower descended from Sara Fina's son, Camilio; and through Margaret's sister, Christina, comes the Naranjo family, all of whom are represented in the Cameros Collection.

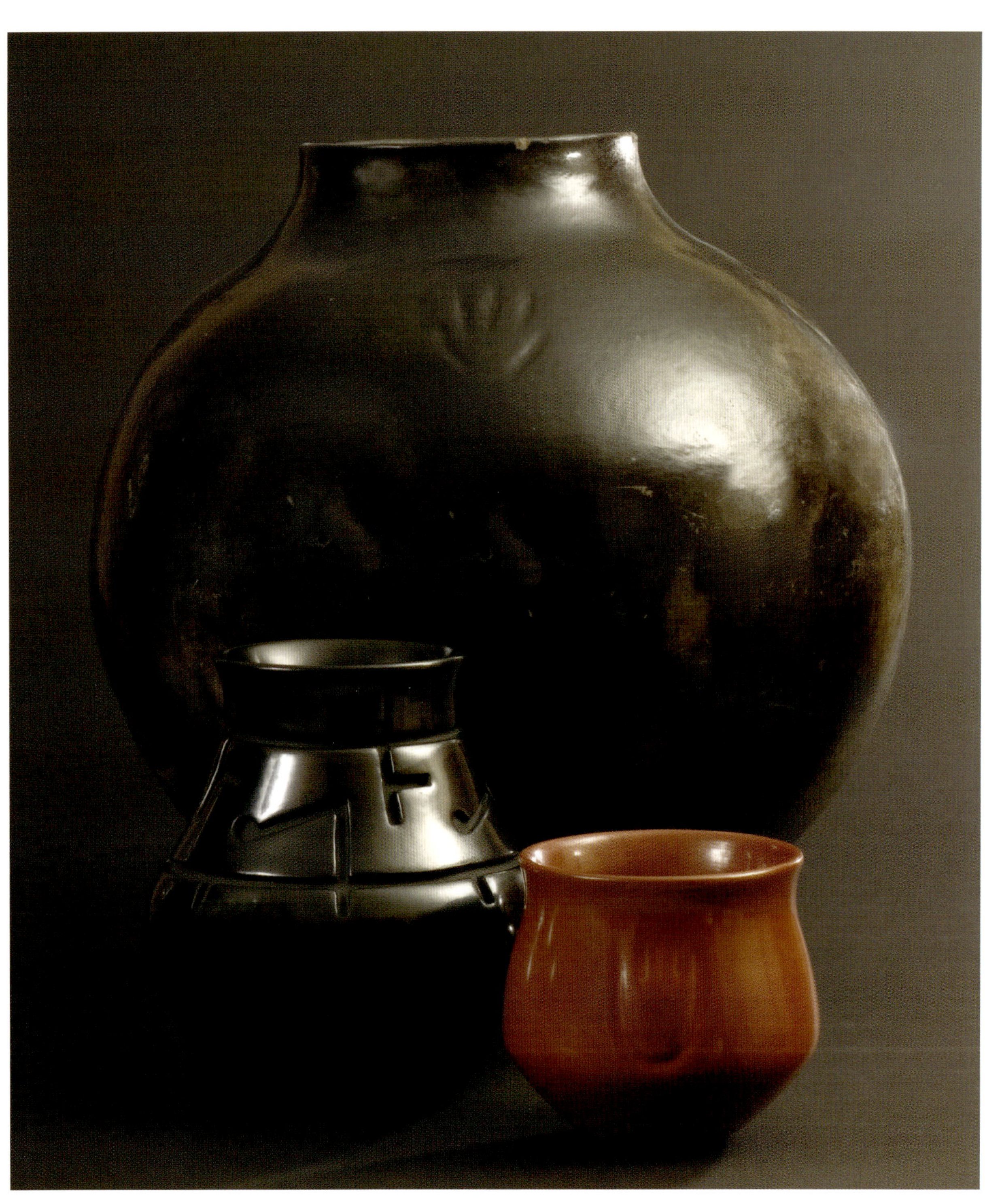

(Clockwise from top) Sara Fina Tafoya, blackware storage jar, c. 1920s; Margaret Tafoya, polished redware with impressed bear paw, c. 1980s and polished blackware jar with carved design, c. 1970s.

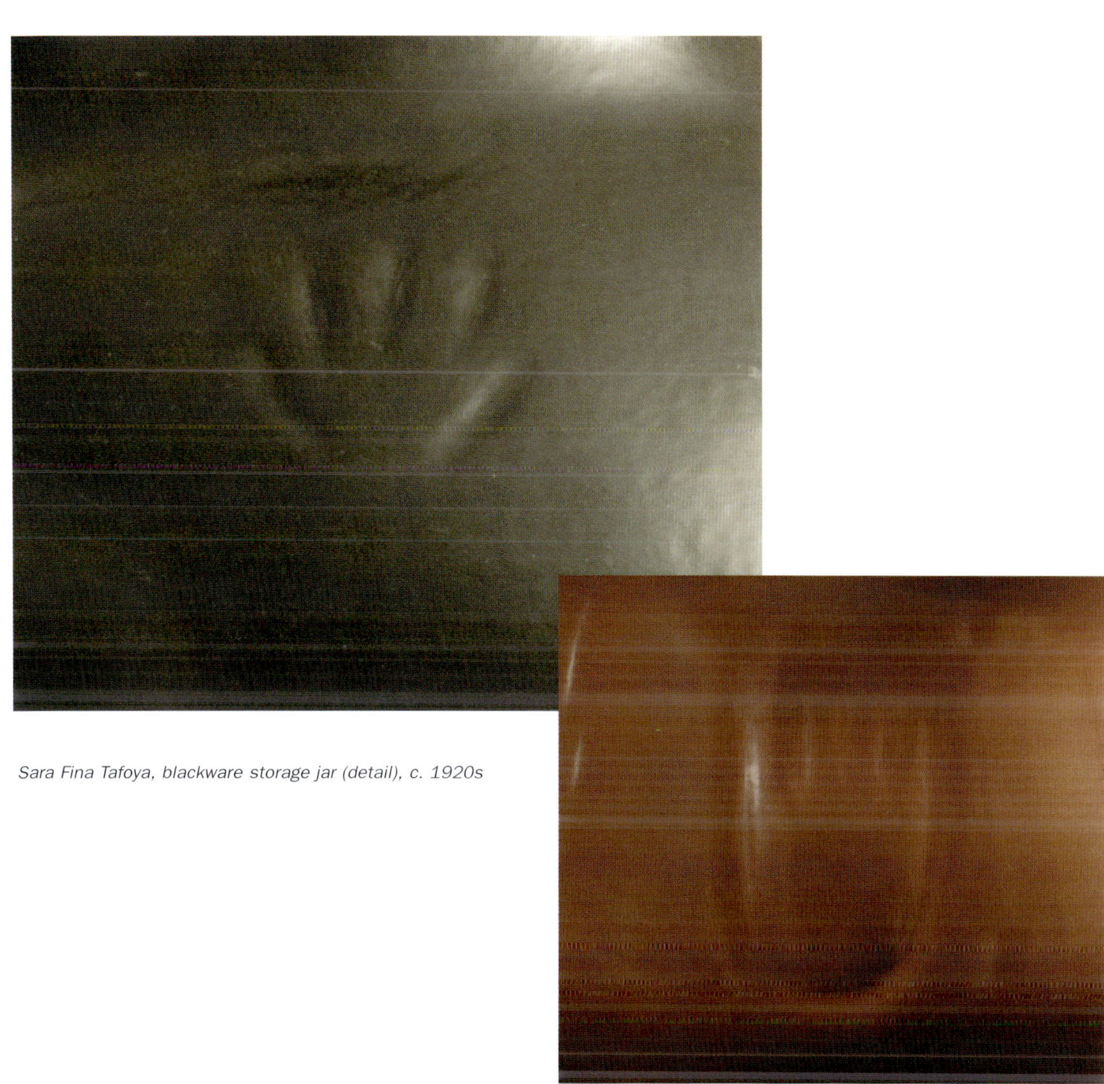

Sara Fina Tafoya, blackware storage jar (detail), c. 1920s

Margaret Tafoya, polished redware with impressed bear paw (detail), c. 1980s.

Lucy M. Lewis (c. 1898-1992) / Acoma

Though a matriarch of her pueblo's pottery tradition, Lucy Lewis's experience was different than that of Nampeyo, Maria Martinez, or the Tafoya women. Lucy was born in the Acoma Pueblo, known as Sky City. As its name implies, this ancient city was built approximately 7,000 feet above sea level atop a 367-foot sandstone mesa. The difficult ascent proved so effective at repelling invaders that it is thought to be the oldest continuously inhabited city in what is now the continental United States.

Naturally segregated from outside influence by the location of her home, Lucy's development as a potter was different from the other Great Mothers. She was not initially motivated by archaeologists, traders, or tourists to create or innovate pottery. Her craft arose from an arguably more innate desire to experiment and improve. Lucy was never formally educated. Instead, she learned pottery-making from her aunt and then became inspired by ancient Mimbres and Anasazi shards that could be found near the Acoma Pueblo, reviving ancient images from both. She was already a talented potter in traditional polychrome designs when she began to incorporate the traditional Zuni design of a deer with a heartline.

It was not until after 1950, when she won the first pottery competition she ever entered, that public attention was drawn to the quality of her work. Soon, her pottery began winning national recognition and showing up in New York art galleries. Today, Lucy's influence is easily recognizable in Acoma pottery. She is best known for two innovations that make Acoma pottery distinctive: Impeccably exact, hand-painted linear and geometric designs, typically accomplished in black on white slip; and, in contrast to this, the use of empty space in designs.

Another differing aspect of Lucy Lewis as matriarch of the Acoma pottery tradition is that she did not work collaboratively. Lacking a formal education herself because there was no school nearby, she insisted that her eight children leave home for schooling. This left Lucy and her husband to farm, and she made pots in her spare time. The simple grace of many of Lucy's pots belies the enormous amount of toil that went into their creation. She harvested her own clay, built and scraped her own vessels, painted her own designs, and fired them in a homemade kiln—a labor giving her every right to the title Great Mother.

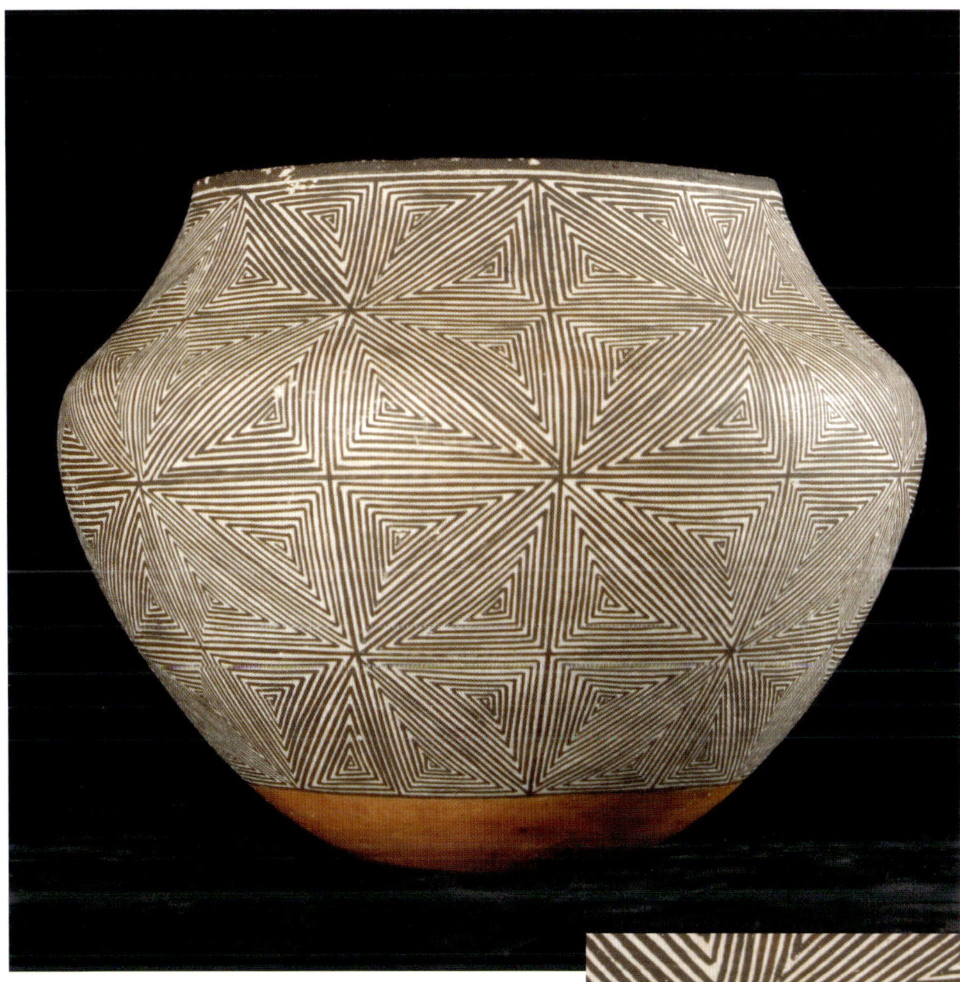

Lucy Lewis, fineline jar, 1953

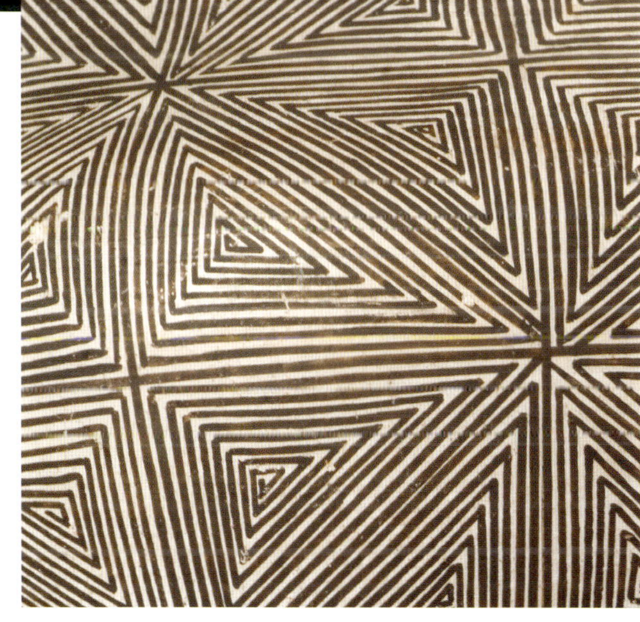

Lucy Lewis, fineline jar (detail), 1953.

(Clockwise from top) Susan Folwell, "Homage to the Pottery Gods," polychrome jar, 2007; Les Namingha, polychrome "mosaic" jar, 2006; Jody Folwell, blackware bowl, c. 1997.

Chapter 2

Artists without Reservation

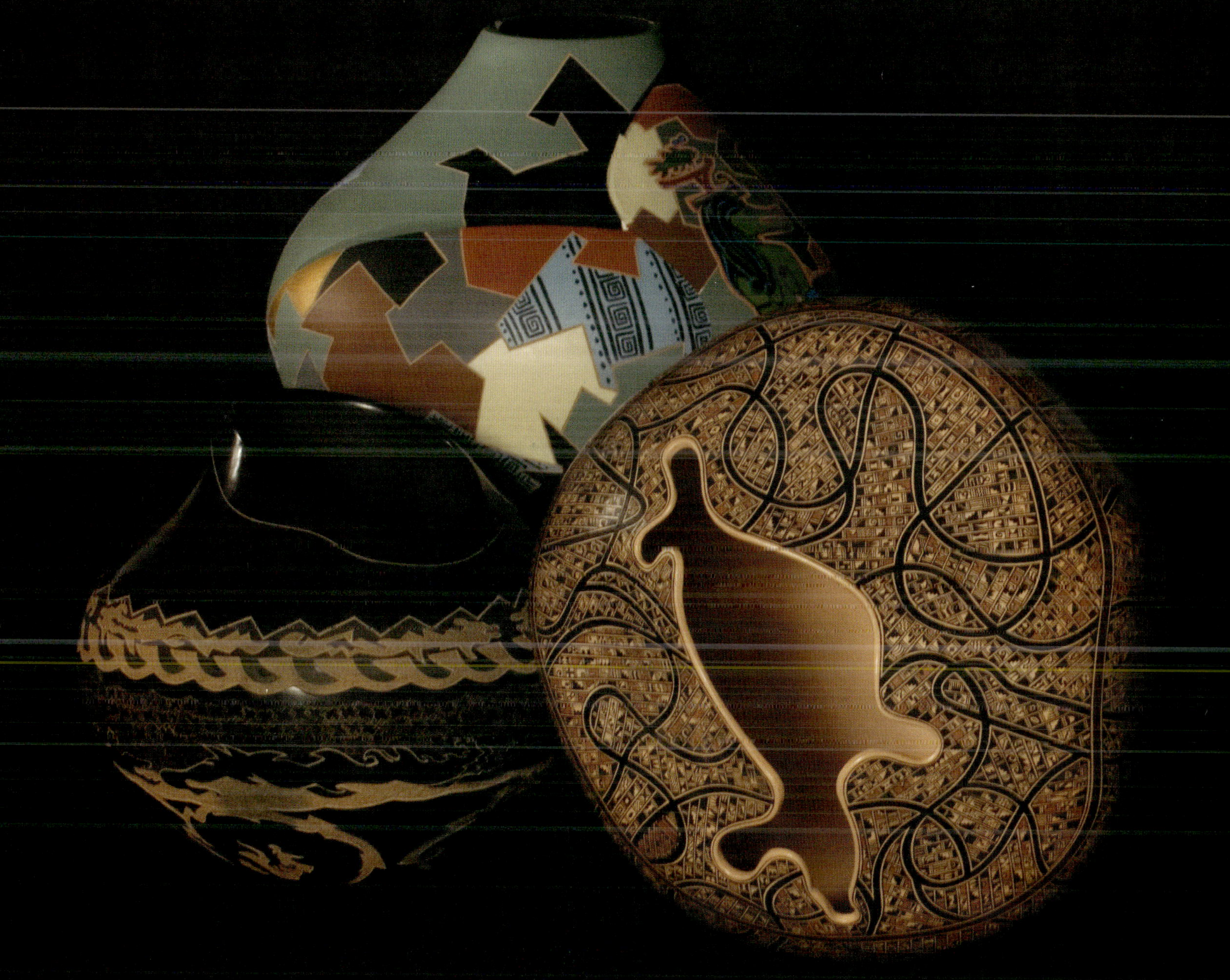

Chapter 2: Artists Without Reservation

Scholars throughout history have viewed innovation as an important gauge for studying the development of any given field. In many cases, innovation is characterized by improvement, giving rise to the idea that innovation is intrinsically superior to tradition. That is not always the case, especially in art.

True innovation is rare, which makes it a desirable distinction for the artist and a beacon to the savvy collector. But newness of form, or mere difference or oddity is not enough to qualify as innovation. In art, innovation is more than segregation from the norm. It is an expression of originality that is recognized as such and accepted to the point of imitation. Call it "survival of the most appealing" since new efforts must be appreciated before they will be replicated.

Nevertheless, labeling artworks and artists as innovative is neither an effort to canonize certain potters over others, nor to argue with unofficial classifications already made by gallery owners, collectors, critics, museums or the artists themselves. This chapter seeks to distinguish trendsetters—those who are or will be imitated. These "Artists Without Reservation" circumvent existing boundaries, be they established artistic methods, conventional tools or media, technological limitations, or merely the recognized styles of their pueblo or reservation. Within the Cameros Collection, there is a wide array of visual idiom. Whereas the next chapter seeks to recognize superior examples of existing styles and techniques, Artists Without Reservation are potters whose work is indicative of things to come.

Popovi Da (1923 - 1971) / San Ildefonso

Popovi Da was regarded for many years as the vanguard of artistry in Southwestern pottery. Born Antonio Martinez to the famed Maria and Julian Martinez, he changed to his native name, Popovi Da (pronounced "day"), which translates to "Red Fox," in 1948. About the same time, he began helping his mother gather clay and temper. By 1956, Popovi had become his mother's partner in pottery creation.[xi] Over the rest of his life, Popovi transformed his pueblo's pottery styles and greatly influenced the rise of Southwestern pottery as a respected art form.

An experimenter at heart, Popovi invented several firing techniques, including those that produced a sienna colored finish, a black and sienna finish called "duotone," and his most famous contribution, a gunmetal finish. Gunmetal in its final appearance is brighter and more lustrous than a blackware finish. The firing process is similar to blackware but involves the incorporation of ash into the fire. A hotter fire is used, and the pottery is exposed to heat for longer than regular blackware. It is the adherence of the ash to the pot's surface that causes the gunmetal effect. The mastery of this technique comes in the timing of removal: If the piece is not left long enough, it will appear as regular blackware; if it is left too long, it will surpass the peak level of shine and become dull gray. Popovi was one of only two known artists who could achieve this effect with consistency.

Popovi is credited with helping to revive polychrome pottery in his pueblo, which had been all but replaced by the popular black-on-blackware his mother and father developed. He is also believed to be the first modern potter to experiment with inlaid stones, specifically turquoise. However, he quickly abandoned this style, leaving it to his son, Tony Da, to develop and master.[xii]

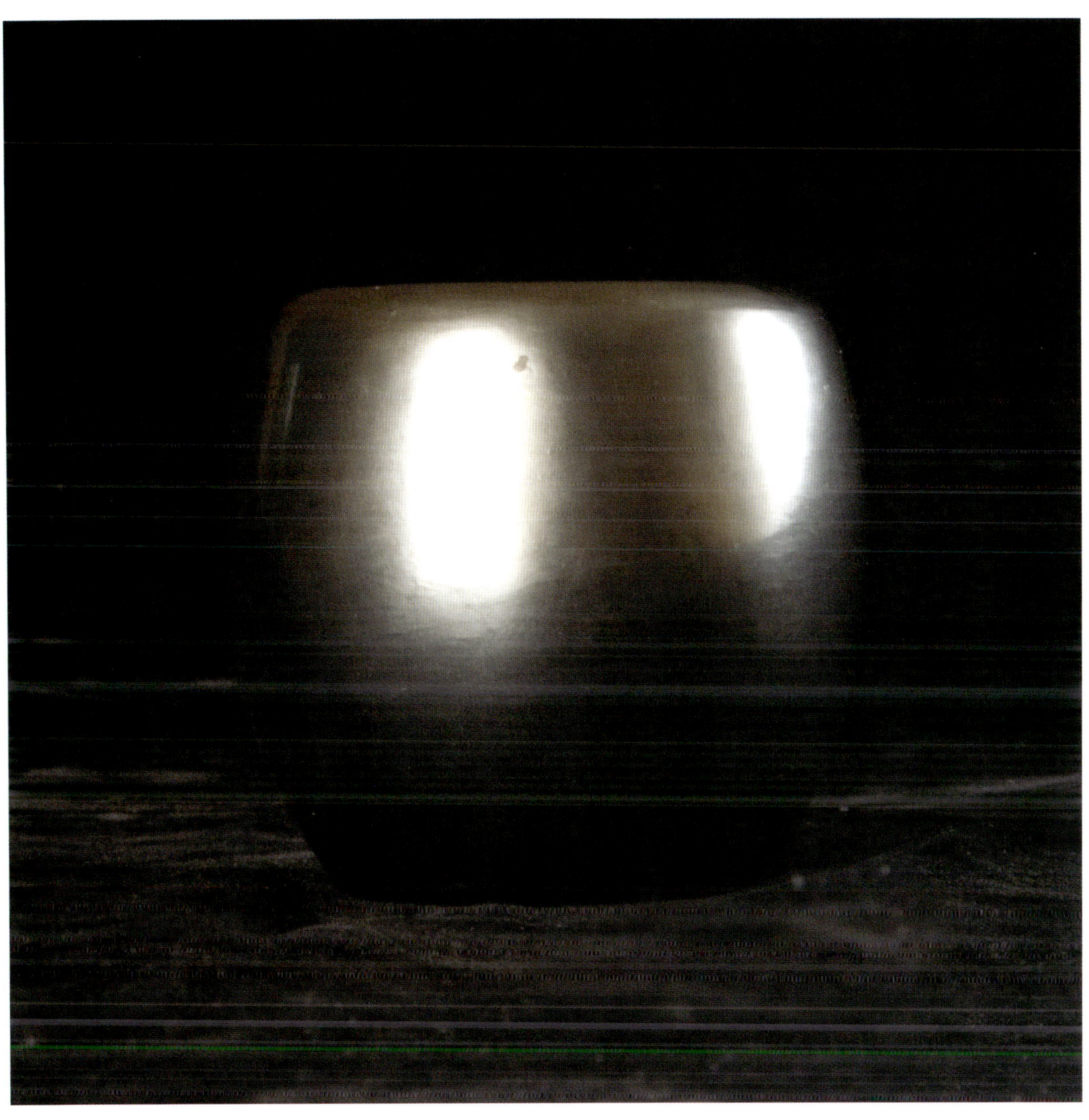

Popovi Da, gunmetal cup, October 1965. Only two artists are said to have mastered the technique that brought about the gunmetal finish: Popovi Da, and his sister-in-law, Santana. For this reason, gunmetalware is rare.

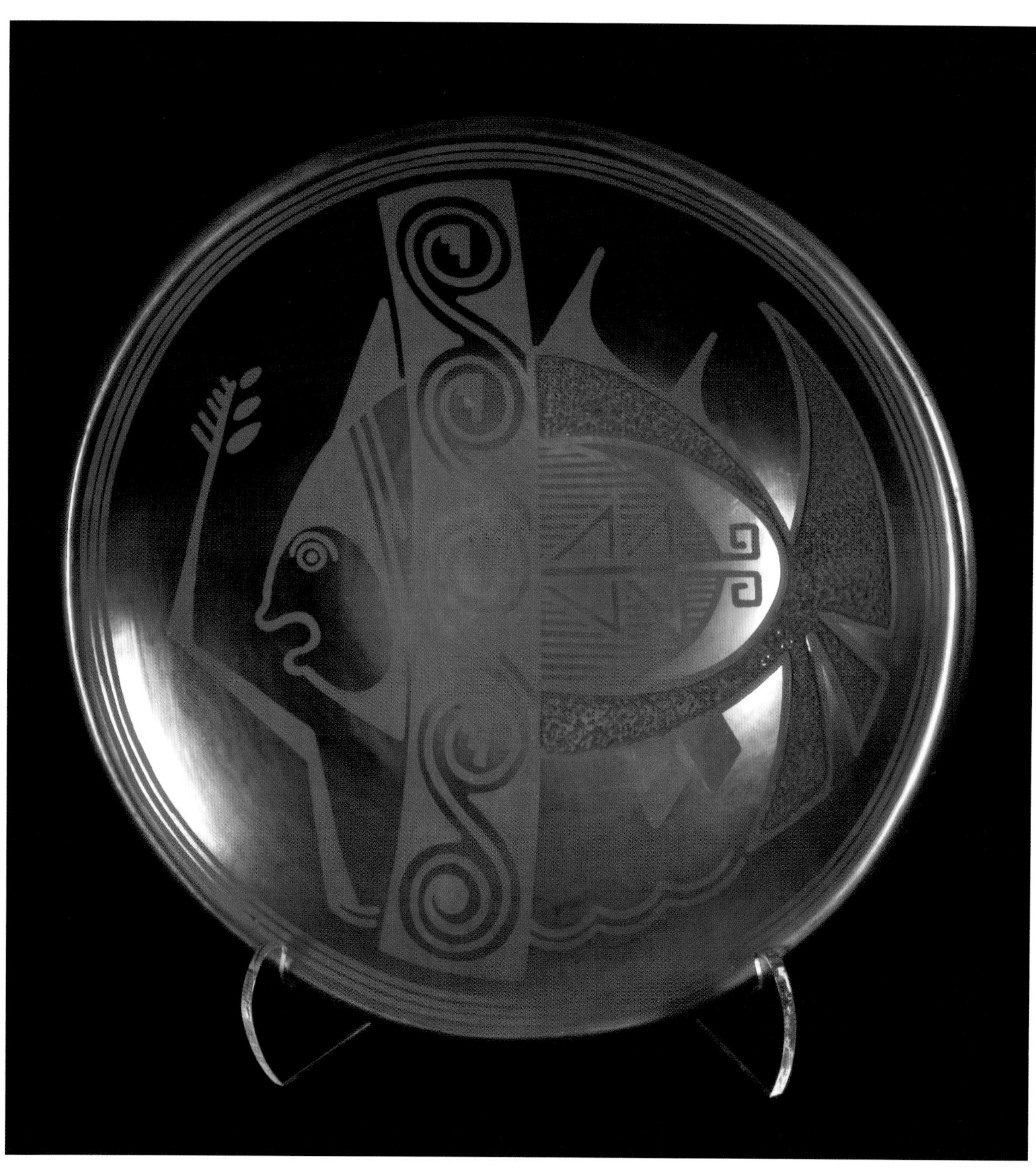

Popovi Da, black-on-blackware plate, June 1960. While Maria and Popovi's collaboration is considered by some to be the height of Maria's artistry and of black-on-blackware, works, like this plate, that are signed by Popovi alone, are rare and highly sought after.

Tony Da (1940 -) / San Ildefonso

Tony Da, son of Popovi Da and grandson of Maria Martinez, had only a brief pottery career from the late 1960s to about 1980 when he was severely injured in a motorcycle crash. In this short span, his contributions to Southwestern pottery were brilliant and continued the legacy of innovation in his famous family's art.

Though he considers himself primarily a painter, Tony was among the first to begin incising the surface of his pottery with small but deep geometric forms. In addition, Tony is believed to have popularized stone inlay on pottery, perfecting what his father had only experimented with. At first, it was a simple piece of turquoise that would contrast brightly with the black-on-blackware, sienna ware, and duotone finishes his family had innovated. Later, he began adding *heishi* (shell beads) and other stones.

Tony's artistry and creativity led him to sculpt forms like large bear fetishes and turtles. On all of these works, he experimented with the juxtaposition of the numerous techniques at his disposal: the matte and shiny surfaces of his family's finishes, both *sgraffito* and deeper incisions into the surface, stone inlay in several colors, and eventually with the use of silver elements.[xiii]

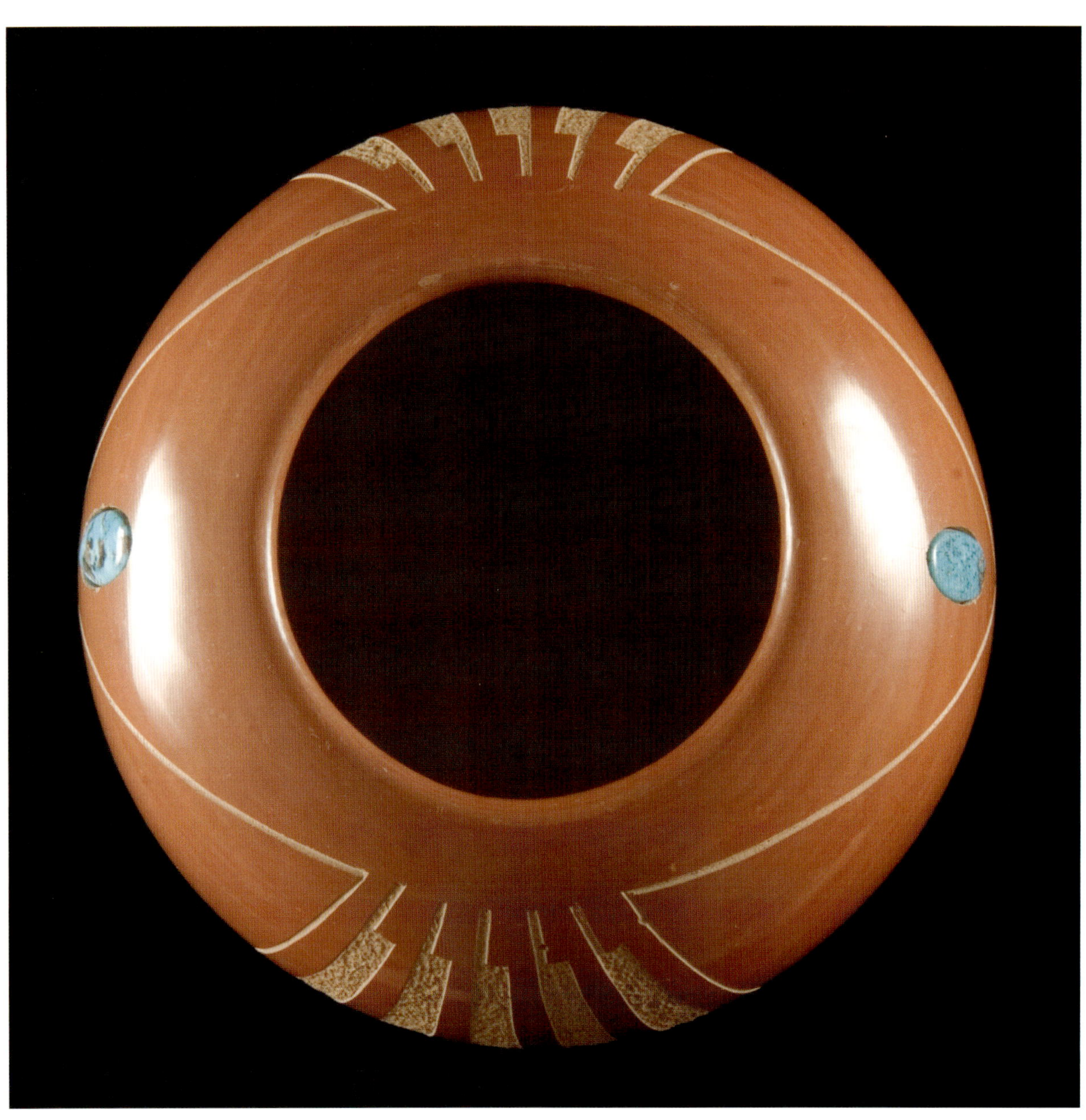

Redware vessel with sgraffito *feather design and turquoise inlay by Tony Da, c. 1970. The feather design is said to have been revived by Tony's grandfather, Julian.*

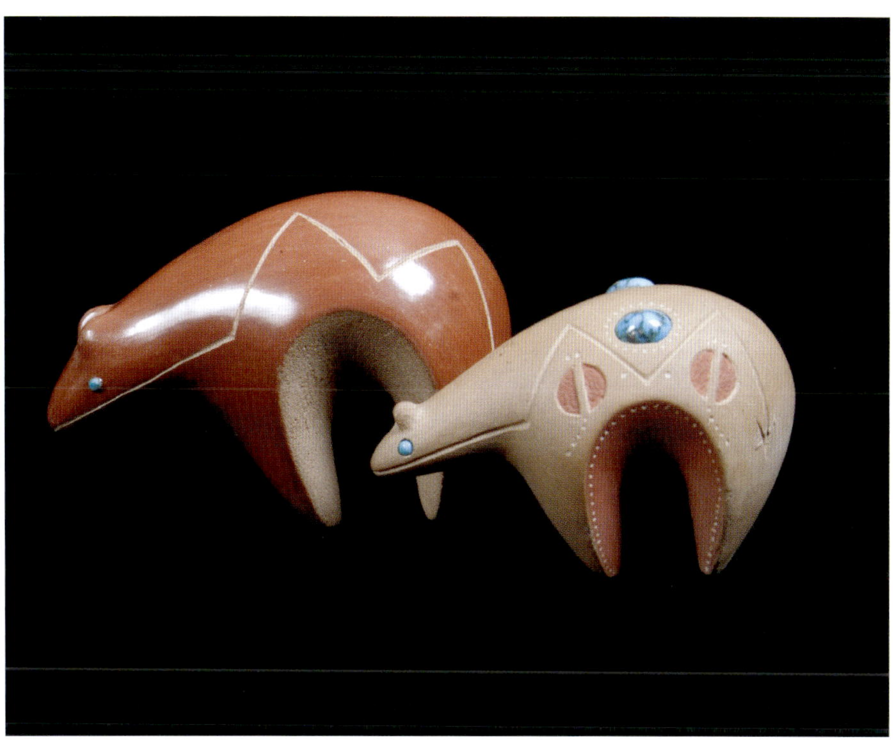

Redware fetish bears by Tony Da, (R) c. 1971-72 and (L) c. 1976-77.
Both feature polished and matte finishes with turquoise inlay.

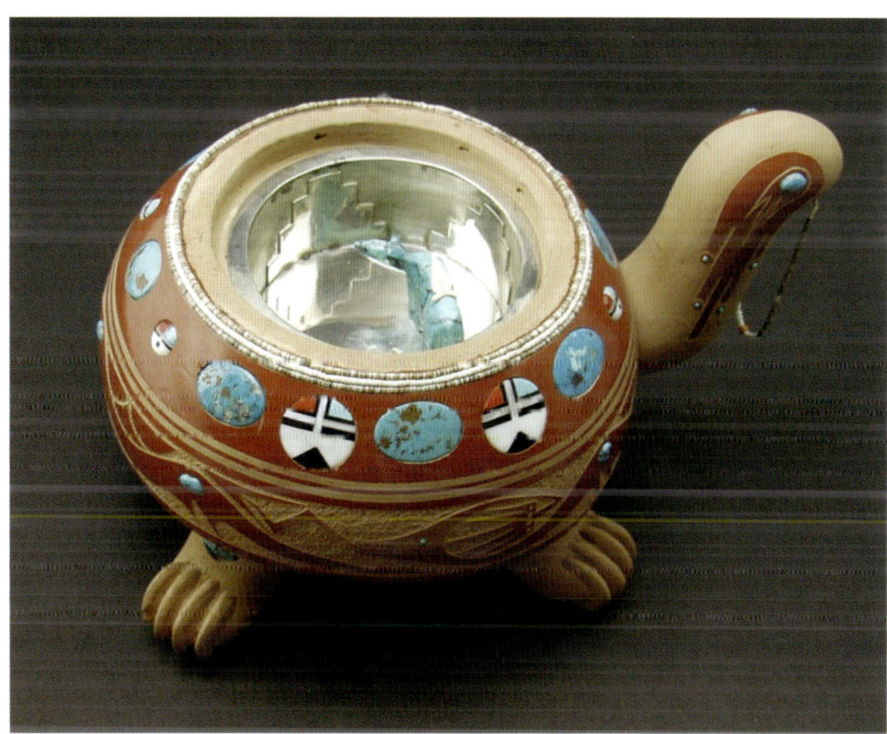

Sculpted redware turtle by Tony Da, c. 1975.
This is a masterpiece of Tony's artistry. Notice the polish and sgraffito avanyu *design circumnavigating the body; the heavy use of inlay, the polish and matte finishes and the use of silver on the interior.*

Dora Tse Pe (1939 -) / Zia / San Ildefonso

When Dora, a Tewa Indian born at Zia Pueblo, married Tse Pe Gonzalez of San Ildefonso, she already knew the pottery-making craft. Her new husband, who went by the name Tse Pe, had been born to the well-known potter Rose Gonzalez and was an accomplished potter in his own right. Their collaboration with each other as well as the influence of Popovi and Tony Da, led Dora to master new pottery techniques.

Dora Tse Pe took what she learned from her fellow San Ildefonsan potters and expanded it. She continues the tradition of stone inlay, incision, and *sgraffito*, but is best known for her novel juxtaposition of different types of clay in the same pot, particularly her use of lustrous micaceous clays alongside polished or matte black and red clays. The creativity of juxtaposing dull surfaced clay that has sparkling elements with clay that has been hand polished to shine like glass takes the original contribution of San Ildefonso—black-on-blackware pottery—to a new level.[xiv]

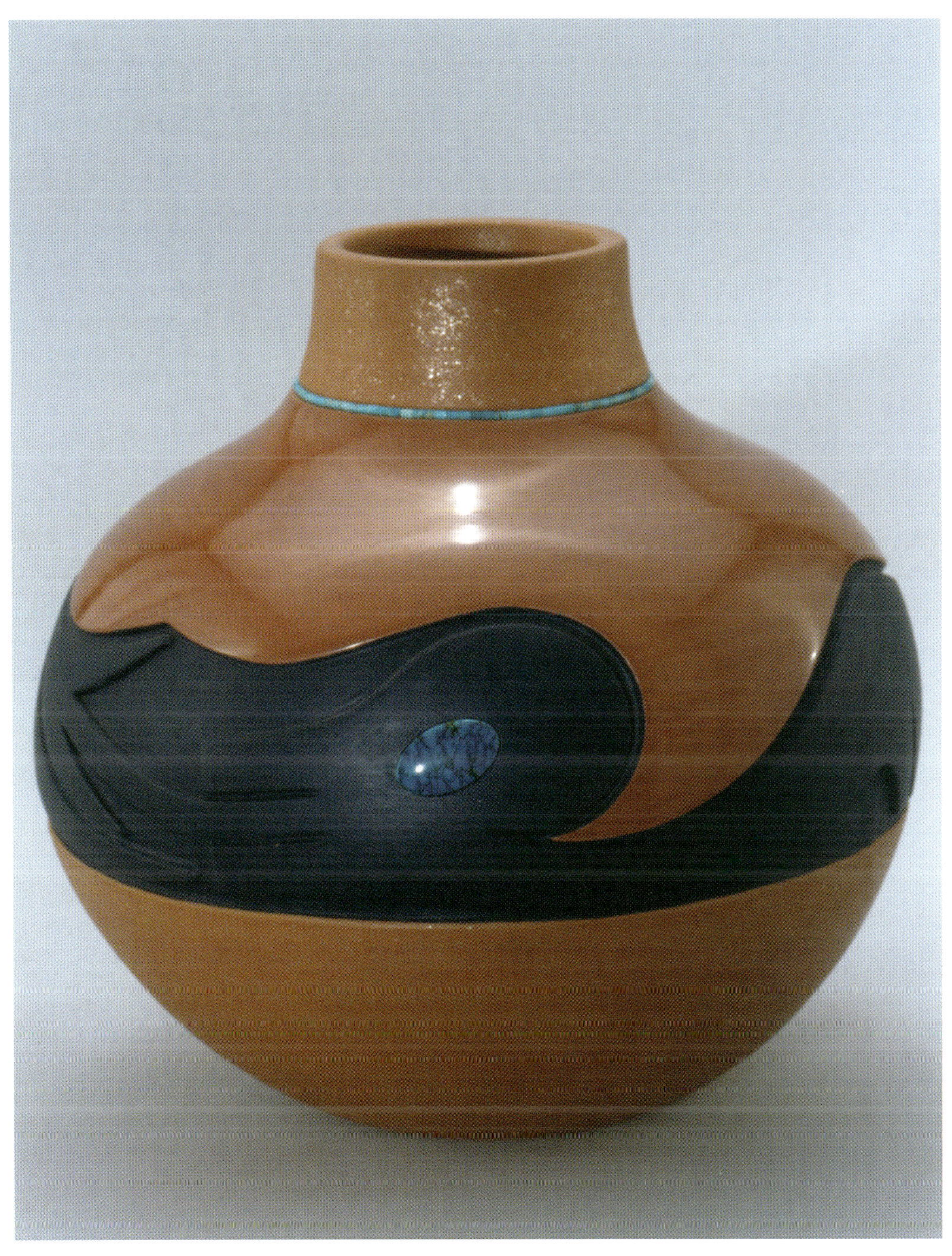

Dora Tse Pe, polished redware, blackware, and micaceous jar with heishi *and turquoise inlay, c. 1990s.*

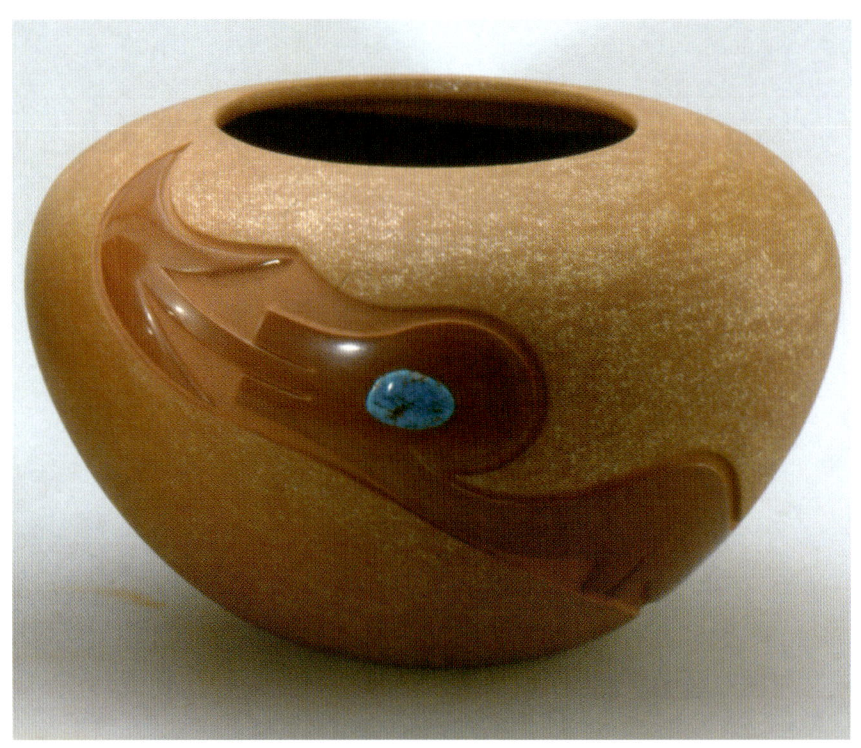

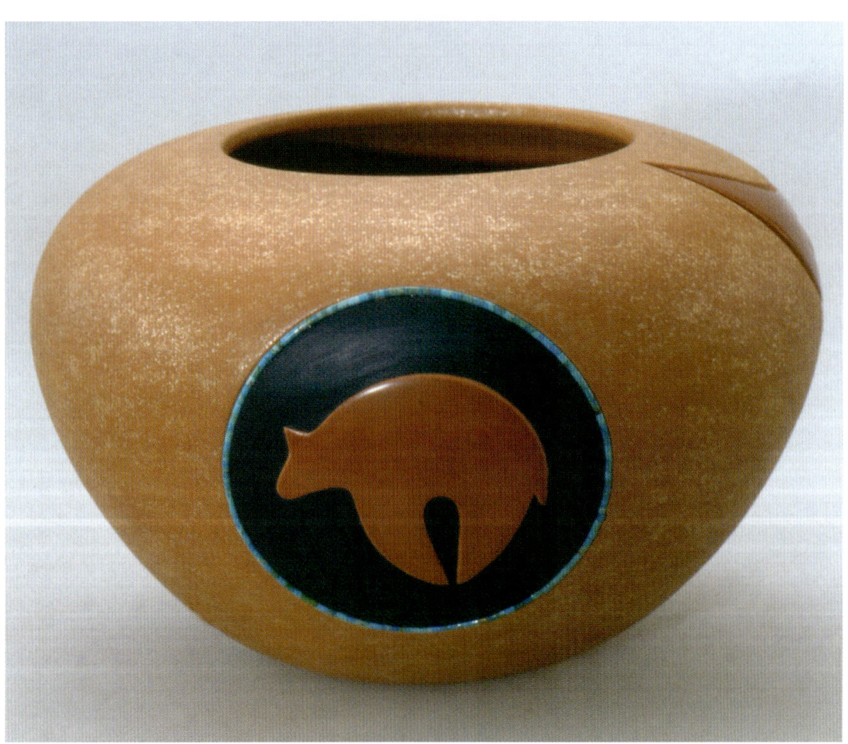

Alternate side views of same red and black ware vessel, Dora Tse Pe, c. 1990s. Dora's use of micaceous clays has helped revived its popularity; the copper and gold colors add a new dimension to contemporary Southwestern pottery.

Joseph Lonewolf (1932 -) / Santa Clara

Along with his father, Camilio Tafoya, and his sister, Grace Medicine Flower, Joseph Lonewolf elevated a simple scratching technique to an art form, initiating a new tradition for his pueblo. Exploiting this technique, called *sgraffito*, Joseph created tiny jewels of pottery, extraordinary not only for their size but also but for the level of precision and artistry employed on each.

Like his father's work, Joseph's miniatures feature animals and subjects rarely found on other pottery. From butterflies to goats, the animals are narrative devices that recall ancient symbols and tales. The storytelling nature of these works harkens to the some of the original intent of pottery—that of a vessel, for things tangible and things not.

Today Joseph's own children, Greg Lonewolf, Rosemary "Apple Blossom" Lonewolf, and Susan "Snowflake" Romero, continue the family's great tradition. Lonewolf family miniatures continue to be highly respected and sought after.

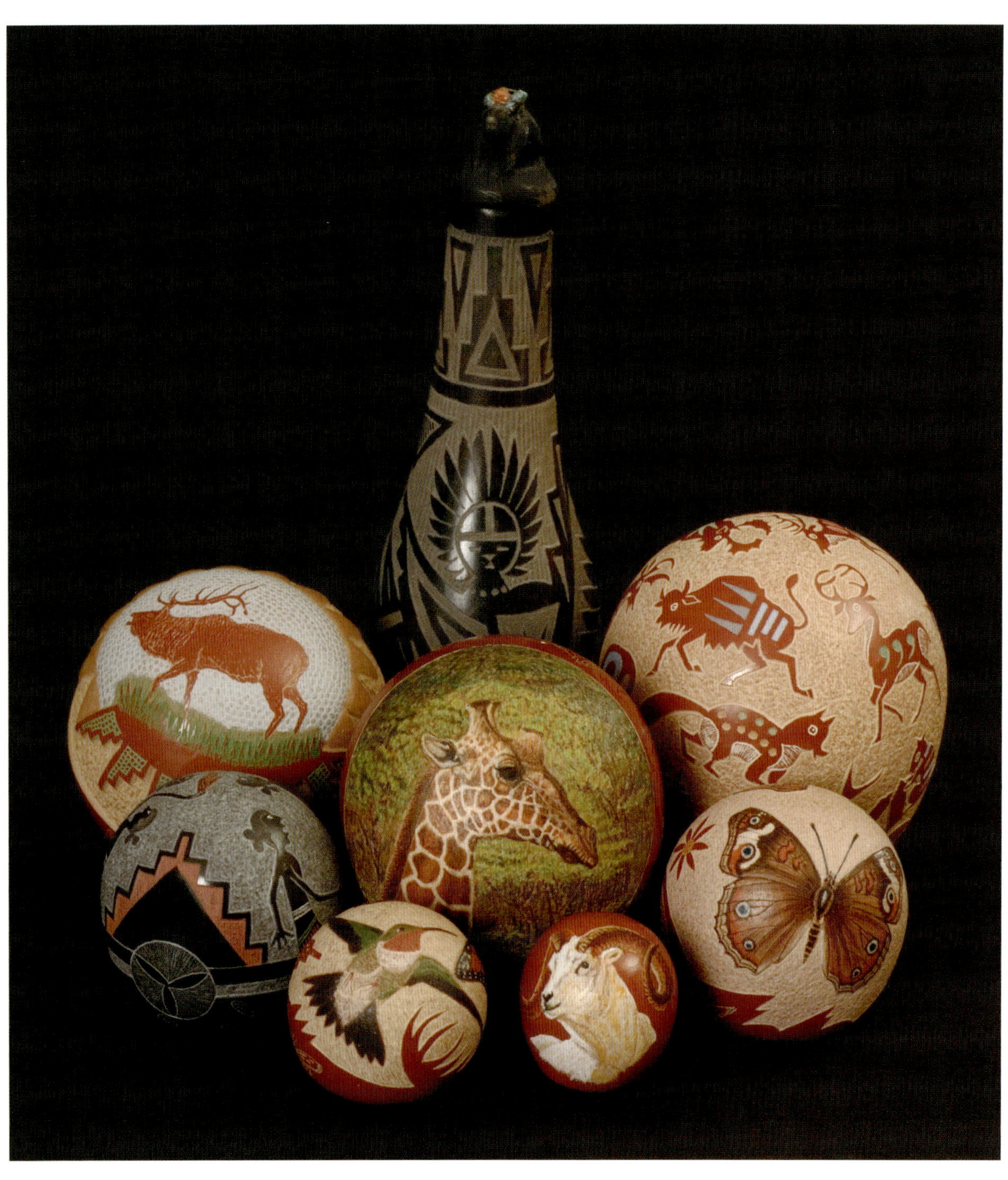

Joseph Lonewolf miniatures in the Cameros Collection

Grace Medicine Flower (1938 -) / Santa Clara

In Greek mythology, the Graces are goddesses of beauty, blossoming, and delight. In Christian theology, grace is divine favor and influence. In art, grace is elegance and beauty of form. The pottery of Grace Medicine Flower embodies all of this and more.

Born into the famous Tafoya family, Grace was privy to exceptional teachers and influences. Along with her brother, Joseph Lonewolf, Grace pioneered the use of *sgraffito*. These Tafoya potters combined this technique for precise etching of the clay surface with both of polished and matte surfaces. Applied after a pot is dried and polished but before it is fired, *sgraffito* leaves no margin for error. Done well, the result is a design more intricate than is possible with any other technique in Southwestern pottery.

While both she and her brother, Joseph, are well known for incorporating intricate *sgraffito* designs onto miniature pottery, Grace is famous for using this technique on larger vessels and in contrast to more deeply carved backgrounds. Eventually, these carved backgrounds yielded completely to Grace's knife and she began to produce vessels-*cum*-sculpture of remarkable form. She found that the strategic absence of clay could be as beautiful as its adornment.

Grace also created the idea for basket weave pieces.[xv] Influenced by prehistoric ware that retained weave impressions from the basket in which the clay was formed and fired, Grace's concept was to create a surface texture on her pottery that appeared as if the clay had fallen away to reveal a basket underneath. But Grace's "basket weave" design is carved not impressed. She incises the individual coils into the clay, then etches the texture of each coil. Finally, she adds a clay slip that mimics the natural color of woven baskets.

Grace is considered one of the best living potters of the Southwest. Her work is possibly the only pottery from Santa Clara that incorporates all styles of Santa Clara redware pottery (micaceous, polychrome, polished, and matte) as well as all the carving techniques (*sgraffito*, incising, and carving). From the shallowest etching to the most sculptural excision, Grace's work pays homage to the beauty of Santa Clara. Her pottery is a manifestation of what can be accomplished in clay with elegance of form and with the divine influence of Clay Mother.

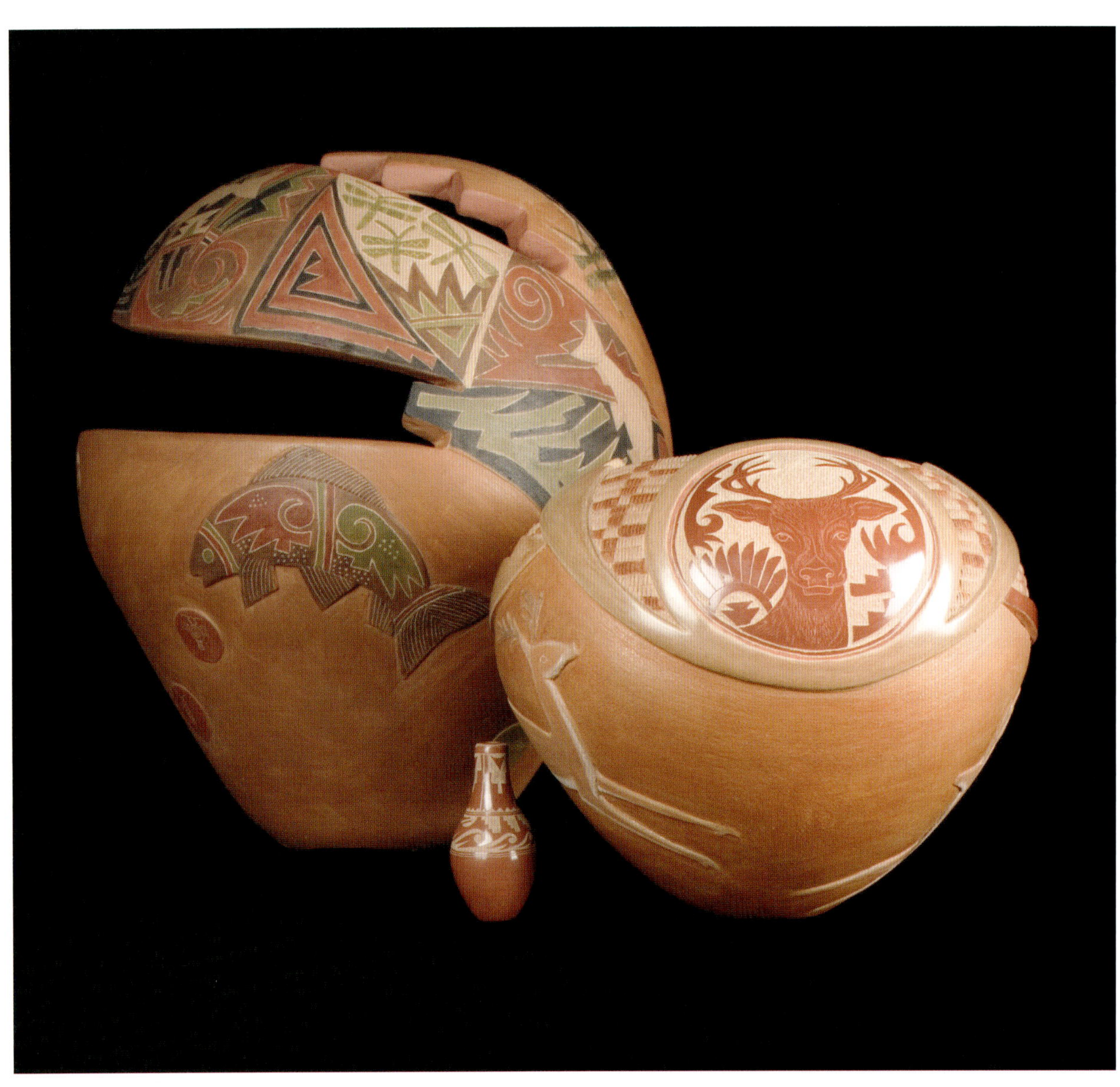

Grace Medicine Flower, redware cut out with polychrome, 2005; redware basketweave bowl, c. 2000; redware miniature, 1994. The "basketweave" bowl gives the effect of an exposed basket lying just underneath the surface of the clay.

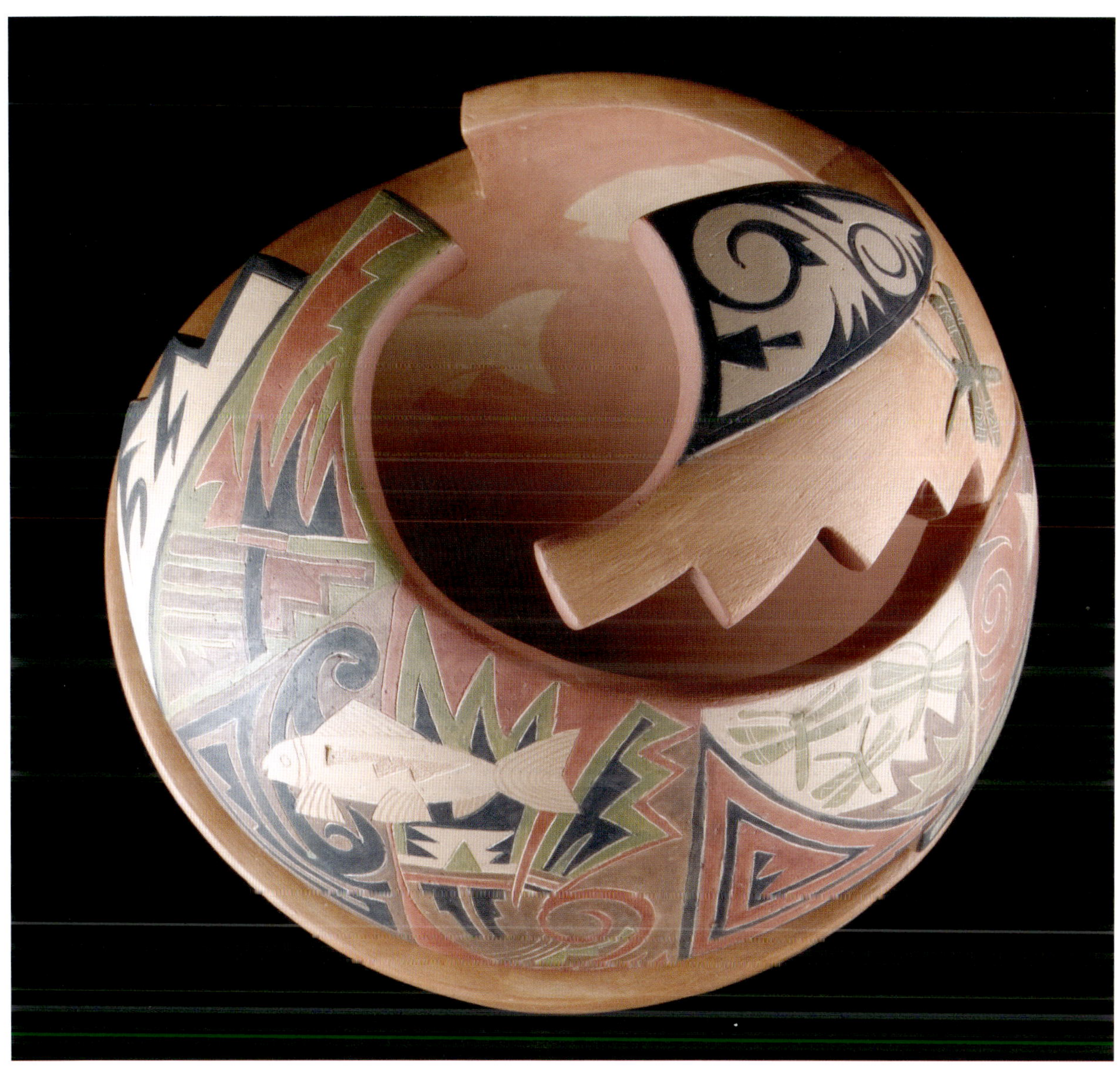

Redware cut out with polychrome (detail) Grace produces fewer than 20 pieces a year, though the demand among collectors for her pieces continues to rise with each new year and innovation.

Nancy Youngblood (1955 -) / Santa Clara

Nancy Youngblood became a perfectionist when she tried to recreate larger pottery in small-scale. But even as she experimented in miniatures, Nancy, granddaughter of Margaret Tafoya, was drawn to her family's older tradition of making large vessels with high polish and deep carving. Calling on these elements, Nancy incorporated their ideals into a new form, the s-swirl ribbed bowl that would become synonymous with her name.

The inspiration for her first swirled "melon" jar, so called because the undulating impressions mimicked those of a gourd or melon, came from her great-uncle, Camilio Tafoya, and her great- grandmother, Sara Fina. Around 1970, Nancy discovered vessels by both relatives in Santa Fe galleries. Each had simple and sparsely placed ribs. Sara Fina's water jar had slanted ribs at the lip of her vessel, and Camilio's had thick ribs that snaked from top to bottom. From those works, Nancy was inspired to create her own version of the swirled melon bowl—first making the ribs deeper, finer, and more numerous, then later curving the ribs provocatively in unrelenting ripples around the vessel.

Aside from the obvious technical challenge of the formation and polishing of these vessels, Nancy has pushed herself to achieve larger vessels in more variety with even more ribs. Her pots, whether they have straight, slanted, or swirling ribs, primarily contain 32 or 64 ribs. Six times now she has tried to carve a 128-ribbed bowl but has not yet overcome the challenge. Nevertheless, few other artists can imitate her efforts, and she has the awards to prove it. She relates a story about the highest honor she ever received: Several years back, before her grandmother passed away, Nancy showed Margaret, matriarch of the Santa Clara style, a tall vase prototype that had ribs with six curves flowing down the form. Famous for not complimenting unworthy pottery, her grandmother studied it closely and said, "I think I could make that, but I doubt I could polish it."[xvii]

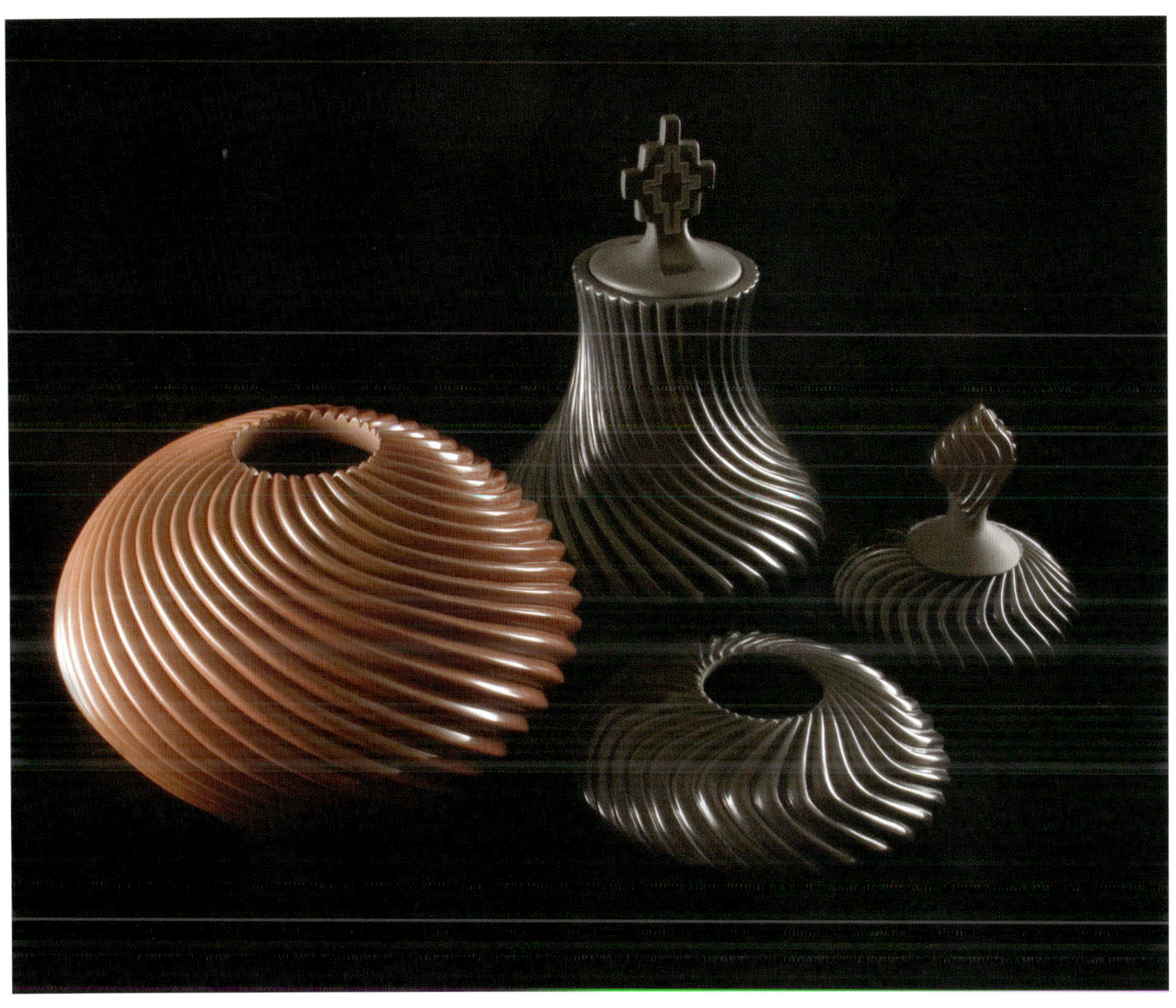

Nancy Youngblood, selection of swirled vessels. Clockwise from left: redware melon bowl, 1993; blackware vase with cruciform lid, 2003; blackware vase with swirled lid, 1991; and blackware bowl, 2003. The Nancy Youngblood pottery in the Cameros Collection are all composed of 32 ribs.

Nathan Youngblood (1954 -) / Santa Clara

Assimilation. Refinement. Perfection. These terms could be used to describe the work of any of our "Artists Without Reservation." For most, they are not the reason they have been included in the category. Nathan Youngblood did not pioneer the use of a certain tool or technique. Nor did he innovate a type of pottery finish. In the longstanding tradition of his famous family, he creates blackware and redware pottery with deeply carved designs. "Every time I sit down to create a pot, it's an act of prayer," the artist says.

While Nathan and his sister, Nancy, were born into the famous Tafoya clan, they did not grow up in the immediate presence of the pottery-making tradition. Instead, their father's military career kept them traveling the world until their teenage years. When his family moved back to Santa Clara Pueblo, Nathan went to live with his grandmother Margaret Tafoya and learned pottery making by literally mirroring everything she did.[xviii]

At first, like his grandmother, Nathan experimented with pottery that was about form and finish, but he also appreciated more figural carving and eventually translated it into large-scale pottery. Over time, Nathan's early globetrotting adventures impacted his art as much as his grandmother's tutelage. As his skills grew, he realized that every great artist, like the ones he had seen in some of the great museums of the world, had a personal style. He wanted to be an artist, not merely a craftsman. In development of that style, Nathan began to leave bare the channels he carved from the clay surface. This practice contrasted with the tradition of painting the carved out sections with thick clay slip. By leaving them exposed, he created cleaner lines. By carving at a drier stage than most potters and by experimenting with modern tools, Nathan sought to enhance the precision of these lines.

As Nathan has embraced his technique and style, he has played with forms and size. Many people who see his work agree that it appears almost Asiatic. The artist himself has claimed to have assimilated these and other cultural influences, yet, no matter who or what the inspiration, it is uniquely Santa Claran and uniquely Nathan Youngblood.

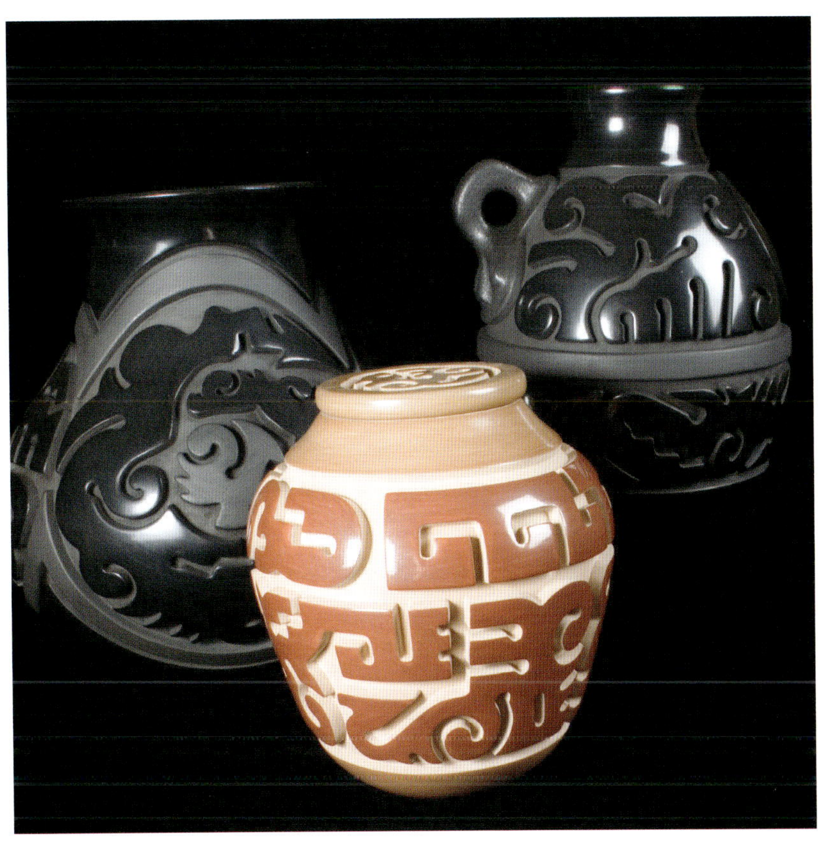

Nathan Youngblood, blackware vase, 1995-2000; redware jar with lid, c. 1995; blackware jug with handle, 2005.

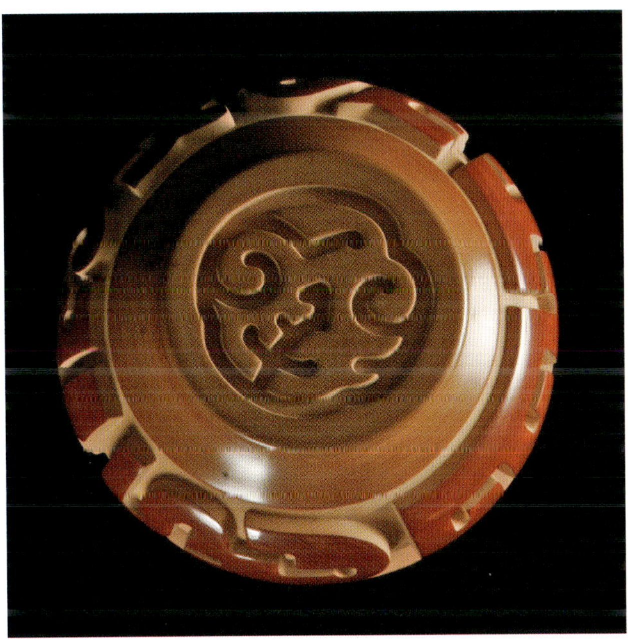

Nathan Youngblood, redware jar with lid (top). It is easy to see the almost Asian influence of Nathan's deep carving.

Autumn Borts-Medlock (1967 -) / Santa Clara

Covered with gardens of flowers and birds, the pottery of Autumn Borts-Medlock is easily distinguishable from the masses of pottery produced in the Southwest. Though the artist has continued to carve floral patterns for more than 10 years now, her technique and product continue to advance. Nancy and Alan Cameros even stood in line overnight to purchase a coveted work of hers so that their collection would reflect the best of her abilities. Yet, flowers have been sculpted into clay before, and many potters are inspired by nature. So, what is it about the pottery of Autumn Borts-Medlock that has transfixed collectors?

The floral scenes in Autumn's pottery transcend tribal design. Her designs appeal to those already passionate about Southwestern pottery as well as others who are looking for pottery that encompasses a broader aesthetic. However, her artwork is more than just well executed pottery with pretty designs. Over the years, Autumn has honed her designs so that they reflect implied motion. Flowers do not just stand in perfect arrangement. They bend and flow with the native grasses, subject to the whim of the wind. Hummingbirds do not pose happily on a twig. They are caught mid-hover, mid-flap. It is her talent for capturing such moments in time that makes her work intriguing and covetable.

Descended from the Tafoya family, Autumn cites many of her accomplished relatives as direct influences on her methods, technique, and style. Her mother, Linda Cain, and her grandmother, Mary Cain, are considered some of the best sculptors of their respective generations. Her sister, Tammy Garcia, is famous as well for her carving and unique designs. Her biggest influence, though, is another major artist who was inspired by the Southwest and its flora.

Years before she was a full-time potter or had included floral designs on her pottery, Autumn found herself waiting in a bus stop in Española, New Mexico, where she was enchanted by a poster of two large petunias advertising a Georgia O'Keeffe exhibition.[xix] Because the poster was stuck to the wall with duct tape, Autumn felt sure it did not have much value to the bus stop. She asked the receptionist if she could have the poster. Decades later, that poster hangs well-framed in Autumn Borts-Medlock's pottery studio.

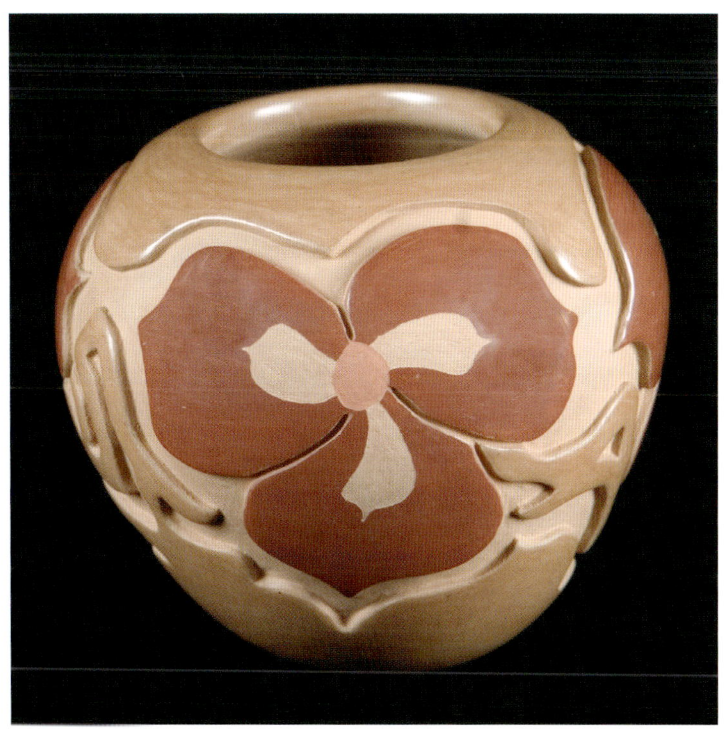

Autumn Borts-Medlock, polychrome redware "flower" jar, 1995.

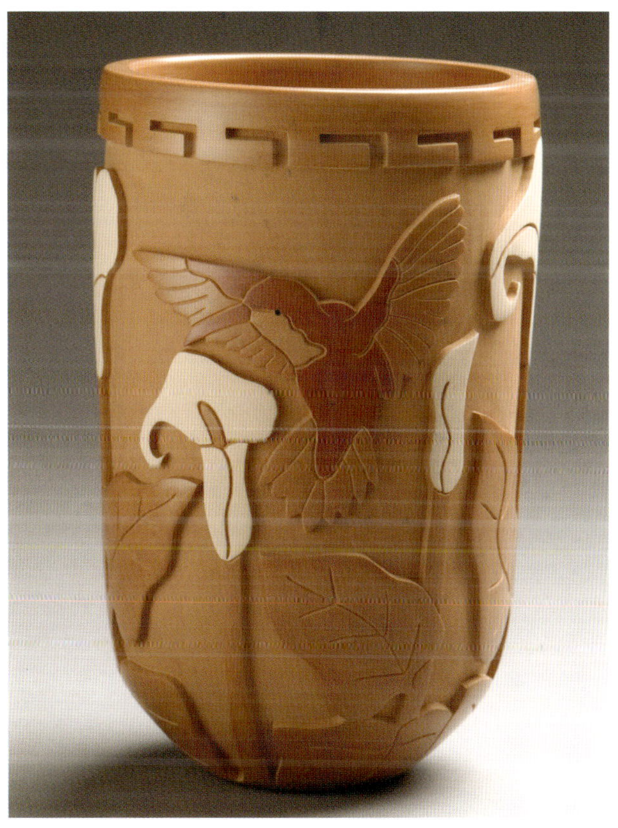

Autumn Borts-Medlock, polychrome redware "hummingbird" vase, 2001.

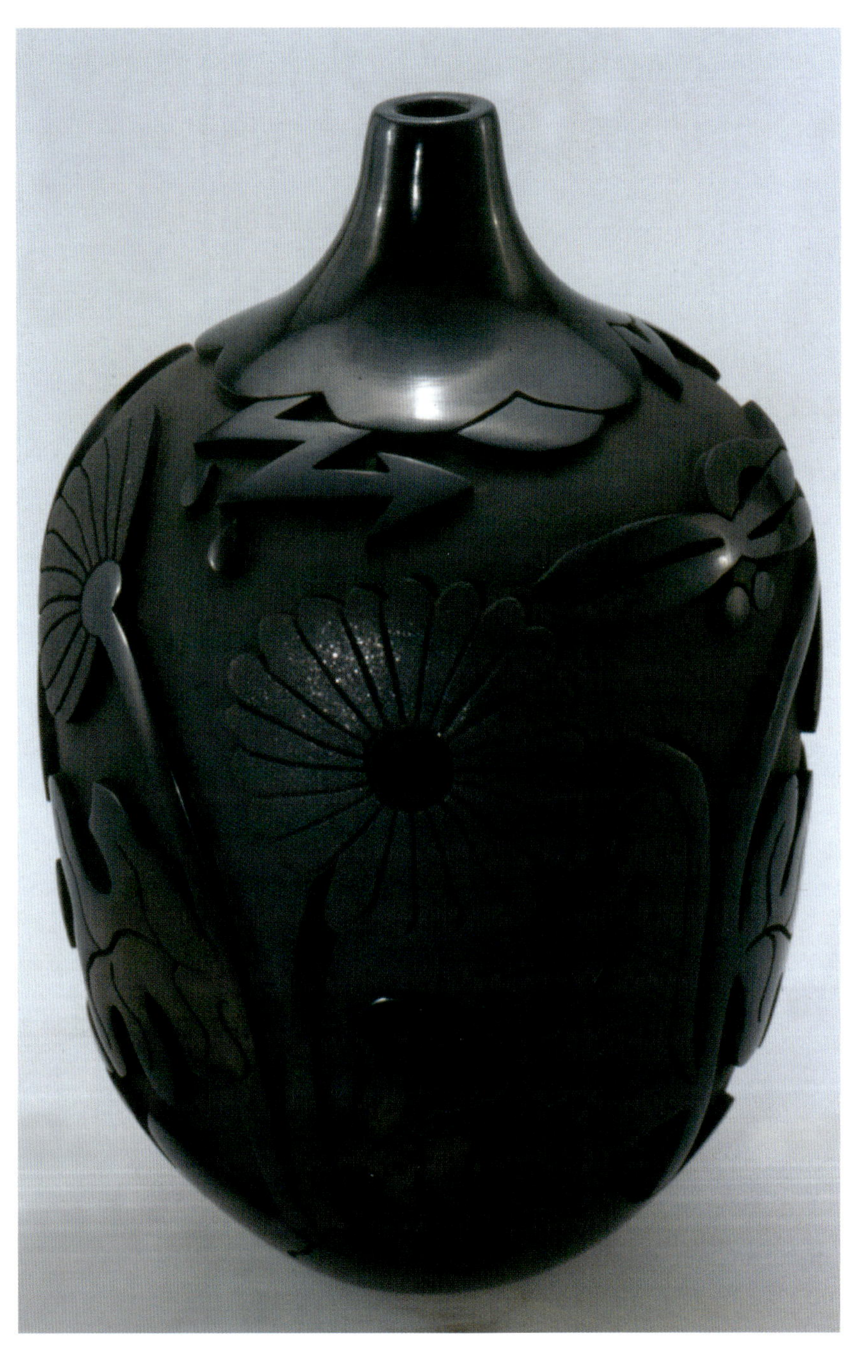

Autumn Borts-Medlock, blackware vase, 2005.

Tammy Garcia (1969 -) / Santa Clara

"Mommy, how do you lose your sense of humor? And if you do, how do you find it?" Tammy Garcia's 5-year-old daughter asked one of those profound-yet-naïve questions that can only come out of the mouths of babes. True to her heritage and artistry, Tammy answered her daughter's question by designing a piece of pottery.

Tammy Garcia is one of the most celebrated potters of her generation. She is descended from a long line of famous potters who collectively have established and extended the Santa Clara pottery tradition. By virtue of her lineage, she has had the opportunity to study with some of the best potters this land has ever known, though it has been her own talent and creativity that has propelled her to the top of her field since she started selling pottery at age 16. She is an exceptional carver who has begun applying her skills to other media such as bronze and glass. She has pushed the limits of her original medium, clay, making pottery of a size that rivals even her great-great-grandmother Sara Fina Tafoya's legendary storage jars.

Simple things like her child's innocent question inspire her. Challenged to find an answer that would satisfy her daughter, Tammy was reminded of *koshari*, pueblo clowns who use humor to teach children right from wrong. Tammy set out to create a pot featuring a *koshari* playing "Guess which hand?" with a small child. In the carvings, the child guesses at which hand holds an apple. True to life, the clown was changing the hand that hold the apple and holding out an empty hand in response to each guess. What the clown did not realize was that there was a horse behind him who was about to eat the concealed apple.

It is this kind of storytelling in the carving tradition that Garcia feels compelled to preserve and promote. Like most of her generation, Tammy learned from observing, and she attributes many of her designs to established motifs like the *koshari*. She has an affinity for prehistoric and historic pottery and feels that most modern scholars overlook the storytelling and record-keeping function of even the simplest piece of pottery. Tammy is trying to keep this function alive while carrying on other Santa Clara traditions.

Carving is one of the longstanding traditions in the Tafoya family. Tammy states that Sara Fina Tafoya was thought to have used her finger to indent a simple *avanyu* (water serpent) form into some of her pieces.[xx] For a time, the more famous indented bear paw practically became a family logo. Many members of the Tafoya clan, Tammy Garcia notably among them, have taken this tradition to new levels of creativity and excellence.

Tammy is doing more than following tradition; she is pushing the limits of the medium and the boundaries of the tradition. Her carving has become more intricate and multilayered and her vessels bigger and bolder in their composition. She is currently working in a scale that is about three-times larger than other potters. To work in such size is to gamble with disaster. The larger the pot, the more fragile it becomes.

In August 2006, the Cameroses commissioned Tammy to create a vessel that would exemplify her skills as a potter. This meant creating a large-scale piece that would ultimately be the largest in their collection. Adding to the significance of the commission, it was to be polished blackware, not redware. Redware pots can be kiln fired, and Tammy was one of the first potters who dared do this in defiance of tradition. Kiln firing offers the artist greater control than the traditional but inherently more precarious process of pit-firing. Blackware, however, must be pit-fired in order to produce the color for which it is named and valued.

Early in the commission, Tammy sat down with the Cameroses to talk about imagery. They knew that they wanted traditional imagery, but they also wanted something unique and relevant to themselves. No stranger to storytelling, Tammy probed with questions about what inspired them. When they told her about their grandson, who kept them on their toes with all of his energy and questions, Tammy was reminded of how her daughter had inspired the first appearance of *koshari* on her pottery.

As of this writing, the Cameros commission has yet to be completed. When finished, it will be a masterful example of both tradition and originality; and in deference to the children who inspire potter and patron alike, the piece will most assuredly feature *koshari*.

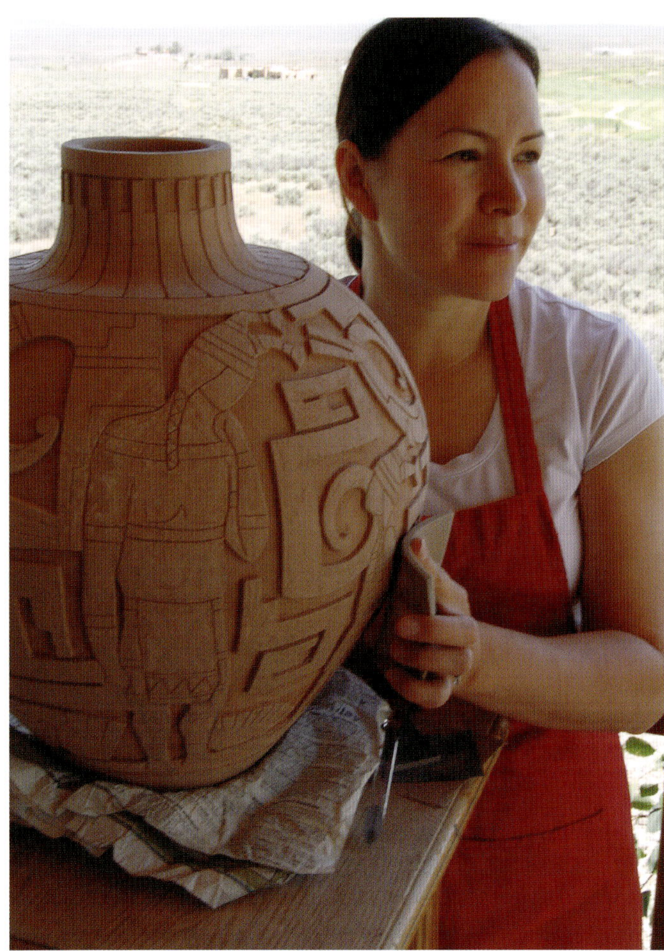

Tammy Garcia with the storage jar commissioned by Nancy and Alan Cameros, 2007.

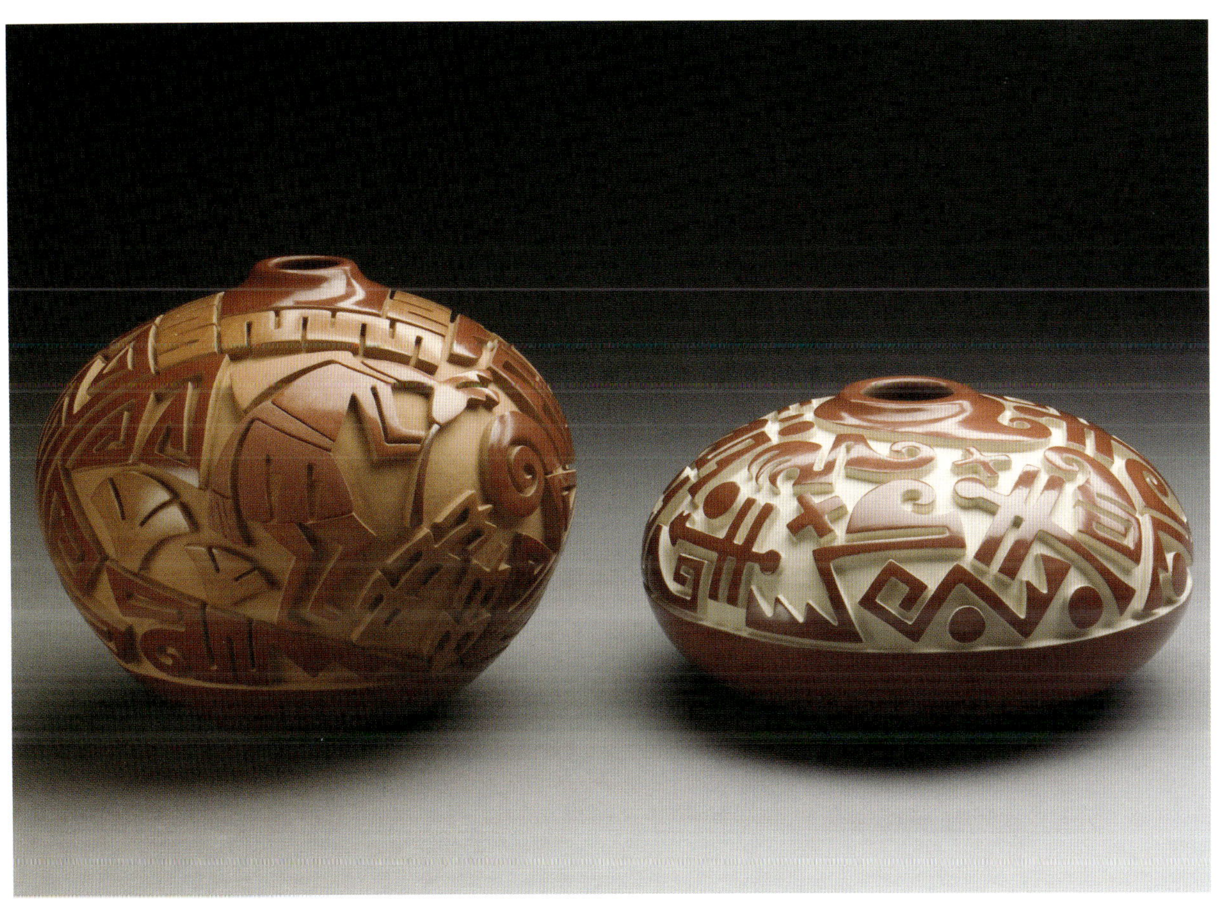

Tammy Garcia, (L) redware heightened with various red slips, c. 1996; (R) redware with white slip and dragonfly motif, 1994.
Tammy has begun using a style of polychrome on redware that relies on different tones of red clay on carved patterns at different levels.

Jody Folwell (1942 -) / Santa Clara

Perhaps more than any other avant-garde artist in this chapter of avant-garde artists, Jody Folwell represents the concept of an Artist Without Reservation. No matter the finish, no matter the clay, no matter the decorative technique, Jody is likely to incorporate it at some time, making her work a courageous deviation from established pottery standards.

No slave to fashion, Jody does not pay heed to what the market dictates—usually repetition of a familiar style—and refuses even to repeat her own work. Nor does she adhere to ancestral styles. Her work is frequently politically or socially motivated, but not always. Her pots are recurrently asymmetrical, but not always. Yet somehow, despite the mercurial design elements and structure, there is still a recognizable Jody Folwell style.[xxi]

What, then, is the hallmark of her work? Some think it is merely its ability to draw attention to its difference. Such an assumption robs the work of its intensity, for it is the artist and the intentions she places behind the creation of these vessels that remain consistent. Not merely a utilitarian or decorative object, each Jody Folwell pot is a statement reflecting the artist's personal and political sensibilities.

Jody is a late bloomer when it comes to pottery. Following her college education, she worked as an educator and began a family. Ten years into her first marriage, Jody returned to the art form she was introduced to as a child. Rather than follow the immensely successful style of her native Santa Clara Pueblo, Jody immediately began to introduce unorthodox shapes and "protest pots." She incorporated wordplay and abstraction, letting designs hover on the surface of the pot as if it were a canvas. She was also one of the first artists to begin displaying brown pottery, a color that is achieved by removing it early from an oxygen-poor manure fire. According to Jody's daughter, Susan, early removal from the firing process was initially a mistake, but the rich-colored result inspired Jody to create more pots in that style.
Remarking on Jody, Scottsdale gallery owner Charles King muses: "It is interesting that in talking about Jody to other artists, I often hear the word 'courageous.' She embarked on many of her artistic stylings in the 1970s, when the impact of Maria [Martinez] may have been at its highest. Yet, she chose to follow her own path."

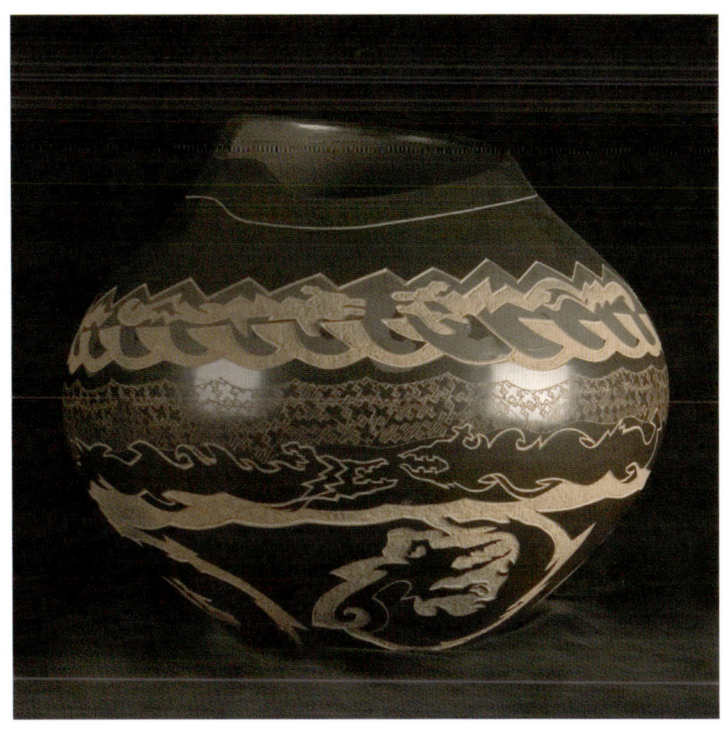

Jody Folwell, blackware bowl, c. 1997.

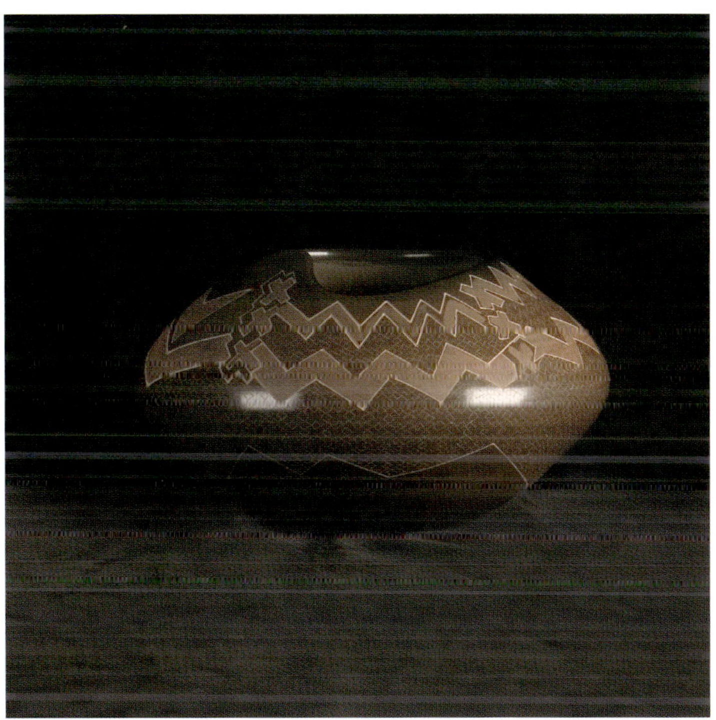

Jody Folwell, blackware bowl, c. 1996. The color variation in this bowl is a testament to Jody's skill at firing her pots.

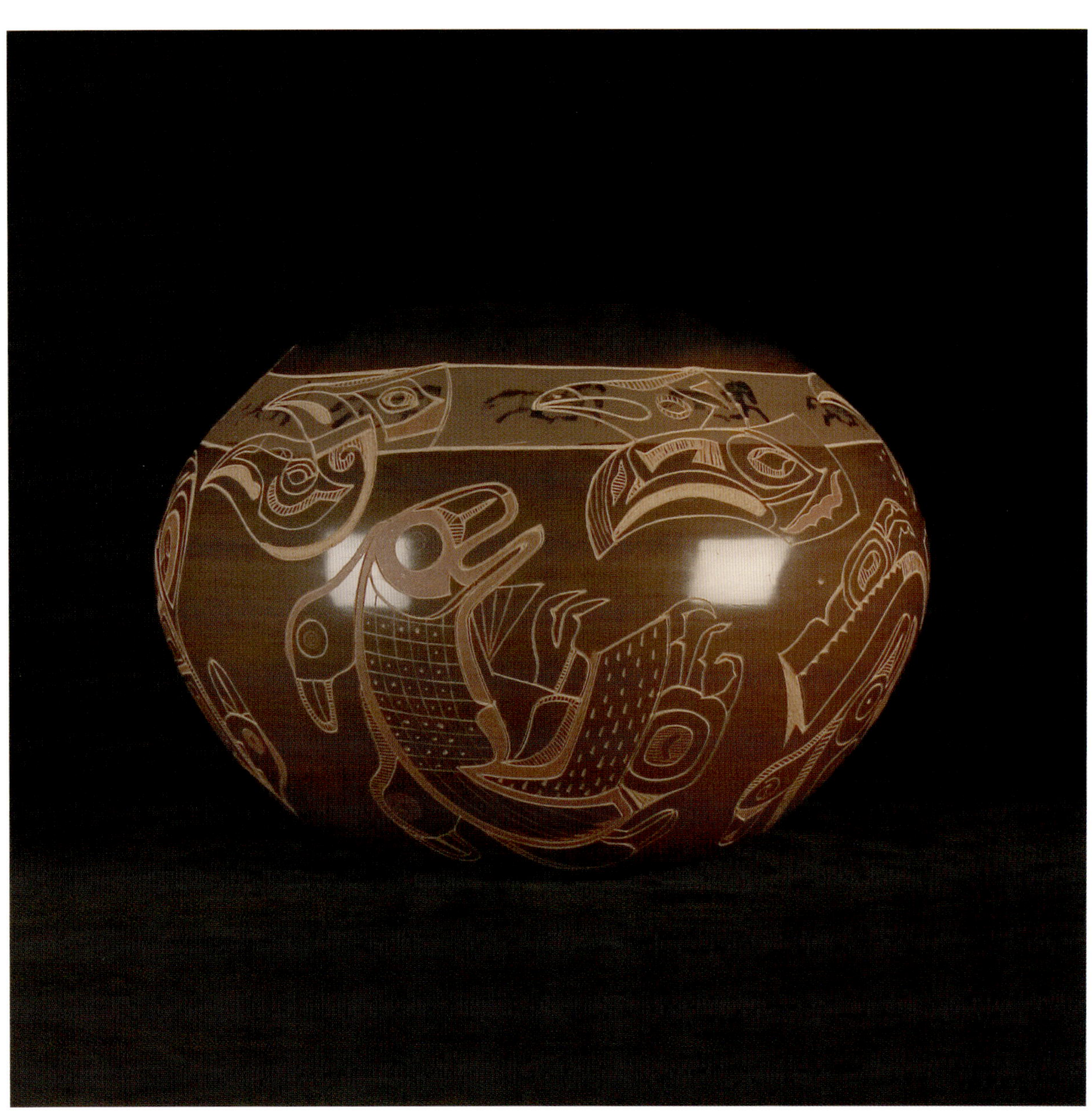

Jody Folwell, brownware bowl, c. 1997. Notice Jody's use of designs inspired by Pacific Northwest tribes.

Susan Folwell (1970 -) / Santa Clara

Ironically, being born into a family of iconoclasts comes with expectations. True to her roots, Susan Folwell is as likely to meet these as defy them. Influenced equally by tradition and rebellion, Susan's pottery is the result of experimentation with established techniques and non-indigenous slips, including the use of wood stains and acrylics. Like her progressive mother, Jody Folwell, Susan is a nonconformist, drawing criticism from some while commanding respect on the whole for her contributions to the art form.

As with many pueblo artists, Susan is influenced greatly by her mother's pottery. That defiant style motivates Susan to incorporate *sgraffito*, high polish, unorthodox figures and words, and asymmetrical forms in her own pottery. Susan transcends her mother's efforts through the addition of vibrant colors. These have become her trademark, but she is just as likely to return to muted, natural clay colors and more symmetrical shapes.

No matter the size, shape, or coloration, Susan's pottery is decidedly graphic. Images from ancient to contemporary are never absent from her wares, whether delicately incised or vividly painted. She has even been known to introduce unexpected elements: Northwest Coast Indian symbols, caricatures of politicians, and even commercial product logos. This reliance on imagery can perhaps be attributed to her earlier education in photography, both at the Center for Creative Studies in Detroit, Michigan, and the Idyllwild School of Music and Arts in California. Regardless of whether particular images appeal to different collectors or admirers of her work, it is obvious that the work itself is a timeless statement reflecting American culture, not just Southwest tradition.

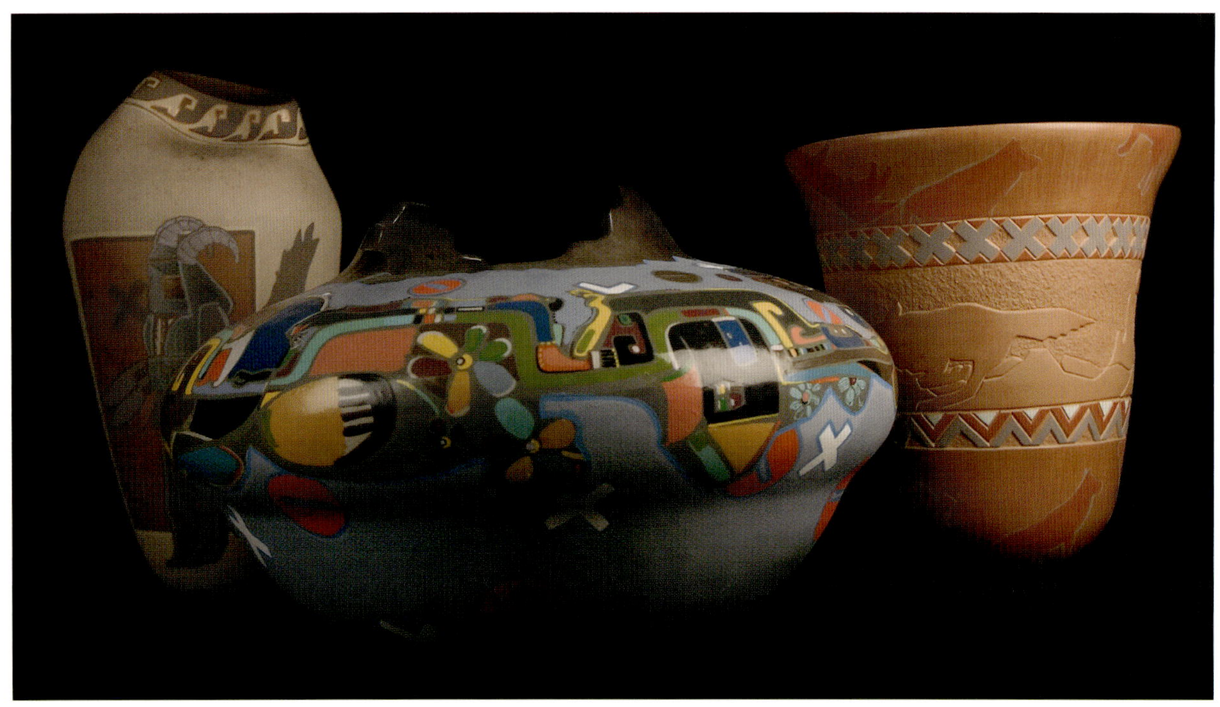

Susan Folwell, L-R: "Medicine Man" polychrome vase, c. 2005; "Slaughter of the Lambs" polychrome bowl, c. 2001; "Coyotes" redware vase with sgraffito *and polychrome, c. 2004. The outstanding variety in Susan's work is obvious from the pieces in the Cameros Collection.*

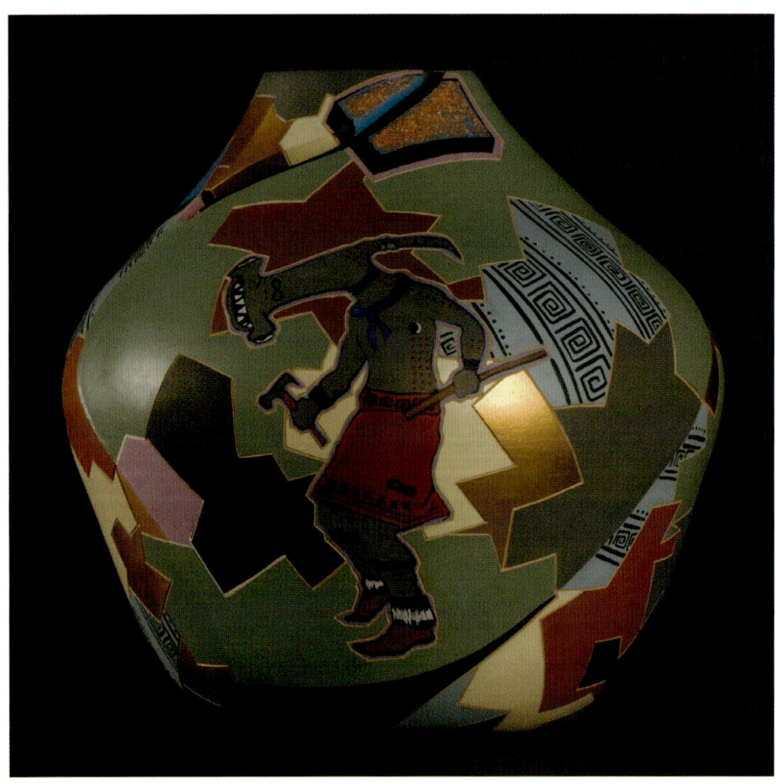

Susan Folwell, "Hommage to the Pottery Gods," polycrome jar, 2007.

Thomas Polacca (1935 - 2003) / Hopi

Grandson of the famous Nampeyo of Hano, Thomas Polacca was one of the first men to practice the Hopi's typically female art of pottery making. So strong was the Hopi indignation at a man who made pottery that Tom veered from making traditional polychrome vessels. Under the conflicting pressures of artistically expressing himself through pottery and perpetrating further cultural offense, Tom created his own unique style.

Like some of his non-Hopi contemporaries, Tom became known for pots with deep incising that separated designs and colors. Unlike others who pioneered this technique, Tom incorporated Hopi designs and vibrant colors. This departure from the Hopi tradition of making smooth vessels adorned with elaborate painted designs established a new trend. Indeed, Tom's pottery appears less like a painted vessel than an amalgamation of assorted clays with many colors and textures. Today, his pottery is immediately recognizable by the colorful, narrative scenes that are incised deeply into the surface.

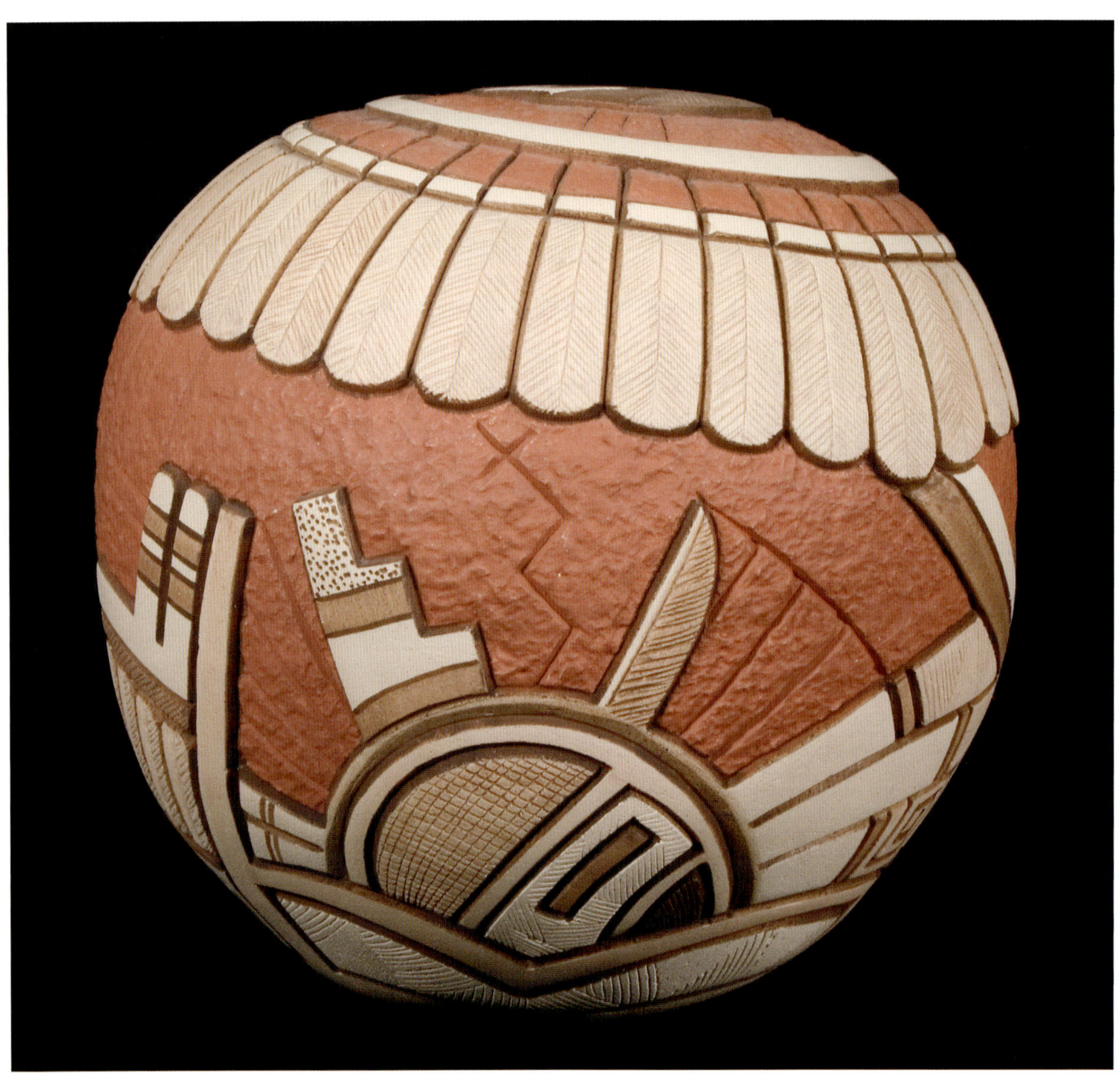

Thomas Polacca, polychrome seed jar, 1992. By incising around figures and creating surface texture with sgraffito, *Tom heightened his colors in a way Hopi tradition had never seen before.*

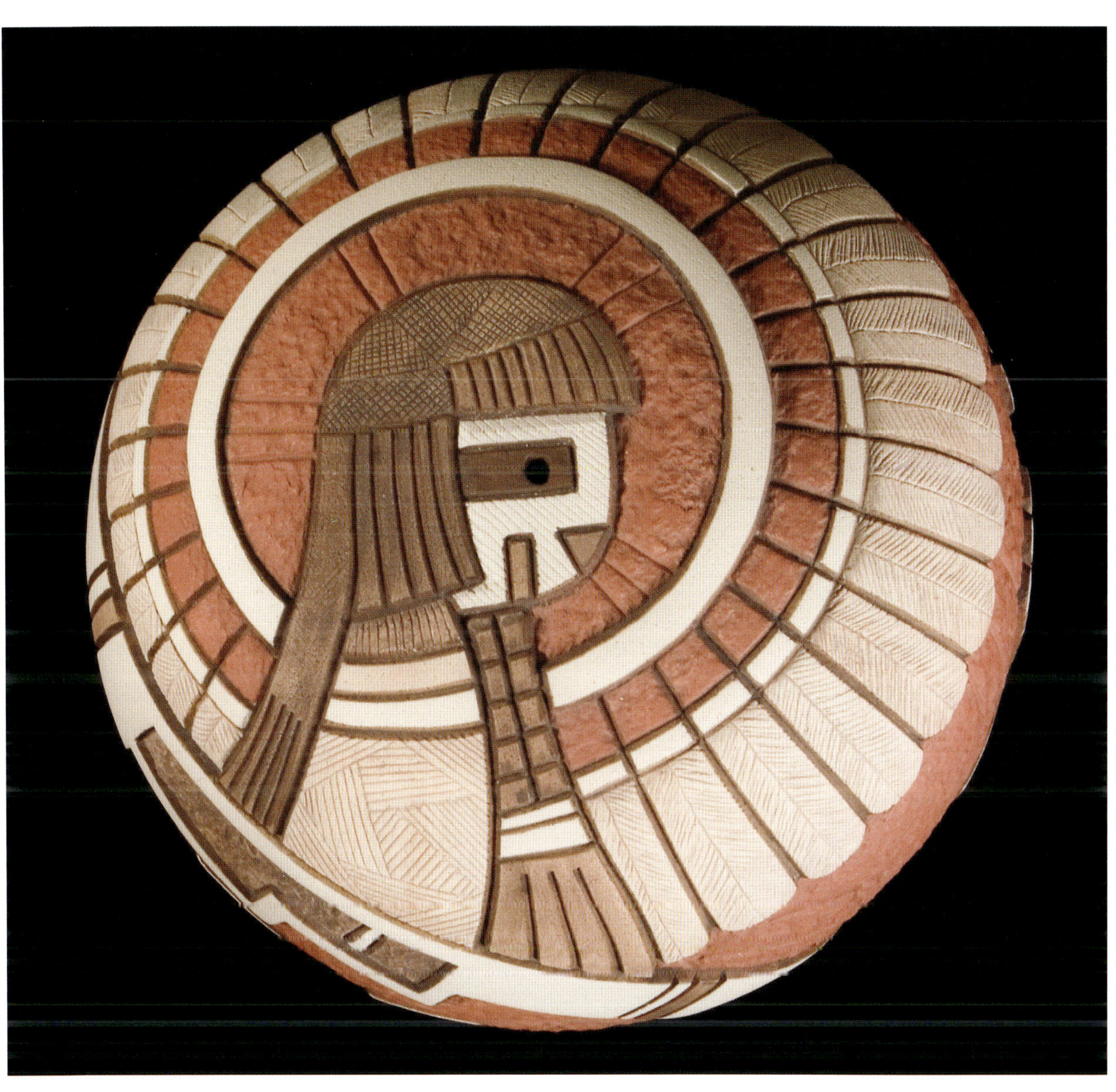

Thomas Polacca, polychrome seed jar, 1992, top view.

Al Qöyawayma (1938 -) / Hopi

Al Qöyawayma is known for creating pale, silken, ceramic vessels with almost classical repoussé figures. Sometimes, the low relief yields to actual sculpture in his minimalist creations, but both techniques invoke the Southwestern cultures. The subtle tones and shadows that dance across the surface recall the ancient lands of his Hopi people with startling power.

His teacher and aunt, Elizabeth White (Polingaysi), once admonished him to "take the best from other cultures and blend with what you already have."[xxii] She should know. As her nephew states, "She made the transition from 'the stone age to modern day."[xxiii] True to her advice, Al Q—as he is widely known—uses the best from his native tradition: local clays, coil construction, and stone polishes, yet is not restricted by these or any traditions. Instead of scraping the clay like most in the Southwest tradition, he pulls it like taffy. While Nampeyo of Hano, matriarch of the Hopi tradition of pottery, helped refine the clay used by the Hopi in pottery, Al does not settle. A scientist at heart, he has created his own clay mixtures based on his Sikyatki cultural roots. As for the repoussé technique, you are more likely to find it on medieval European reliquaries[xxiv] than other Southwestern pottery.

Like his pieces that transcend tradition and ancestry, Al Q defies description as a potter or artist. "Renaissance man" might be a more accurate label. Poet, potter, sculptor, scientist, educator... Al Q creates pottery stemming from many traditions and none. He calls on his ancestral tradition to a certain degree when considering subject matter for his artwork but abandons and exceeds it when it comes to what he creates. His recent turn to polychrome slips is homage to the strong Hopi tradition of polychrome pottery.

Born and raised in Los Angeles, the background of this Southwest potter was already destined to be different than those who grew up in the pueblos and reservations. Al Q's creativity is blended with an analytical ability that propelled him into other fields. He holds degrees in engineering from California State Polytechnical University San Luis Obispo and the University of Southern California. He holds co-patents worldwide on Inertial Guidance Systems for military and passenger aircraft. He was a Fulbright Fellow to the Maori people of New Zealand. He formed and managed the environmental department of the Salt River Project, Central Arizona's primary electric and water utility, and he co-founded the American Indian Science and Engineering Society, a group that has grown in membership to over one half million.[xxv]

How does one define a man of such expansive ability? The words "thinker" and "medium" come to mind, for those two characteristics govern all he does. In the world of Southwestern pottery, they befit a true innovator.

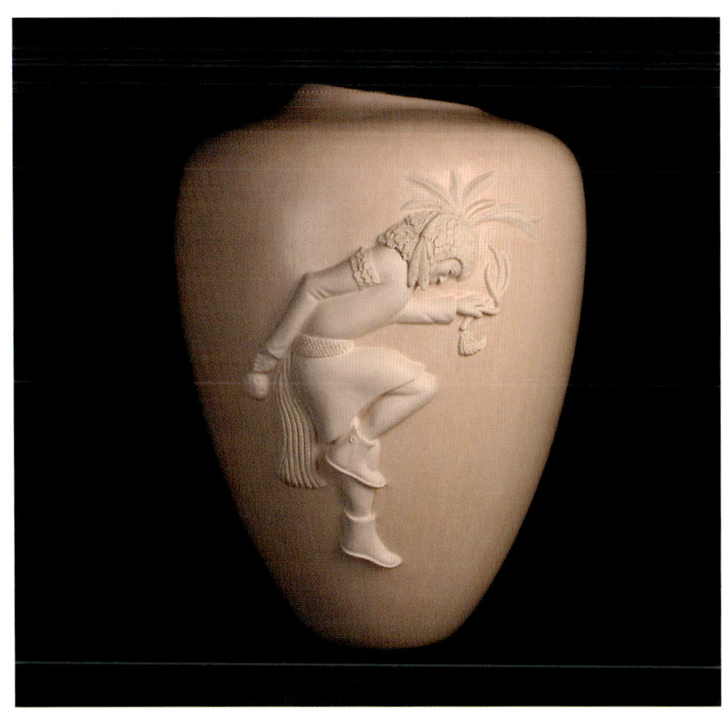

Al Qöyawayma, buffware vase with buffalo dancer, 1991.

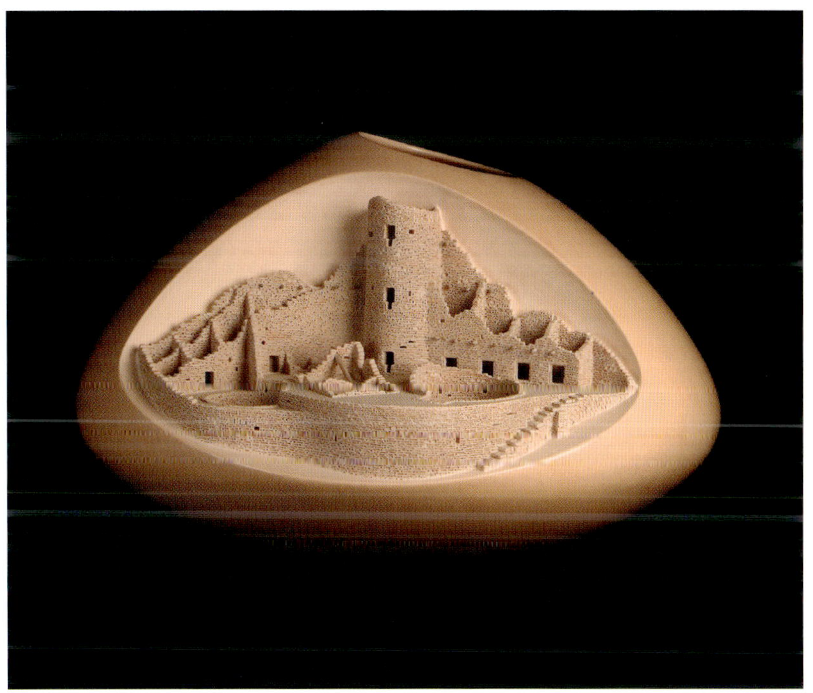

Al Qöyawayma, Mesa Verde series buffware vessel with high relief dwelling, 1992. Vessels such as these are carved out or carved in to a single piece of clay after it has been formed into its basic shape. The only additional application of clay would be in forming the outside walls of the dwelling. The artist states that because of the high sculptural relief, shadow creates realism in the replicated architecture.

Preston Duwyenie (1951 -) / Hopi

Despite the extensive Hopi tradition of elaborate painted designs, Preston Duwyenie has found a niche in the creation of minimalist forms that show off the texture and beauty of the clay, augmented with judiciously placed bits of silver inlay. It is difficult to say which is the vehicle for which: the silken luster of polished clay to underscore the barest embellishment of precious metal, or vice versa. The juxtaposition of the two and the resultant art are the perfect vehicle for Preston's exceptional aesthetic.

Schooled as a potter and jeweler, Preston's work combines these crafts with unique skill and beauty. Metal inlay is rare in pottery, and Preston seems to perceive metal differently than other jewelers might. Rather than viewing silver as the frame for a gemstone, this potter uses it sparingly as the crown jewel of his creations.

For the past decade, Preston has experimented with textures of both clay and inlay, trying to recreate each in the other. He opposes and sometimes complements textures in each—the silver invoking patterns of rippling water, the sand recalling windblown dunes. The artist relates the story[xxvi] of how these simple elements came to be represented in his pottery. At a low point in Preston's life, he went walking in the dunes around the Hopi Reservation, seeking guidance. As he prayed, he came upon a small rock in the sand. By the patterns in the sand around it, Preston noticed how the tiny pebble had forced both the wind and sand to alter their courses. “It was a tiny island in a sea of sand,” reflects the artist. In that rock, he saw himself and the fortitude he sought. Preston would later give this same stone to his second wife, Debra, in a symbolic gesture of giving himself to her for safeguarding. Debra keeps that stone with her in a small pouch that also contains cornmeal, a traditional Hopi prayer offering.

Shortly after he found the stone, Preston adopted the stone and the rippling sand patterns into his art. Indeed, this texture has become something of a hallmark in his recent work. It is hard to imagine something as ubiquitous as sand becoming a hallmark for anyone in the Southwest, but Preston's work readily merits it. Like the sandy landscapes, his work is stark, simple, and infused with powerful elements. While he continues to use ancient pottery-making techniques, Preston, like his rock, has clearly established a path of his own.

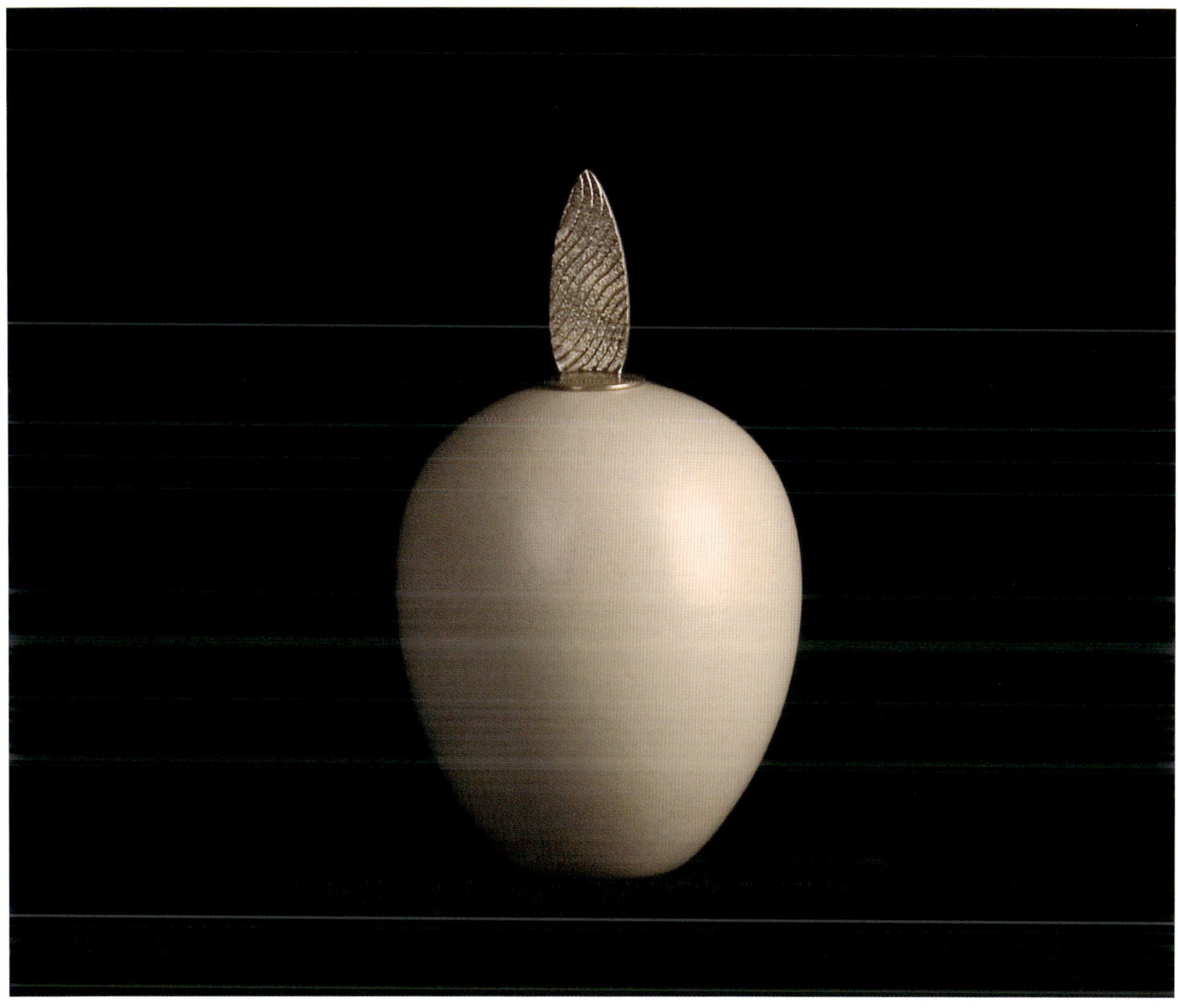

Preston Duwyenie, Shifting Sands series, buffware seed jar with silver lid, c. 1998-99. In this series, the clay represents Mother Earth; the silver stopper symbolizes the water of Heaven, which is considered a masculine force in Hopi tradition. The two elements unite to germinate the precious seeds within.

Les Namingha (1968 -) / Hopi

Taught by his famous aunt, Dextra Quotskuyva Nampeyo, Les Namingha learned to create Hopi pottery with thin walls, fine finishes, and family designs. His artistic sensibility would continue to develop through a series of unusual experiences. Eager to expand their child's horizons, Namingha's parents encouraged him to participate in the Indian Placement Program with a Mormon family. Though he returned to the reservation every summer and participated in his Native religious ceremonies, Les became sufficiently involved in the Church of Jesus Christ of Latter Day Saints to attend Brigham Young University in Utah. During that time, he worked for two years as a missionary in England and earned a degree in design.[xxvii]

He has taken his contemporary training in design and applied it to his family tradition, making his pottery a heady combination of the traditional and innovative. Bold, abstract designs inspired by the likes of Sol Lewitt and Jasper Johns[xxviii] appear on his wares as if the pottery surface itself were a painted canvas. Even the shapes of some of his pots reveal modernist sensibilities, though all are wrought in traditional fashion.

The pieces by Les Namingha in the Cameros Collection exemplify some of his finest work and an important step toward the more colorful and abstract work he does today. The expressionistic ribbons that swirl around these pots simultaneously divide the pots into multiple sections and unify the whole. Designs painted in miniature act as parts of a larger mosaic. These “Mosaic Pots” were inspired by the Shard Pattern created by Les's aunt, Dextra, and by the subsequent body of work by Hopi potter Rondina Huma. Elements like a carved, undulating lip do not seem out of place in traditional Hopiware, even while being strikingly original.

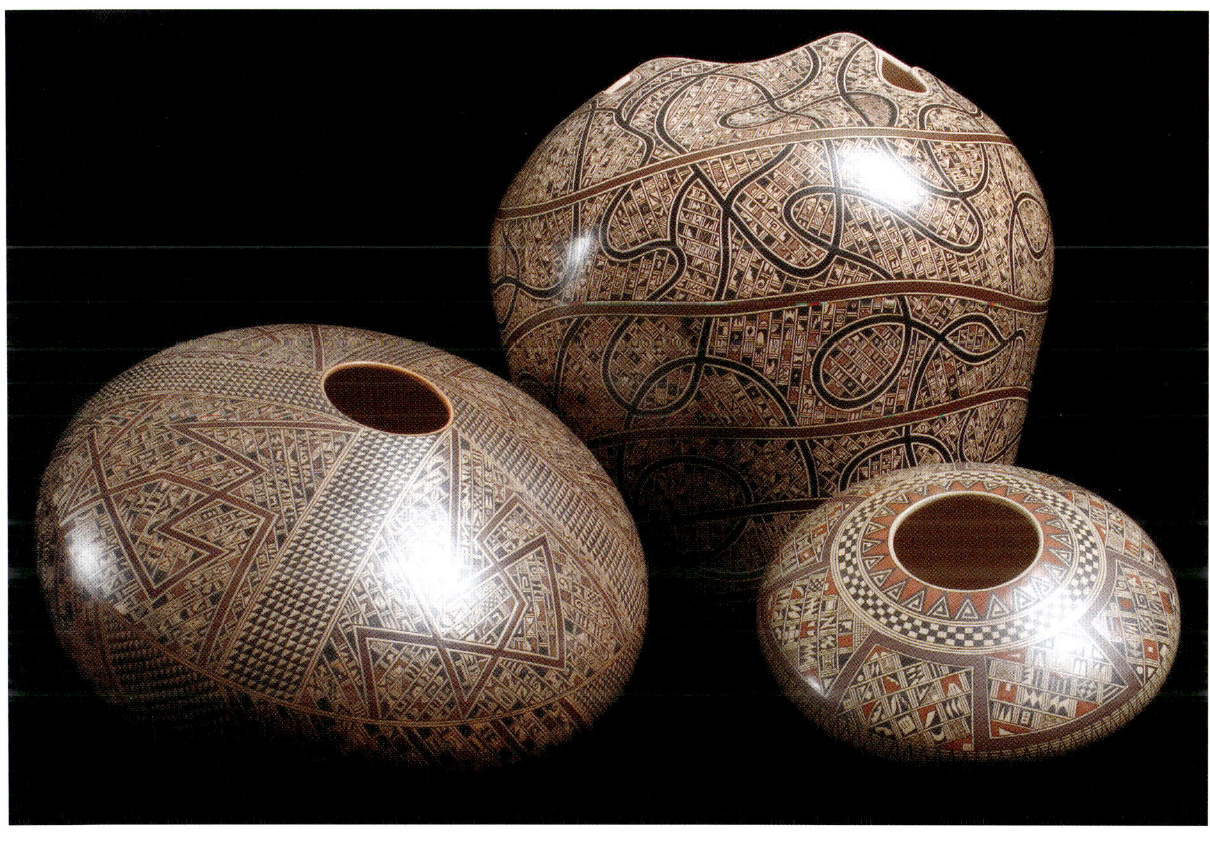

(L-R) Les Namingha, polychrome "mosaic" jars, c. 2005 and c. 2006; and Rondina Huma, polychrome mosaic jar, 2001.

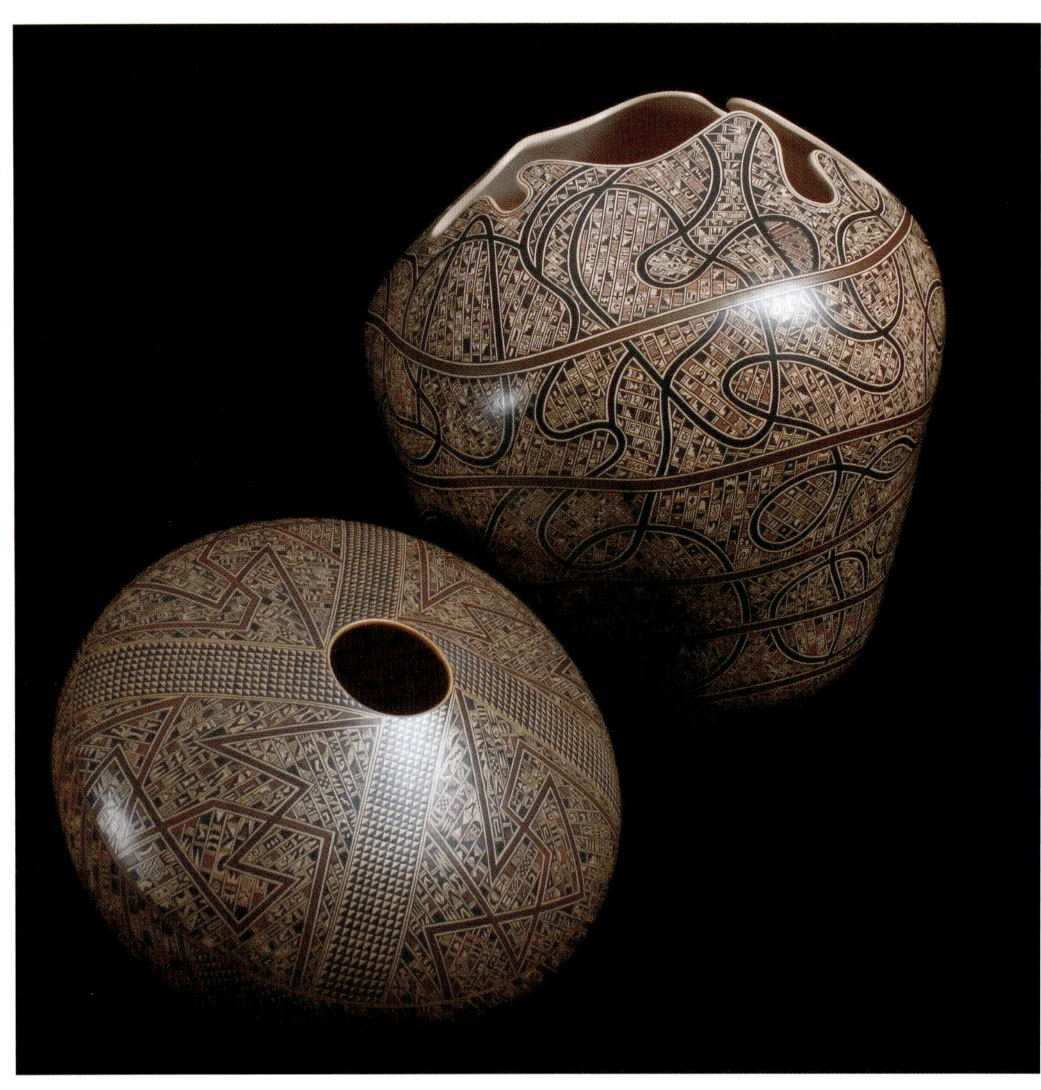

Les Namingha, polychrome "mosaic" jars, c. 2005 and c. 2006 (L-R).

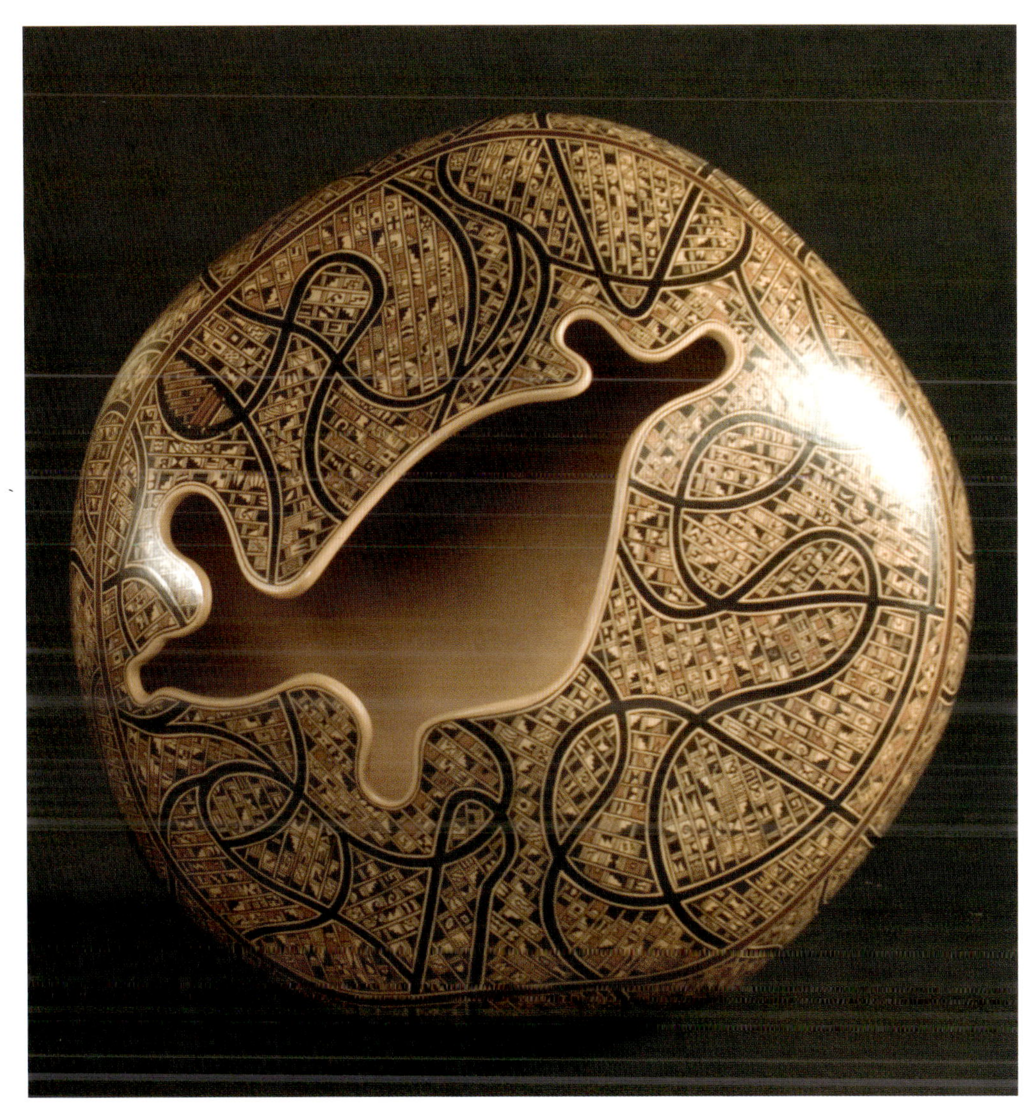

Les Namingha, detail of carved lip on polychrome "mosaic" jar, c. 2006.

Alice Cling (1946 -) / Navajo (Diné)

During the late 19th and early 20th century, the Navajo Reservation, because of its geography, was largely bypassed by the forces that gave birth to contemporary Southwestern pottery. Free from the influence of demand that brought other pottery types to the fore, Navajo pottery remained an almost strictly utilitarian, minor craft form.

Primarily unadorned, traditional Navajo pottery was made of rather unexceptional brown clay and was coated with pine pitch for waterproofing. Alice Cling, a groundbreaking potter from Tonalea region on the Navajo Reservation, raised this craft to fine art. Along with her mother, Rose, Alice began to refine crude utilitarian forms and pay attention to how the local clay fired. While still simple, in that they are unadorned, Alice's pots exhibit a mastery of elegant forms.

The aesthetic contribution of Alice's work is the magnificent coloration that she achieves in her pottery during the firing process. Similar to pottery-making in other reservations and the pueblos, the Navajo technique is arduous. It requires the clay to be dug, dried, sifted to remove impurities, mixed with temper, formed, scraped, polished, and, of course, fired. It is this last step (as combined with the local clay) that lends a unique character to Alice's work. After covering her pottery with a red slip Alice burns local juniper wood in an outdoor kiln to coax dark fire clouds to bloom over the red surface that also gives hints of purple. Then, following Navajo custom, she applies warm pine pitch to the pots as they exit the fire. The pitch saturates every pore of the clay surface. This tradition imparts a waterproof quality to porous wares. Alice takes it one aesthetic step further and burnishes the pitch to produce the final gloss that distinguishes her work.

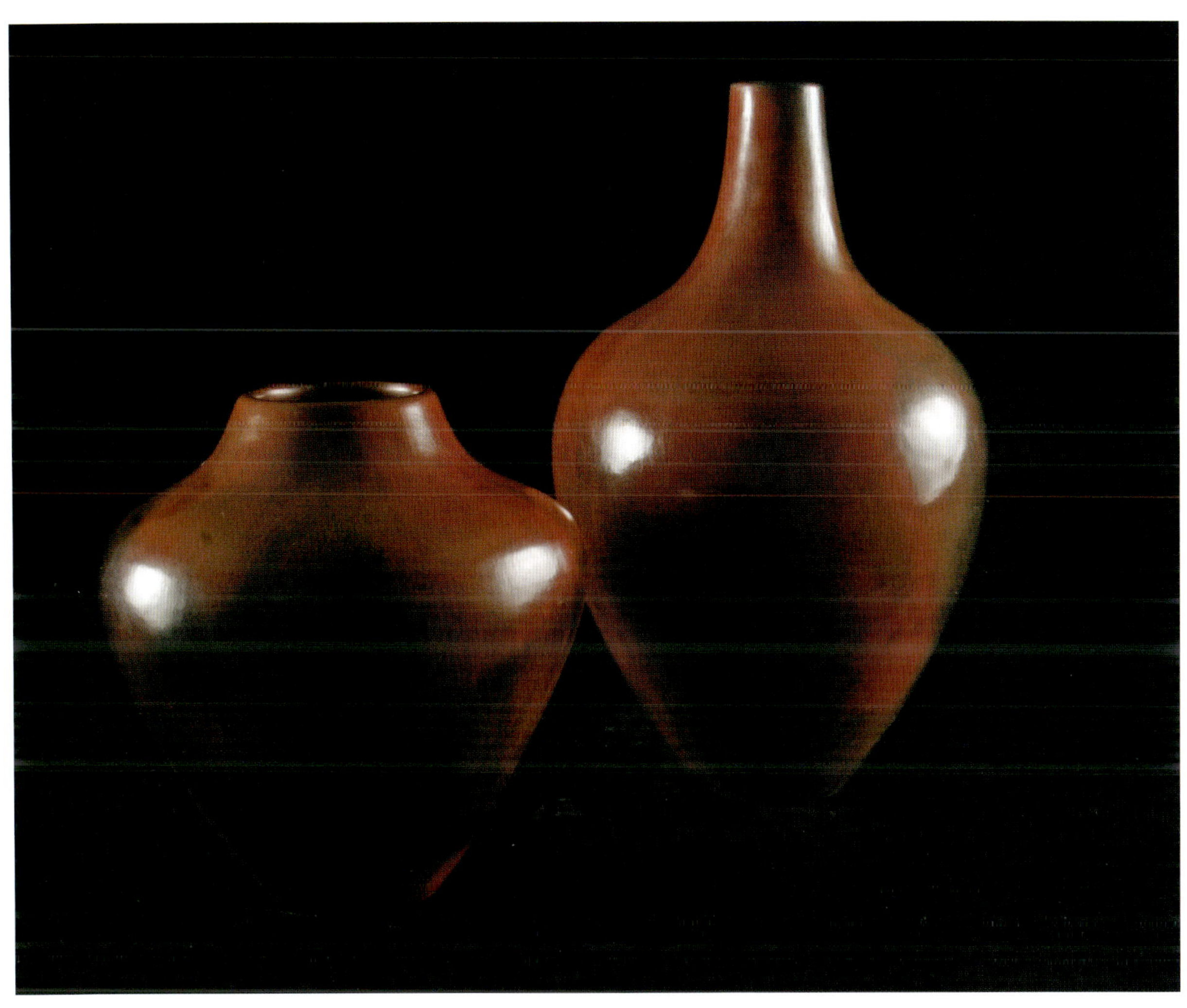

Alice Cling, polished brownware vessels, both 2004.

Richard Zane Smith (1955 -) / Wyandot

Of Wyandot ancestry, Richard Zane Smith perhaps seems out of place among the Southwestern pueblo potters. Sometimes Richard's work is not initially recognized as pottery because of its unique textures and colors. Nevertheless, everything about Richard's pottery glorifies the Southwest pottery-making tradition, and his efforts deserve to be catalogued in its annals of innovation.

At first glance, Richard's finely-textured, subtly-hued, matte pottery appears as anything but clay; a second glance does not clarify. Even when understood to be pottery, it appears as though the clay has been carefully incised over the entirety of the surface. This is misleading. Richard's pottery is actually constructed out of tiny, almost threadlike coils of clay. Most Southwestern potters still build their pots in the traditional manner of layering thick, snake-like coils that are then scraped smooth, a process that obliterates evidence of the coils. Although Richard abides by the hand-coil method, he does so by vastly reducing the thickness of his coils then leaving them exposed—unscraped and unpolished in a manner reminiscent of prehistoric corrugated ware. His intent was to revive this method, to "take an ancient root, and grow something from it."[xxix]

Ancient corrugated ware was sometimes pressed or pinched with patterns beyond a straight coil, but was otherwise unadorned. Richard's contemporary versions include subtly-varied, colored slips that absorb into the clay to provide muted half tones and shading. Unpolished, the colors remain understated yet create distinct patterns that imply volume and depth. In some of his pottery, as with the piece in the Cameros Collection, the delicate, shingle-lapped coils are scored with an interlocking geometric pattern, uniting patterns and colors to yield an illusory texture. By combining the illusion of three dimensions on a two-dimensional surface that constructs a three-dimensional vessel, the artist produces an utterly inimitable style. Part of Richard's pottery philosophy is collaboration between the artist and the material. For this reason, Richard avoids pottery competitions, believing them to be an artificial impetus, a temptation to perfect a "product", rather than let the clay's own nature reveal itself within the work. So he is content to honor the material; in return, it clearly honors him.

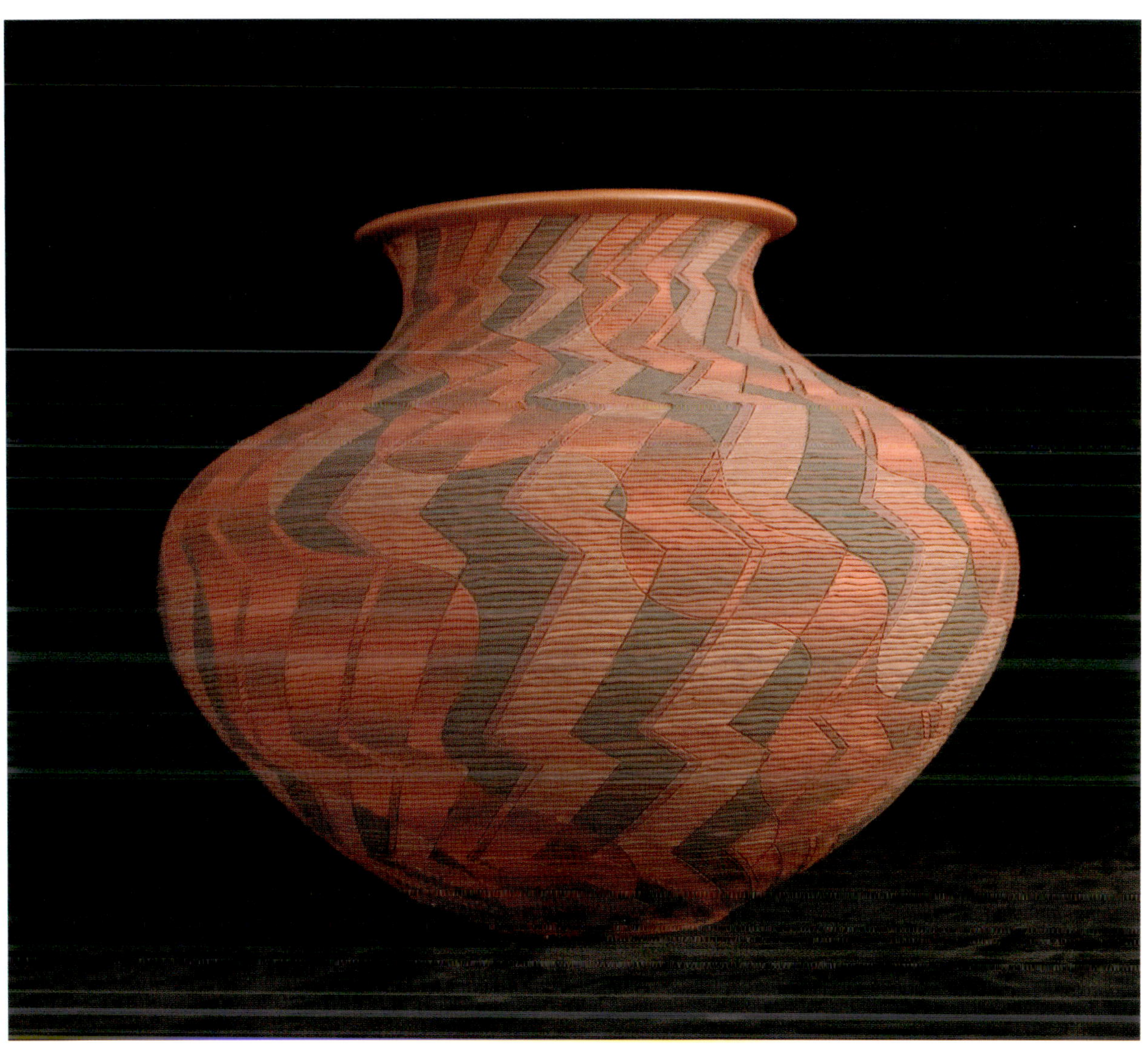

Richard Zane Smith, polychrome olla, 2003.

Hubert Candelario (1965 -) / San Felipe

Born into a pueblo without a strong pottery-making tradition, Hubert Candelario was compelled to teach himself this art around the age of 20. After much experimentation, Hubert began incorporating inspiration from some of the great potters like Maria Martinez into pots made with micaceous clay from the San Felipe pueblo. His use of micaceous clay is neither original nor unique, but this gold-flecked coral clay paired with the shapes of his pots has made Hubert's work both noticeable and notable.

Within the Cameros Collection, the few pieces by Hubert Candelario illustrate the originality and evolution of his work. To the swirl design as conceived by other artists, Hubert has added new dimension by including sharper ribs and the fantastic texture of the simultaneously matte and shimmering micaceous clay. A second miniature vessel in this collection alludes to another direction in Hubert's pottery. In this miniature, the shallow, continuously-carved channel appears almost as a jigsaw puzzle of pottery shards.

It is these shards or puzzle pieces that Hubert has begun to selectively remove, piercing his pots with ever more holes. While potters have experimented with carving and removing sections of their pottery before, Hubert's work is reminiscent of architecture in its complexity and daring. He has become increasingly bold in what he removes from the clay. His efforts have resulted in lacy, delicate, sculptural pots that are formed sometimes with only the barest suggestion of clay. Sometimes referred to as "Holey Pots," they are perhaps better referred to as "holy" as it seems that only divine intervention could help the potter defy the physics of clay as he does.

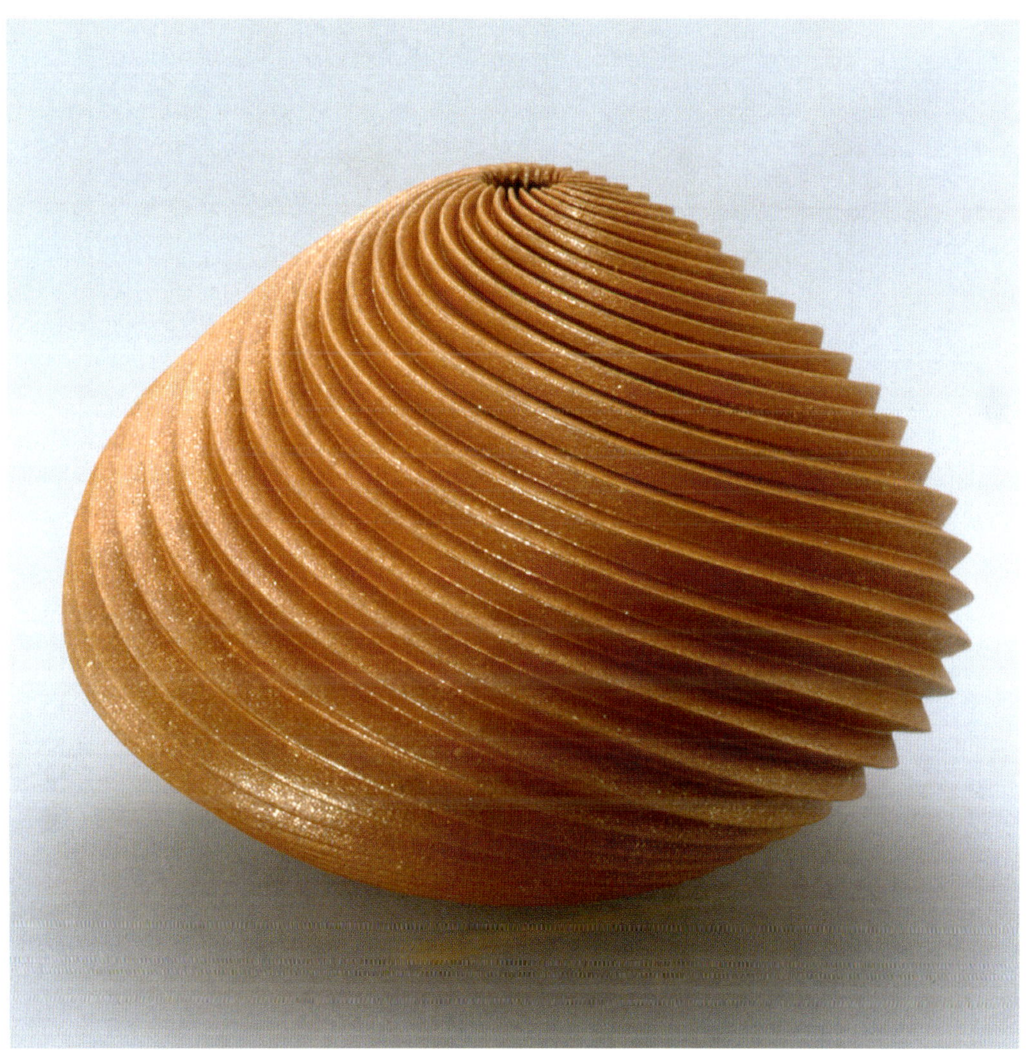

Hubert Candelario, micaceous swirled melon jar, 2006.

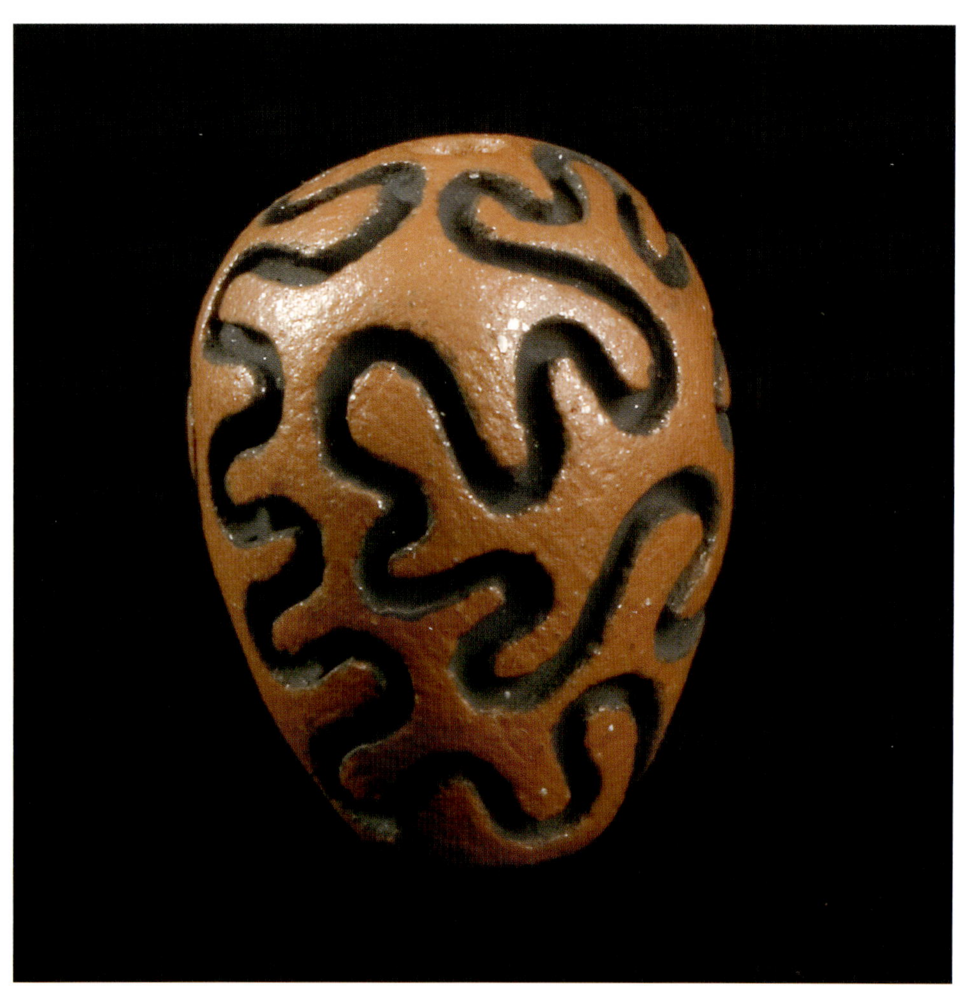

Hubert Candelario, micaceous miniature puzzle pot, 2001.

Virgil Ortiz (1969 -) / Cochiti

Clay was merely the beginning for Virgil Ortiz. He was born to a family of potters in the Cochiti Pueblo, where the pottery style is markedly different from other pueblos. Characterized by bold black designs with splashes of orange on pale clay, Cochiti pottery takes the form of vessels as well as figures. Early figures called *munos* are a tradition that can be dated to around 400 C.E. Discouraged by missionaries after the Spanish invasion, *munos* made a return in the late 19th century when tourists and traders started venturing through the Southwest. The ceramic characters lampooned the stream of foreigners flowing into the region. While the creation of these figures flagged after about 1910, Cochiti pottery never lost its playfulness or distinctiveness.

This sense of whimsy characterizes the work of Virgil Ortiz. When he learned to make pottery, he sought to replicate traditional Cochiti designs. After years of practice, he realized that what he was doing was art, not craft. This realization caused him to blossom as a designer, absorbing traditions from Ancient Greek to Art Nouveau and taking them in unique directions. According to the artist, he does not like to appropriate or recycle clichés in art but infuses pueblo tradition with external influences.[xxxi] In the late 1980s, Virgil visited a munos collector and was inspired to recreate the old figures for a modern world.[xxxii] Today, he has gained international fame for applying his sinuous, tattoo-like patterns not only to exceptional pottery and figurines but also to video, graphic design, and *haute couture*.

Around 2002, his vessels and early forays into clothing design attracted the attention of New York-based fashion designer Donna Karan. The artists collaborated to create designs for five dresses for Karan's Spring 2003 clothing line. From that experience, Virgil's own line, *Indigene*, was born. Luxury handbags, outerwear, and jewelry now bear Virgil Ortiz's sophisticated patterns. He has since added the *Renegade Collection*—high end t-shirts that portray Ortiz's modern interpretation of the Native Warrior and Femme Fatale.

Early in Virgil's life, his mother warned him and his brothers to stay true to their heritage and not give it up for money. True to this admonition, Virgil continues to make pottery, both figural and vessel, and does not rely on apprentices to form or paint his pottery. If anyone helps, it is his nieces and nephews who have the privilege of learning directly from their uncle.

"The most important things for Cochiti people are the language and the art," Virgil states.[xxxiii] And so both language and art animate his designs wherever they turn up. Likewise, they infuse other aspects of his life. His success has given him the ability to give back to his community, which he does by devoting time to Cochiti youths. When his new studio is complete, he will invite as many children as possible to "learn whatever they are interested in learning" from him. For now he continues to teach Cochiti children their native Keres language. In return, they have inspired him: He wants to create a movie and video game that will feature his clay figurines as Keres-speaking superheroes. While artistic prowess is not the defining trait of most superheroes, it is not hard to imagine that the Cochiti children think of the multi-talented Virgil Ortiz in this way.

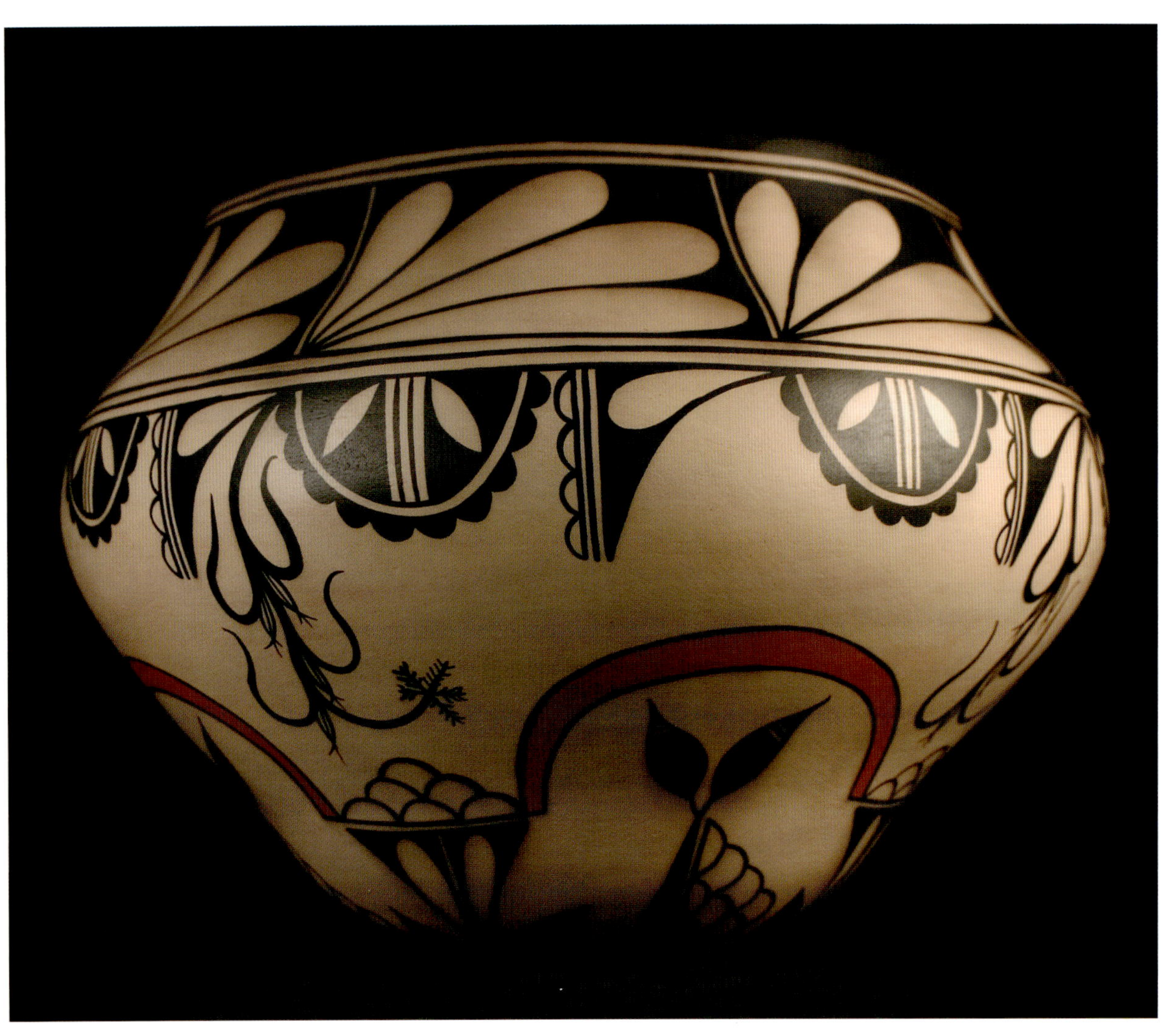

Virgil Ortiz, polychrome jar, 2002.

Russell Sanchez (1966 -) / San Ildefonso

Many potters who came before Russell Sanchez were perfectionists, but his uncanny ability to combine and execute various techniques makes his pottery exceptional. Influenced by some of the great potters in the San Ildefonso tradition, he credits them all for his success: His great-aunt, Rose Gonzalez, for showing him how to make pots; his aunt, Dora Tse Pe, for teaching him to be a perfectionist; Popovi Da for stimulating his use of colored slips; Tony Da for influencing his use of turquoise and *heishi* inlay; and Jody Folwell for the impetus to constantly experiment. He also credits nature for inspiring his designs.

Among the various elements that contribute to the individuality of his pots, Russell includes the use of clays with colors that range well beyond the traditional. Many artists are strict about using clays native to their ancestral pueblo, or at least their region. An avid outdoorsman, Russell never ceases to hunt for new clays, whether visiting exotic countries or hiking the familiar mesas near his home. Subsequent experimentation often reveals varied and surprising properties of these clays, which become part of the rareness of his art.

Most potters use a single kind of clay and either fire it in a manner that exposes different colors (duotone, for example) or paint on different slip to add or alter color. Although Russell uses these techniques, he is unafraid of combining clays of different color in a single pot. He has also taken to adding copper inlay in some of his wares—the only potter so far known to do so. The results befit a potter of the San Ildefonso tradition where Russell asserts, “Innovation is part of our tradition.”[xxxiv]

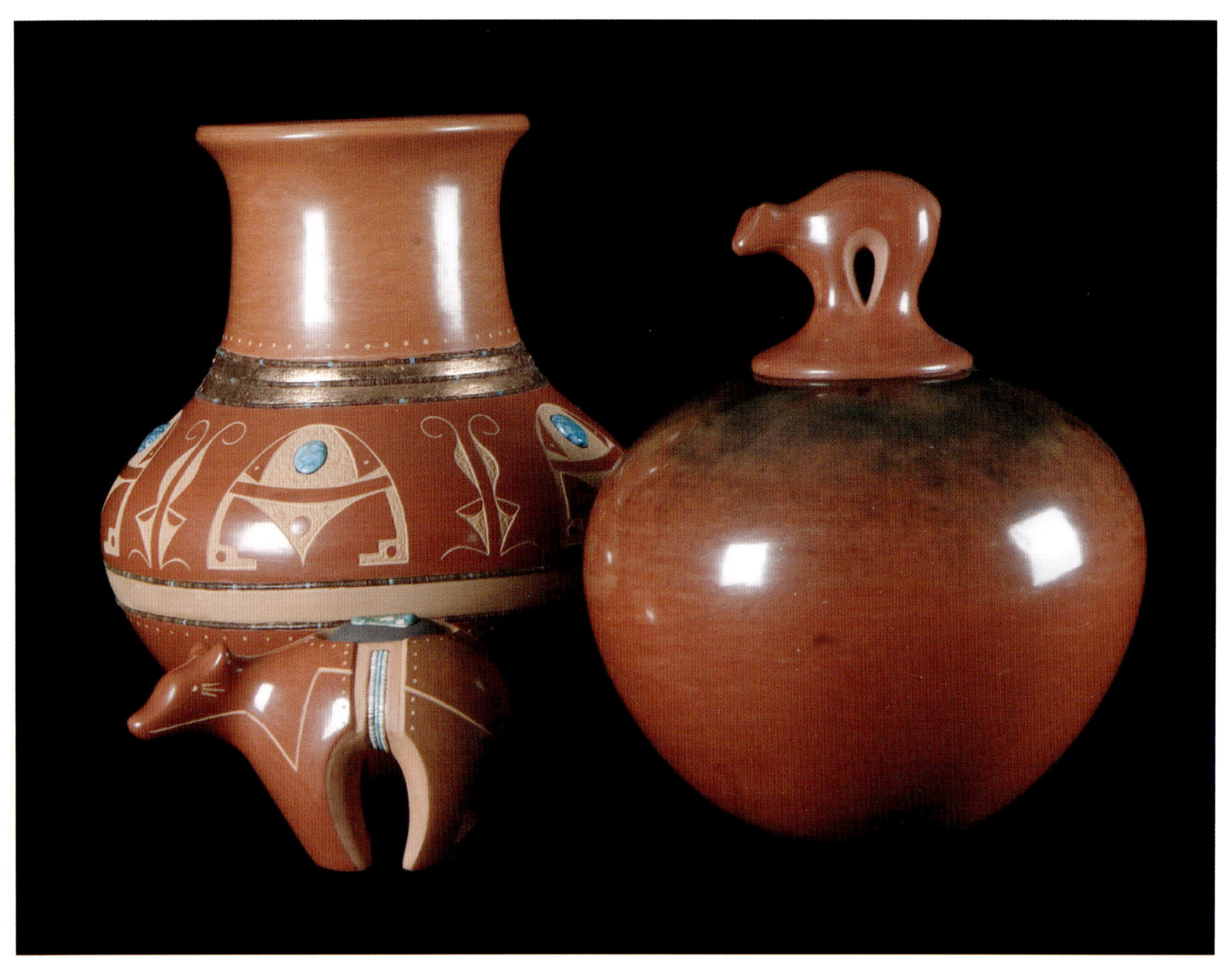

Russell Sanchez, (L-R) polished redware jar with copper bands and turquoise and heishi inlay, 2006; polished redware bear with turquoise and heishi *inlay, c. 1995-2000; polished redware jar with carved lid, 1995.*

(Clockwise from top) Dextra Quotskuyva, polychrome jar with Migration Pattern, c. 1980-85; Steve Lucas, polychrome jar, c. 2001-02; Quotskuyva, polychrome vase, c. 1980-85; Jake Koopee, polychrome seed jar, n.d.; Lucas, polychrome jar, 2003; Quotskuyva, polychrome vase, c. 1980-85.

Chapter 3

Keepers of Tradition

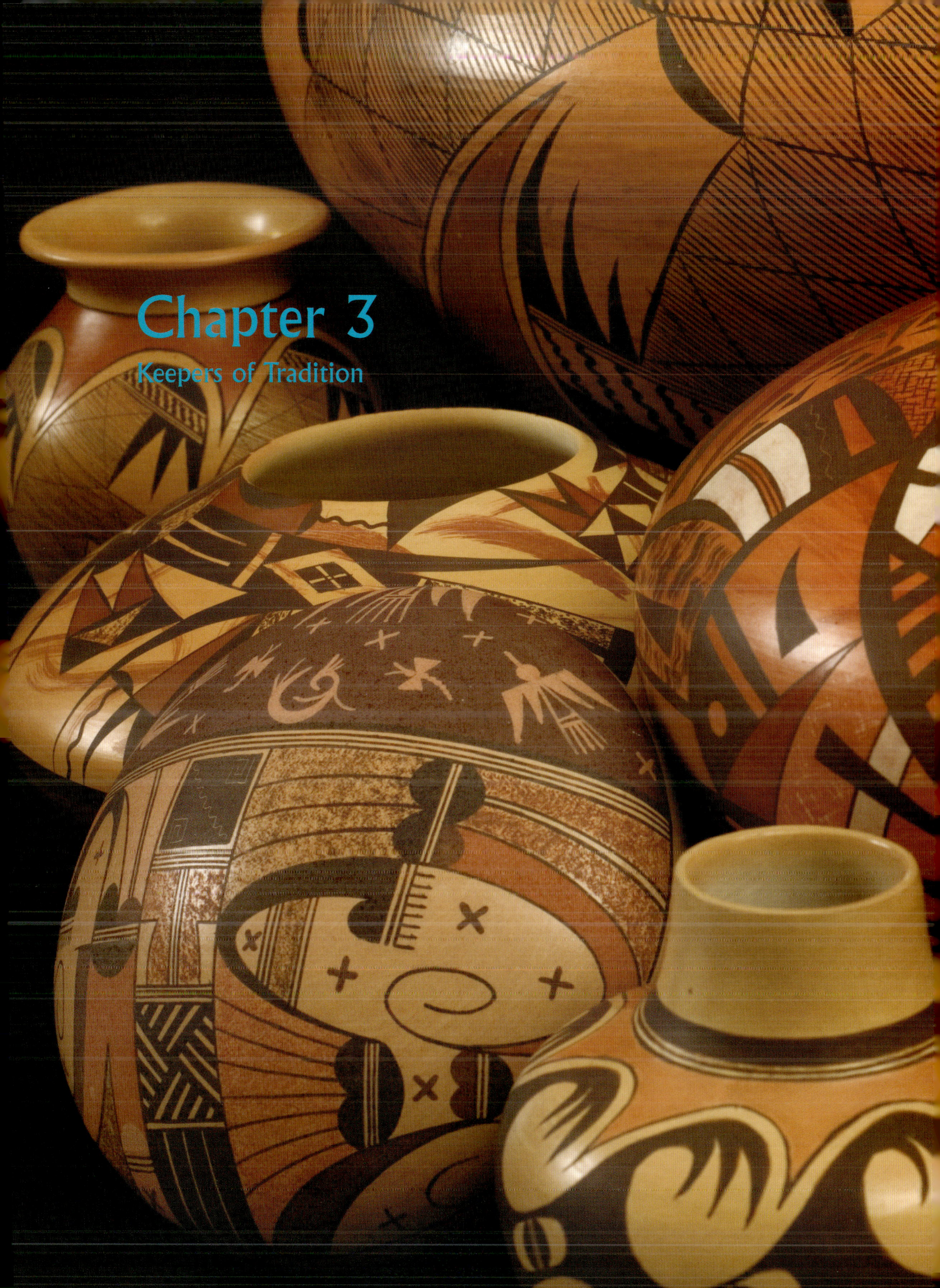

Chapter 3: Keepers of Tradition

Tradition is not immutable. It is not "stuck" in one era or another, nor does it necessarily imply an origin far in the past. We know that some artistic traditions in the Cameros Collection stem from antiquity, others from modern artisans. Traditions do share at least one common element: The strength of their nature and what that nature communicates about its culture.

Tradition is the name we give to information that is transmitted through generations. In the tradition of Southwestern pottery, every vessel contains generations of experience that, taken together, tell a story. It may be difficult to imagine a simple but beautiful piece of pottery telling a story when the surface is unadorned except for its polish. But imagine the journey a pot takes, and imagine how it is intertwined with the journey of the potter who created it.

Speak to almost any Native American potter and they will tell you that they learned their art from family members. They did not read a book on pottery making, and most did not have formal schooling on the subject (or, if they did, it was after they had long been practicing their craft). The more typical story is of a fascinated child looking on in wonder as his or her kin fashions pots from coil to fire. When the child's interest becomes desire, he or she is given a scrap of clay from which to fashion a toy or favorite animal. Later, perhaps, the child is shown where the family digs its clay and taught how to murmur thanks and praise to Mother Clay for her blessings. The rest, as they say, is history.

The essence of all such stories is what is transferred and transformed into every vessel, no matter how simple. Further decoration supplements this narrative and distinguishes cultural elements. Though tradition is sometimes overlooked in favor of novelty, the potters who are "Keepers of Tradition" should be revered as mediums for the spirits of the past, storytellers for the generations, and guardians of culture.

In this chapter, the reader will explore many stylistic traditions. Many are particular to one pueblo or reservation. Others cross geographical boundaries. But they are grouped here based on appearance. The previous chapters illustrated the origins of many of these styles; here we see the culmination of generations of tradition.

Undecorated Pottery

The tradition of leaving pottery undecorated dates to the earliest days of the craft. As one can imagine, the earliest pots were experiments in structure and utility. They were simple vessels intended for common use. As with most crafts, practitioners started simply and talented individuals contributed new ideas and techniques over time, sometimes elevating craft to art.

Painting, carving, stone inlay—all these things have helped propel Southwestern pottery forward as fine art. However, when all but the barest adornment is absent from pottery, form and texture emerge from the clay. Its essential beauty is laid bare by the potter's hands. Pottery of this sort is a testament to the potter's skill, first as a craftsman forcing the clay to take shape, then as an artist coaxing from it a beauty that transcends and unifies.

In the current age of pottery, the Santa Clara Pueblo is best known for its unadorned yet spectacularly beautiful pottery. These blackware and redware pots are typically polished to a sheen that resembles glass. This lustrous texture could betray every flaw but instead highlights the perfection of the form. Early works by Sara Fina and Margaret Tafoya (see page 34) sometimes bore minimal indentation of *avanyu* and bear paw forms. Later artists from other pueblos and reservations follow this or their own traditions, contributing new examples of rare beauty to the art form.

Within the Cameros Collection there are many excellent examples:

Helen Shupla (1928 - 1985) grew up in Santa Clara where she was schooled in the art of exceptionally polished blackware and redware. Her pots were always meticulously shaped and polished, and occasionally included pressed or incised motifs. In extension of this style, Helen became well known for her melon jars. After marrying a Hopi man, she spent time on the Hopi Reservation where the local clay had greater plasticity. This allowed her to develop the technique of pushing the clay out from the inside of the pot, instead of carving the form into the surface. The technique took great patience so as to not puncture the pot and be forced to start over.

Helen taught this technique to her son-in-law, Alton Komalestewa, a Hopi also related to Nampeyo of Hano through his father. Though Alton lived on this reservation famed for its pottery, he only learned pottery-making from Helen Shupla. Unlike the Hopi wares, Alton's pottery regularly exhibits a pushed-out melon jar form as well as his mother-in-law's painstaking polish so well-known in the Santa Clara Pueblo.

Both Helen's and Alton's melon bowls can be distinguished by their interiors. Because their technique requires the clay to be pressed from within, the inside of the pot follows the curves of the exterior. The earlier technique for making melon jars was to carve the ribs out of the thickness of the clay pot, leaving the interior smooth. Helen and Alton's work can usually be distinguished from each other by the mouths of the vessels; Helen's were always large enough to fit her entire hand, unless she was working in miniature.

Lonnie Vigil (1949-) from the Nambe Pueblo is another artist who is trying to preserve and perfect historical art forms from his pueblo's tradition. A self-taught artist who has worked in blackware, redware, and occasionally buff slips, Lonnie is known primarily for his micaceous pottery. Though well known for pottery today, Lonnie's path to the art form was indirect. After nearly 10 years working for the Bureau of Indian Affairs in both Santa Fe, New Mexico, and Washington, D.C., he was jolted into realizing that his life was not spiritually fulfilling. During a performance of *Night of the First Americans* at the Kennedy Center, a Sioux elder of the Lakota Tribe dismissed the audience in his native language. Lonnie did not understand the words, but he was convinced of their meaning. He immediately tendered his resignation and returned to Nambe. For a year, he contemplated new paths for his life before it became clear that pottery was his true calling. Though he had never made pottery, he felt that it was somehow fused with his existence. Since 1989, he has dedicated himself to creating pottery from the sparkling Nambe clays.

While many artists create pottery solely for collectors, Lonnie feels strongly that pottery should be functional as well as decorative to fulfill the original intent of pottery. While he humbly calls it "cookware," his collectors still recognize the simplest of Lonnie's utilitarian ware as sculpture. No matter the label, Lonnie's pottery stands out as homage to Clay Mother. There is no obvious adornment, just naked clay in its glittering surface and form. “It is not about elaborating on the clay,” the artist insists, “but rather getting to the essence of it.”[xxxv]

Today, the rich copper color of Lonnie's work sparkles with golden flecks of mica and usually somewhere on his pottery is a seemingly intentional “fire cloud.” This accidental effect of outdoor firing is often avoided as a blemish, but Lonnie seems to have mastered its presence on his wares. At least his fire clouds appear in aesthetically perfect positions. Flaws or not, the fire clouds, perhaps like the artist's life, take the path that Mother Clay intends for them. The artist is wise enough not to argue.

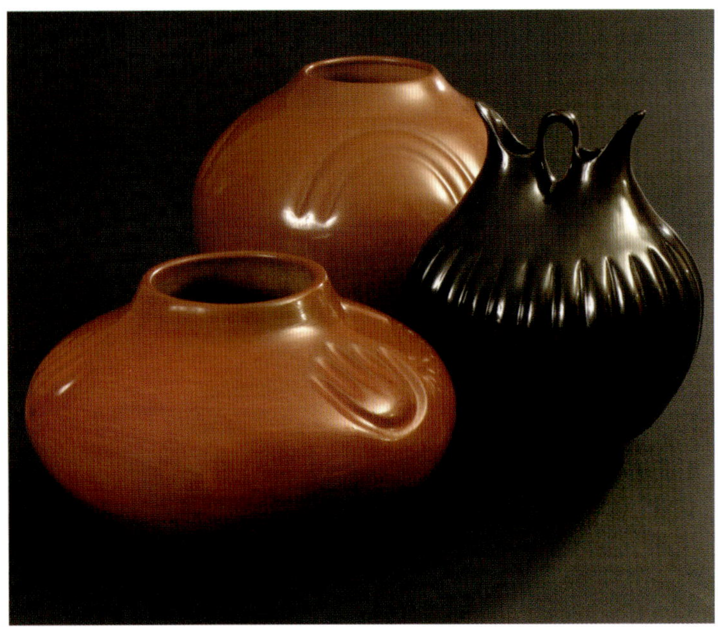

(Clockwise from top) Alton Komalestewa, redware jar with rainbow impression, c. 1980s; blackware "pushed out" melon wedding vase, c. 1990s; Helen Shupla, polished redware bowl with avanyu *impression, c. 1970s.*

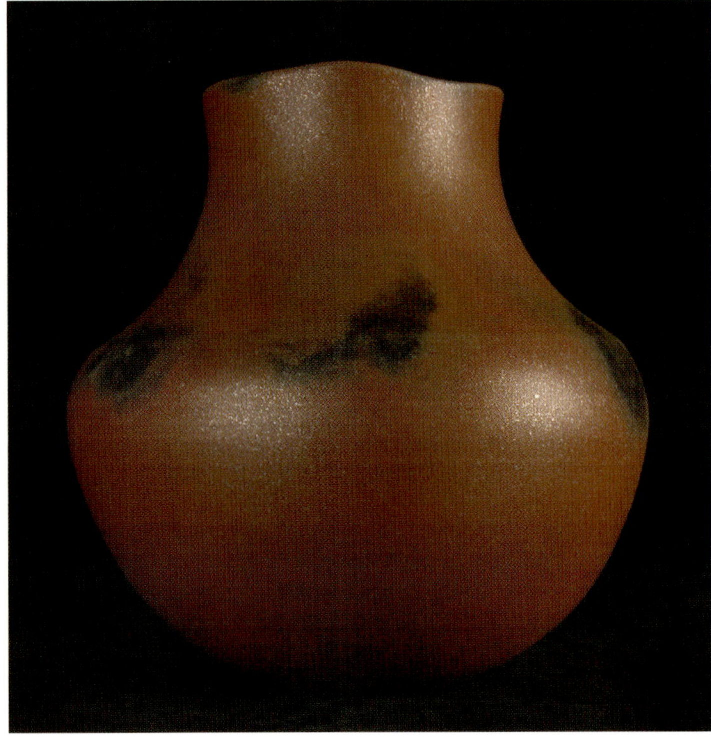

Lonnie Vigil, micaceous storage jar, c. 1998.

Polished and Carved Pottery

If unadorned pottery is where tradition begins, then decorated pottery is the first step of evolution. From basic clay shaped into utilitarian forms, potters began to focus more seriously on the aesthetics of their wares by experimenting with shapes. Later, some of the pueblo potters began to exhaustively polish the surface of their wares to enhance the appearance of both the form and the clay color. Stemming from this, since Sara Fina Tafoya first used her finger to impress a simple *avanyu* into one of her highly polished pots, Santa Clara potters have honed and perfected that tradition, producing numerous skilled carvers.

Among them are Teresita Naranjo (1919 - 1999), granddaughter of Sara Fina Tafoya, and Linda Cain (1949-), niece of Teresita and mother of Tammy Garcia and Autumn Borts-Medlock, two other exceptional carvers featured in the Cameros Collection. Both Teresita and Linda have created beautifully formed and polished redware and blackware pottery, just as Sara Fina's daughter, Margaret, had done (see page 34). Also following tradition, Teresita and Linda painted matte slips where they carved away clay to further define the sometimes-lyrical, sometimes-geometric designs that adorn their pottery. Occasionally on Linda's redware, the buff slip is replaced by a whiter slip that her daughter, Tammy Garcia, says is a time-consuming endeavor. Tammy used this same technique in her own work for a time (see page 65) but eventually abandoned it because the white slip required 10 or more applications before it became opaque enough to remain white on top of the red clay.

Harrison Begay, Jr. (1961-) was born in the small Navajo community of Jeddito near Keams Canyon, Arizona. Though this area has a particularly strong history in pottery, Harrison was taught pottery making in Santa Clara upon marrying into a Santa Clara family of potters. While married, his pottery clearly incorporated Santa Clara designs. Since his marriage ended, he has turned his attention to Navajo imagery. Today, his pottery is a stunning hybrid. Beginning with the traditional Santa Clara method of creating his vessel, Harrison embellishes it with Navajo mythological symbols. Unlike the Santa Clara potters, however, Harrison does not carve clay away from his designs, letting them rise to the surface. Instead, his pottery features deep, v-shaped channels carved around figures. So-called backgrounds are left at the same level as the design, merely separated by the channels, then further distinguished by Harrison's use of matte slip. Harrison's pottery is fired to create redware and blackware following the initial methods he learned. More recently, he has been exploring the beauty of brownware, which is more commonly seen in his native Navajo pottery tradition. In contrast to Navajo pottery-making tradition, Harrison does not add pine pitch after firing, but he emulates the same shine that can be achieved with pitch by stone polishing his pottery in the Santa Clara way.

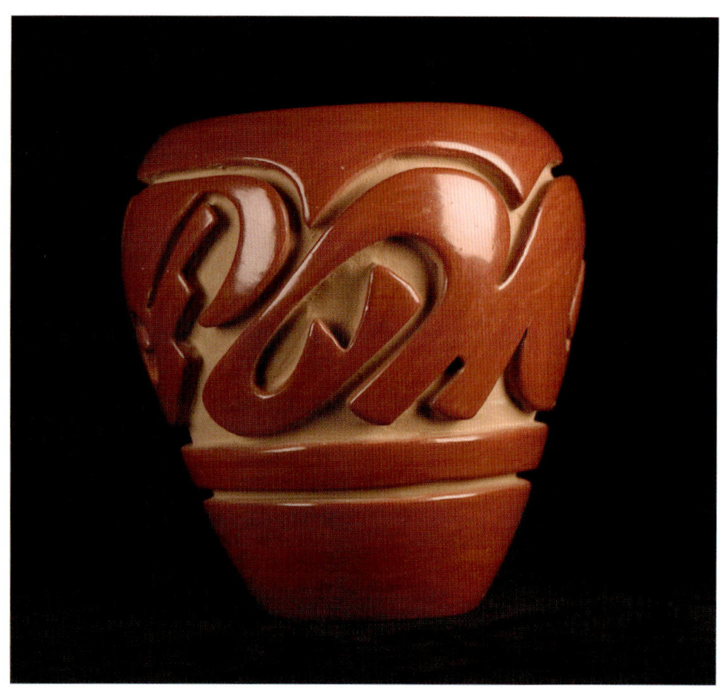

Teresita Naranjo, carved redware vase, c. 1980s.

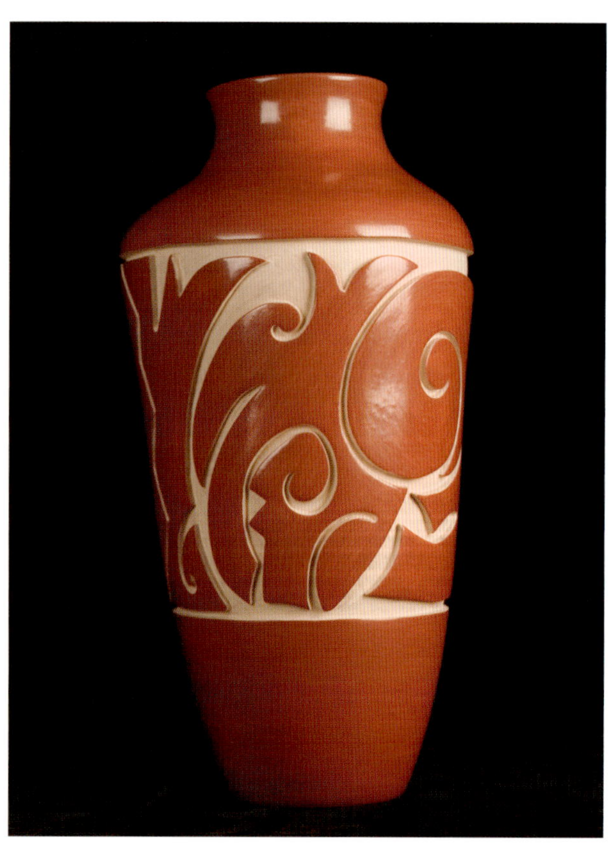

Linda Cain, carved redware vase with white slip inpainting, 2002.

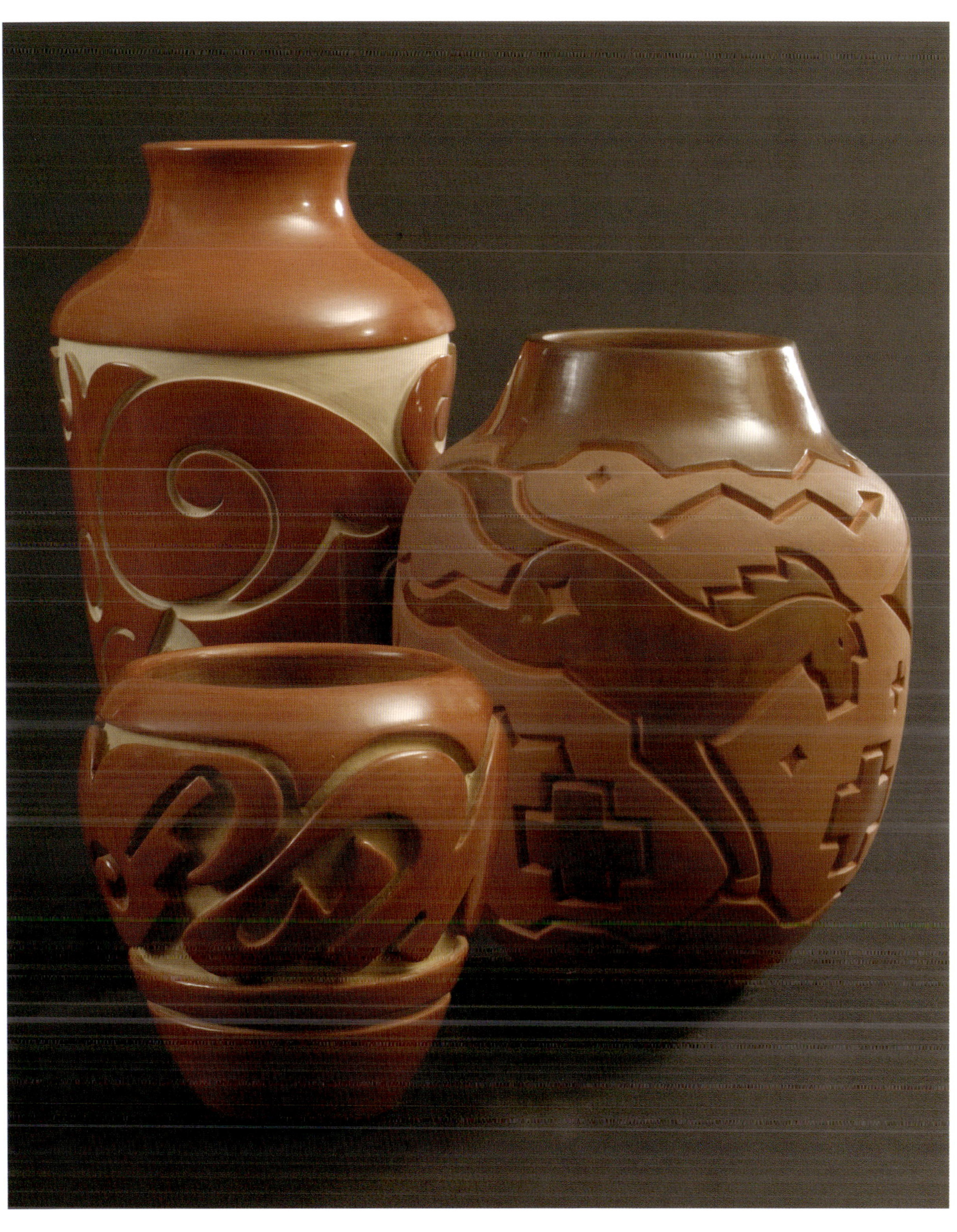

(Clockwise from top) Linda Cain, carved redware vase with white slip inpainting, 2002; Harrison Begay, brownware vase, 2001; Teresita Naranjo, carved redware vase, c. 1980s.

Pottery with Inlay

Popovi Da is thought to be the first modern potter to experiment with the inlay of semiprecious turquoise into pottery. However, it was his son, Tony, who popularized the technique (see page 46.) Starting with a single piece of turquoise to punctuate a vessel or complement its colors, this style has evolved like all others, being combined at various times with sculptural or *sgraffito* elements, different color slips and painted designs, or even multiple varieties of stone.

While stone inlay has become more common, flawless execution remains important in the overall quality of the pottery. Choice and placement of stones, as well as the different technical elements with which they are combined, all dictate the quality of the piece. Within the Cameros Collection, there are numerous excellent examples. Some we have already seen with the Da family, Russell Sanchez (see page 92) and Dora Tse Pe (see page 49). But there are others within this collection that serve as excellent and even rare examples of the use of stone inlay.

Barbara Gonzales (1947-) is a descendant of Julian and Maria Martinez through their son Adam and his wife, Santana. Barbara has both followed and expanded on family tradition in both redware and blackware but is best known for her intricately etched pottery with inlaid stones. She commonly uses small pieces of turquoise and coral to punctuate her delicate designs.

Though he was born at San Ildefonso Pueblo, John Gonzales (1955-) is only distantly related to either Barbara Gonzalez or to the Maria Martinez family of potters. After living away from the pueblo most of his life, John sought to return to pueblo life in the early 1990s. With help and inspiration from his father and sister, John learned to make pottery, and eventually mastered it. Today, he is known for his skill at making plates. These are typically adorned with extensive turquoise and *heishi* (shell bead) inlay, surrounded by *sgraffito* design.

Until her recent death, Carmelita Dunlap (1925 - 2000) was considered the last living protégé of her aunt, Maria Martinez. Her pottery closely follows the traditions her aunt and other relatives established, exhibiting flawless form and excellent polish in both redware and blackware. She was also a skillful painter and created beautiful designs on her pottery. The piece in the Cameros Collections is a rarity. Though indisputably inscribed and dated by Carmelita, it is anomalous to her body of work because of the turquoise inlay.

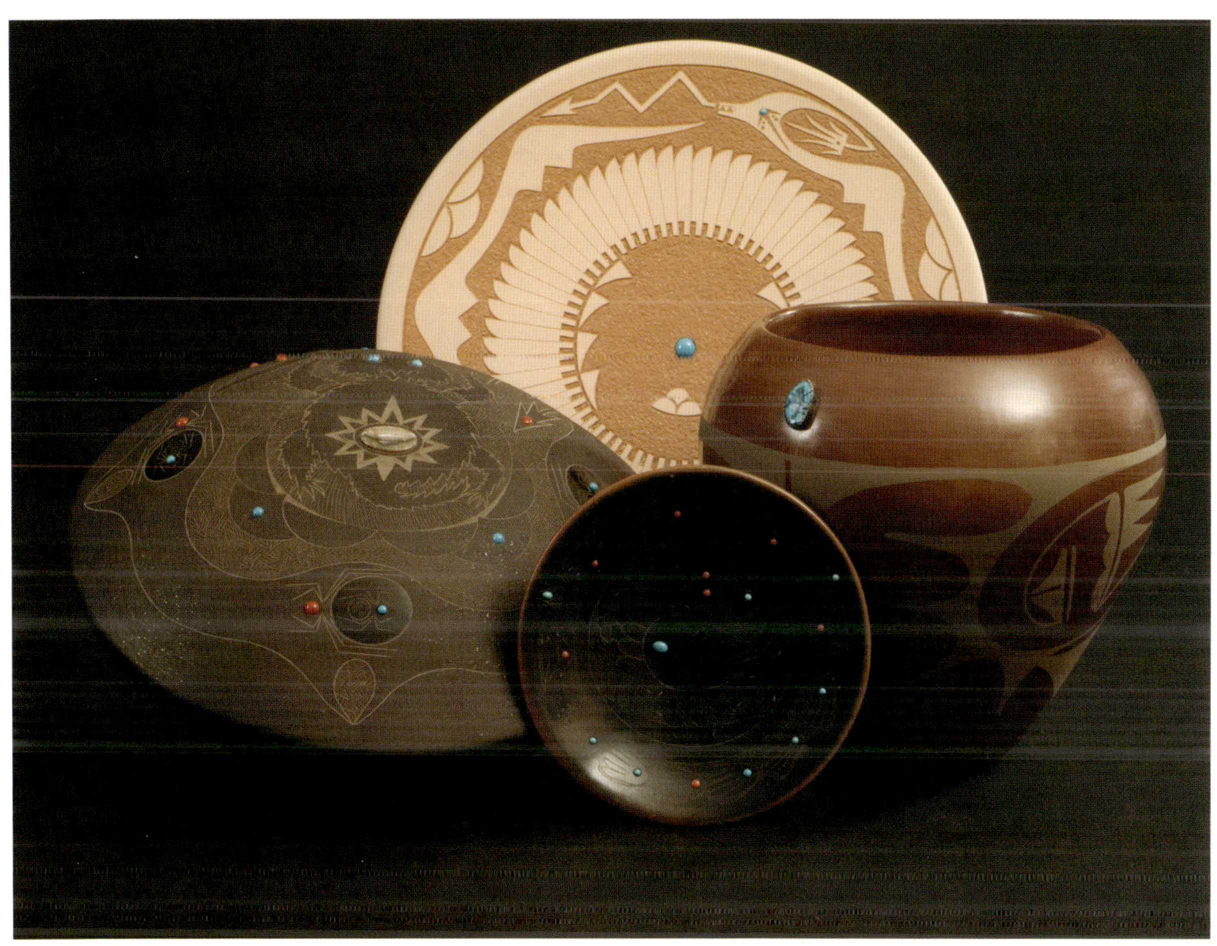

(Clockwise from top) John Gonzalez, redware plate with turquoise inlay, 2004; Carmelita Dunlap, polished redware vase with turquoise inlay, 1982; Barbara Gonzalez, blackware plate with turquoise and coral inlay, 1992; Barbara Gonzalez, blackware vessel with turquoise, coral and shell inlay, c. 2000.

Pottery with Sgraffito and Polish

Glass-like polish on pottery brought renewed attention to the surface of the clay. With the introduction of *sgraffito*, a new level of intricacy could be imparted to decoration. When the sleek luster of the one was juxtaposed with the rough, matte texture of the other, an impressive style was produced. Below are some of the potters within the Cameros Collection who explore the combination of these two aesthetic traditions. The beauty of these works only begins to touch upon the talent that lies behind them.

The pottery of Paul Naranjo (1957 - 2002) is exceptional not just for its polish and form but for his style of covering large vessels with *sgraffito* images. An avid outdoorsman,[xxxvii] Paul turned regularly to wildlife themes. Perhaps because of intimate experience with the majestic creatures of the wild, he would not allow himself to recreate them in diminutive form on miniatures as many of his fellow potters have done. Instead, the animal figures invade expansive pottery surfaces, the finely etched lines that define them giving way to exceptional polish on occasion.

Like many of the current generation of potters, Jody Naranjo (1969-) continually seeks ways to blend tradition and modern influences. Combining the elements of high polish, for which her pueblo is known, with designs both new and old etched into the surface, Jody accomplishes just that. Jody's jar in the Cameros Collection is a beautiful example of this blend—a large redware piece built and fired in the traditional manner. To this piece, she has added figures on horseback inspired by the Crazy Horse Monument as well as her own kiva-stepped diamond pattern. Where *sgraffito* has not etched the surface into a design, a modern checkerboard pattern fills the space. The artist breaks with tradition in the application of this pattern, as the matte squares are not painted slip. Rather, the polish is lightly scraped away to reveal the naked clay beneath.[xxxviii]

In another variation on tradition, Jody is unsatisfied with making starkly red or black ware. Both styles arise from the same clay; it is the firing technique that alters its appearance to red or black. Traditionally, blackware is achieved by reducing the oxygen content of a fire by adding manure. Instead of firing a piece of pottery with one method or the other, Jody will add manure midway through the firing to the parts of her pottery that she wants to turn black or grey. The result is a distinctly modern take on the ancient.

Jennifer Tafoya Moquino (1977-) is one of the few artists to pair *sgraffito* with the use of polychrome on blackware, a style inspired by the polychrome work of her father and mother, Ray and Emily Tafoya. Yet, the realism of her wildlife scenes is perhaps better likened to that of her father-in law, Corn Moquino. Jennifer's accomplishment has been to combine the strengths of these family traditions by enhancing the precision of her *sgraffito* with the application of natural, colored slips after firing. She frames her scenes with elegant traditional pottery forms and historic Santa Clara geometric patterns. As can be seen on the Jennifer Moquino vase in the Cameros Collection, one of the artist's favorite motifs is trout, the depiction of which has almost become trademark. Jennifer loves to fish and be a part of nature. The artist has familiarized herself with the great variety of trout species, in order to be as accurate as possible in their depiction. Her use of color emphasizes the subtle differences among them.

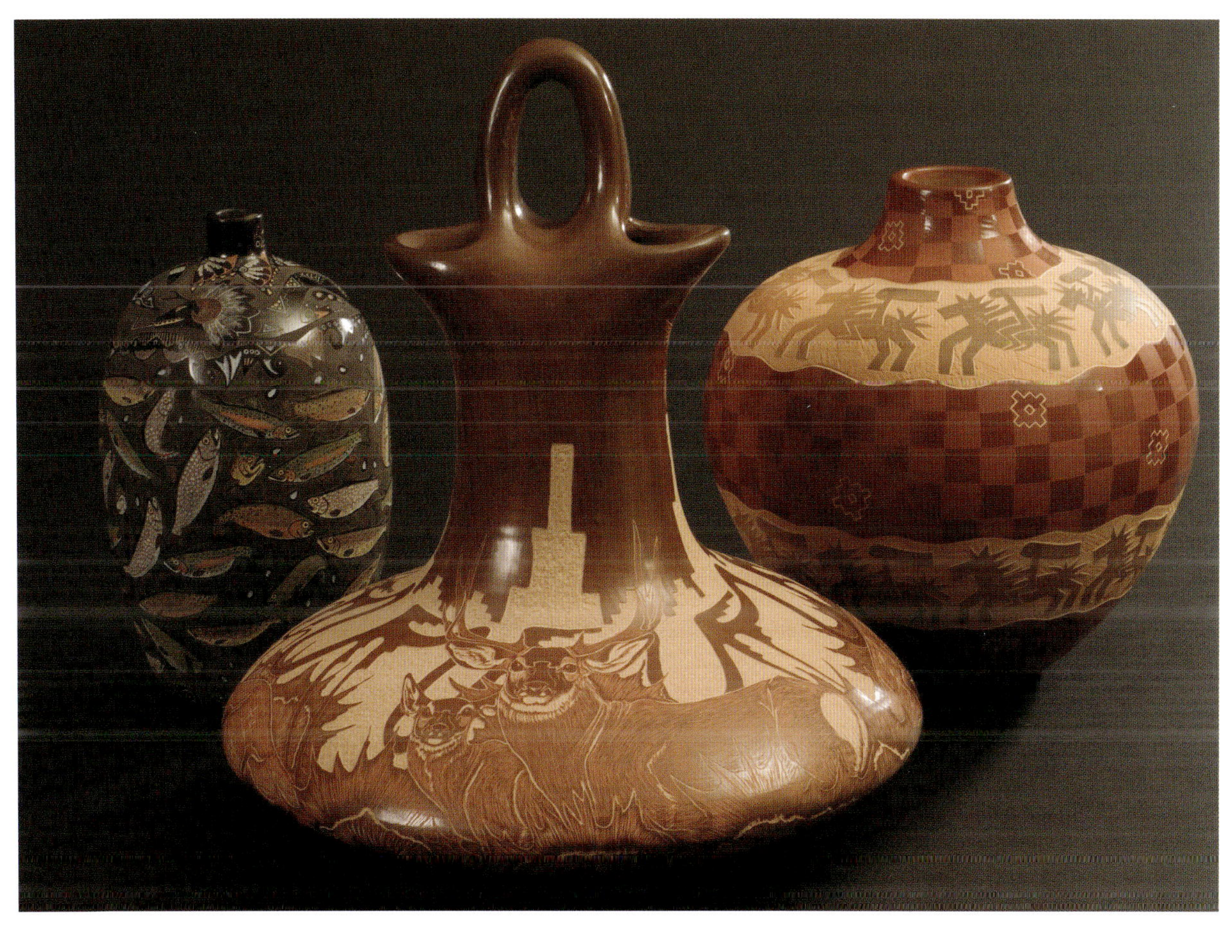

Jennifer Tafoya Moquino, blackware and polychrome vase, c. 2002-04; Paul Naranjo, brownware wedding vessel, c. 1990-95; Jody Naranjo, redware jar with sgraffito, *2006.*

Miniature Pottery

Until artists like Joseph Lonewolf raised the status of clay miniatures, diminutive Southwestern pottery was either crafted by pueblo children to learn the art of pottery making from scraps that were not to be wasted, or created as small, less expensive items for the tourist trade. Miniatures have since become more highly regarded as they represent a significant challenge to the artist, who must maintain the detailed precision of larger forms and designs while shifting to a small scale. Many of these miniatures take the form of "seed jars," tiny vessels with a hole at the top or bottom big enough only for a single seed to pass though. The typically convex surface further challenges the artists to manipulate their designs so that they can be read as if on a flat surface.

Along with his children, Joseph Lonewolf and Grace Medicine Flower, Camilio "Sunflower" Tafoya (1902 - 1995) put his indelible mark on Southwestern pottery. The whole Camilio Tafoya family is known for its pioneering work in *sgraffito*. Early in his career, Camilio followed the trend of his famous mother, Sara Fina, and sister, Margaret, by creating larger pottery. However, because he also tended to carve intricate designs over the entire surface, the time-consuming nature of creating large vessels, then decorating their expansive surfaces, gave rise to his serious pursuit of miniature pottery. Miniatures became the ideal artistic vehicle for the meticulous and detailed carving process of *sgraffito*.[xxxix] Camilio's son, Joseph, created such beautifully carved and painted miniatures that they were often referred to as "Pottery Jewels."[xl] Joseph's children continue this tradition. The whole family is well-represented in the Cameros Collection.

Greg "Greywolf" Lonewolf (1952-) follows Camilio's and his father Joseph's styles closely, combining unique colors with *sgraffito*. Like his father, Greg also celebrates a Native American communion with the natural world through his depictions of wildlife. As a child, Greg thought that the whole of the Santa Clara pueblo were potters—an easy mistake to make when one descends from the Tafoya line. But he soon realized that each family and each individual added something special to the community. Greg now pursues interests aside from pottery but still makes a couple miniatures a year. He also experiments with other ceramic methods like Asian Raku and porcelain. He is confident that he will return to making miniatures on a more regular basis in due time.[xli] Greg's two talented sisters continue their family's tradition in their own ways.

Miniaturist is only the start for Rosemary "Apple Blossom" Lonewolf (1953 -). World traveler, lecturer, artist in residence, public artist, scholar...from her pueblo's tradition of pottery making, this multifaceted woman continues to carve out a niche for herself in the larger art world. Her brother, Greg, states that Rosemary has the enviable ability of infusing her work with her life story. When one's life is as exceptional as Rosemary's, the artwork that arises from it is equally impressive. For example, working under both an Artist Fellowship and Project Grant from the Arizona Commission on the Arts, Rosemary researched clay composition at Arizona State University in Tempe. Clay from different regions has different properties, and she was looking for one that would not deteriorate if continuously exposed to the elements as a work of public art. To find the appropriate "clay body," she had to concoct it herself. She now has a recipe for architectural clay that will transfer from the freezer to boiling water without cracking or spalling. This clay has allowed her to construct monumental art and outdoor murals, yet she continues to make miniatures as time allows. Is it any wonder, then, that of all the miniatures in the Cameros Collection, hers is the largest?

Of the Lonewolf clan, Susan "Snowflake" Romero (1955 -) is the only one to avoid the use of polychrome on her miniatures. In collaboration with her husband, Mike Romero, another talented potter from Santa Clara, they more than make up for omitting this convention with their technical excellence in polishing and intricacy in *sgraffito*. The level of detail they accomplish in their work eliminates any conceivable need for the addition of color. Susan states that under the tutelage of her father, she was taught to polish so well that it is able to replace painted color. Instead, she controls the level of polish to reveal different tones of the clay's own natural hues. Her sister adds that Susan is "the best polisher in the family."[xlii]

Greg relates a story about how Camilio, Joseph, Rosemary, Susan, and he decided to each make a miniature depicting a hummingbird. At the completion of everyone's pieces, they compared them. Greg recalls being flattered that his family confused his pottery with his father's. He also remembers how each family member admired the different talents that the others brought to the same type of pottery.[xliii]

Like several of the Lonewolf clan, Wallace Nez, Jr. (1972-) is known for wildlife depictions on polychrome and sgraffito miniatures, but do not think that his work is mimicry. The young potter grew up far away from the Lonewolfs on the Navajo Reservation in Utah where he started making pottery in the time-consuming traditional process at the age of 12. Wallace eventually began using commercial and native paints to enhance his intricately detailed miniatures and developed a style that is immediately recognizable as his own. He creates exquisite portraits of animals surrounded by radiating circles of etched detail. He manages to convey majesty in the portraits despite their diminutive size by framing them with meticulous repetitive patterns. This spotlight effect reflects his reverence for the animals.

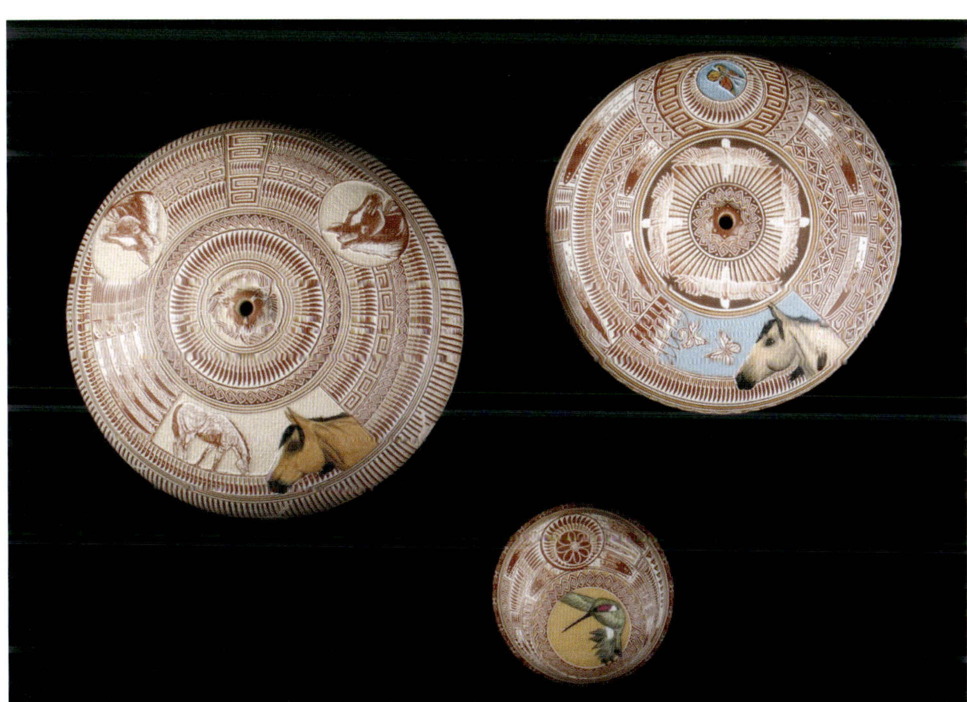

Miniatures by Wally Nez, Jr.

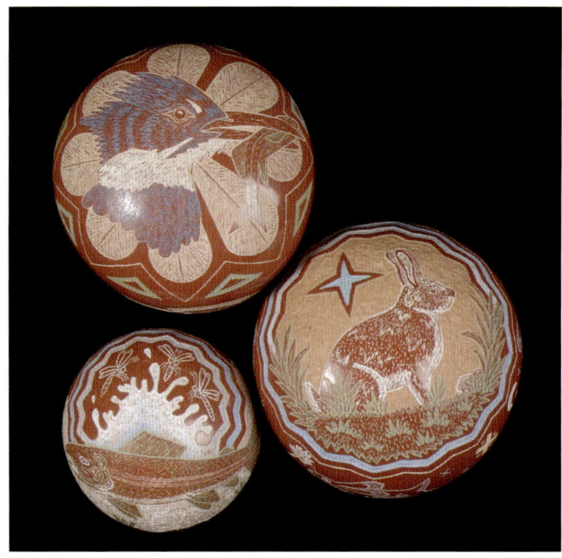

Undated miniatures by Greg Lonewolf.

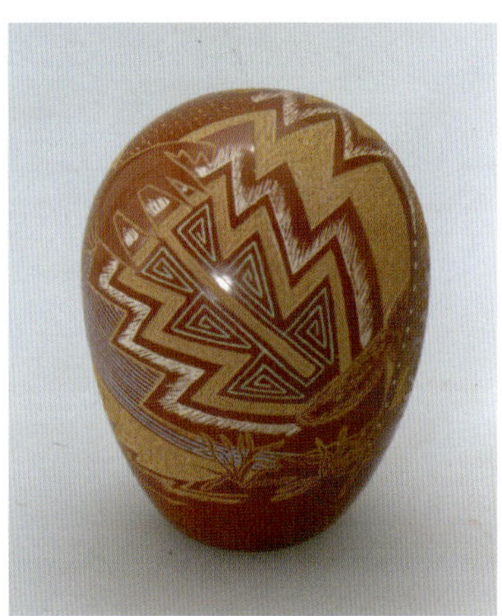

Rosemary "Apple Blossom" Lonewolf miniature,
"What the Big Bad Wolf is Really Afraid of," c. 2006.

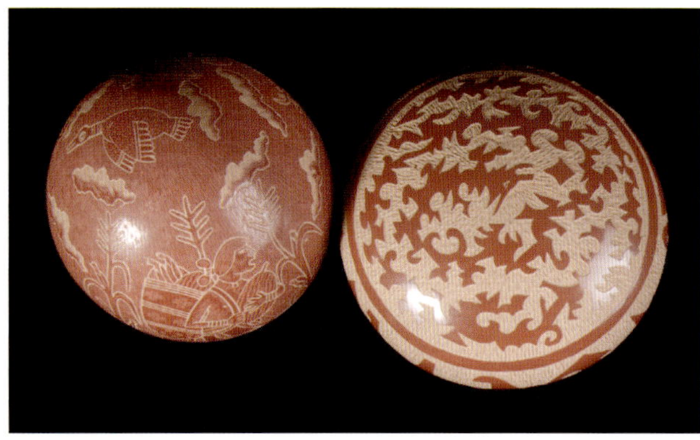

Susan Romero, redware miniatures, both c. 1997.

Pottery with Emergent Figures

From simple impression, to *sgraffito*, incision, and carving, manipulating the clay's surface has a long tradition in Southwestern pottery. In pursuit and extension of this tradition, contemporary potters follow new methods to endow their works with a sculptural quality. Artists represented in the Cameros Collection have used both low- and high-relief, as well as the occasional addition of a color to the sculpted figures that project from their pottery.

Though a descendant of Nampeyo of Hano, Iris Youvella Nampeyo (1944-) was unable to rely on the traditional Sikyatki revival designs made popular by her famous grandmother because she did not know how to paint.[xlv] In an effort to encourage his young daughter just learning to make pottery, her father said, "Why don't you paint a corn on the ladle."[xlvi] This simple symbol of their clan (Corn Clan) should have been easy to paint, but young Iris understood that she should fashion the ear of corn from the clay—thus giving birth to her trademark. Since this initial misinterpretation, Iris has perfected her wares with the symbol that has now become synonymous with her work—a sculpted ear of corn, flanked by receding husks, emerging from silky, flesh-colored clay. In the process, she has inspired other artists to apply and extend her technique, most notably Al Qöyawayma.[xlvii]

Jeff Roller (1963-) takes the carving process one step further by surpassing low-relief in order to achieve fully three-dimensional sculpture on his pottery. His figures are sculpted in complete form on the lids of his pottery, or they take the shape of animal busts erupting from the clay. Part of Santa Clara's famous Tafoya family, Jeff uses traditional methods and materials to create his sculpted wares.

In extension of the monochromatic work of Iris Youvella Nampeyo and Jeff Roller, Zuni artist Deldrick Cellicion adds polychrome paint to enhance the appliqué figures that rise out of (and scurry across) his pottery. Zuni pottery is similar to that of the nearby Acoma Pueblo in its use of fine lines, complicated use of geometric pattern, and most especially in the appearance of animal figures. It is no wonder that Deldrick's pottery consistently features animal motifs. His elegant, stylized salamander designs in relief have drawn the attention of pottery enthusiasts and collectors in recent years.

Like these other artists, Betty Manygoats, the mother of Elizabeth Manygoats, was inspired to add relief images to her traditional Navajo brownware pottery a few decades ago. Today, of Betty's nine daughters who carry on the tradition of appliquéd figures in Navajo pottery, it is Elizabeth who has stretched this inspiration to its zenith. She does not stop with appliqué. From low-relief to free-standing characters, she spins elaborate stories that seem to bring her pots to life. Aptly called "Lifestyle Pots," these figures are often stylized to resembled figures from the more famous Navajo art form of weaving and are painted in similarly bright colors that make the figures seem to leap off the pot.

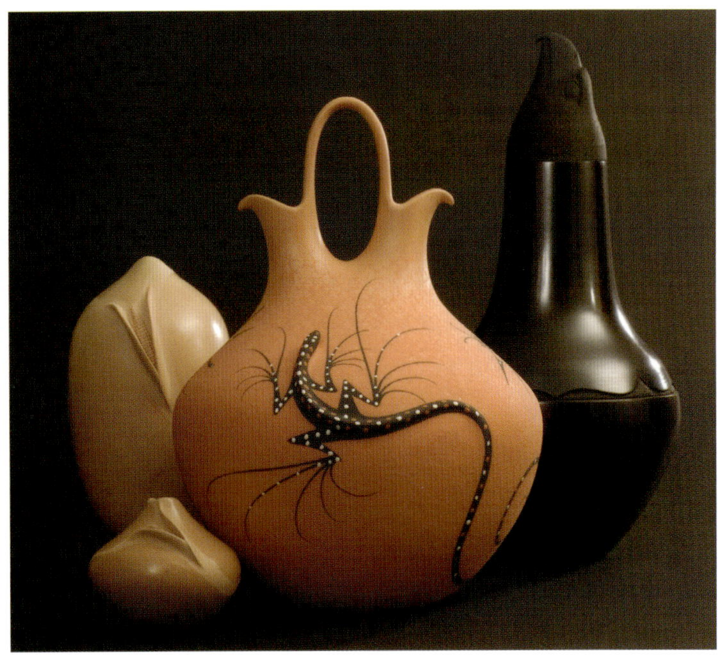

(L-R) Iris Youvella Nampeyo, buffware jar, c. 2002 and buffware vase, n.d.; Deldrick Cellicion, redware wedding vase with polychrome salamander, c. 1990s; Jeff Roller, blackware jar with carved lid, 1999.

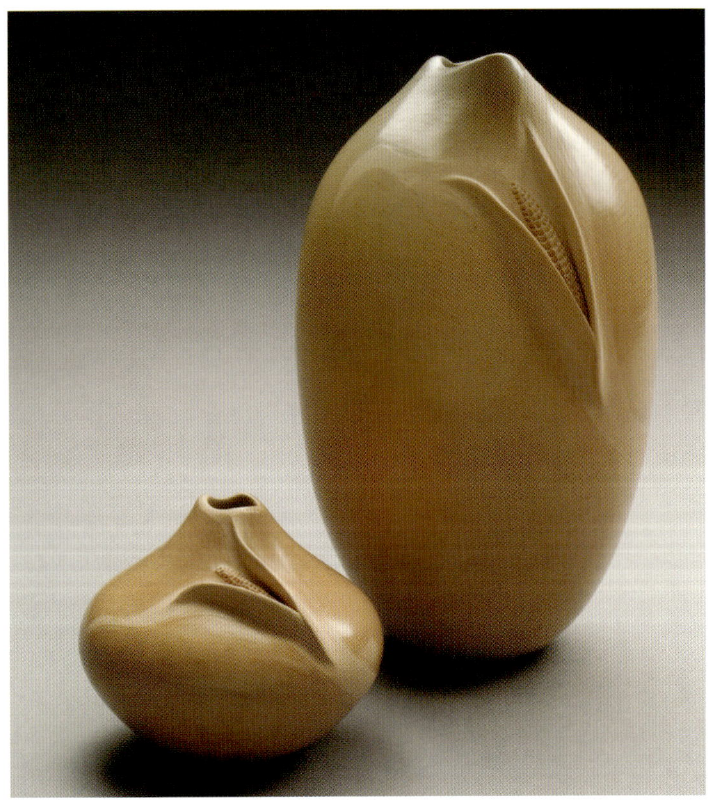

Iris Youvella Nampeyo, buffware vessels with Corn Clan symbols, (L) 2002 and (R) n.d.

Fine Line Pottery

There are other pueblos where potters employ fine line painting and eye-boggling geometric design, but pottery from the Acoma Pueblo seems to represent these aesthetics most starkly. Known primarily for pottery of sharp black patterns over brilliant white slip, Acoma pottery has exploited this sharp contrast to create a new tradition of intricate, repetitive patterns. Though Acoma has produced excellent polychrome pottery that includes animals and scroll designs, Acoma fine line pottery seems to be a product of constant competition to produce the smallest, most intricate optical illusions possible. It has even been called "op art" in reference to the mid-20th century movement exploring the perceptual experience of vision. While Acoma pottery designs evolved independently, the reference is nevertheless accurate. Both Acoma fine line pottery and optical canvas or sculptural art rely on a discordant foreground/background where the two planes compete for primacy.

Dorothy Torivio (1946-) is the standard by which Acoma "op art" pottery is judged. Extrapolating from the newer Acoma tradition established by Lucy M. Lewis and Marie Chino[xlviii] as well as the ancient Anasazi and Mimbres geometric designs, Dorothy developed the idea of repeating a single motif over the surface of an entire pot.[xlix] She paints her vessels freehand, mentally segmenting the vessel to visualize how she will accomplish her mathematically perfect design. As the shape of the pottery expands, so do the patterns, becoming almost kinetic and seeming to pulsate across the surface. Dorothy's four-pointed diamonds, seen in both of her works in the Cameros Collection, represent the four cardinal directions, or snowflakes when red-orange dots are placed around them.

The fine line pottery of Rebecca Lucario (1951-) is easily recognized. The thin walls of her pots are rivaled only by the tiny, threadlike lines Rebecca uses to embellish the surfaces. She paints using a traditional yucca brush, sometimes with only one fibrous strand. However, Rebecca's plates are the real marvel. Up to 30 inches in diameter, the plates are an exercise in precision and perfection. Rebecca's meticulous geometric designs seem to vibrate on the flat, round shape—an effect that one slip of her yucca brush would ruin, distracting the eye rather than dazzling it.

Sandra Victorino (1958-) is the niece and protégé of Dorothy Torivio. Studying her aunt's skill taught her patience and traditional technique. Sandra has wound those into her own take on the Acoma's "op art" pottery. Though in every other way she follows tradition, she has been known to use a sharp lid from a can of Spam and a butter paddle as tools. Inspired by the spiraling pattern of repetitious motifs that her famous aunt occasionally explores in her own work, Sandra experiments with the addition of figures and heavier use of color—the red-orange also found in Acoma polychrome. This intense color punctuates the black patterns that wind dizzyingly around pots of all sizes. Her newer works are distinguished by a continuation of pattern inside the lip of the vessel.

While Acoma is already known for its eggshell-thin pottery, Shana Garcia-Rustin (1969-), in collaboration with her husband, Patrick (Apache), create some of the thinnest pottery being made. An accomplishment by itself, the delicate nature of this pottery is only one aspect of Shana's artistry. Like many of the best Acoma artists, she plays off the illusory repetition of black and white patterns. Hers encompass the pot to culminate in an inventively wrapped and color-splashed mouth at the top of the vessel.

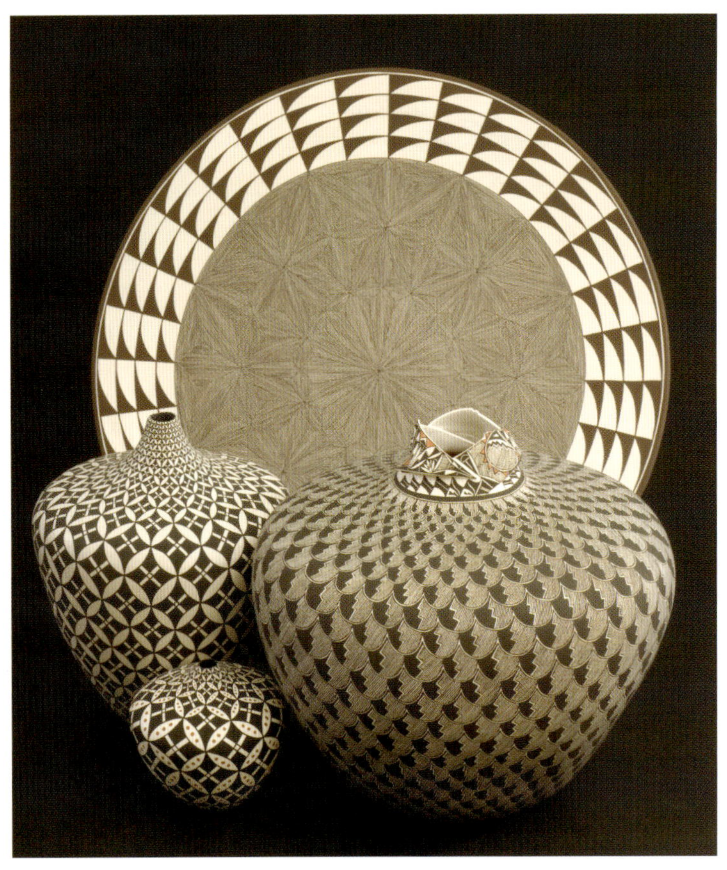

(Clockwise from top) Rebecca Lucario, fine line plate, c. 2005; Shana Garcia-Rustin, fineline jar, c. 2000; Dorothy Torivio, "Snowflake Jar", 1996, and vase, c. 1995.

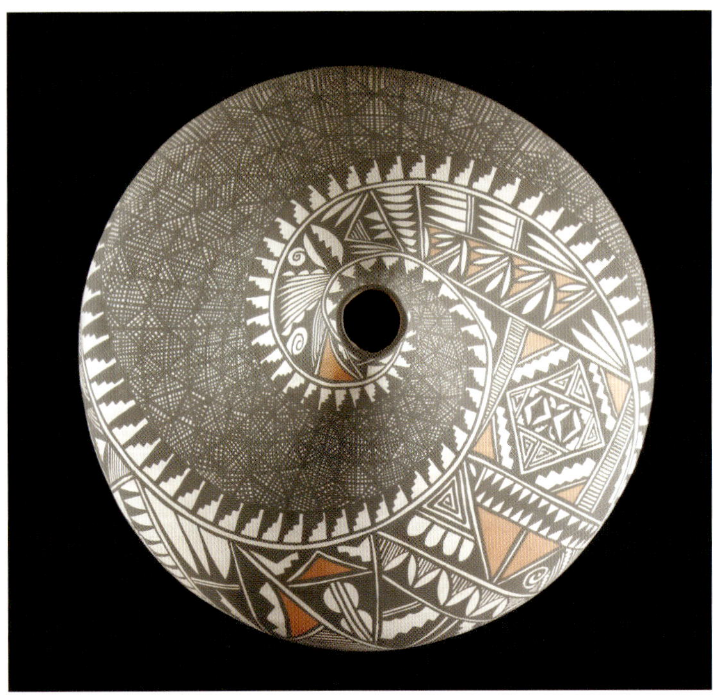

Sandra Victorino, whiteware with swirled fine line pattern, 2000.

Hopi Polychrome and Nampeyo's Designs

In the simplest terms, "polychrome" means "many colors." This term has been applied to any Southwestern pottery style, ancient or modern, that exhibits a palette of at least three colors. The pigments are typically derived from native plants and minerals and produce a range of paints that fire to a variety of reds, browns, yellows, and blacks. White slip and paint has also been produced from a local type of kaolin clay. Contemporary artists are able to achieve a broader range of colors by resorting to non-native pigments.

In the Hopi tradition, polychrome is usually applied directly to fine-textured pottery that fires to a range of warm hues. Unfired pots are dull grey, but the intense heat of outdoor kilns coaxes out colors from pale cream to intense orange-reds depending on the iron, manganese, and titanium oxide content in the clay. The lighter colors frequently blush with darker fire clouds. The more intermediate yellow colors are readily associated with a Hopi origin. These yellows were the dominant color of the ancient pottery shards that inspired Nampeyo to experiment with different clays until she could recreate the same color. She found that pots fired outside with sheep dung and soft coal provided this sought-after background for recreating the ancient polychrome designs.

Exploring the prehistoric symbols of the Sikyatki as well as their constitution led to an important stylistic evolution in Hopi pottery. The ancient styles featured curvilinear abstractions of animals, insects, and other images inspired by the natural environment. At the forefront of the evolution, Nampeyo adapted these designs and continued to recreate several of them throughout her life. According to family legend, Nampeyo's husband, Lesou,[li] copied several of these designs into a notebook and sought permission from tribal elders to use them, effectively transferring a sort of copyright of these images to his and Nampeyo's family. Among the images that the family considers theirs are:

Eagle Feather (or Eagle Tail) Design: Typically appearing on wide-shouldered pots where the top is nearly flat, the Eagle Feather Design begins with a wide square around the mouth of the vessel that represents the four corners of the Earth.[lii] Feather patterns, representing prayers, protrude from each side of the square. This pattern has evolved under the brush of many artists, sometimes being distilled to the barest essence of its original form.

Migration Pattern: This pattern is not so-named because it migrates evenly across the surface of the pottery. Rather, the fine line hatching found throughout represents the paths taken by clans as they migrated to the Hopi mesas. The long, angular features are said to be bird or bat wings. Because of the artistic dexterity required to achieve the hatched lines and even spacing of the pattern, many scholars believe that Nampeyo was unable to paint this pattern late in her life without help from family members due to failing eyesight.

Parrot Design: Archeologists have determined that the ancestors of the Hopi had a lively trade with Mesoamerica. Parrots and parrot feathers were a significant part of this commerce. Nampeyo's version of this design adapted well to round and linear pottery shapes.

With its colorful array of clays and paints and the vast number of designs arising from tradition, Hopi pottery becomes easily distinguishable. The combinations are infinite and have provided substantial opportunity for potters past and present to accomplish significant feats of creativity and still remain within the borders of tradition. Within the Cameros Collection several potters stand out.

Polychrome on Yellow

Jean Sahme[liii] Nampeyo (1948-) continues the Nampeyo family tradition of using Sikyatki designs on hand-coiled pottery. Her favorite designs are the Migration Pattern, the butterfly, and rain clouds. She has continued to refine her use of these images on her wares and feels that her life and artistry are meant to convey the history of her people and their traditions.

Though she lived a traditional Hopi life, Grace Chapella[liv] (1874 - 1980) saw 106 years of great change in the Southwest and, more important, in her village of Hano. This was partially because the world was rapidly changing everywhere, but it was also because of the attention Grace's famous neighbor, Nampeyo, brought to the village with her pottery. Taking advantage of this circumstance, Grace learned pottery-making from Nampeyo as well as from her own mother. Perhaps as a means of sanctuary in the midst of change, Grace adhered to tradition in her pottery, employing prehistoric methods and symbols revived by Nampeyo. Grace's pottery was usually formed from clay that fired to a cream color. As she became recognized for the color and quality of her wares,[lv] she also became known for the symbols she employed. Among her favorite motifs were the rain bird and butterfly. The latter has been so strongly connected to Grace that her descendants have absorbed it into their own tradition of iconography.

Grace Chapella passed her knowledge of Hopi pottery on to many students, including her great-grandson, Mark Tahbo (1958-). Through this connection, Mark was steeped in the tradition of Sikyatki revival designs. He applies them to the same fine clay that Grace used. Now that his great-grandmother has passed away, he occasionally strays from traditional patterns. Still, he remains rooted in his cultural heritage—the influences at times explicit, at others implied. Some of his most notable designs are his depictions of Katsina faces, a practice long associated with Hopi pottery and even said to be on some of the earliest works of Nampeyo.[lvi]

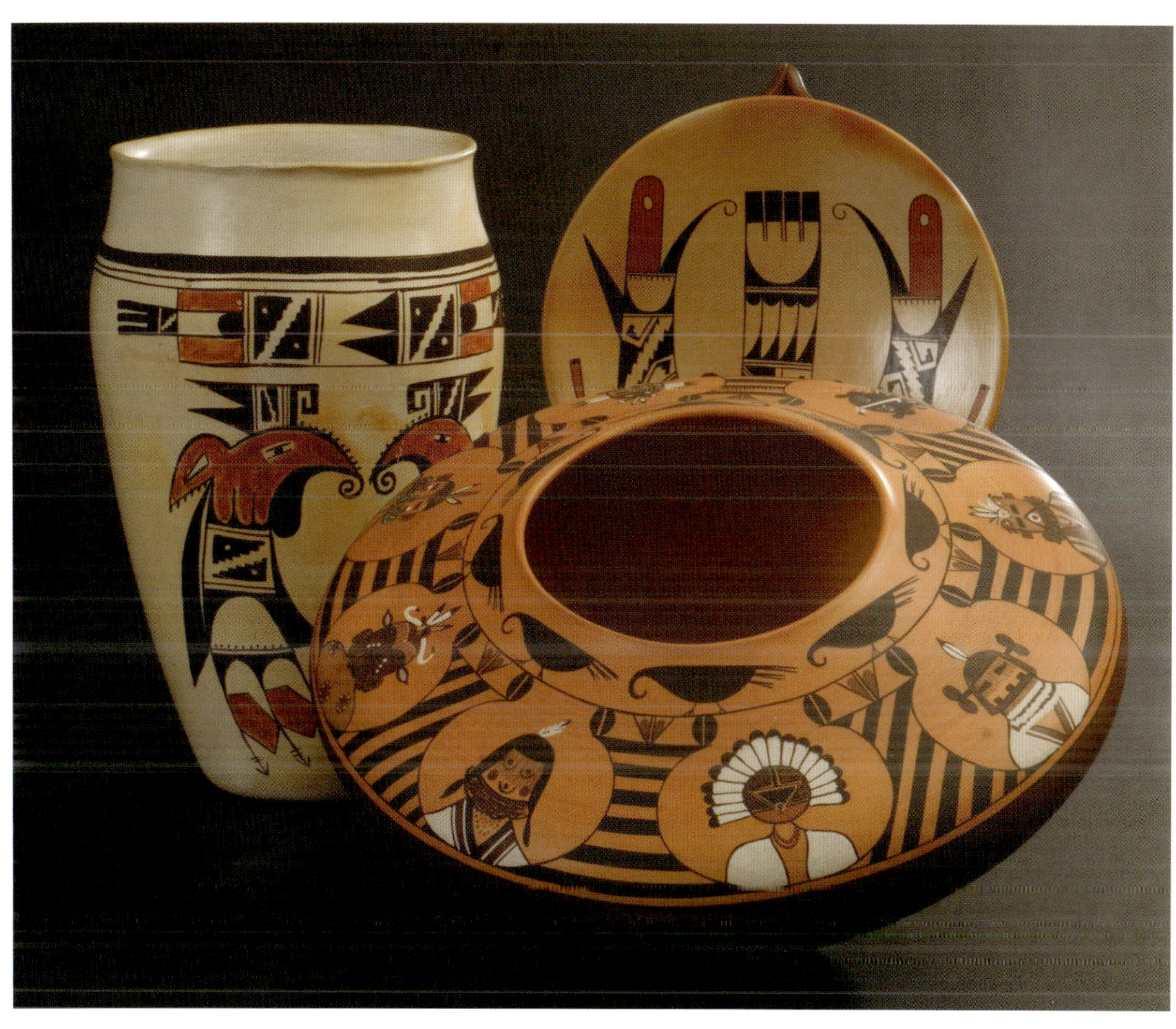

(L-R) Grace Chapella, polychrome cylinder vase with Parrot Design, c. 1950; Mark Tahbo, polychrome Katsina Pot, 2005 and polychrome plate, 1994.

Polychrome on Red

Paqua "Frogwoman" Naha (1890 - 1955), whose first name means "frog" in Spanish, signed her pottery with a painted image of a frog, giving rise to her unusual nickname. Paqua's daughter, Joy Navasie, whose pottery would also gain recognition, would become known as the second "Frogwoman." Throughout Paqua's career, she produced polychrome designs on yellow or cream colored pottery, though occasionally, as with her work in the Cameros Collection, she would use clay that fired to a deeper red.

Descended from the Navasie side of the Naha-Navasie clan of potters, Stetson Setalla (1962-), grandson of Paqua, follows his family tradition closely. He recreates ancient designs on the various warm colors of Hopi clay. In the examples of his work in the Cameros Collection, he accomplishes a deep red hue for his pottery and then embellishes it with darker, vegetal colors. Stetson is an introspective artist who rids himself of negativity before beginning any pot, believing it will corrupt the final product.[lvii]

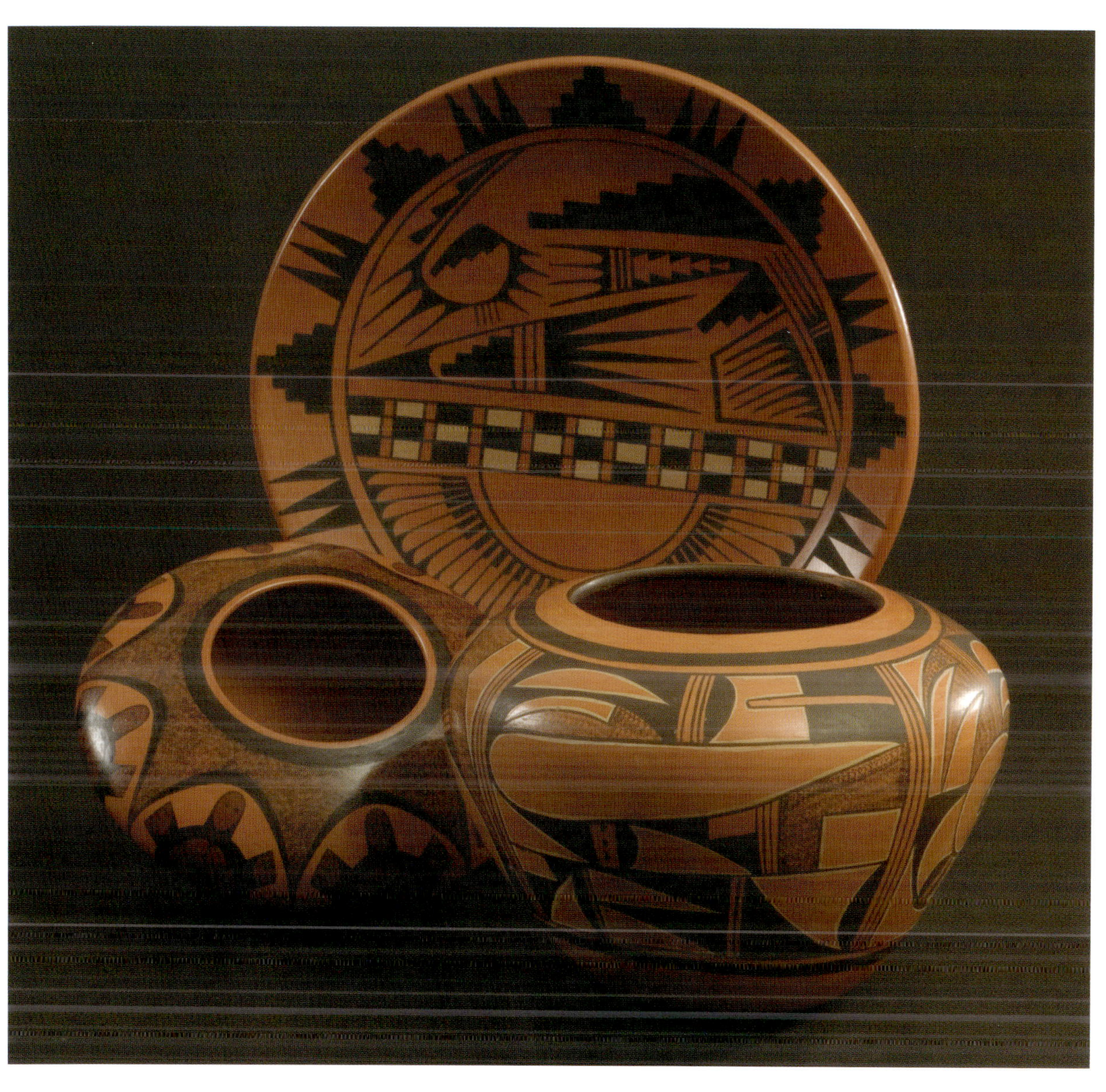

(L-R) Stetson Setalla, polychrome Turtle Pot, c. 2000; Blue Corn, polychrome plate, c. 1980; Paqua "Frogwoman" Naha, polychrome jar, c. 1940s.

Polychrome on White

Helen "Featherwoman" Naha (1922 - 1993) was best known for breaking with the Hopi tradition of applying polychrome paint to unslipped pottery that ranged in color from cream to orange. Since being revived by Nampeyo, this had become the dominant Hopi pottery style. Helen returned to using slip on her pottery, a step unnecessary since Nampeyo's rediscovery of finer clays. Helen also chose to paint her designs primarily in black on white slip, only occasionally adding color. This was also a significant departure from the more varied palette of then-current Hopi style. Unlike Nampeyo's designs, Helen's were inspired by the nearby Awatovi ruins rather than the Sikyatki ones. Since Helen, her Naha and Navasie relatives have become the dominant producers of what is termed whiteware. Largely self-taught, Helen also learned pottery making skills from her mother-in-law, Paqua Naha, the first "Frogwoman." Between them, these two women have launched another famous dynasty of Hopi pottery makers.

Burel Naha (1944-) is the son of Helen Naha and follows in her whiteware tradition. Though he relied on some of the same traditional designs as his mother, he has become famous for his frequent depiction of a lifelike spider on a web (not to be confused with the abstract Spider Design that the Nampeyo clan claims as its own). While he is in fact descended from the Spider Clan of the Tewa, his use of the spider image was inspired by his daughter's computerized rendering of a spider for a school project.[lviii] Black dominates Burel's design, but he also uses a polychromatic palette to add subtle color variations to his realistic images.

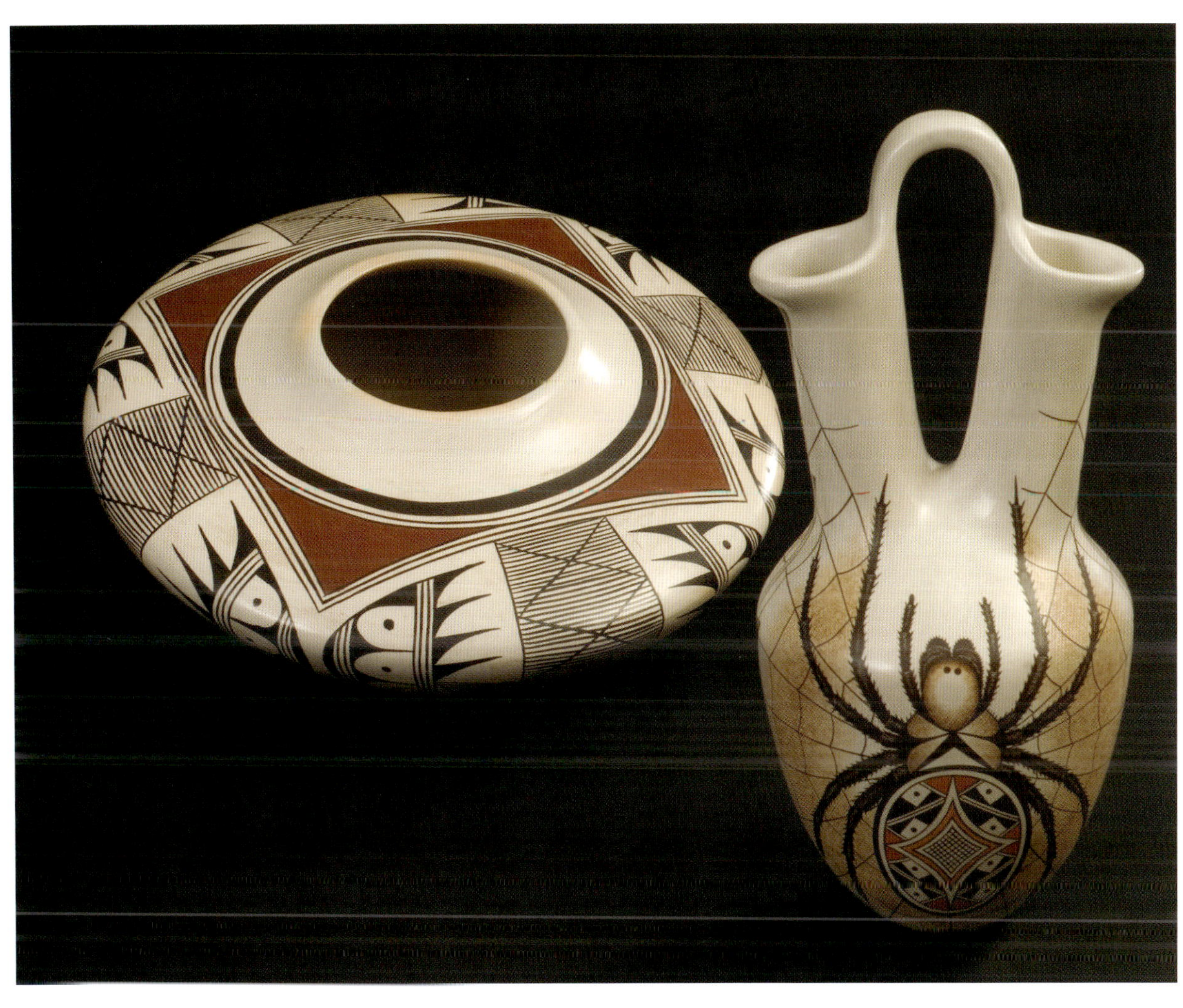

(L-R) Helen "Featherwoman" Naha, polychrome whiteware jar, c. 1985; Burel Naha, polychrome whiteware wedding vessel, n.d.

Variations on Nampeyo's Designs

The great-granddaughter of Nampeyo, Dextra Quotskuyva (1928-) is possibly the most influential Hopi potter living today. Dextra has made it her life's work to study all the known Nampeyo and prehistoric Hopi pottery. She commits their designs to memory so as to summon them into her own pottery. She adheres to classic forms and traditional methods of creation, and passes on her knowledge to a new generation of potters, including her daughter, Hisi Nampeyo, and nephews Les Namingha and Steve Lucas. She cautions her students to "use the old [designs] first, they have a lot of power, then later add your own ideas."[lix]

This approach to pottery makes Dextra especially difficult to categorize. Is she a Keeper of Tradition or an Artist Without Reservation? It is true that every Dextra design is an original, never repeated. "I don't do the same design ever,"[lx] says the artist. This fact alone forces Dextra to be ever creative in her embellishment of pottery. Yet, whether she is painting a motif that is obviously Hopi, or a pattern's Hopi heritage is disguised by a modern sense of flourish and creativity, Dextra's images are anchored in custom. Indeed, much of her work is about elaborating or simplifying Hopi designs. She may try to create a kaleidoscope effect on a wide-shouldered jar[lxi] as no other artist has yet done, or leave vast sections of a vessel unadorned, but these are visual choices. Different from Nampeyo's artistic preferences, they reflect the guidance of the same aesthetic that the great matriarch of Hopi tradition established, not an effort to break from it.

More than a century ago, Nampeyo re-established what is today considered "classic" Hopi. Today, no one could disagree that Dextra is an enormous part of, if not the current definition of, that same concept. To try to reclassify such an enormously influential artist as a mere trendsetter would be to rob her of the reputation she has earned for creating exceptional work that reveres and extends her cultural heritage.

Steve Lucas (1955-), great-great-grandson of Nampeyo, begins decorating his pottery with a preconceived design based in Hopi tradition. He primarily uses vegetal paints and clay slips to create the palette of polychrome for which he is well known. From there, he lets the clay guide him. The pottery shape dictates the extension and expression of his patterns, but the designs themselves take on new life as he is influenced by new ideas, such as landscapes viewed from the air.[lxii] By adapting these and other designs, he is in the process of developing a new Hopi iconography.

Inspired by the work of Dextra, Jake Koopee (1970-) was motivated to look closely at prehistoric Sikyatki shards found near his home on the First Mesa of the Hopi Reservation and put his own creativity into traditional Hopi designs. The shards have primarily provided symbols for the artist to incorporate into his pottery. To these he has added his own symbols. While Jacob is known for making some of the largest traditional Hopi pottery, his miniatures are exceptional in their own right.

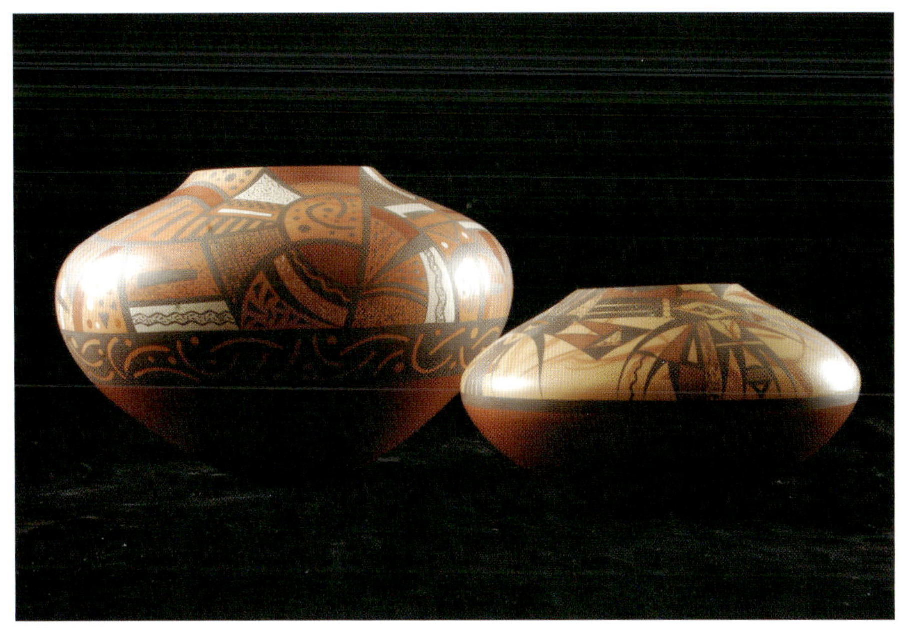

Steve Lucas, polychrome jars, c. 2001-02 and, 2003.

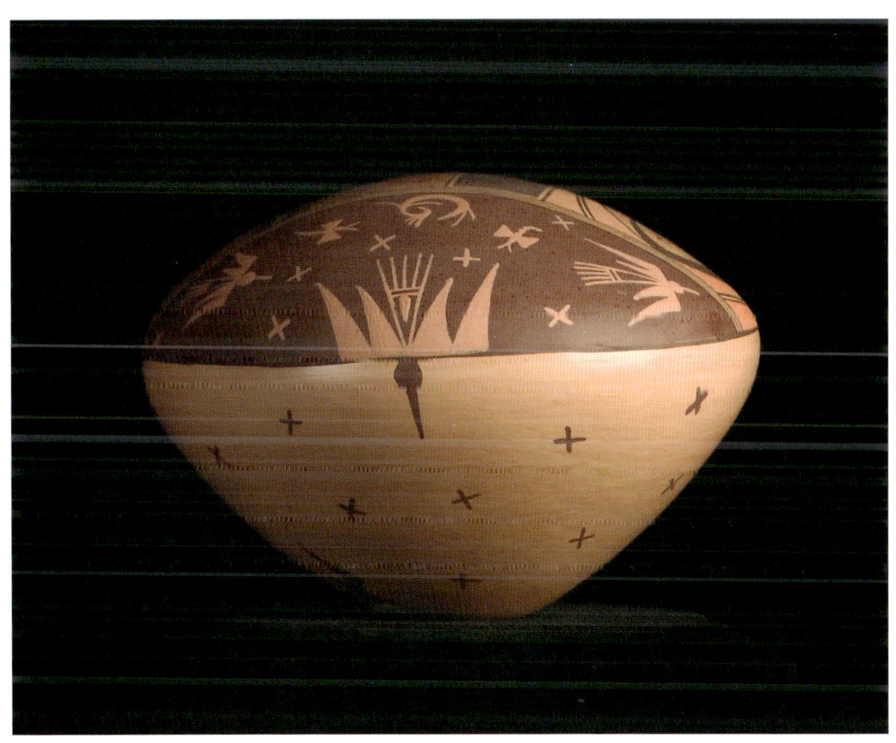

Jake Koopee, "Under the Stars," polychrome seed jar, c. 2004.

Polychrome Shard Pattern

It was Dextra Quotskuyva who created the so-called Shard Pattern. A single piece of pottery, it is painted to look like as if it was constructed from hundreds of fragments. Perhaps the pattern is influenced by the broken prehistoric pottery so prevalent around the Hopi Reservation, or by the ancient Mimbres tradition of purposefully breaking a piece out of pots.[lxiii] In any case, the idea of fragments reunited alludes beautifully to the sciences of ethnology and archeology that have tried to piece together Native history, as well as to the cultural mosaic that is today's pottery tradition. In each section, or "shard," a different symbol is painted and remains inimitable throughout the whole. The artist likens it to the universe filled with unique individuals.[lxiv] Of all her one-of-a-kind patterns, Dextra's Shard Pattern has gained as much admiration from potters as pottery enthusiasts. Two notable potters have put their own unique perspective on it: Les Namingha's in his mosaic patterns (see page 79), and Rondina Huma.

Rondina Huma (1947-) is one of the few artists who has the skill and patience to pursue Dextra's lead in the Shard Pattern category. While it would be nearly impossible to recreate Dextra's work, Rondina has become famous for her own shard pots (see page 79). Using a deep burgundy palette and microcosmic segments, Rondina pieces together hundreds of tiny Sikyatki designs to comprise an entire mosaic. Though of Tewa and Hopi descent, Rondina did not have the advantage of learning from a family of famous potters. She is self taught and has earned her reputation through precision and perfection. She even takes the time and risk to fully polish the insides of her bowls—a trait uncommon in Southwestern pottery.

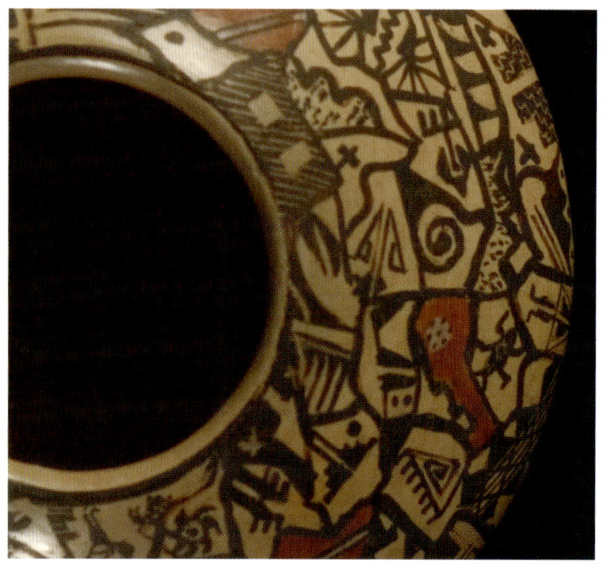

Dextra Quotskuyra, polychrome shard miniature, c. 1980.

Variations on the Shard Pattern

Rainy Naha (1949-) is descended from a family of famous Tewa potters. Like her mother, Helen Naha, and brother, Burel, she carries on the tradition of working in white slipped Hopi clay. Rainy has also created her own style of pottery. Not quite accurately described as Shard Pattern, for her segments are not random, her pottery is nonetheless segmented into tiny frames for designs. Each design may reappear within the same pot but with no discernable pattern. Her vessels are also sometimes divided into quadrants by dark bands that intersect at the mouth of the pot. These bands contain their own symbols, frequently depicting phases of the moon that denote a "Solstice Pot."

Most of the pottery of Lawrence Namoki (1949-) would not fall into the category of Shard Pattern. Its varied surface texture and use of color is more likely to call to mind the pottery of Tom Polacca. Interestingly enough, Lawrence's first foray into Hopi art was carving sacred Katsina dolls following in his father's vocation. It was only later in life that he tried his hand at pottery. For several years, he taught himself the age-old method of pottery making. Then, in 1985, he introduced his pottery at the Eight Northern Indian Pueblos Arts and Crafts Fair at San Ildefonso Pueblo in New Mexico. Its obvious infusion of a sculptor's background and Katsina imagery garnered the award for Best in Show.[lxv]

Almost 20 years later, the artist would persuade Nancy and Alan Cameros to purchase a work from him that had not yet been created. It would be similar to his masterpiece of 1985 in that it would be divided into quadrants and be based on Hopi legend—this time on the story of Creation. On Lawrence's "Creation Pot," the symbols overlap, at times half obscured by one another. At the microcosmic level, everything appears chaotic and disjointed. Only when it is viewed as a whole do the parts unify, invoking order, much like creation itself must have taken place. It is this simultaneous segmentation and unification that earns this piece a place in this subcategory of Hopi polychrome. Call them shard or call them chaos, the pieces come together neatly under the creative force of the artist.

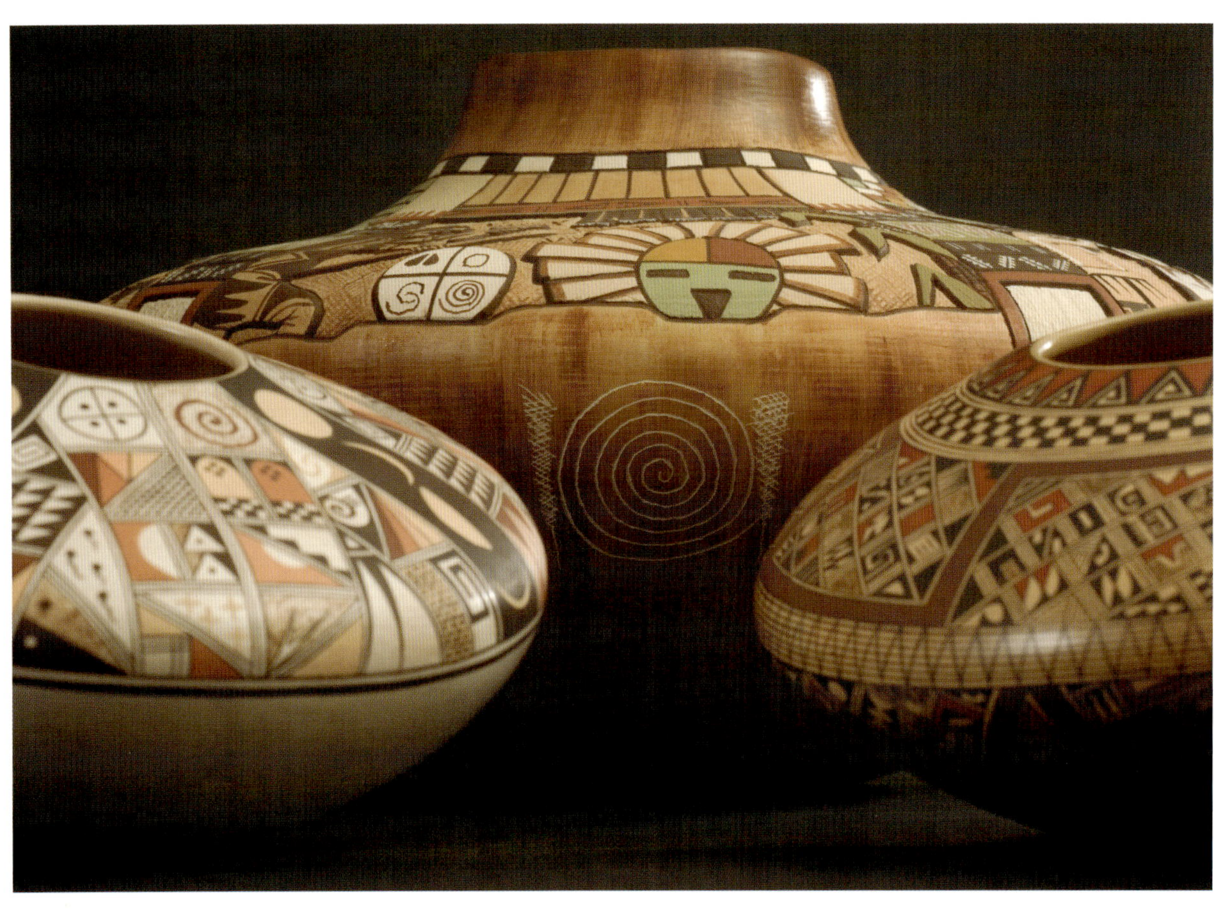

(L-R) "Solstice" by Rainy Naha, polychrome on whiteware, c. 2000-02; "Creation" by Lawrence Namoki, incised polychrome, 2005; Rondina Huma, polychrome mosaic jar, 2001.

Pueblo Polychrome Traditions

Born in San Ildefonso, Crucita "Blue Corn" Gonzalez (1921 - 1999) was ushered into a world of pottery that had been redefined by fellow villager Maria Martinez and her family. So great was the fame of the Martinez pottery, especially the black-on-blackware, that it had almost overshadowed older pueblo styles. In respectful defiance of these new traditions, Blue Corn, as she is commonly known, purposefully avoided the influence of the Martinez family and pursued older styles to influence her work. Blue Corn experimented with colors created from mineral and vegetal sources and used them to paint the ancient motifs that she had studied onto pottery coated with a cream colored slip. For her initiative, she is credited with helping to revive polychrome in San Ildefonso.[lxvi]

Emma Lewis Mitchell (1931 -) is one of the daughters of the late Lucy M. Lewis, matriarch of the current Acoma pottery tradition. Emma feels strongly about not deviating from the methods and aesthetic her mother re-established so as to keep the tradition of her ancient ancestors alive. Purposely avoiding contemporary influences, Emma continues to create well established designs such as the lightning bolt and the deer with a heartline, an ancient Zuni symbol adopted long ago by Acoma puebloans. The heartline is the red arrow pointing from the deer's mouth to its middle. Heartlines are thought to serve as a reminder of the life of the animal whose spirit was captured within the representation. More contemporary meanings portray the heartline as a symbol of long life or the power of healing. The heartline also resembles the symbols for snake and lightning, two extremely powerful forces in pueblo mythology.

Margaret Gutierrez (1936-) & Luther Gutierrez (1911 - 1987) were sibling potters from Santa Clara Pueblo. They worked in contrast to the better known Santa Clara tradition of high-polish blackware and redware, continuing their parents' style of polychrome wares. Their early designs centered on traditional motifs like the *avanyu*, but in the 1970s they began to paint polychrome caricatures of animals on their pottery. These whimsical creatures were deftly painted in an extensive palette of colors, for which the two artists became well known. Since Luther died, Margaret has continued to make pottery with other relatives, but without their collective influence, there are few who continue the polychrome tradition for Santa Clara.

Joseph (1947 -) & Barbara (1951 -) Cerno are a husband and wife team that creates traditional Acoma polychrome *ollas*. Joseph fashions these water jars, some of the largest among the pueblos,[lxvii] and Barbara, of Hopi descent, paints them in vibrant colors. They use the white Acoma clay and employ traditional motifs, though recently they have begun exploring more whimsical designs. The most famous of these is the locomotive, which is anachronistic to the ancient patterns. Its appropriation into Southwestern pottery is understandable because the completion of the Santa Fe Railroad around 1880 represented an important turning point in the value and status of pueblo wares.

Married to Hopi potter Steve Lucas, Yvonne Lucas (1959 -) is actually of Laguna descent. Encouraged by her husband, as well as by his famous teacher and aunt, Dextra Quotskuyva,[lxviii] Yvonne tried her own hand at pottery-making. At first, she worked in Hopi-style polychrome but has since begun reviving traditional Laguna patterns. The results are a stunning marriage of elegant construction and lyrical composition.

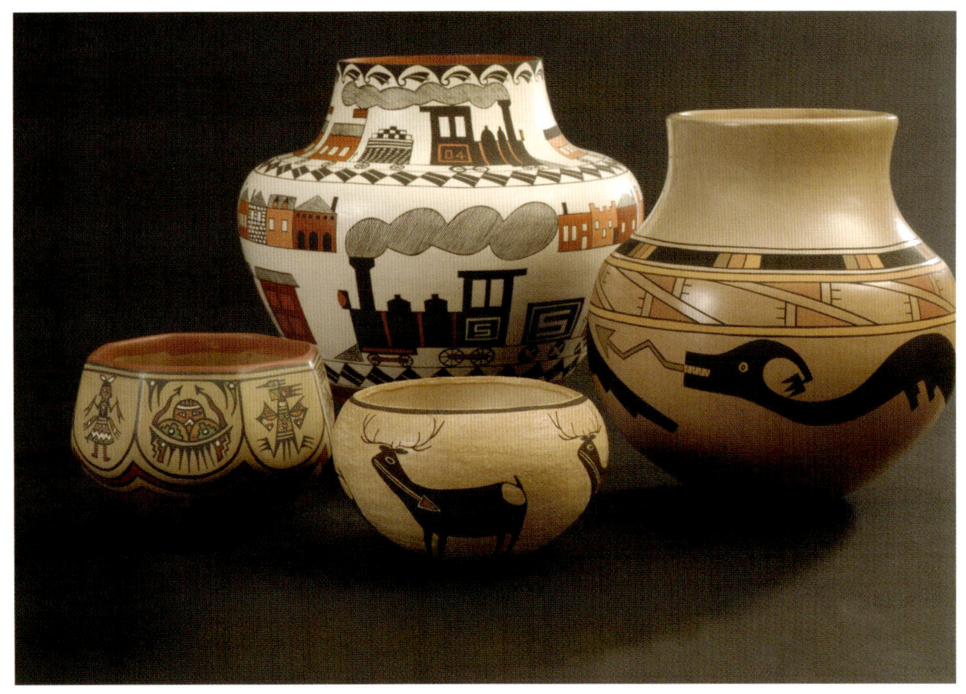

(Clockwise from top) Joseph Cerno, polychrome jar, April 2003; Blue Corn, polychrome vase, c. 1965; Emma Lewis Mitchell, polychrome bowl with heartline deer, c. 1965-70; Margaret and Luther Gutierrez, polychrome bowl, c. 1975.

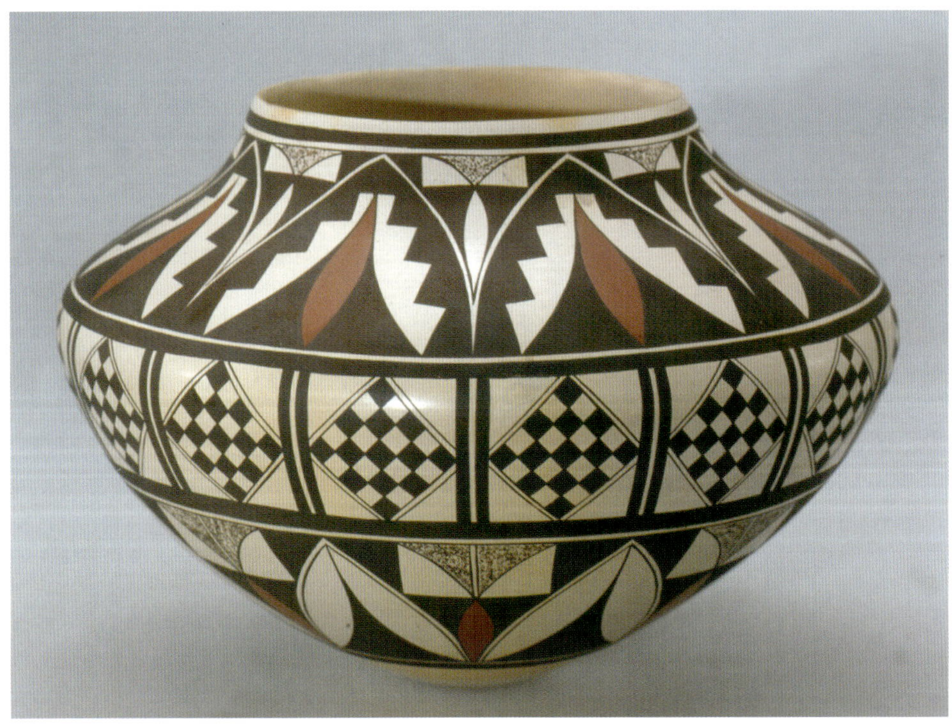

Yvonne Lucas, polychrome jar, 2000.

Endnotes

i Jung, p. 26.

ii Wright, “Nampeyo,” in Cohen, p. 35

iii Kramer, p. 62.

iv *ibid.*

v Spivey, p. 15.

vi *ibid.*, p. 77.

vii From interview between the author and Tammy Garcia March 27, 2007.

viii McCoy, “Sarafina Tafoya and Margaret Tafoya,” in Cohen, p. 42.

ix Whittington, Susan Roller. Eulogy for Margaret Tafoya.

x Douglas.

xi Spivey, pp. 53, 82.

xii *ibid.*, p. 86.

xiii *ibid.*, p. 108.

xiv Peterson,“Pottery of American Indian Women: The Legacy of Generations,” p. 206.

xv From ongoing conversations between the author and Charles King.

xvi From an interview between the author and Nancy Youngblood, June 5, 2007.

xvii *ibid.*

xviii From an interview between the author and Nathan Youngblood, June 30, 2007.

xix From an interview between the author and Autumn Borts-Medlock, June 4, 2007.

xx From an interview between author and Tammy Garcia, May 27, 2007.

xxi From ongoing conversations between the author and Charles King.

xxii Ron McCoy, “Al Qöyawayma,” in Cohen, p. 80.

xxiii Al Qöyawayma quoting his aunt, Elizabeth White Poligaysi, in an interview with the author, June 22, 2007.

xxiv The artist points out that a type of repoussé has been discovered within the Chavin culture (c. 1900 BC) from around Valdivia, Equador.

xxv From the artist's autobiographical website: http://www.alqpottery.com/biography.html

xxvi From an interview between the author and Preston Duwyenie, June 22, 2007.

xxvii From an interview between the author and Leo Namingha, June 30, 2007.

xxviii *ibid.*

xxix From an interview between the author and Richard Zane Smith, June 29, 2007

xxx Clark, p. 81.

xxxi From an interview between the author and Virgil Ortiz, June 20, 2007.

xxxii *ibid.*

xxxiii Fauntleroy, Gussie, “Swirling with Success,” pp. 92-8.

xxxiv Gussie Fauntleroy, “Translating Tradition,” p. 95.

xxxv From an interview between the author and Lonnie Vigil, June 12, 2007.

xxxvi From an interview between the author and Tammy Garcia, March 27, 2007.

xxxvii Naranjo.

xxxviii From an interview between author and Jody Naranjo June 14, 2007.

xxxix Dillingham, “Fourteen Families in Pueblo Pottery,” p. 205.

xl “The Pottery Jewels of Joseph Lonewolf.”

xli From an interview between the author and Greg Lonewolf, June 15, 2007.

xlii From an interview between the author and Rosemary Lonewolf, June 20, 2007.

xliii *ibid.*

xliv Gussie Fauntleroy, “The Ones to Watch,” p. 175.

xlv Dillingham, “Fourteen Families in Pueblo Pottery,” p. 25.

xlvi *ibid.*

xlvii From an interview between the author and Al Qöyawayma, June 22, 2007.

xlviii Not represented within the Cameros Collection.

xlix Roberta Burnett, “Dorothy Torivio,” in Cohen, p. 122.

l Collins, “Nampeyo, Hopi Potter,” p. 13.

li From an unpublished essay by Steve Lucas on Nampeyo of Hano.

lii Struever, p. 54.

liii According to a quote by Jean Sahme in Dillingham, “Fourteen Families of Pueblo Pottery,” she states that she leaves the 'i' out of her last name “because it is simpler for [her] to spell it that way,” p. 46.

liv A transliteration of Grace's Native name, “Tsepela,” meaning “White Squash Blossom,” from Collins, “Hopi Traditions in Pottery and Painting Honoring Grace Chapella.”

lv *ibid.*, Reference to “White Pottery Lady.”

lvi Kramer, p. 65.

lvii Schaaf, “Hopi- Tewa Pottery,” pp. 152-3.

lviii Dillingham, “Fourteen Families in Pueblo Pottery,” p. 73.

lix *ibid.*, p. 56. Quote from Les Namingha.

lx Struever, p. 18.

lxi From a conversation between the author and Martha Hopkins Struever June 2007.

lxii Struever, p. 33.

lxiii Referred to as a “kill hole” since the holes were introduced to the pots for mortuary purposes and placed over the faces of the deceased.

lxiv *ibid.*, p. 21.

lxv Indyke.

lxvi Schaaf, “Pueblo Indian Pottery: 750 Artist Biographies,” pp. 161-2.

lxvii Schaaf, “Pueblo Indian Pottery: 2000 Artist Biographies,” p. 75.

lxviii Streuver, p. 97.

Exhibition Checklist

Harrison Begay, brownware vase, 2001, 10 x 7.5 inches.

Blue Corn, polychrome plate, c. 1980, 14 inches.

Blue Corn, polychrome vase with avanyu design, c. 1965, 10 x 8.5 inches.

Autumn Borts-Medlock, blackware vase, 2005, 10.5 x 7 inches.

Autumn Borts-Medlock, polychrome redware "Hummingbird" vase, 2001, 10 x 6 inches.

Linda Cain, carved redware vase with white slip inpainting, 2002, 12.5 x 6 inches.

Hubert Candelario, micaceous swirled melon jar, 2006, 7.5 x 8 inches.

Hubert Candelario, micaceous miniature puzzle pot, 2001, 1.5 x 1.25 inches.

Deldrick Cellicion, redware wedding vase with polychrome salamander, c. 2004, 14 x 9.25 inches.

Joseph Cerno, polychrome jar, April 2003, 11 x 11 inches.

Grace Chapella, polychrome cylinder vase, c. 1950, 13.5 x 8 inches.

Alice Cling, polished brownware vase, 2004, 10 x 6 inches.

Alice Cling, polished brownware jar, 2004, 6 x 5.5 inches.

Tony Da, sculpted redware turtle with turquoise, heishi and silver inlay, c. 1975, 8 x 10 inches.

Tony Da, redware jar with sgraffito and turquoise inlay, c. 1970, 5 x 5 inches.

Tony Da, sculpted redware bear with turquoise inlay, c. 1976-77, 1.5 inches.

Tony Da, polished redware bear with turquoise inlay, c. 1971-72, 2 inches.

Popovi Da, gunmetal cup, October 1965, 2.5 x 2.25 inches.

Popovi Da, black-on-blackware plate, June 1960, 12 inches.

Carmelita Dunlap, polished redware vase with turquoise inlay, 1982, 8 x 8 inches.

Preston Duwyenie, Shifting Sands series buffware seed jar with silver lid, c. 1998-99, 5 x 3 inches.

Jody Folwell, blackware bowl, c. 1997, 9.5 x 9.5 inches.

Susan Folwell, "Slaughter of the Lambs" polychrome bowl, c. 2001, 11 x 16 inches.

Susan Folwell, "Medicine Man" polychrome vase, c. 2005, 14.5 x 7 inches.

Tammy Garcia, Redware with white slip and dragonfly motif, 1994, 5.5 x 7.5 inches.

Tammy Garcia, redware heightened with various red slips, 1996, 6.5 x 7 inches.

Tammy Garcia, blackware storage jar, 2007, 18.5 x 15.75 inches.

Shana Garcia-Rustin, fine line jar, c. 1995-2000, 11 x 10.5 inches.

Barbara Gonzalez, blackware vessel with turquoise, coral and shell inlay, c. 2000, 6 x 12 inches.

Barbara Gonzalez, blackware plate with turquoise and coral inlay, 1992, 6.25 inches.

John Gonzalez, redware plate with turquoise inlay, 2004, 12 inches.

Margaret & Luther Gutierrez, polychrome bowl, c. 1975, 4.5 x 7 inches.

Rondina Huma, polychrome mosaic jar, 2001, 4.5 x 7.5 inches.

Alton Komalestewa, blackware "pushed out" melon wedding vase, c. 1990, 9.5 x 8 inches.

Jake Koopee, "Under the Stars," polychrome seed jar, c. 2004, 4.5 x 5 inches.

Lucy Lewis, fine line jar, 1953, 6 x 7.5 inches.

Greg Lonewolf, polychrome miniature, n.d., 1.5 x 1.5 inches.

Greg Lonewolf, polychrome miniature, n.d., 1.5 x 1.5 inches.

Greg Lonewolf, polychrome miniature, n.d., 2 x 1.5 inches.

Joseph Lonewolf, polychrome miniature, 1976, 3.5 x 1.5 inches.

Joseph Lonewolf, polychrome miniature, 1986, 2.125 x 2 inches.

Joseph Lonewolf, polychrome miniature, 1997, 0.875 x 0.75 inches.

Joseph Lonewolf, polychrome miniature, 1977, 1.75 x 1.5 inches.

Joseph Lonewolf, polychrome miniature, n.d., 1 x 1 inches

Joseph Lonewolf, polychrome miniature, n.d., 1.875 x 1.5 inches.

Joseph Lonewolf, polychrome miniature, n.d., 1.25 x 1.25 inches.

Joseph Lonewolf, polychrome miniature, n.d., 1.25 x 1.25 inches.

Rosemary Lonewolf, polychrome miniature, 1996, 4 x 3 inches.

Rebecca Lucario, fine line plate, c. 2005, 16 inches.

Steve Lucas, polychrome jar, 2003, 4.5 x 6.5 inches.

Steve Lucas, polychrome jar, c. 2001-02, 7 x 8.5 inches.

Yvonne Lucas, polychrome jar, 2000, 8 x 11 inches.

Elizabeth Manygoats, polychrome vessel with carved figures, 2006, 9 x 9 inches.

Maria Martinez and Popovi Da, polychrome jar, 1959, 7.75 x 9 inches.

Maria Martinez, blackware bowl, c. 1950, 3.5 x 4.25 inches.

Maria Martinez & Popovi Da, black-on-blackware feather plate, June 1960, 12.5 inches.

Maria & Julian Martinez, polychrome jar, c. 1920, 8.75 x 10.25 inches.

Grace Medicine Flower, redware cut out with polychrome, 2005, 10 x 8 inches.

Grace Medicine Flower, redware basketweave bowl, c. 1995-2000, 6 x 7 inches.

Grace Medicine Flower, redware miniature, 1994, 2 x 1 inches.

Emma Lewis Mitchell, polychrome bowl with heartline deer, c. 1965-70, 4 x 6 inches.

Jennifer Tafoya Moquino, blackware and polychrome vase, c. 2002-04, 9.5 x 5 inches.

Burel Naha, polychrome whiteware wedding vessel, 2004, 12 x 5.5 inches.

Helen "Featherwoman" Naha, polychrome whiteware jar, c. 1985, 5 x 11.5 inches.

Paqua "Frogwoman" Naha, polychrome jar, c. 1940s, 7.5 x 10 inches.

Rainy Naha, "Solstice," polychrome on whiteware, c. 2000-02, 4.5 x 8 inches.

Les Namingha, polychrome "mosaic" jar, c. 2006, 14 x 12 inches.

Les Namingha, polychrome "mosaic" jar, 2005, 7.5 x 10.5 inches.

Lawrence Namoki, "Creation," incised polychrome, 2005, 8 x 13 inches

Nampeyo of Hano (attributed to) and polychrome bowl, c. 1915-20, 2.5 x 5 inches.

Nampeyo of Hano (attributed to) polychrome cylinder jar, c. 1915-20, 11.5 x 6 inches.

Nampeyo of Hano (attributed to) polycrome bowl, c. 1905, 4 x 9.5 inches

Iris Youvella Nampeyo, buffware jar, c. 2002, 4 x 4 inches.

Iris Youvella Nampeyo, buffware vase, n.d., 8.25 x 5 inches.

Jody Naranjo, redware jar with sgraffito, 2006, 9 x 8 inches.

Paul Naranjo, brownware wedding vessel, c. 1990-95, 13.5 x 11 inches.
Teresita Naranjo, carved redware vase, c. 1980s, 6 x 5.25 inches.
Wally Nez Jr., polychrome miniature, 2000, 2 x 3.25 inches
Wally Nez Jr., polychrome miniature, 2003, 1 x 3.25 inches.
Wally Nez Jr., polychrome miniature, c. 2001, 1.375 x 3.25 inches.
Virgil Ortiz, polychrome jar, 2002, 11.5 x 15 inches.
Thomas Polacca, polychrome seed jar, 1992, 9 x 9 inches.
Dextra Quotskuyva, polychrome jar, c. 1980-85, 12.5 x 15 inches.
Dextra Quotskuyva, polychrome vase, c. 1980-85, 4.25 x 4.25 inches
Dextra Quotskuyva, polychrome vase, c. 1980-85, 5.25 x 4 inches
Dextra Quotskuyva, polychrome shard miniature, c. 1980, 2 x 3 inches.
Al Qöyawayma, Mesa Verde series buffware vessel with high relief, 1992, 13 x 14 inches.
Al Qöyawayma, buffware vase with Buffalo Dancer, 1991, 12 x 8 inches.
Jeff Roller, blackware jar with carved lid, 1999, 8.5 x 4.75 inches.
Jeff Roller, blackware jar with carved eagle head lid, 2000, 15.5 x 7 inches.
Susan Romero, redware miniature, c. 1997, 1.5 x 2 inches.
Susan Romero, redware miniature, c. 1997, 2.5 x 1.75 inches.
Jean Sahmie, polychrome cylinder vase, 2004, 13.5 x 6 inches.
Russell Sanchez, polished redware jar with carved lid, 1995, 8.75 x 6.5 inches.
Russell Sanchez, polished redware bear with turquoise and heishi inlay, c. 1995-2000, 3 x 4 inches.
Russell Sanchez, polished redware jar with copper bands and turquoise and heishi inlay, 2006, 6.25 x 8.5 inches.
Stetson Setalla, polychrome Turtle Pot, c. 2000, 5.75 x 9 inches.
Helen Shupla, polished redware bowl with bear claw impression, c. 1970s, 7 x 11 inches.
Helen Shupla, polished blackware wedding vessel with bear claw impression, c. 1970s, 9.5 x 7 inches.
Richard Zane Smith, polychrome olla, 2003, 10.25 x 12 inches.
Camilio Tafoya, polychrome miniature, c. 1985-90, 1.75 x 1.25 inches
Margaret Tafoya, polished blackware jar with carved design, c. 1970s, 9 x 9 inches.
Margaret Tafoya, polished redware with impressed bear paw, c. 1980s, 5.75 x 6 inches.
Sara Fina Tafoya, blackware storage jar, c. 1920s, 22 x 19 inches.
Mark Tahbo, polychrome plate, 1994, 10 inches.
Mark Tahbo, polychrome Katsina Pot, 2005, 3.75 x 6 inches.
Dorothy Torivio, vase, c. 1995, 9 x 7 inches.
Dora Tse Pe, micaceous and redware bowl with avanyu and turquoise inlay, c. 1990s, 8 x 10 inches.
Dora Tse Pe, micaceous black and redware bowl with avanyu, c. 1990s, 9 x 8 inches.
Sandra Victorino, whiteware with swirled fine line pattern, 2000, 7 x 7.25 inches.
Lonnie Vigil, micaceous storage jar, c. 1998, 14.5 x 13 inches.
Nancy Youngblood, blackware vase with swirled lid, 1991, 6.25 x 4.25 inches.
Nancy Youngblood, blackware vase with cruciform lid, 2003, 10 x 6 inches.
Nancy Youngblood, swirled blackware melon bowl, 2003. 3.5 x 6 inches.
Nancy Youngblood, swirled redware melon bowl, 1993, 6.5 x 9 inches.
Nathan Youngblood, redware jar with lid, c. 1995, 6.75 x 6 inches.
Nathan Youngblood, blackware jug with handle, c. 2003-05, 10.5 x 6.5 inches.
Nathan Youngblood, blackware vase, 1995-2000, 10.25 x 8.5 inches.

Illustrated Catalogue of the

The Nancy & Alan Cameros Collection of Southwestern Pottery

Holdings as of June 2007

Acoma
- The Lewis Family

Cherokee

Cochiti

Hopi
- The Nampeyo Family
- The Naha Family
- The Chapella Family

Jemez

Laguna

Nambe

Navajo (Diné)

Sandia

San Felipe

San Ildefonso
- The Martinez Family
- The Gonzales Family

Santa Clara
- The Tafoya Family
- The Gutierrez Family

Santo Domingo

Wyandot

Zuni

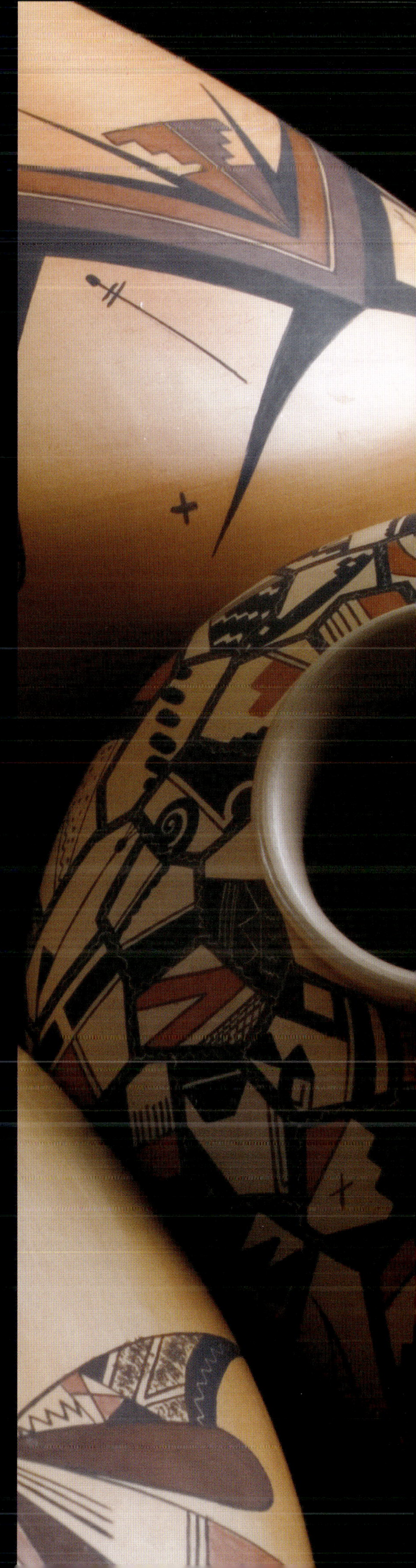

Acoma Pueblo

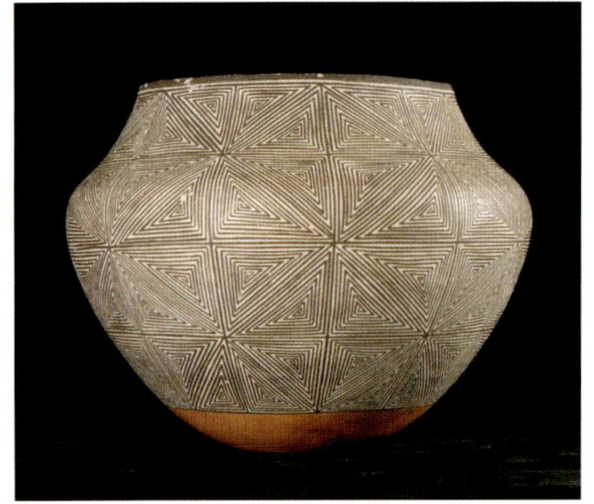

Artist: **Lewis, Lucy** (c. 1900 - 1992)
Date: 1953
Pueblo: Acoma
Family: Lewis
Height: 6 inches
Diameter: 7.5 inches

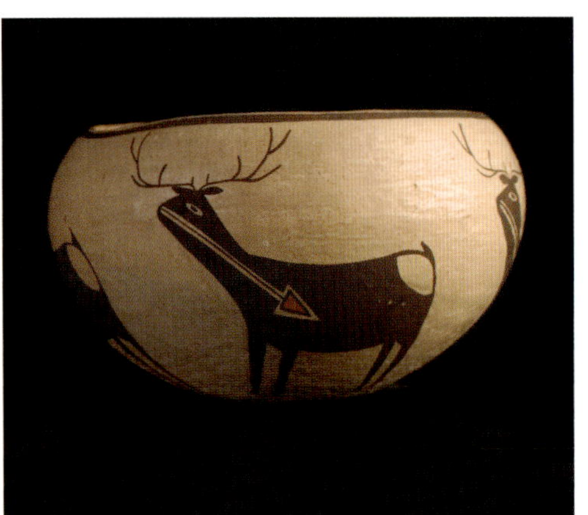

Artist: **Lewis, Emma** (1931 -)
Date: c. 1965-1970
Pueblo: Acoma
Family: Lewis
Height: 4 inches
Diameter: 6 inches

Other Acoma Potters

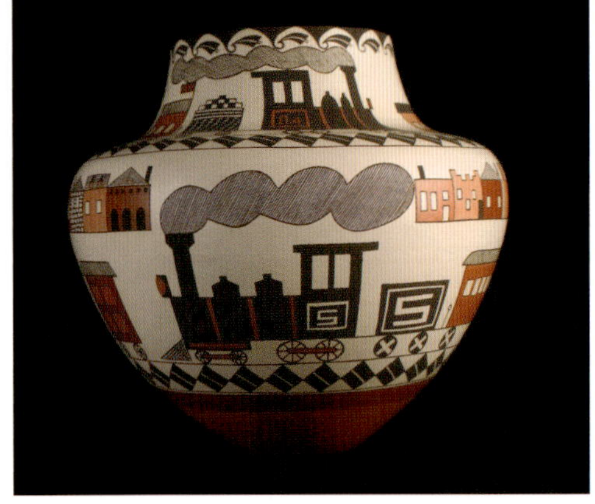

Artist: **Cerno, Joseph** (1947 -)
Date: April 2003
Pueblo: Acoma
Height: 11 inches
Diameter: 11 inches

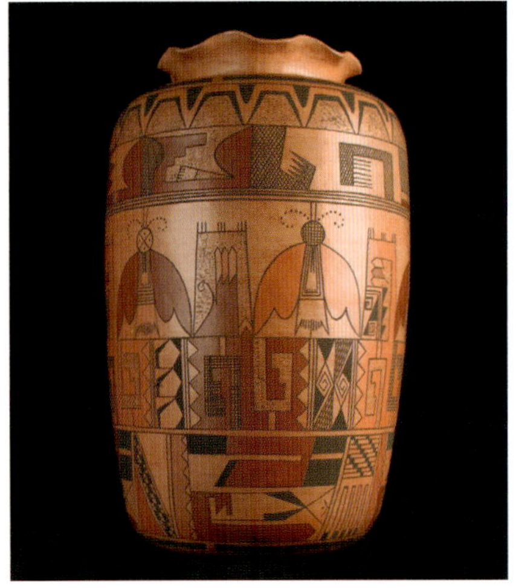

Artist: **Cerno, Barbara Hyzah** (1951 -)
Date: 2000
Pueblo: Acoma
Height: 13.5 inches
Diameter: 8 inches

Acoma Pueblo

Artist: **Garcia-Rustin, Shana** (1969 -)
Date: c. 1995-2000
Pueblo: Acoma
Height: 11 inches
Diameter: 10.5 inches

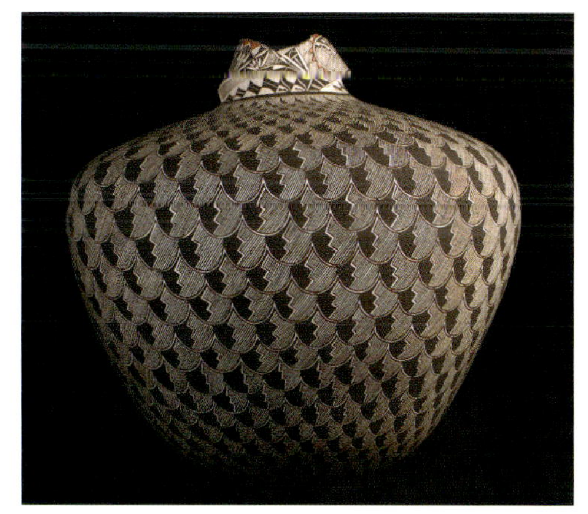

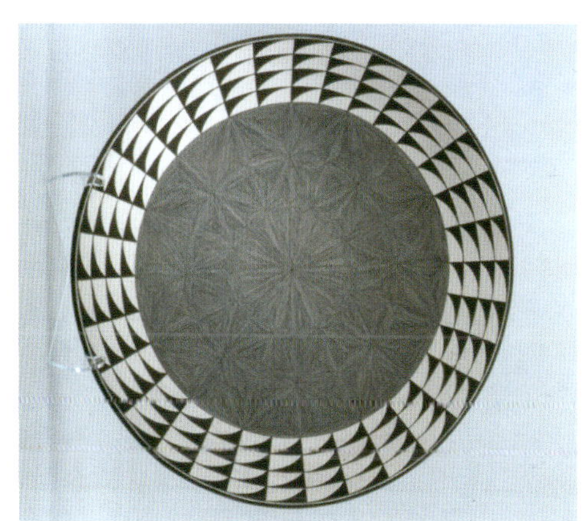

Artist: **Lucario, Rebecca** (1946 -)
Date: c. 2005
Pueblo: Acoma
Diameter: 16 inches

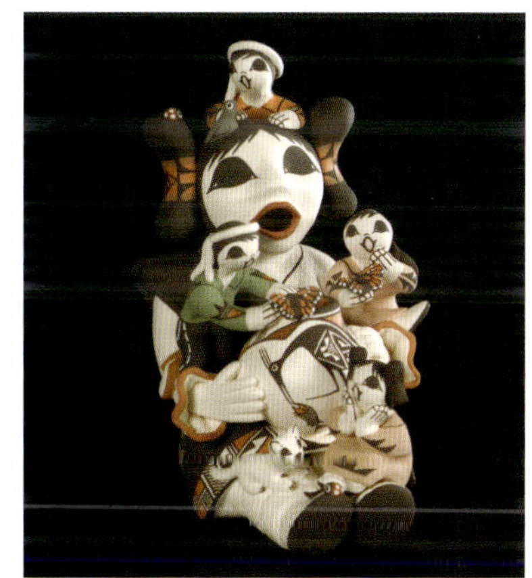

Artist: **Ray-Henderson, Marilyn** (1954-)
Date: 2007
Pueblo: Acoma
Height: 7.5 inches
Diameter: 4.5 inches

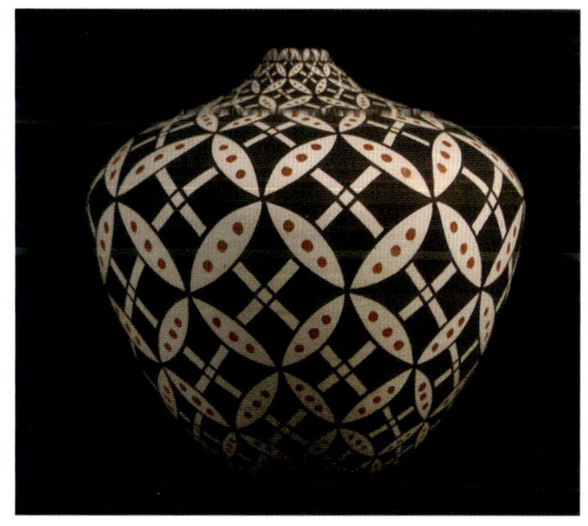

Artist: **Torivio, Dorothy** (1946 -)
Date: 1996
Pueblo: Acoma
Height: 4.75 inches
Diameter: 4.25 inches

Acoma Pueblo

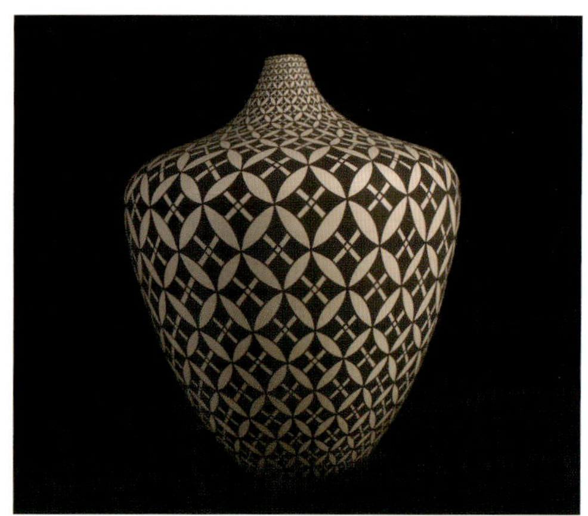

Artist: **Torivio, Dorothy** (1946 -)
Date: c. 1995
Pueblo: Acoma
Height: 9 inches
Diameter: 7 inches

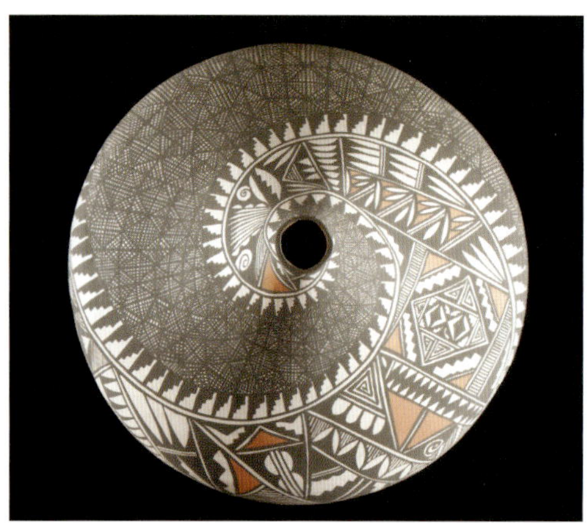

Artist: **Victorino, Sandra** (1958 -)
Date: c. 2000
Pueblo: Acoma
Height: 7 inches
Diameter: 7.5 inches

Cherokee

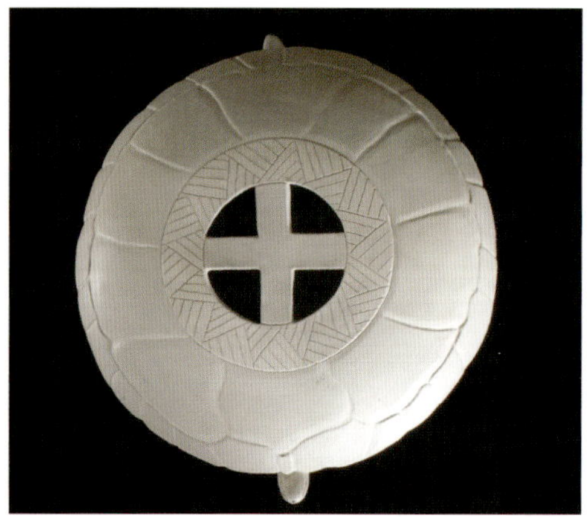

Artist: **Osti, Jane** (1945 -)
Date: 2003
Tribe: Cherokee
Height: 4 inches
Diameter: 14 inches

Cochiti Pueblo

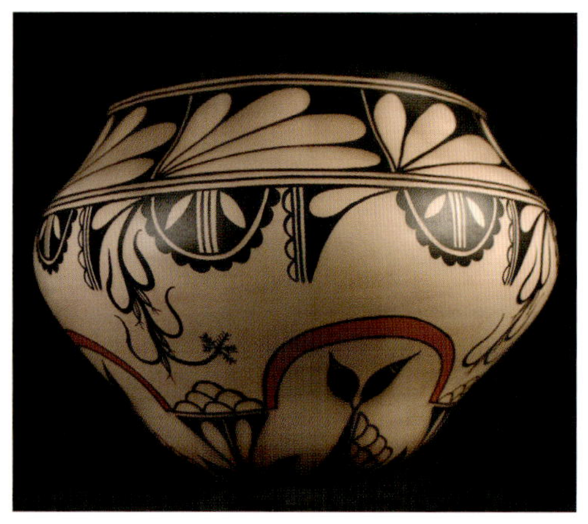

Artist: **Ortiz, Virgil** (1969 -)
Date: 2002
Pueblo: Cochiti
Height: 11.25 inches
Diameter: 15 inches

Hopi Reservation

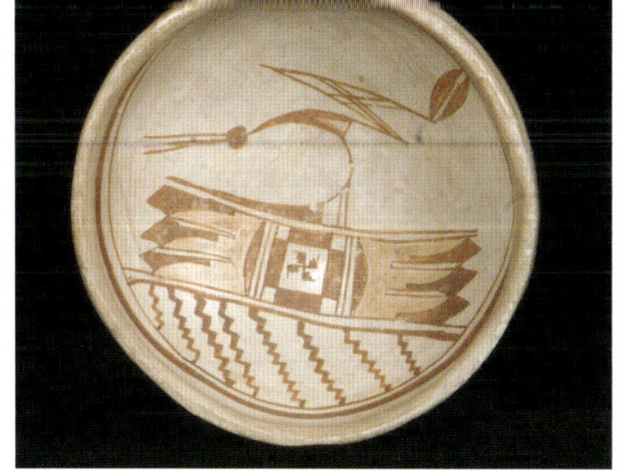

Artist: **Attributed to Nampeyo of Hano** (1859 - 1942)
Date: 1910
Tribe: Hopi-Tewa
Family: Nampeyo (Matriarch)
Height: 2.5 inches
Diameter: 5 inches

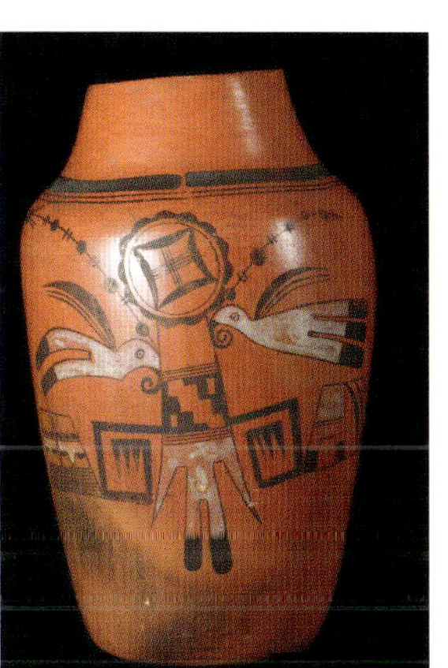

Artist: **Attributed to Nampeyo of Hano** (1859 - 1942)
Date: c. 1915-1920
Tribe: Hopi-Tewa
Family: Nampeyo (Matriarch)
Height: 11.5 inches
Diameter: 6 inches

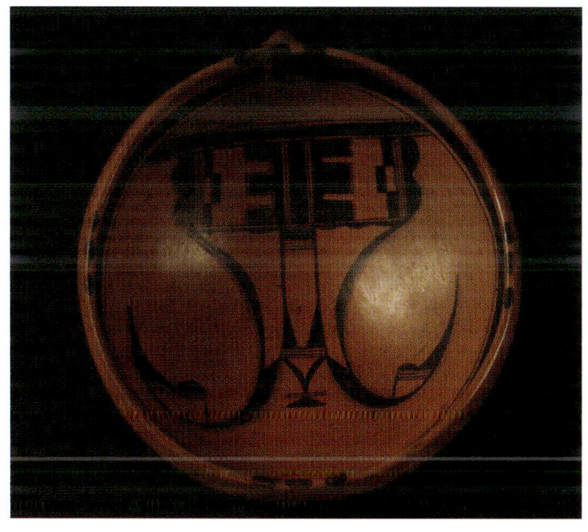

Artist: **Attributed to Nampeyo of Hano** (1859 - 1942)
Date: c. 1905
Tribe: Hopi-Tewa
Family: Nampeyo (Matriarch)
Height: 4 inches
Diameter: 9.5 inches

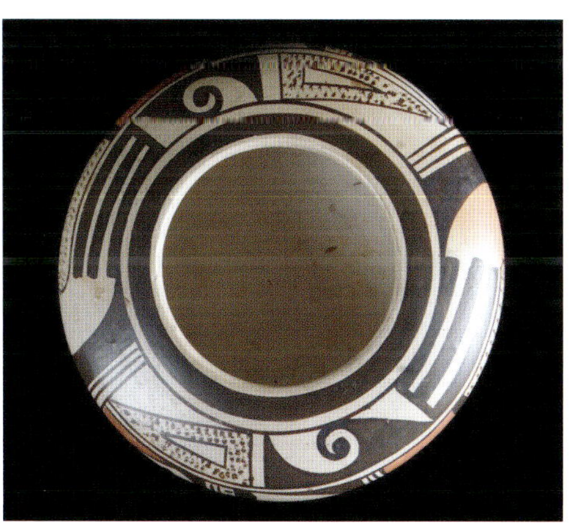

Artist: **Polacca Nampeyo, Fannie** (1904 - 1987)
Date: c. 1960s
Tribe: Tewa
Family: Daughter of Nampeyo
Height: 3 inches
Diameter: 5.5 inches

Hopi Reservation

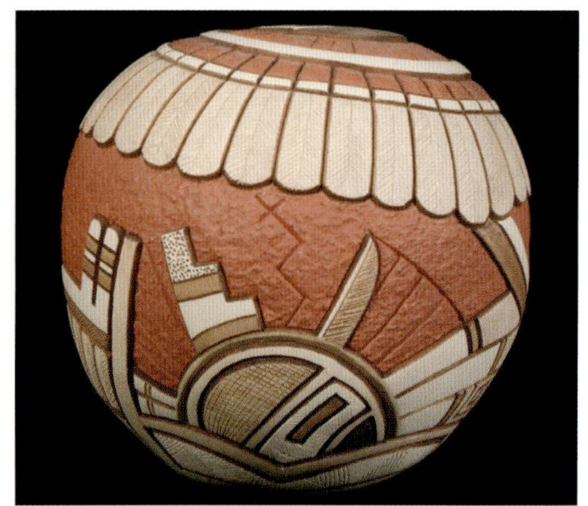

Artist: **Polacca, Thomas** (1935 - 2003)
Date: 1992
Tribe: Tewa
Family: Grandson of Nampeyo
Height: 9 inches
Diameter: 9 inches

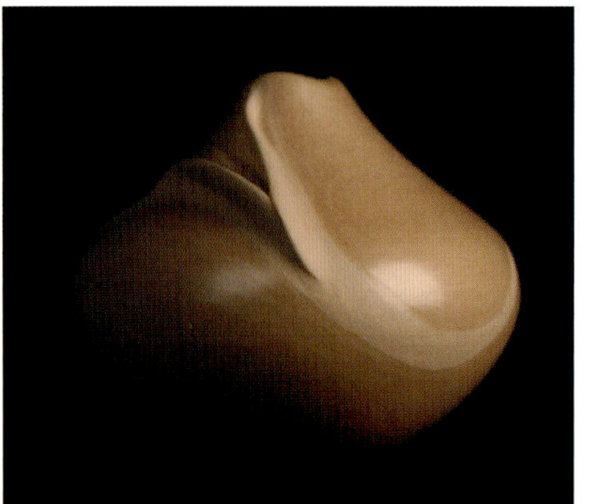

Artist: **Nampeyo, Iris Youvella** (1944 -)
Date: c. 2002
Tribe: Tewa
Family: Granddaughter of Nampeyo
Height: 4 inches
Diameter: 4 inches

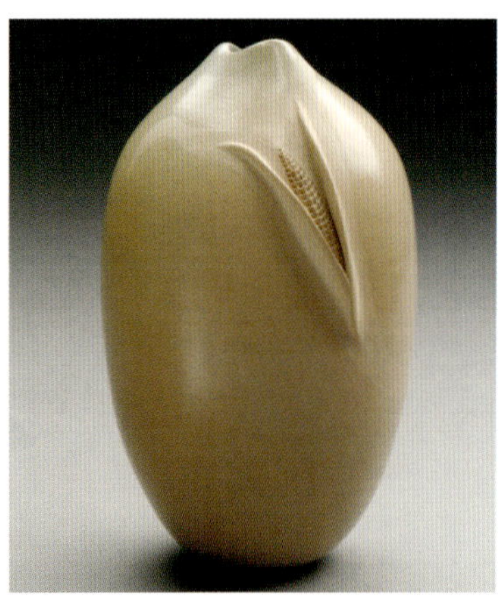

Artist: **Nampeyo, Iris Youvella** (1944 -)
Date: c. 2005
Tribe: Tewa
Family: Granddaughter of Nampeyo
Height: 8.25 inches
Diameter: 5 inches

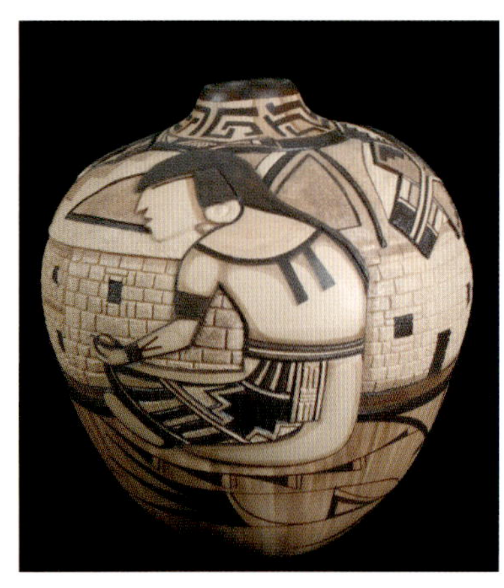

Artist: **Polacca, Gary** (1955 -)
Date: c. 2004
Tribe: Hopi-Tewa
Family: Great-grandson of Nampeyo
Height: 10.5 inches
Diameter: 9 inches

Hopi Reservation

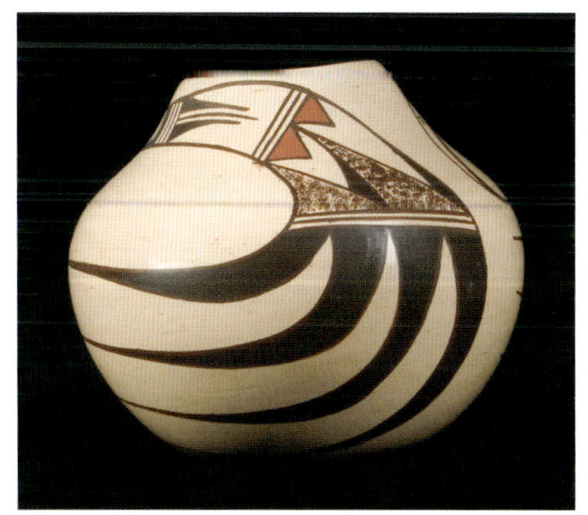

Artist: **Polacca, Fannie L.** (a.k.a. Fannie Myron)
Date: n.d.
Tribe: Hopi-Tewa
Family: Great-granddaughter of Nampeyo
Height: 2.5 inches
Diameter: 3 inches

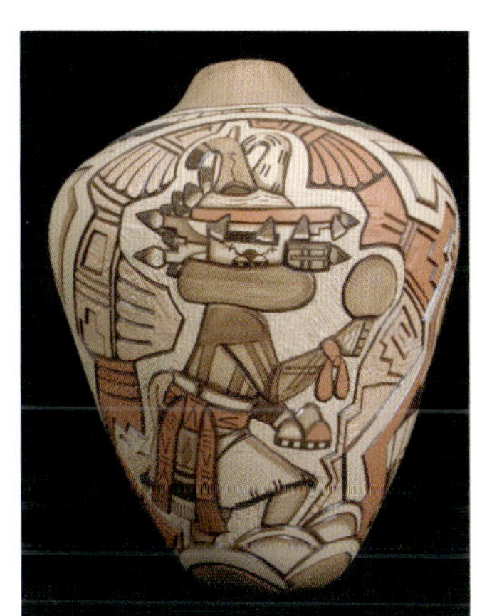

Artist: **Nampeyo, Marty & Elvira** (1970 -) & (1968 -)
Date: c. 2004
Tribe: Hopi
Family: Great-granddaughter of Nampeyo and husband
Height: 12 inches
Diameter: 9 inches

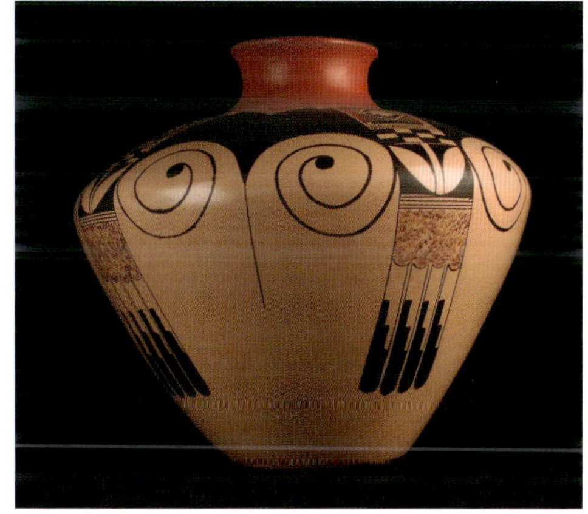

Artist: **Polacca, Clinton** (1958 -)
Date: c. 2003
Tribe: Pima-Tewa
Family: Great-grandson Nampeyo
Height: 11 inches
Diameter: 10.5 inches

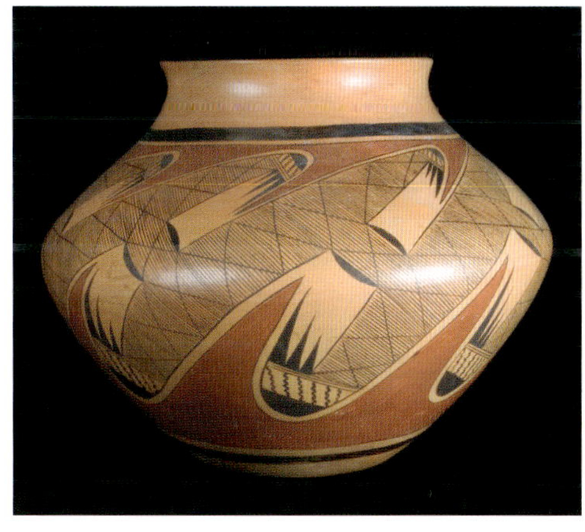

Artist: **Quotskuyva, Dextra** (1928 -)
Date: c. 1980-85
Tribe: Tewa
Family: Great-granddaughter of Nampeyo
Height: 12.5 inches
Diameter: 15 inches

Hopi Reservation

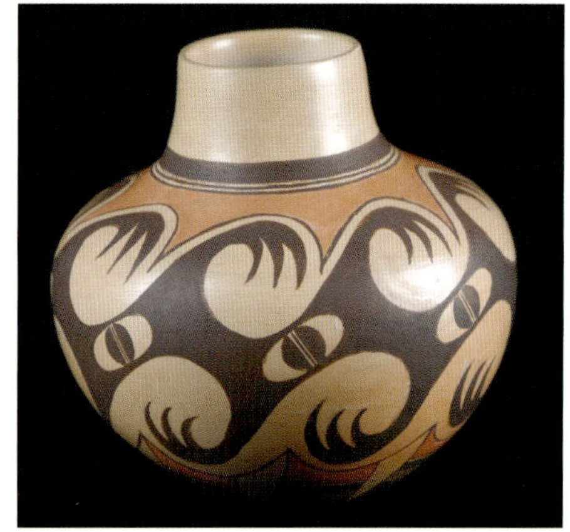

Artist: **Quotskuyva, Dextra (1928 -)**
Date: c. 1980-85
Tribe: Tewa
Family: Great-granddaughter of Nampeyo
Height: 4.25 inches
Diameter: 4.25 inches

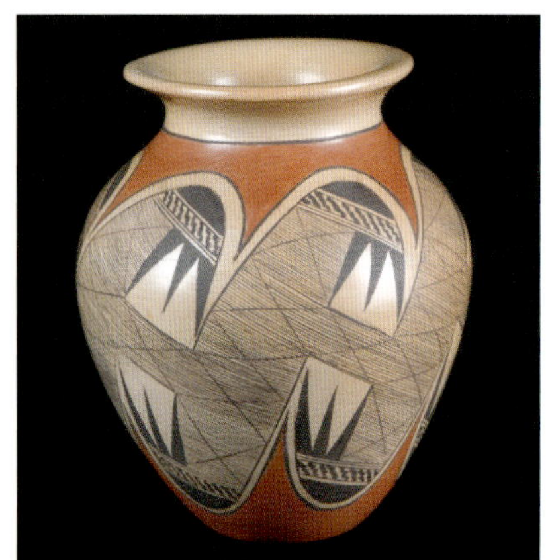

Artist: **Quotskuyva, Dextra** (1928 -)
Date: c. 1980-85
Tribe: Tewa
Family: Great-granddaughter of Nampeyo
Height: 5.25 inches
Diameter: 4 inches

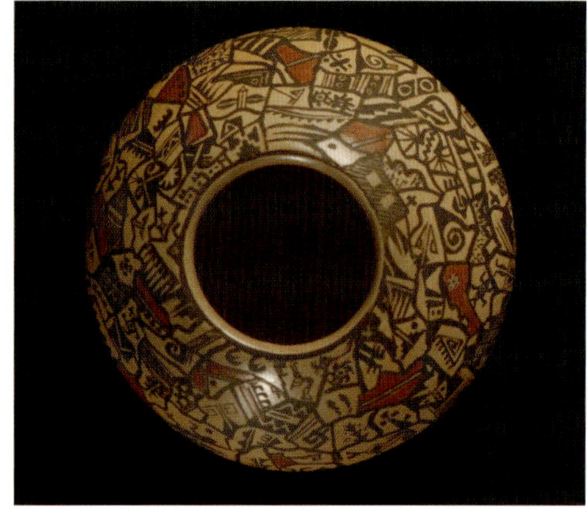

Artist: **Quotskuyva, Dextra** (1928 -)
Date: c. 1980
Tribe: Tewa
Family: Great-granddaughter of Nampeyo
Height: 2 inches
Diameter: 3 inches

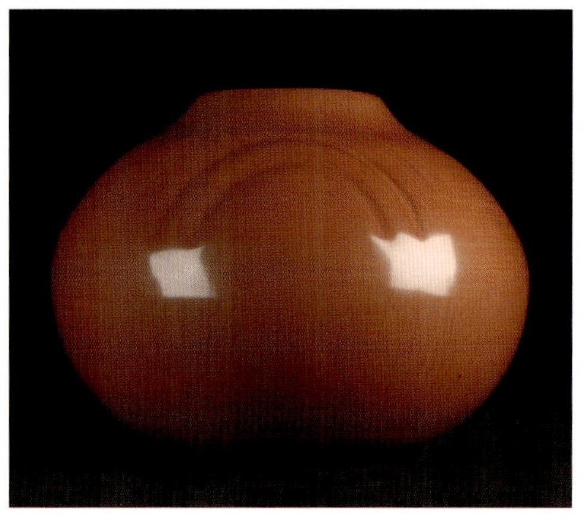

Artist: **Komalestewa, Alton** (active 1970 - present)
Date: c. 1980s
Tribe: Hopi-Tewa
Family: Great-grandson of Nampeyo
Height: 8.5 inches
Diameter: 12 inches

Hopi Reservation

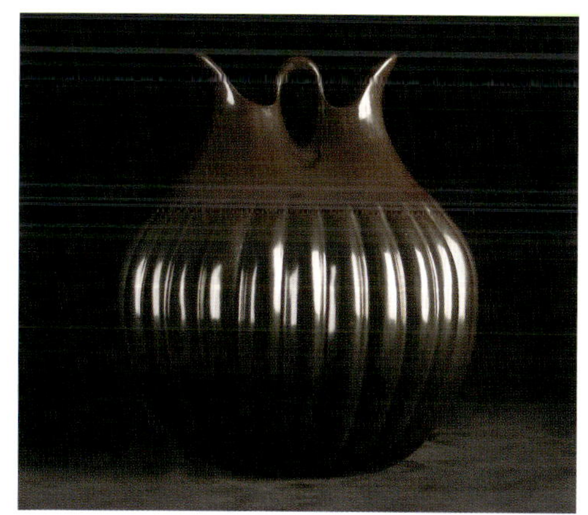

Artist: **Komalestewa, Alton** (active 1970 - present)
Date: c. 1990s
Tribe: Hopi-Tewa
Family: Great-grandson of Nampeyo
Height: 9.5 inches
Diameter: 8 inches

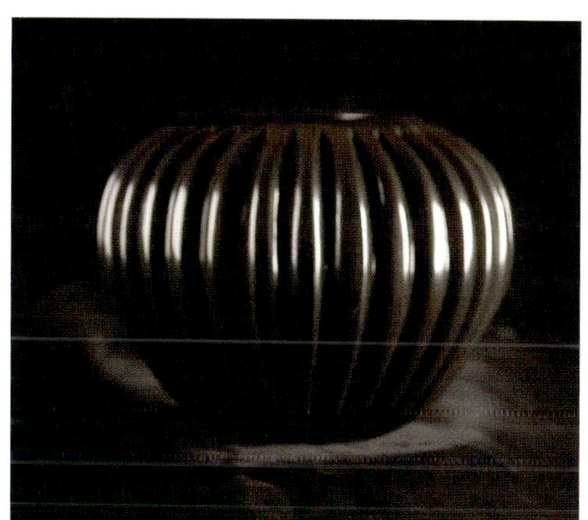

Artist: **Komalestewa, Alton** (active 1970 - present)
Date: c. 2000
Tribe: Hopi-Tewa
Family: Great-grandson of Nampeyo
Height: 4.5 inches
Diameter: 5 inches

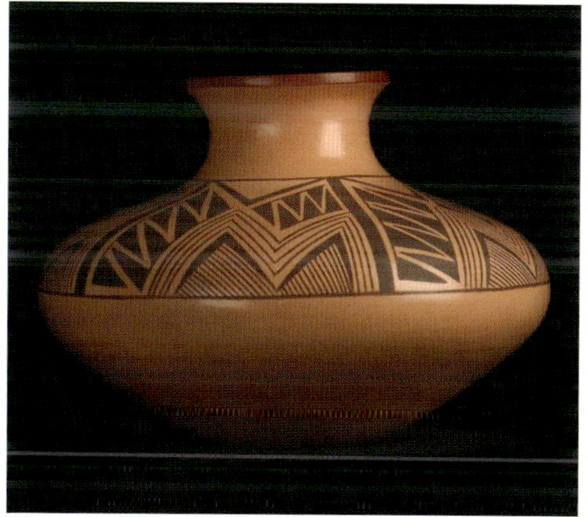

Artist: **Nampeyo, Hisi** (1964 -)
Date: 2002
Tribe: Tewa
Family: Great-great-granddaughter of Nampeyo
Height: 4 inches
Diameter: 5 inches

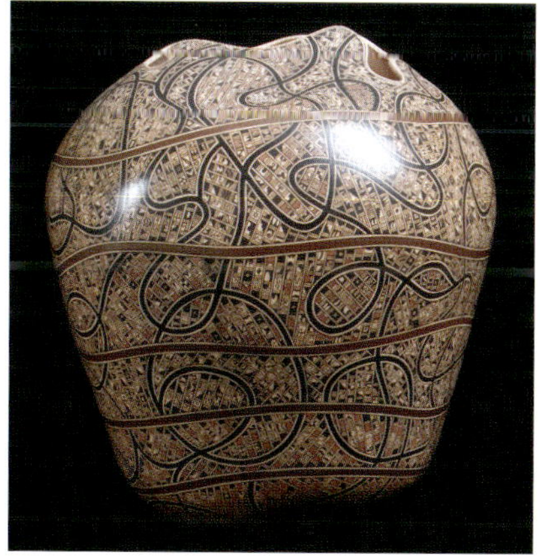

Artist: **Namingha, Les** (1968 -)
Date: c. 2006
Tribe: Tewa-Zuni
Family: Great-great-grandson of Nampeyo
Height: 14 inches
Diameter: 12 inches

Hopi Reservation

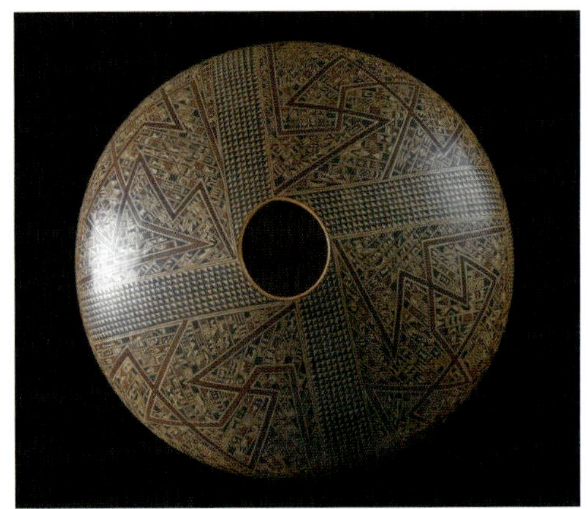

Artist: **Namingha, Les** (1968 -)
Date: c. 2005
Tribe: Tewa-Zuni
Family: Great-great-grandson of Nampeyo
Height: 7.5 inches
Diameter: 10.5 inches

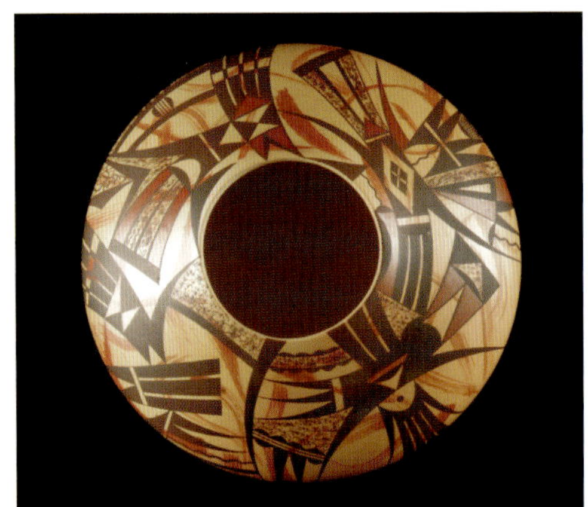

Artist: **Lucas, Steve** (1955 -)
Date: 2003
Tribe: Tewa
Family: Great-great-grandson of Nampeyo
Height: 4.5 inches
Diameter: 6.5 inches

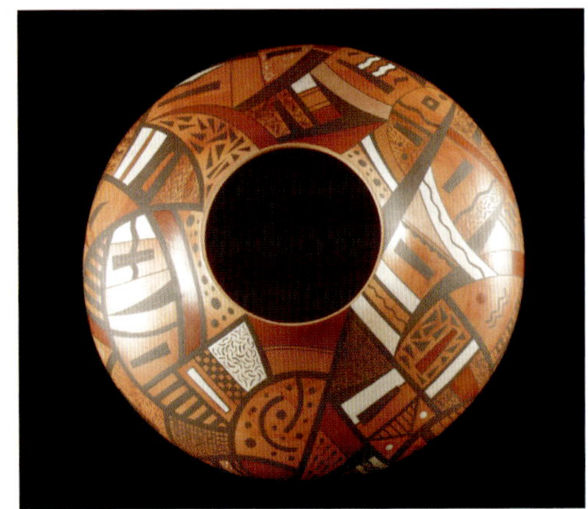

Artist: **Lucas, Steve** (1955 -)
Date: c. 2001-02
Tribe: Tewa
Family: Great-great-grandson of Nampeyo
Height: 7 inches
Diameter: 8.5 inches

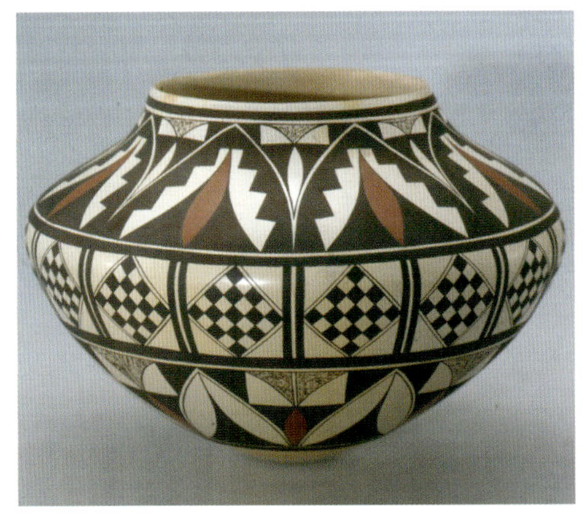

Artist: **Lucas, Yvonne** (1959 -)
Date: 2000
Tribe: Tewa (originally Laguna)
Family: Married to Steve Lucas
Height: 8 inches
Diameter: 11 inches

Hopi Reservation

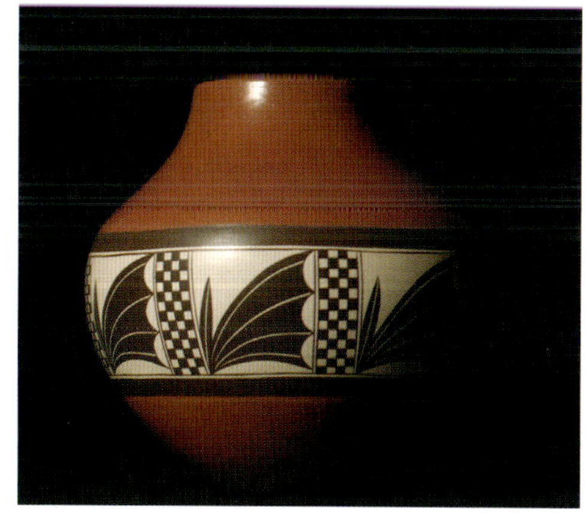

Artist: **Lucas, Yvonne** (1959 -)
Date: 2007
Tribe: Tewa (originally Laguna)
Family: Married to Steve Lucas
Height: 6 inches
Diameter: 6 inches

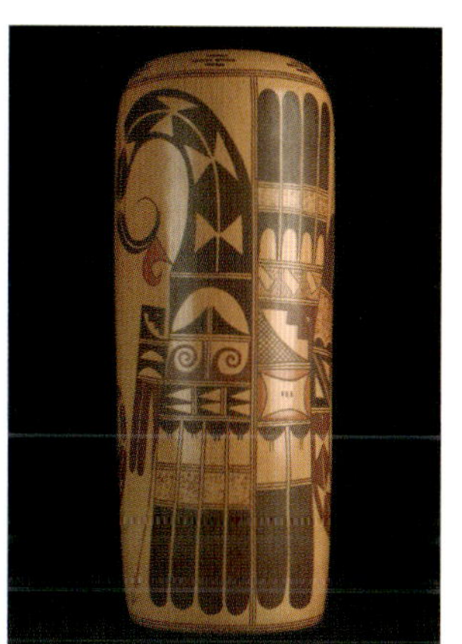

Artist: **Sahmie, Jean** (1948 -)
(a.k.a. Jean Sahme Nampeyo)
Date: 2004
Tribe: Tewa
Family: Great-great-granddaughter of Nampeyo
Height: 13.5 inches
Diameter: 6 inches

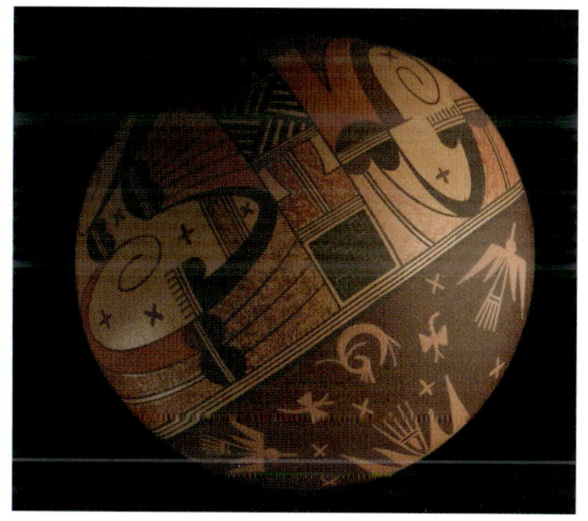

Artist: **Koopee, Jake** (1970 -)
Title: "Under the Stars"
Date: c. 2004
Tribe: Hopi-Tewa
Family: Great-great-great-grandson of Nampeyo
Height: 4.5 inches
Diameter: 5 inches

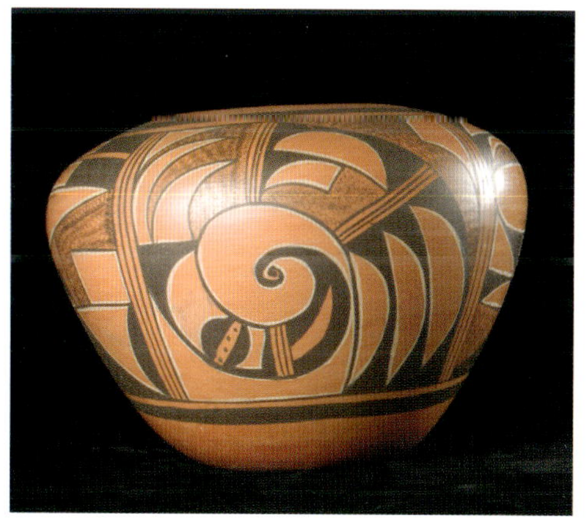

Artist: **Naha, Paqua "Frogwoman"** (c. 1890 - 1955)
Date: c. 1940s
Tribe: Tewa
Family: Naha/Navasie (Matriarch)
Height: 7.5 inches
Diameter: 10 inches

Hopi Reservation

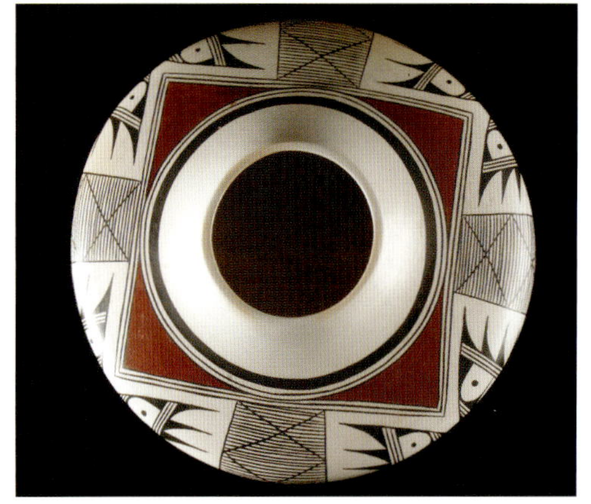

Artist: **Naha, Helen "Featherwoman"** (1922 - 1993)
Date: c. 1985
Tribe: Tewa
Family: Daughter-in-law of Paqua Naha
Height: 5 inches
Diameter: 11.5 inches

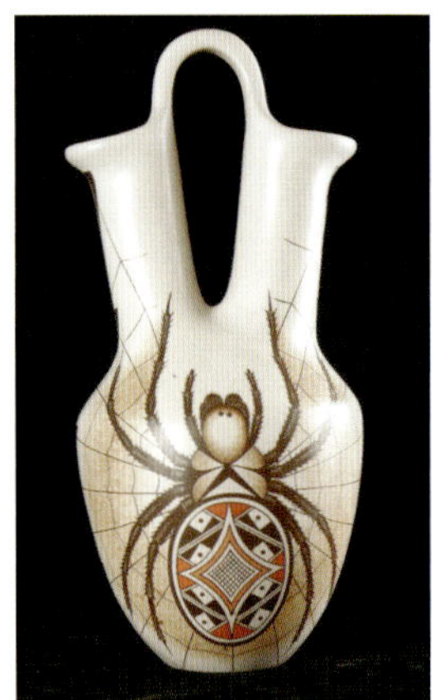

Artist: **Naha, Burel** (1944 -)
Date: c. 2004
Tribe: Tewa
Family: Grandson of Paqua Naha
Height: 12 inches
Diameter: 5.5 inches

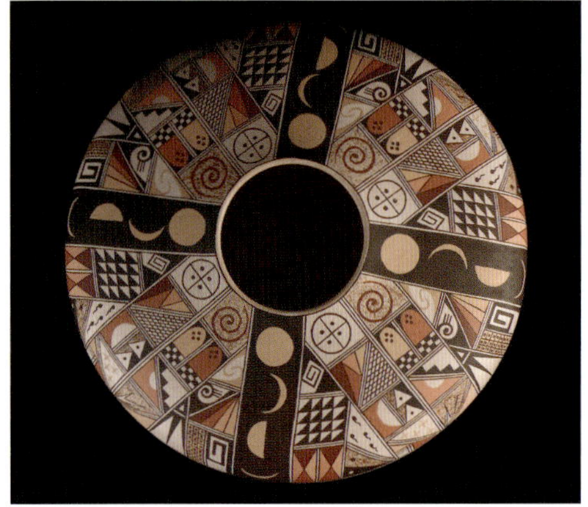

Artist: **Naha, Rainelle** (a.k.a. Rainy, 1949 -)
Date: c. 2000-02
Title: "Solstice"
Tribe: Tewa
Family: Granddaughter of Paqua Naha
Height: 4.5 inches
Diameter: 8 inches

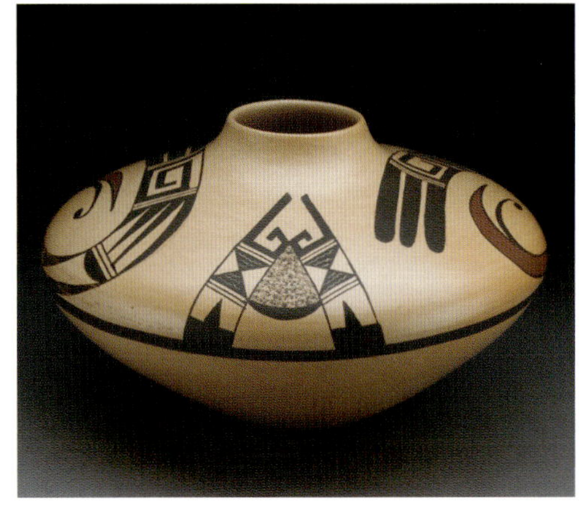

Artist: **Navasie, Fawn** (1959 -)
Date: c. 2004
Tribe: Hopi
Family: Granddaughter of Paqua Naha
Height: 12 inches
Diameter: 7.5 inches

Hopi Reservation

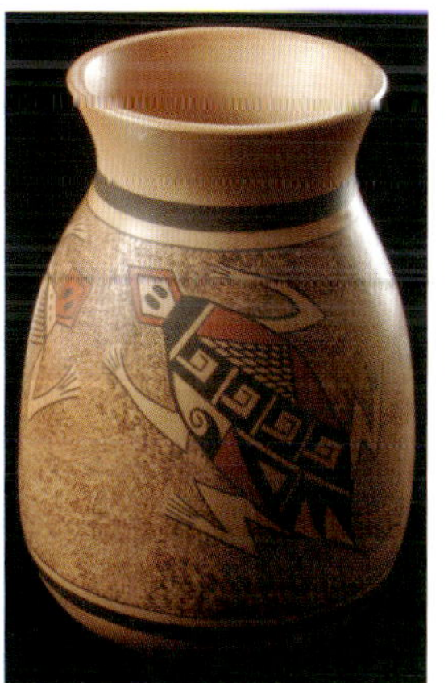

Artist: **Navasie, Dawn** (1961 -)
Date: c. 2004
Tribe: Hopi
Family: Granddaughter of Paqua Naha
Height: 7 inches
Diameter: 10 inches

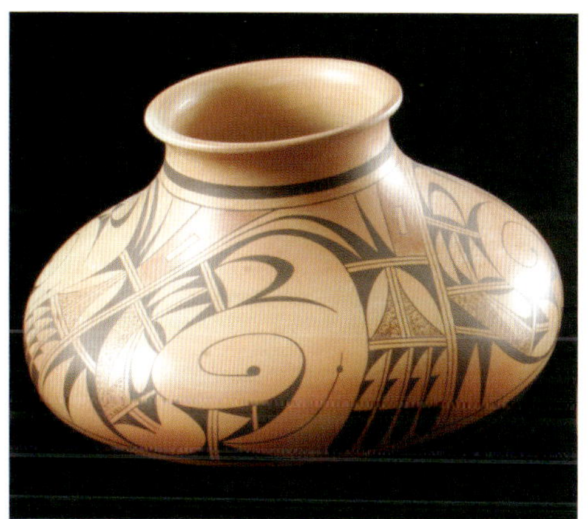

Artist: **Navasie, Dawn** (1961 -)
Date: c. 2004
Tribe: Hopi
Family: Granddaughter of Paqua Naha
Height: 7.5 inches
Diameter: 5 inches

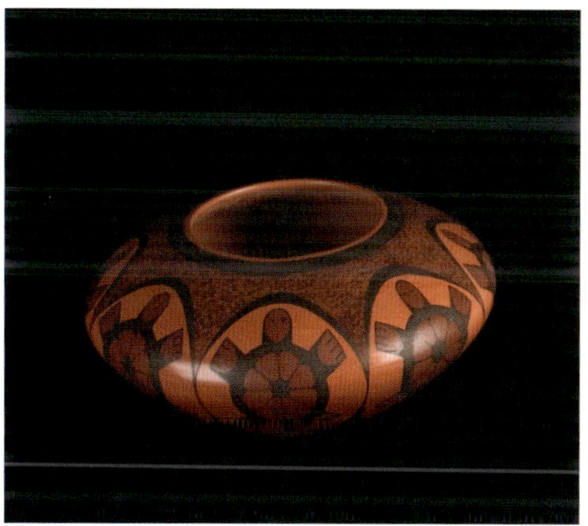

Artist: **Setalla, Stetson** (1962 -)
Date: c. 2000
Tribe: Hopi
Family: Grandson of Paqua Naha
Height: 5.75 inches
Diameter: 9 inches

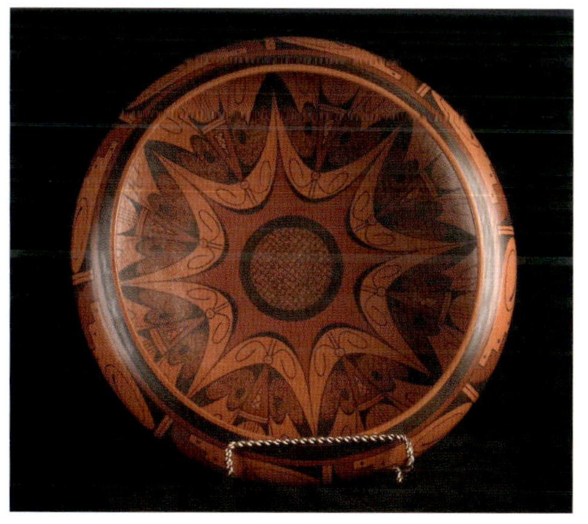

Artist: **Setalla, Stetson** (1962 -)
Date: c. 2000
Tribe: Hopi
Family: Grandson of Paqua Naha
Height: 4 inches
Diameter: 14 inches

Hopi Reservation

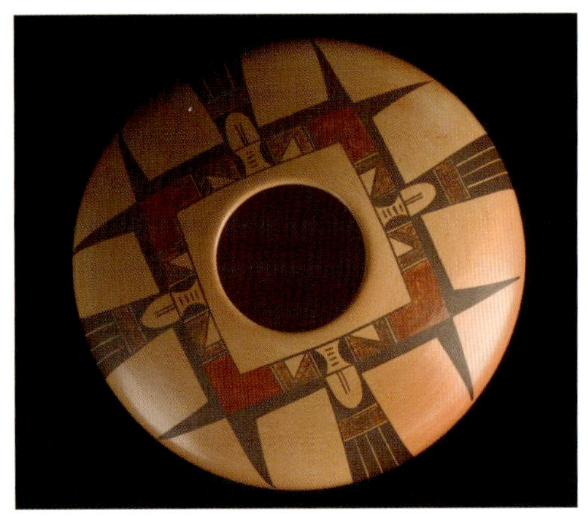

Artist: **Navasie, Dolly Joe "White Swan"** (1964 -)
Date: c. 2004
Tribe: Hopi
Family: Granddaughter of Paqua Naha
Height: 4 inches
Diameter: 7 inches

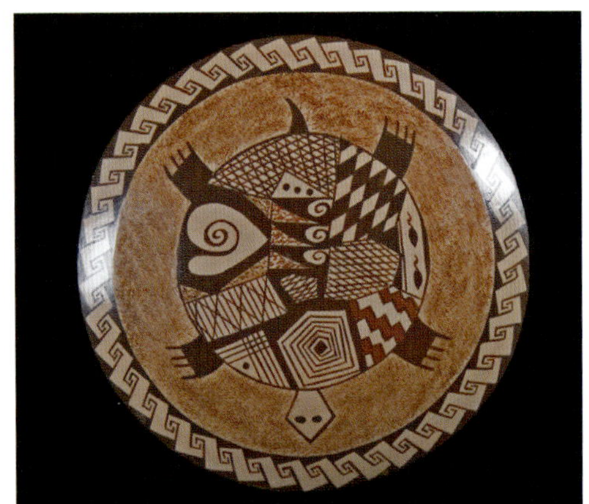

Artist: **Naha, Nona** (1958 -)
Date: c. 2004
Tribe: Tewa-Hopi
Family: Related by marriage to Terry Naha
Height: 1 inch
Diameter: 4.75 inches

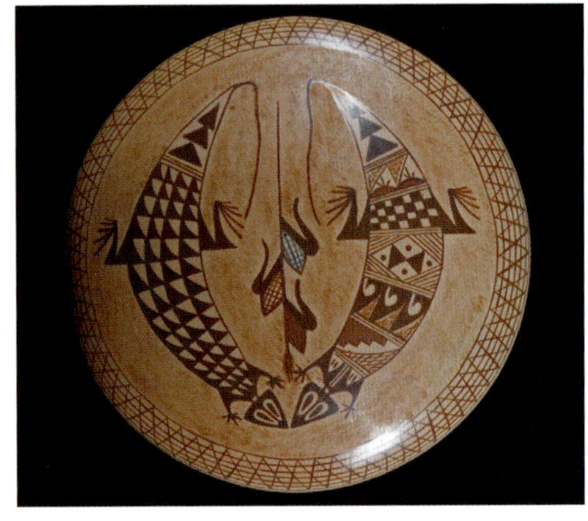

Artist: **Naha, Nona** (1958 -)
Date: c. 2004
Tribe: Tewa-Hopi
Family: Related by marriage to Terry Naha
Height: 2 inches
Diameter: 5.25 inches

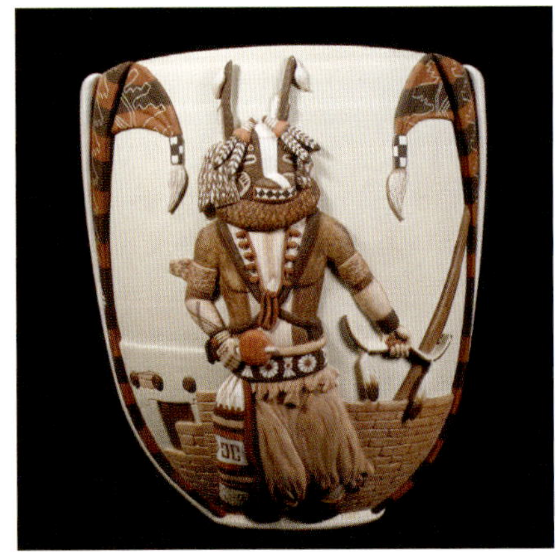

Artist: **Jim, Harrison**
Date: 1966
Tribe: Hopi-Tewa
Family: Related by marriage to Marianne Navasie
Height: 9.5 inches
Diameter: 9 inches

Hopi Reservation

Artist: **Chapella, Grace** (1874 - 1980)
Date: c. 1950
Tribe: Tewa
Family: Matriarch
Height: 13.5 inches
Diameter: 8 inches

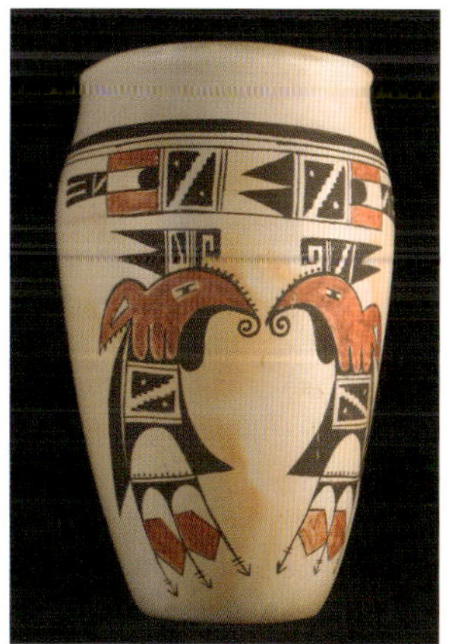

Artist: **Tahbo, Dianna** (1960 -)
Date: 1998
Tribe: Tewa
Family: Great-granddaughter of Grace Chapella
Height: 3 inches
Diameter: 6 inches

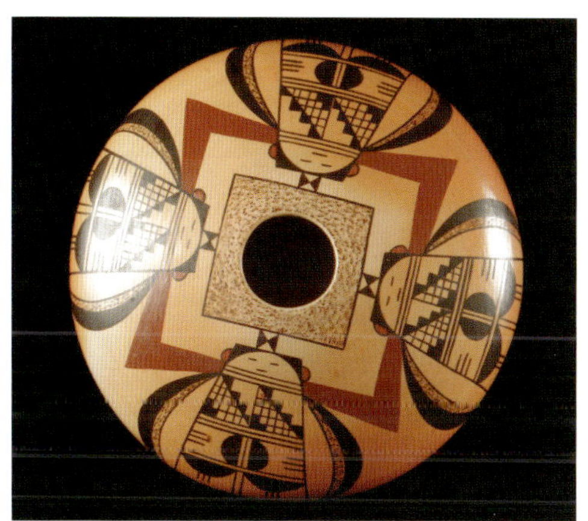

Artist: **Tahbo, Mark** (1958 -)
Date: 1994
Tribe: Tewa
Family: Great-grandson of Grace Chapella
Diameter: 10 inches

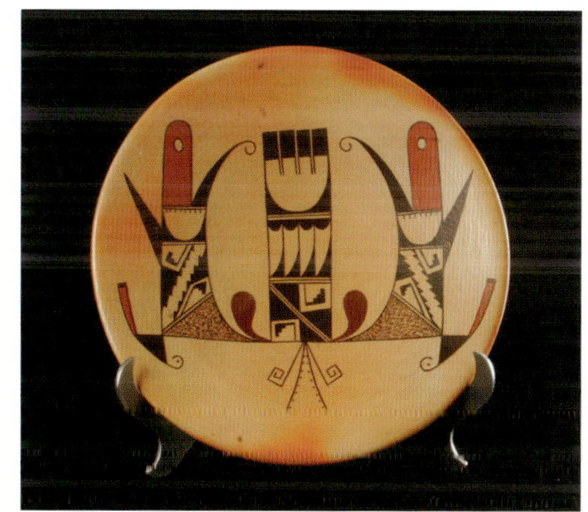

Artist: **Tahbo, Mark** (1958 -)
Date: 2004
Tribe: Tewa
Family: Great-grandson of Grace Chapella
Height: 8.25 inches
Diameter: 15 inches

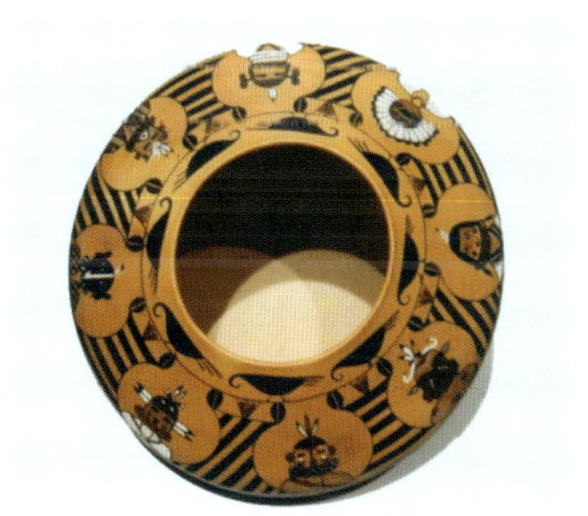

Hopi Reservation

Artist: **Tahbo, Mark** (1958 -)
Date: 2005
Tribe: Tewa
Family: Great-grandson of Grace Chapella
Height: 3.75 inches
Diameter: 6 inches

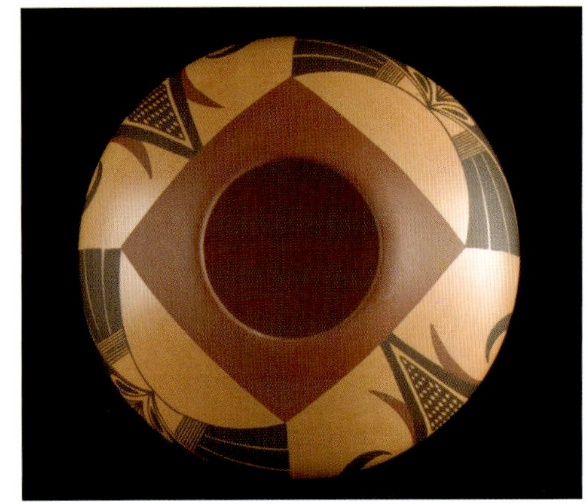

Other Hopi-Tewa Potters

Artist: **Abeita, Karen** (1960 -)
Date: c. 2000
Tribe: Hopi
Height: 4 inches
Diameter: 13 inches

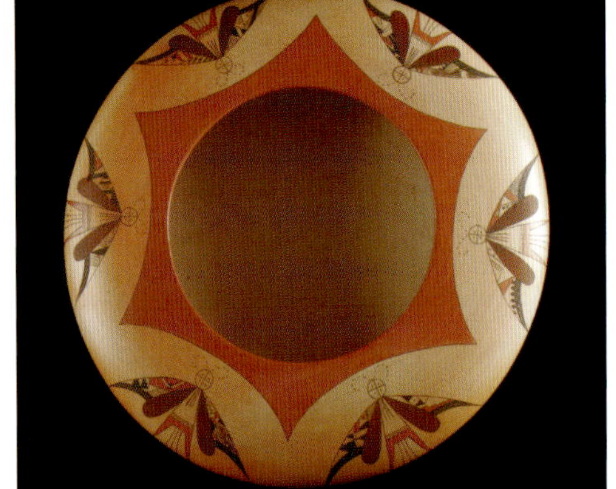

Artist: **Abeita, Karen** (1960 -)
Date: c. 1998
Tribe: Hopi
Height: 6.75 inches
Diameter: 11 inches

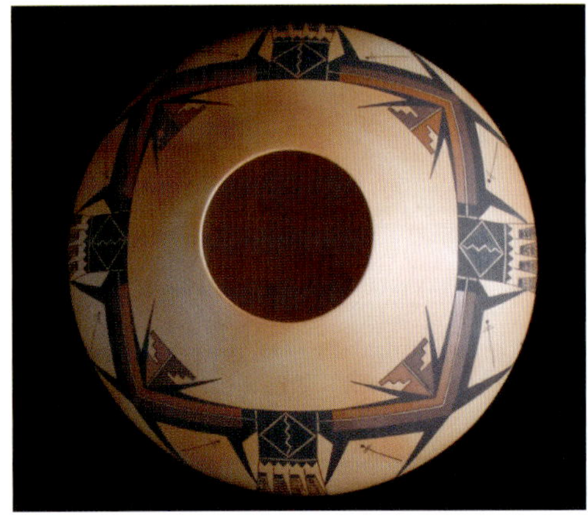

Artist: **Abeita, Karen** (1960 -)
Date: c. 2004
Tribe: Hopi
Height: 5.25 inches
Diameter: 6 inches

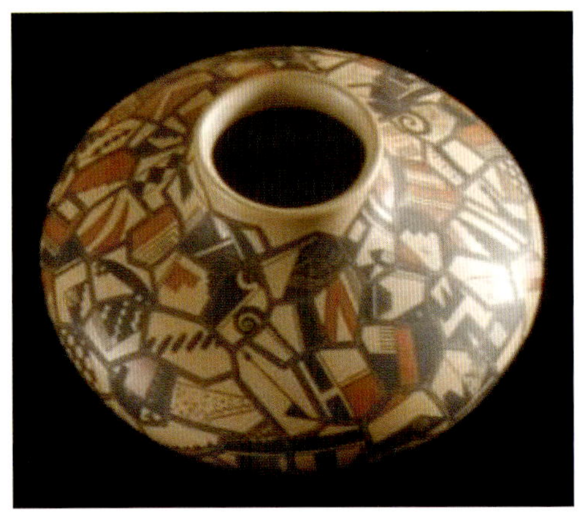

Hopi Reservation

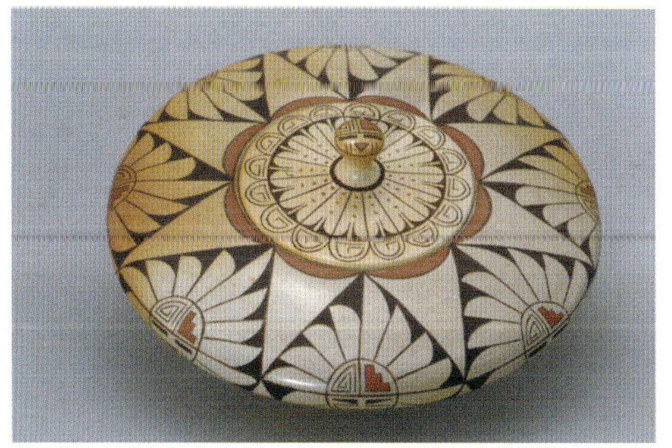

Artist: **Adams, Kathy**
Date: n.d.
Tribe: Hopi-Tewa
Height: 2.5 inches
Diameter: 6 inches

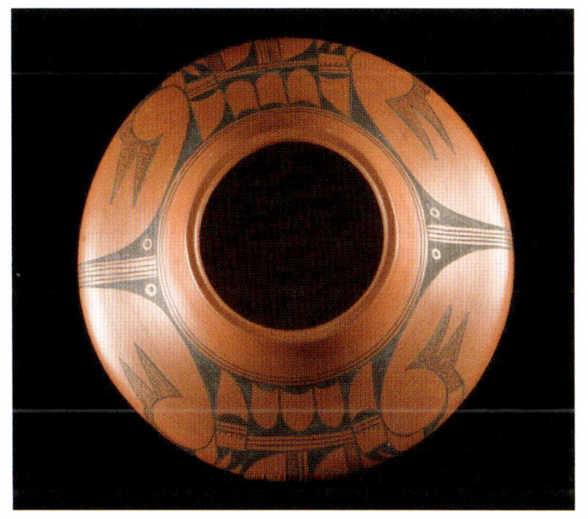

Artist: **Adams, Sadie "Flower Woman"** (1905-1995)
Date: c. 1970s
Tribe: Tewa
Height: 6 inches
Diameter: 9.5 inches

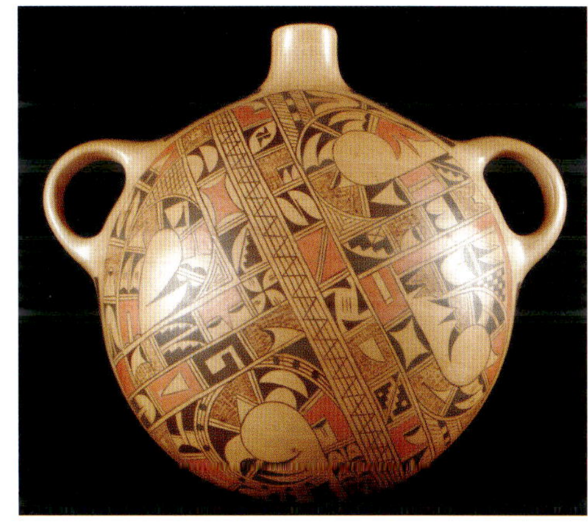

Artist: **Charley, Karen Kahe** (active 1980-present)
Date: 2004
Tribe: Hopi
Height: 11 inches
Diameter: 11 inches

Artist: **Cheeda, Zella "Antelope Woman"** (attributed to) (active 1950 - 1980)
Date: c. 1930s
Tribe: Hopi
Height: 4 inches
Diameter: 12 inches

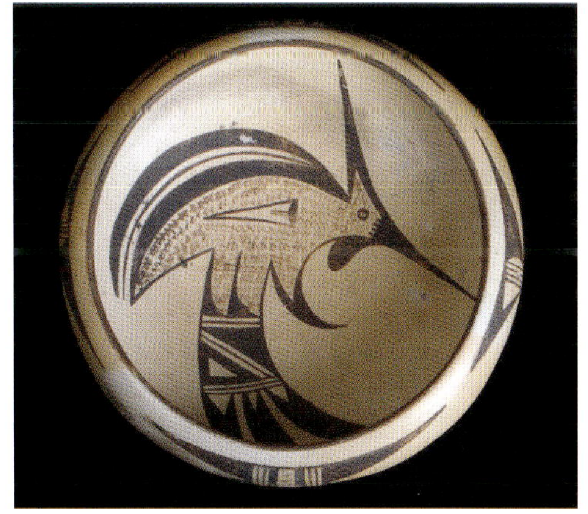

Hopi Reservation

Artist: **Dallas, Tony** (1956 -)
Date: 2007
Tribe: Hopi (Married into a Cochiti family)
Height: 16 inches
Diameter: 5 inches

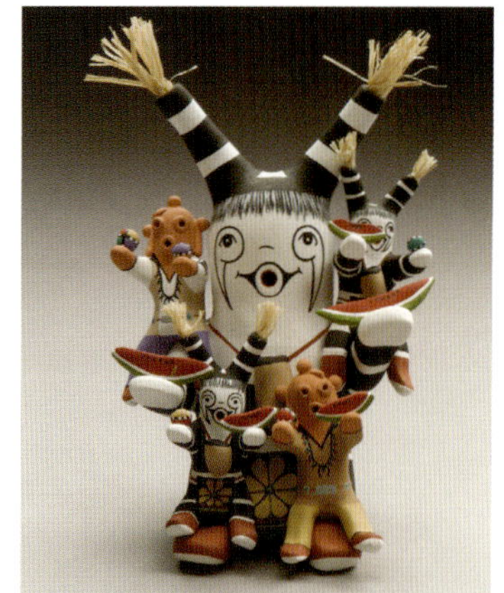

Artist: **Duwyenie, Preston** (1951 -)
Date: c. 1998-99
Tribe: Hopi
Height: 5 inches with lid
Diameter: 3 inches

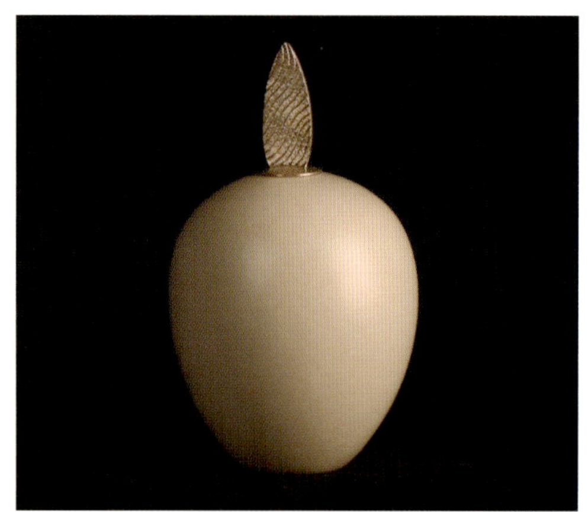

Artist: **Huma, Rondina** (1947 -)
Date: 2001
Tribe: Tewa
Height: 4.5 inches
Diameter: 7.5 inches

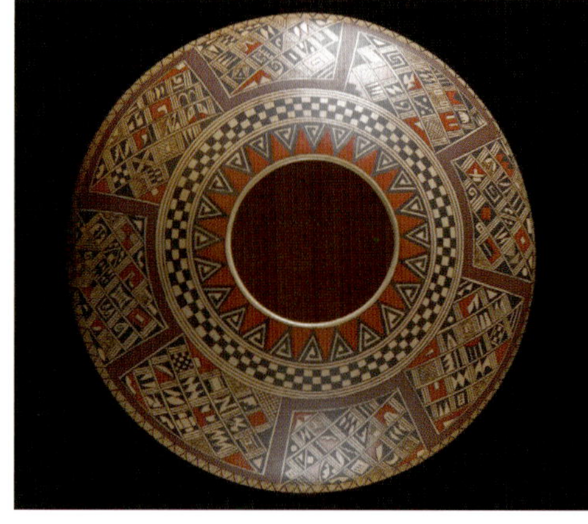

Artist: **Leslie, Rena** (c. 1920 -1980)
Date: c. 1940
Tribe: Hopi
Height: 3.5 inches
Diameter: 13 inches

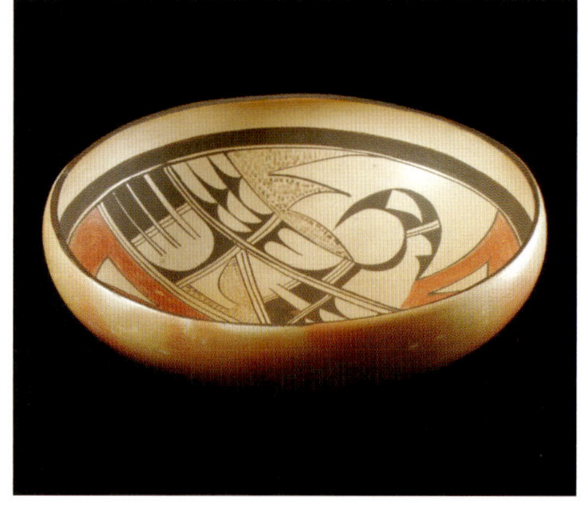

Hopi Reservation

Artist: **Maho, Garrett**
Date: 1985
Tribe: Hopi
Height: 5 inches
Diameter: 7 inches

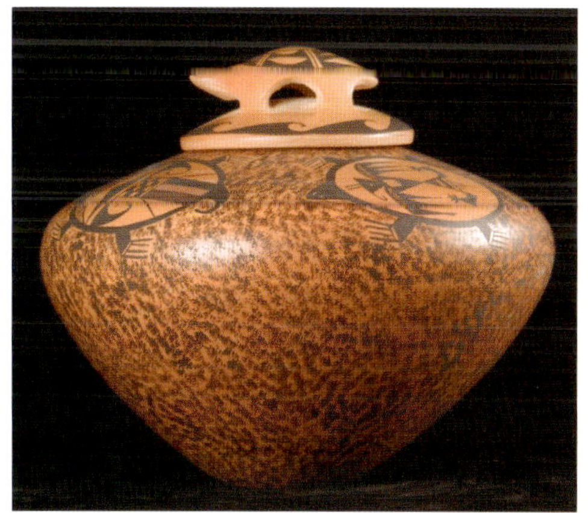

Artist: **Namoki, Lawrence** (1949 -)
Title: "Longhair 2"
Date: c. 2000
Tribe: Hopi
Height: 2.5 inches
Diameter: 2.25 inches

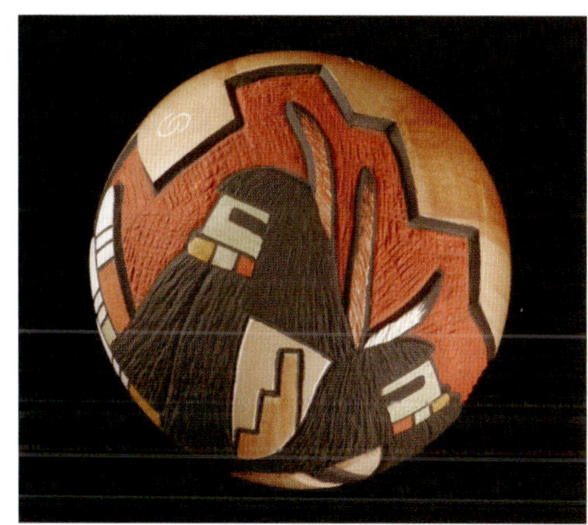

Artist: **Namoki, Lawrence** (1949 -)
Date: 2005
Tribe: Hopi
Height: 4 inches
Diameter: 5.5 inches

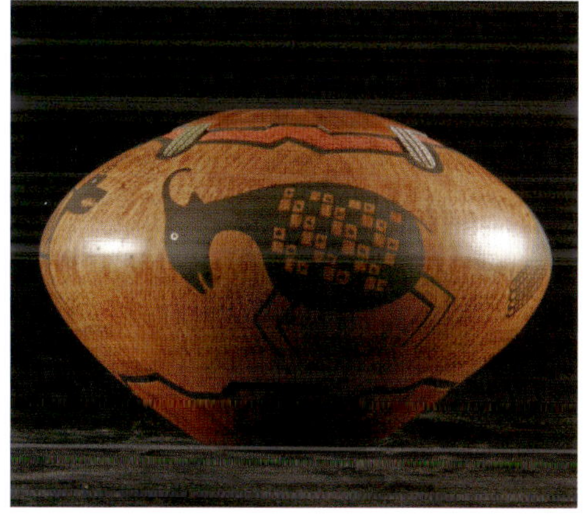

Artist: **Namoki, Lawrence** (1949 -)
Date: 2005
Title: "Creation"
Tribe: Hopi
Height: 8 inches
Diameter: 13 inches

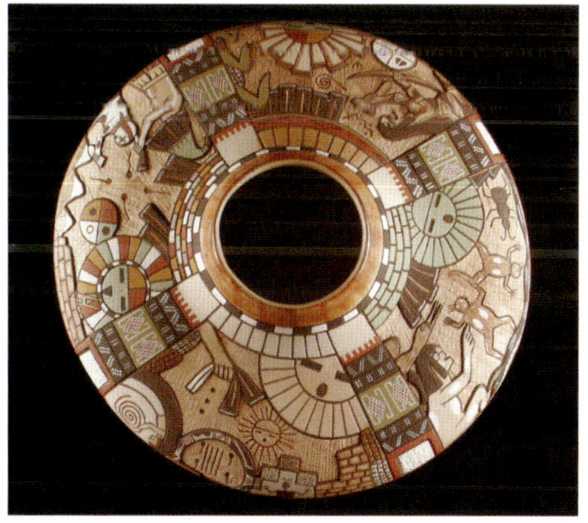

Hopi Reservation

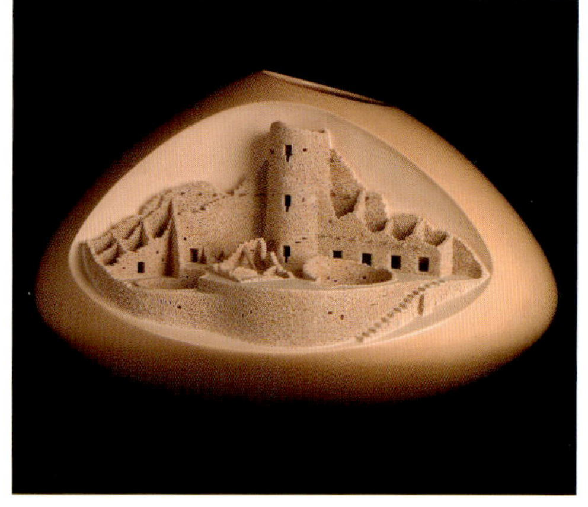

Artist:	**Quöyawayma, Al** (1938 -)
Date:	1992
Tribe:	Hopi
Height:	13 inches
Diameter:	14 inches

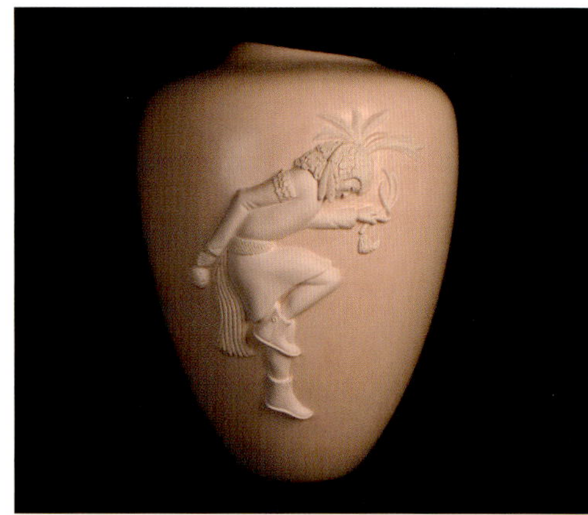

Artist:	**Quöyawayma, Al** (1938 -)
Date:	1991
Tribe:	Hopi
Height:	12 inches
Diameter:	8 inches

Jemez Pueblo

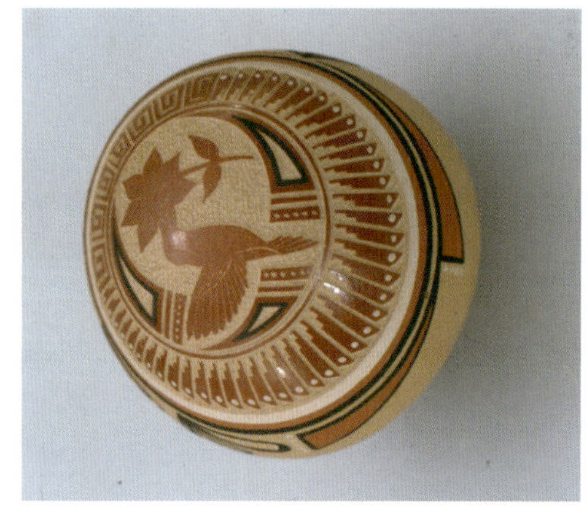

Artist:	**Fragua Daubs, Glendora** (1958 -)
Date:	1988
Pueblo:	Jemez
Family:	Fragua
Height:	2.25 inches
Diameter:	2.25 inches

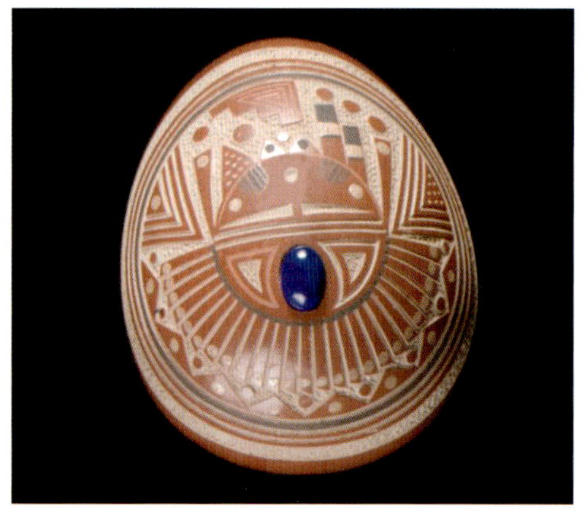

Artist:	**Fragua Daubs, Glendora** (1958 -)
Date:	c. 1980s
Pueblo:	Jemez
Family:	Fragua
Height:	2 inches
Diameter:	2.25 inches

Jemez Pueblo

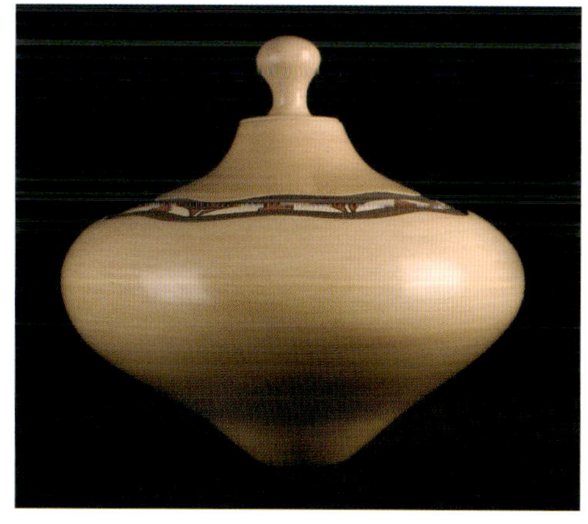

Artist: **Fragua, B.J.** (1962 -)
Date: c. 1997
Pueblo: Jemez
Family: Fragua
Height: 9 inches with lid
Diameter: 11 inches

Laguna Pueblo

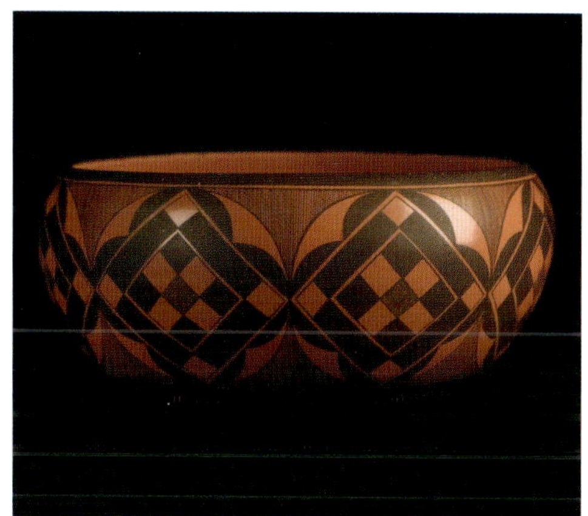

Artist: **Analla, Jr., Calvin**
Date: c. 1990
Pueblo: Laguna
Height: 3.5 inches
Diameter: 7 inches

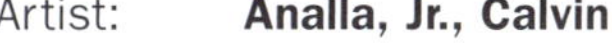

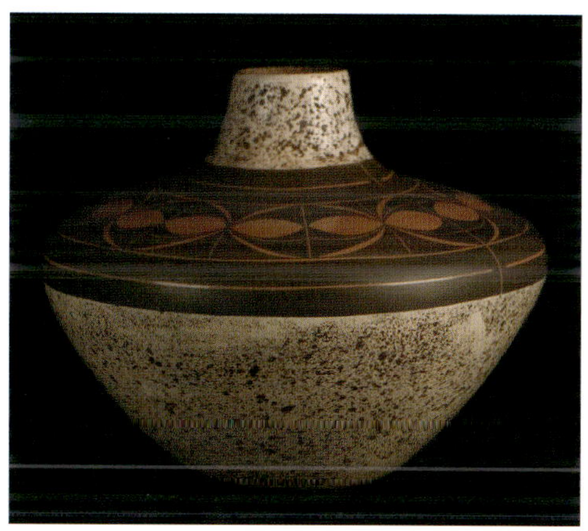

Artist: **Analla, Jr., Calvin**
Date: c. 1995
Pueblo: Laguna
Height: 7 inches
Diameter: 8 Inches

Nambe Pueblo

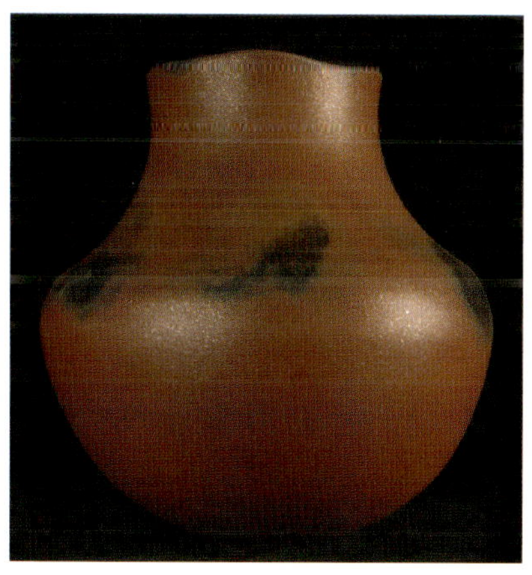

Artist: **Vigil, Lonnie** (1949 -)
Date: c. 1998
Pueblo: Nambe
Height: 14.25 inches
Diameter: 13 inches

Navajo Reservation

Artist: **Begay, Harrison** (1961 -)
Date: 2001
Tribe: Navajo (Diné)
Height: 10 inches
Diameter: 7.5 inches

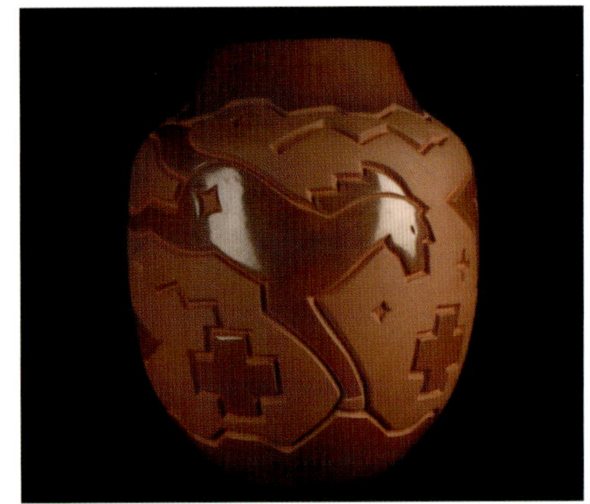

Artist: **Begay, Harrison** (1961 -)
Date: 2002
Tribe: Navajo (Diné)
Height: 8.5 inches
Diameter: 6.25 inches

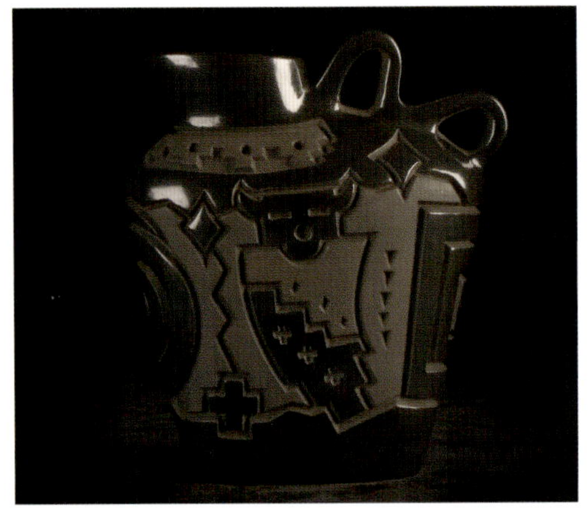

Artist: **Begay, Harrison** (1961 -)
Date: 1995
Tribe: Navajo (Diné)
Height: 5.5 inches
Diameter: 5 inches

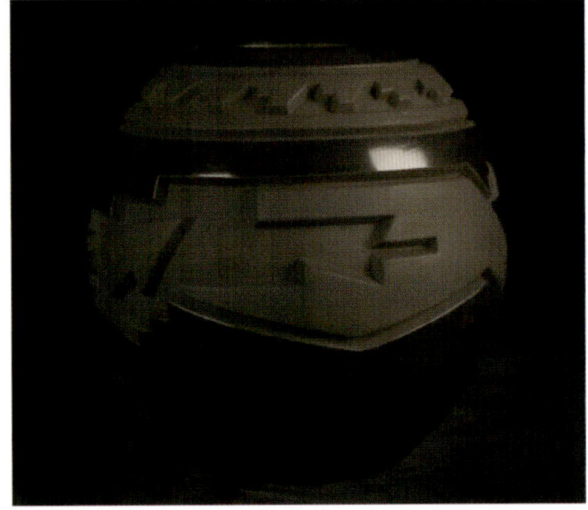

Artist: **Cling, Alice** (1946 -)
Date: 2004
Tribe: Navajo (Diné)
Height: 6 inches
Diameter: 5.5 inches

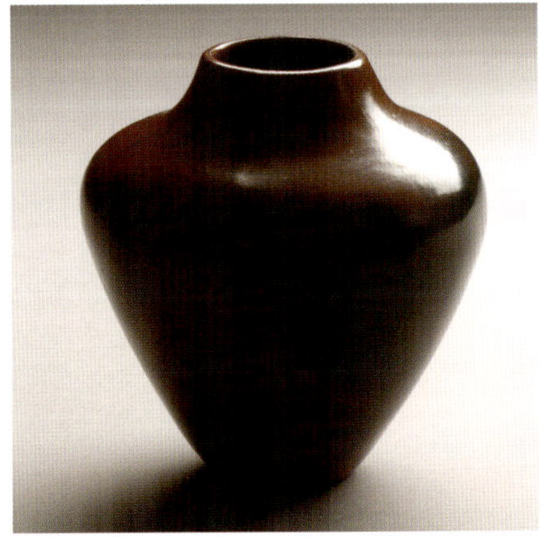

Navajo Reservation

Artist: **Cling, Alice** (1946 -)
Date: 2004
Tribe: Navajo (Diné)
Height: 10 inches
Diameter: 6 inches

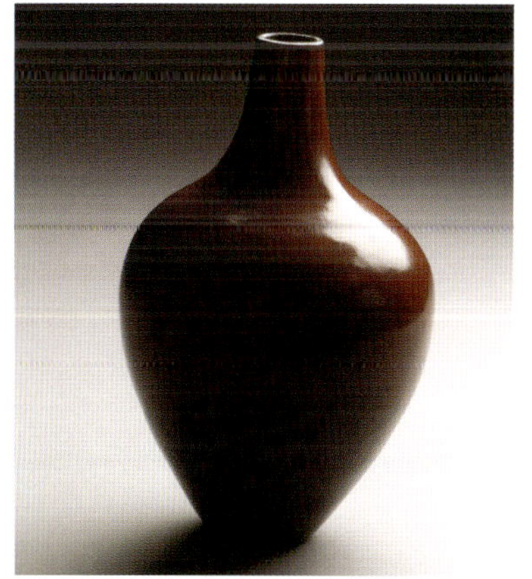

Artist: **Lansing, Bob** (1966 -)
Date: 2003
Tribe: Navajo (Diné)
Height: 1 inch
Diameter: 5.25 inches

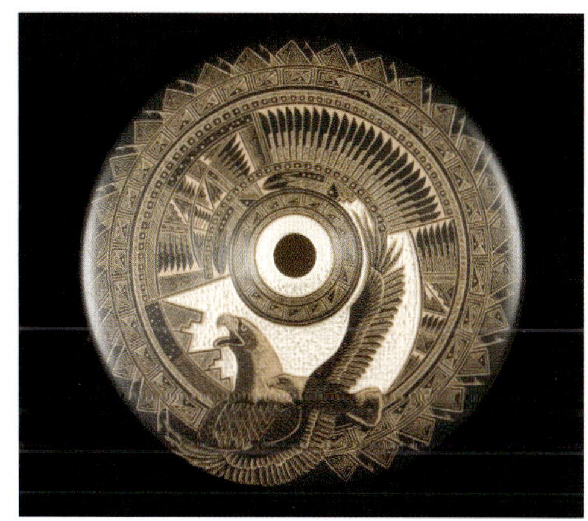

Artist: **Manygoats, Elizabeth**
Date: 2006
Tribe: Navajo (Diné)
Height: 9 inches
Diameter: 9 inches

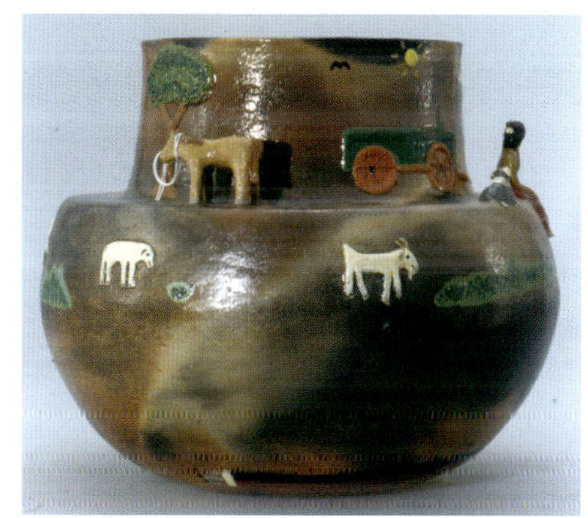

Artist: **Manymules, Samuel** (1969 -)
Date: 2007
Tribe: Navajo (Diné)
Height: 6 inches
Diameter: 8 inches

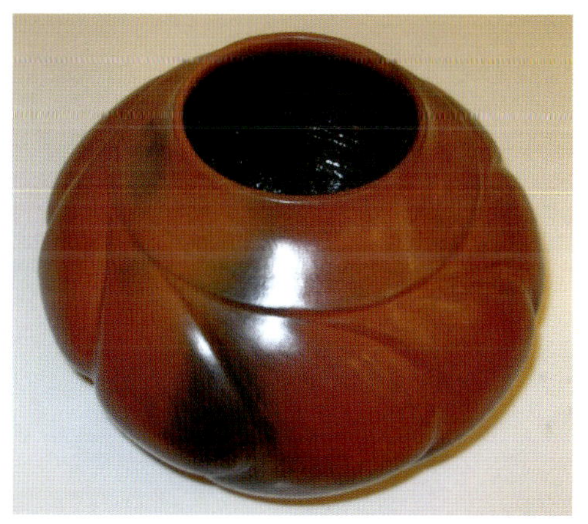

Navajo Reservation

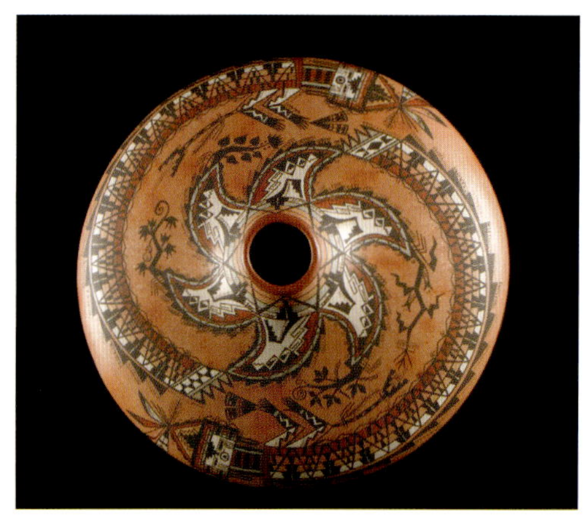

Artist: **McKelvey, Celinda K.** (1977 -)
Date: c. 2001
Title: "Whirling Rainbow Goddess"
Tribe: Navajo (Diné)
Height: 6 inches
Diameter: 12 inches

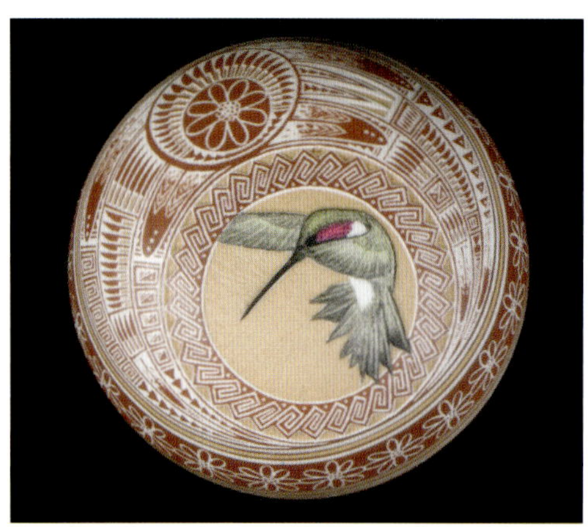

Artist: **Nez, Jr., Wallace** (1972 -)
Date: 2003
Tribe: Navajo (Diné)
Height: 1 inch
Diameter: 3.25 inches

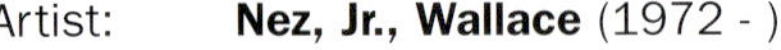

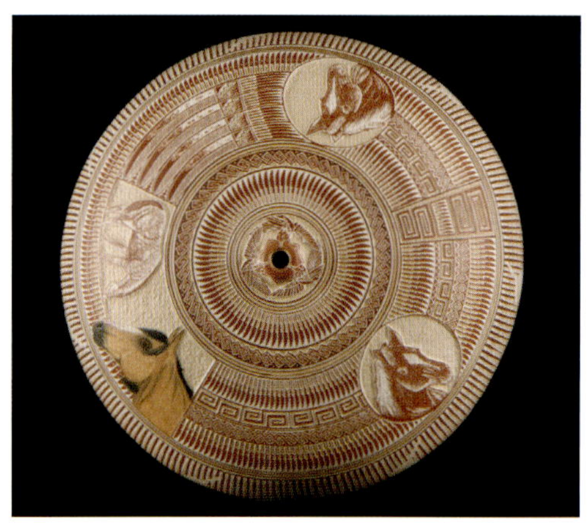

Artist: **Nez, Jr., Wallace** (1972 -)
Date: 2000
Tribe: Navajo (Diné)
Height: 2 inches
Diameter: 3.25 inches

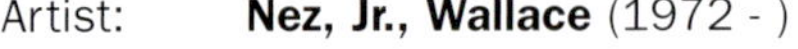

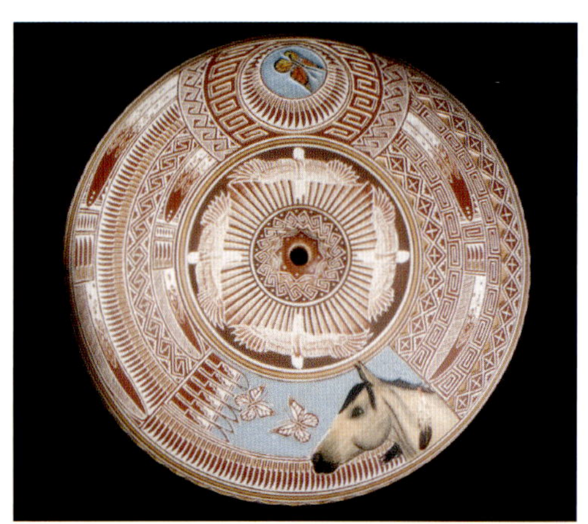

Artist: **Nez, Jr., Wallace** (1972 -)
Date: 2003
Tribe: Diné (Navajo)
Height: 1.375 inches
Diameter: 3.25 inches

Sandia Pueblo

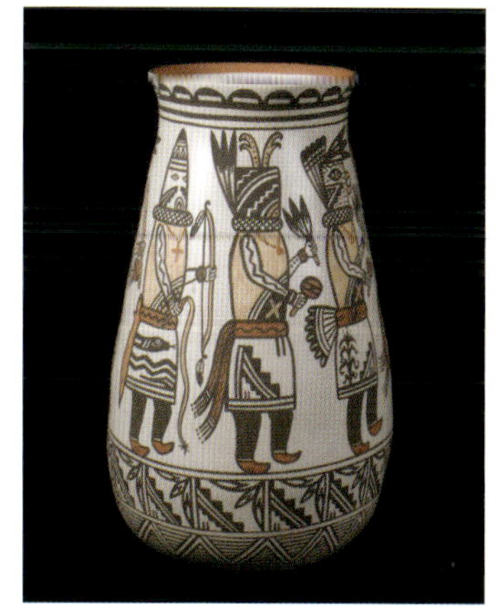

Artist: **Montoya, John** (1960 -)
Date: 2003
Pueblo: Sandia
Height: 11.5 inches
Diameter: 7 inches

San Felipe Pueblo

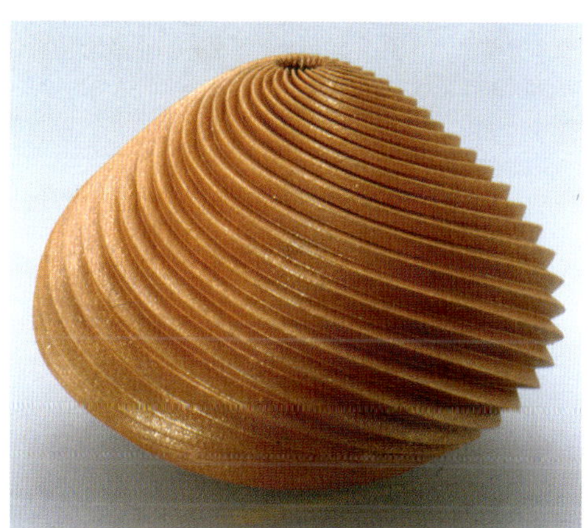

Artist: **Candelario, Hubert** (1965 -)
Date: 2006
Pueblo: San Felipe
Height: 7.5 inches
Diameter: 8 inches

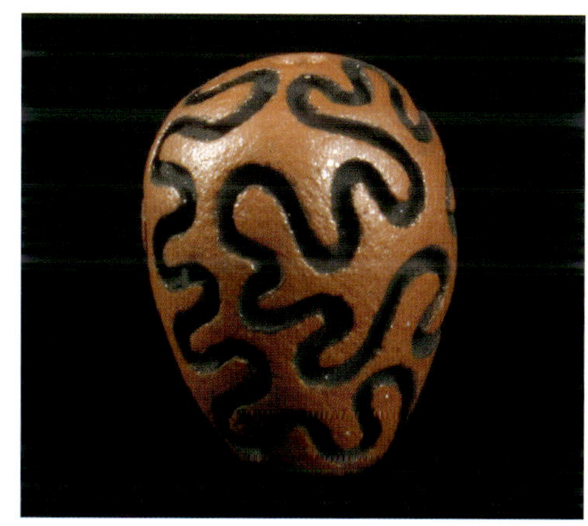

Artist: **Candelario, Hubert** (1965 -)
Date: 2001
Pueblo: San Felipe
Height: 1.5 inches
Diameter: 1.25 inches

Artist: **Candelario, Hubert** (1965 -)
Date: 2007 (in progress)
Pueblo: San Felipe

No Photo Available

San Felipe Pueblo

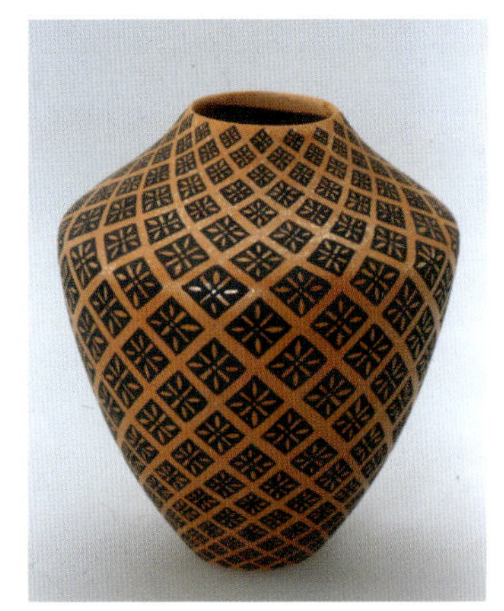

Artist: **Trancosa, Kevin** (1968 -)
Date: 1997
Pueblo: San Felipe
Height: 8 inches
Diameter: 6 inches

San Ildefonso Pueblo

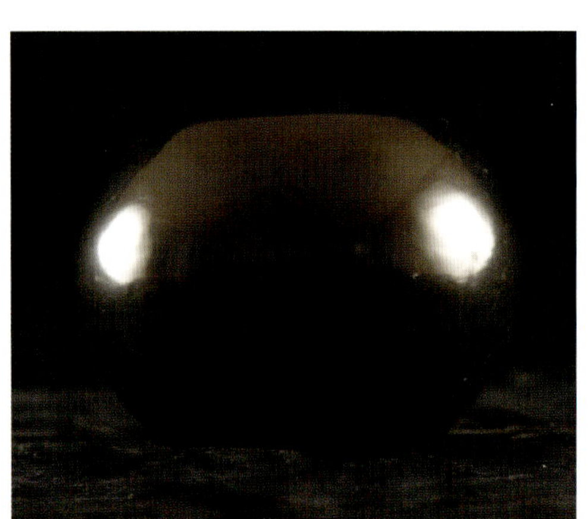

Artist: **Martinez, Maria** (1887 - 1980)
Date: c. 1950s
Pueblo: San Ildefonso
Family: Martinez (Matriarch)
Height: 3.25 inches
Diameter: 4.25 inches

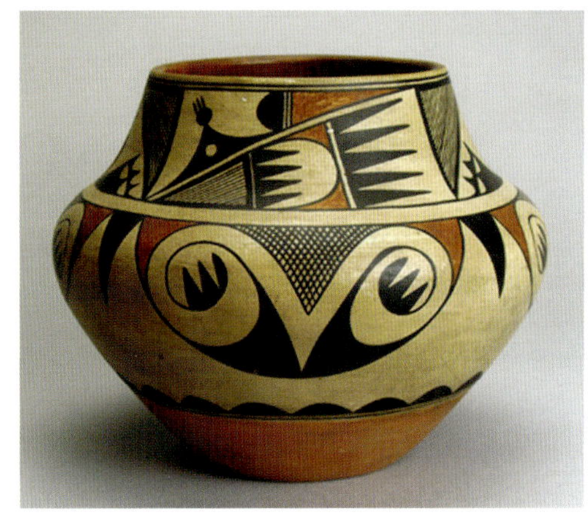

Artist: **Martinez, Maria & Julian** (1887 - 1980)
Date: c. 1920
Pueblo: San Ildefonso
Family: Martinez (Matriarch)
Height: 8.75 inches
Diameter: 10.25 inches

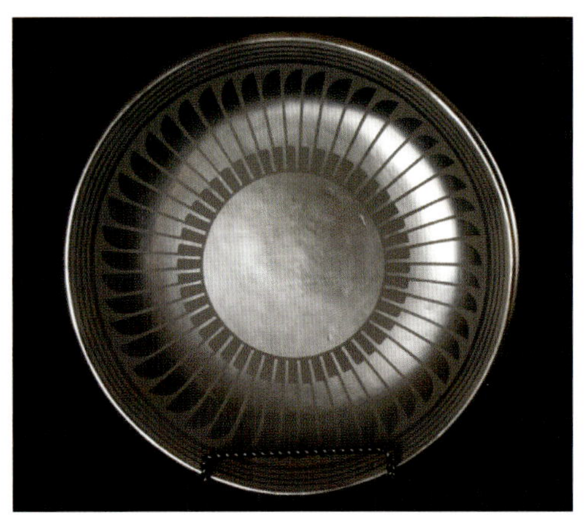

Artist: **Martinez, Maria & Popovi Da** (1887 - 1980) & (1923 - 1971)
Date: June 1960
Pueblo: San Ildefonso
Family: Martinez (Matriarch)
Diameter: 12.5 inches

San Ildefonso Pueblo

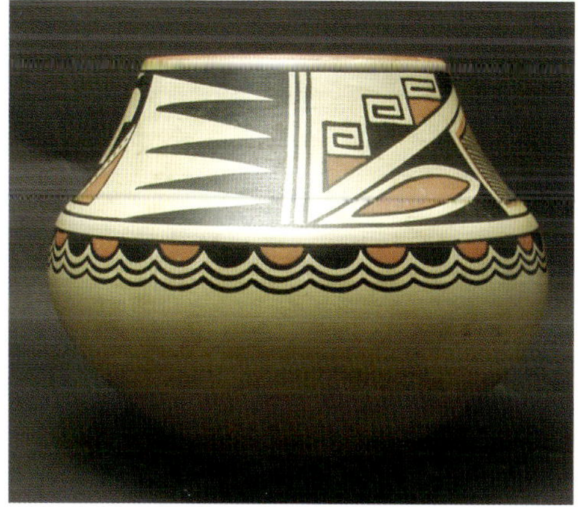

Artist: **Martinez, Maria & Popovi Da**
(1887 - 1980) & (1923 - 1971)
Date: 1959
Pueblo: San Ildefonso
Family: Matriarch and son
Height: 7.75 inches
Diameter: 9 inches

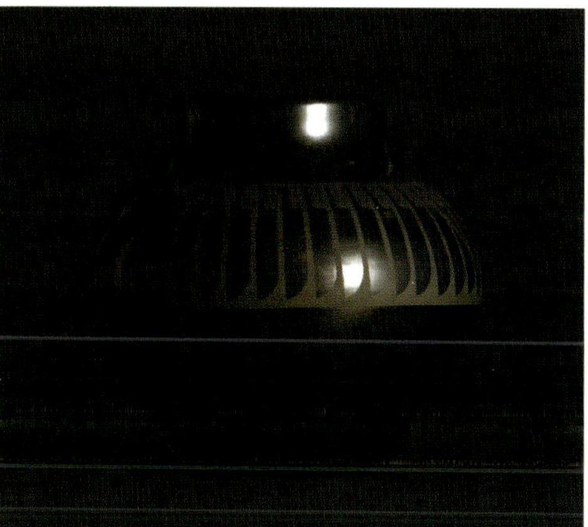

Artist: **Martinez, Maria & Popovi Da**
(1887 - 1980) & (1923 - 1971)
Date: April 1962
Pueblo: San Ildefonso
Family: Matriarch and son
Height: 6.5 inches
Diameter: 7 inches

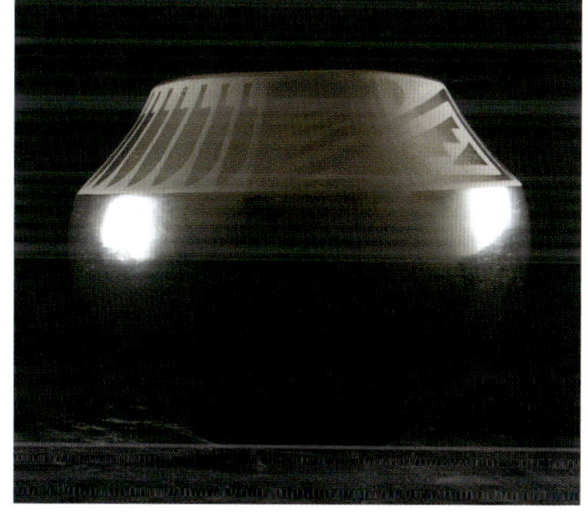

Artist: **Sanchez, Desideria** (1889 - 1992)
Date: n.d.
Pueblo: San Ildefonso
Family: sister to Maria Martinez
Height: 7.5 inches
Diameter: 9 inches

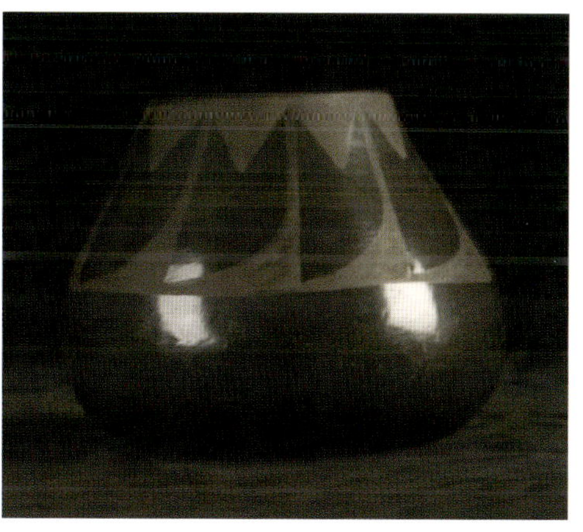

Artist: **Gonzalez, Juanita "Wo-peen"** (1909-1988)
Date: n.d.
Pueblo: San Ildefonso
Family: Cousin to Maria Martinez by marriage
Height: 5 inches
Diameter: 6 inches

San Ildefonso Pueblo

Artist: **Da, Popovi** (1923 - 1971)
Date: October 1965
Pueblo: San Ildefonso
Family: Son of Maria Martinez
Height: 2.5 inches
Diameter: 2.25 inches

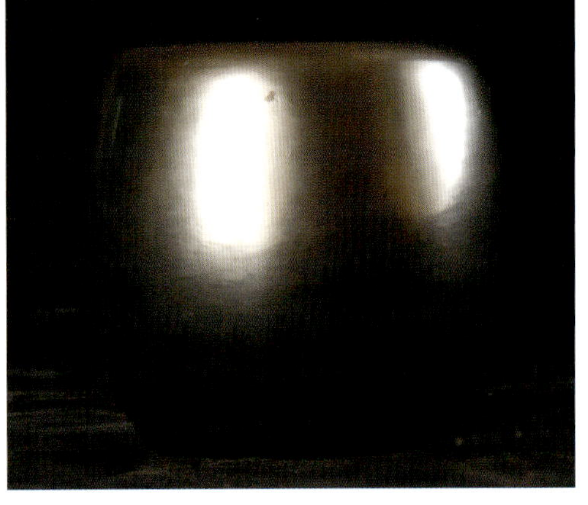

Artist: **Da, Popovi** (1923 - 1971)
Date: April 1968
Pueblo: San Ildefonso
Family: Son of Maria Martinez
Diameter: 12 inches

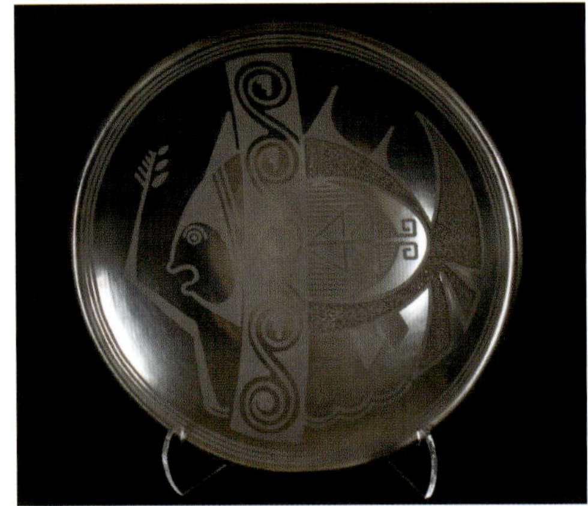

Artist: **Martinez, Maria & Santana** (1909 - 2002)
Date: c. 1950
Pueblo: San Ildefonso
Family: Matriarch and daughter-in-law
Height: 5 inches
Diameter: 6 inches

Artist: **Martinez, Adam & Santana**
(1903 - c. 2000) & (1909 - 2002)
Date: 1988
Pueblo: San Ildefonso
Family: Son and daughter-in-law of Maria Martinez
Height: 6.5 inches
Diameter: 7.5 inches

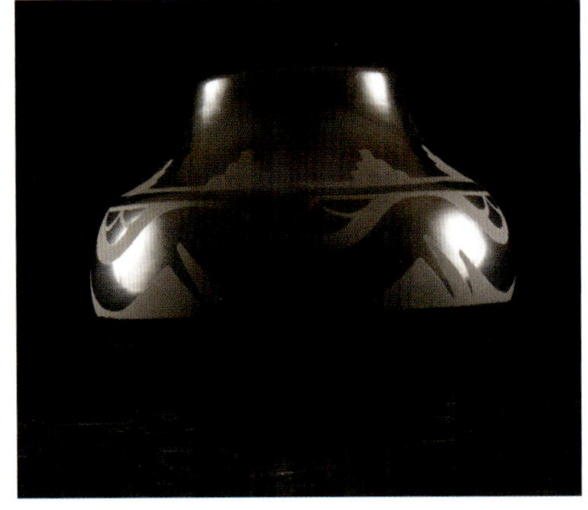

San Ildefonso Pueblo

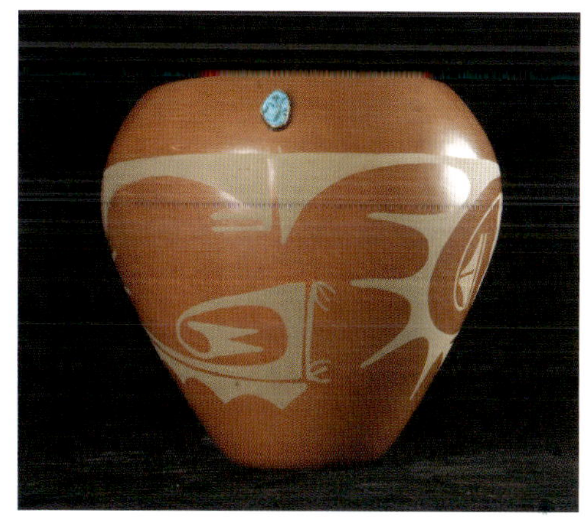

Artist: **Dunlap, Carmelita** (1925 - 2000)
Date: 1982
Pueblo: San Ildefonso
Family: Niece of Maria Martinez
Height: 8 inches
Diameter: 8 inches

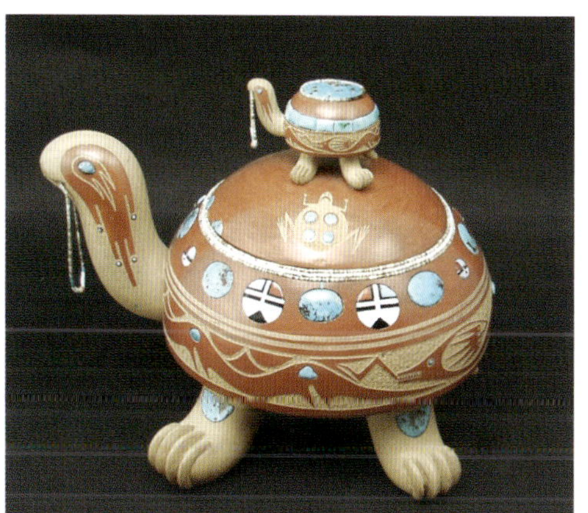

Artist: **Da, Tony** (1940 -)
Date: c. 1975
Pueblo: San Ildefonso
Family: Grandson of Maria Martinez
Height: 7.5 inches
Diameter: 8 Inches

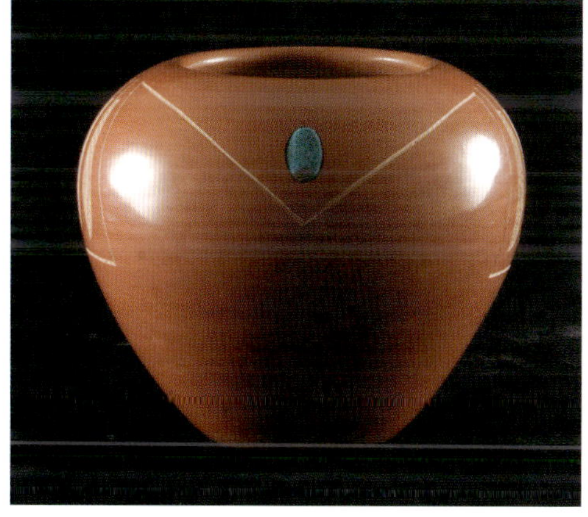

Artist: **Da, Tony** (1940 -)
Date: c. 1970
Pueblo: San Ildefonso
Family: Grandson of Maria Martinez
Height: 5 inches
Diameter: 5 inches

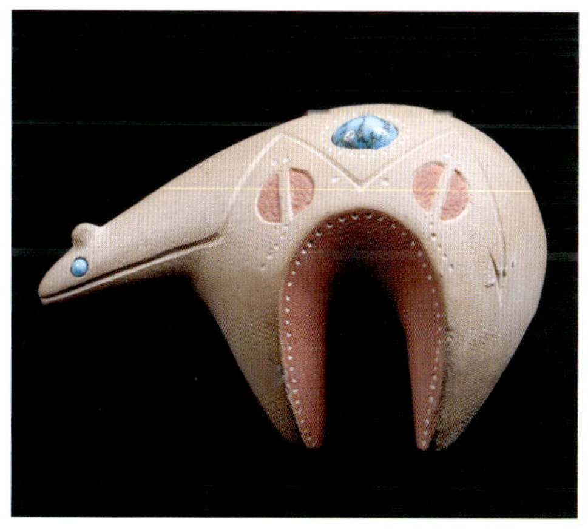

Artist: **Da, Tony** (1940 -)
Date: c. 1976-77
Pueblo: San Ildefonso
Family: Grandson of Maria Martinez
Height: 1.5 inches

San Ildefonso Pueblo

Artist: **Da, Tony** (1940 -)
Date: c. 1971-72
Pueblo: San Ildefonso
Family: Grandson of Maria Martinez
Height: 2 inches

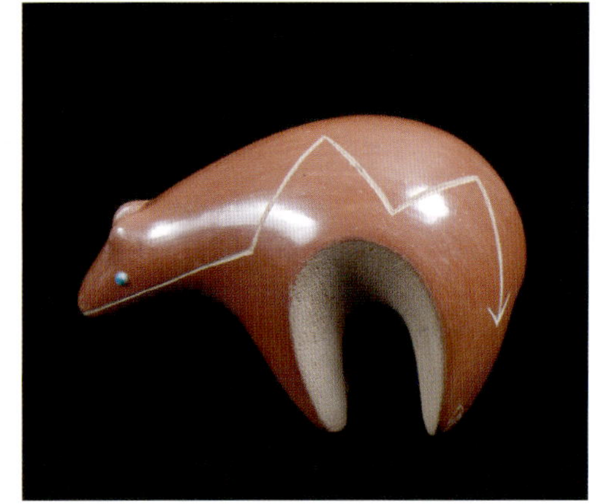

Artist: **Gonzales, Barbara** (1947 -)
Date: c. 2000
Pueblo: San Ildefonso
Family: Great-granddaughter of Maria Martinez
Height: 6 inches
Diameter: 12 inches

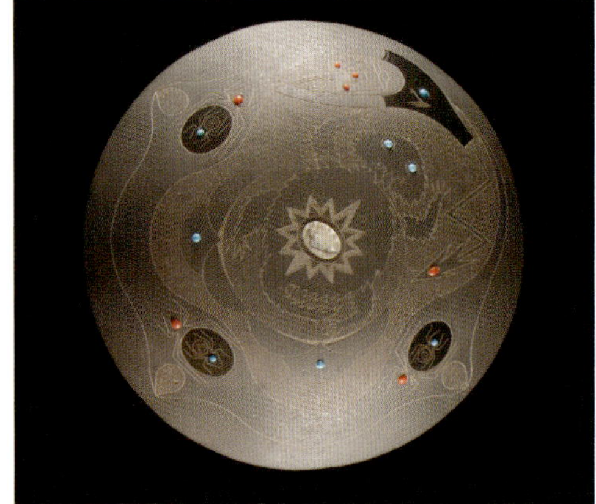

Artist: **Gonzales, Barbara** (1947 -)
Date: 1992
Pueblo: San Ildefonso
Family: Great-granddaughter of Maria Martinez
Diameter: 6.25 inches

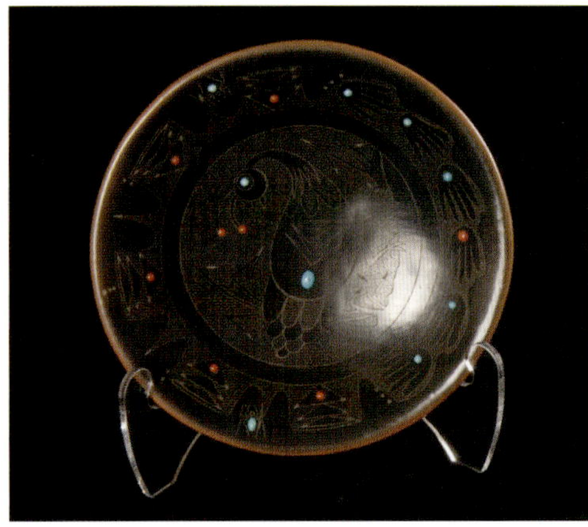

Artist: **Gonzales, John** (1955 -)
Date: 1999
Pueblo: San Ildefonso
Family: Third cousin of Maria Martinez
Height: 2.25 inches
Diameter: 5 inches

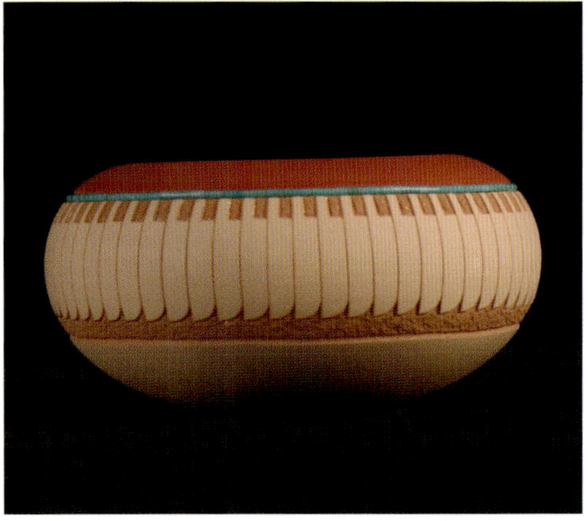

San Ildefonso Pueblo

Artist: **Gonzales, John** (1955 -)
Date: 2004
Pueblo: San Ildefonso
Family: Third cousin of Maria Martinez
Diameter: 12 inches

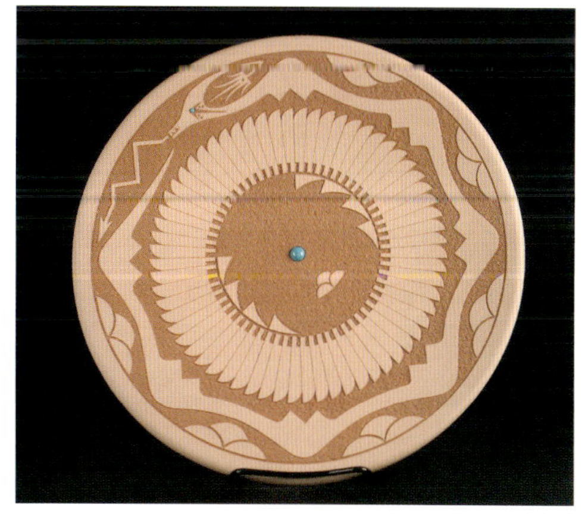

Artist: **Tse Pe** (1940 - c. 2000)
Date: c. 1970
Pueblo: San Ildefonso
Family: Son of Rose Gonzales
Height: 12 inches with lid
Diameter: 8.5 inches

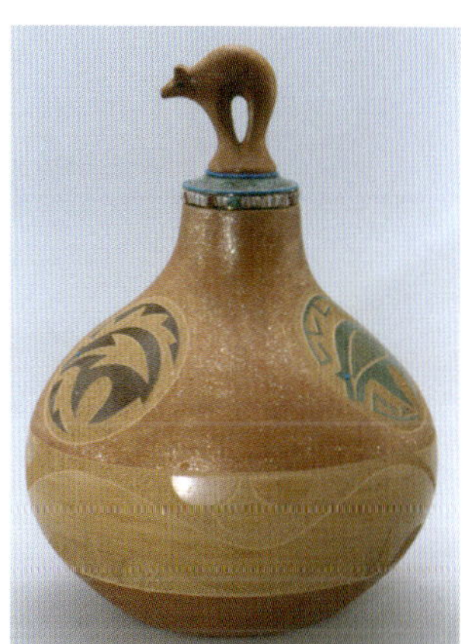

Artist: **Tse Pe** (1940 - c. 2000)
Date: c. 1995
Pueblo: San Ildefonso
Family: Son of Rose Gonzales
Height: 6.25 inches
Diameter: 4.75 inches

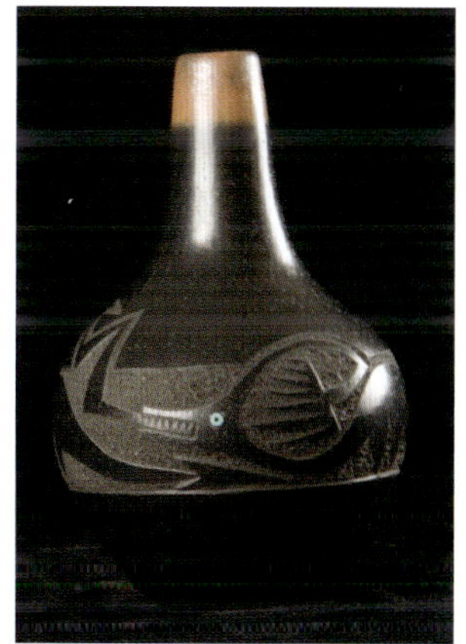

Artist: **Tse Pe, Dora** (1939 -)
Date: 1974
Pueblo: San Ildefonso (originally Zia)
Family: Daughter-in-law of Rose Gonzales
Height: 2.75 inches
Diameter: 3 inches

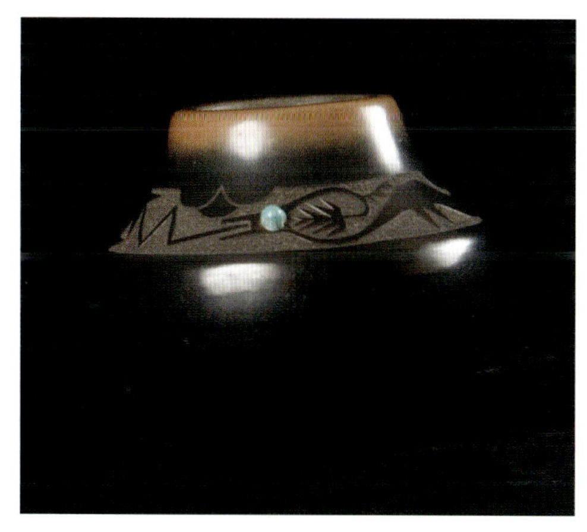

San Ildefonso Pueblo

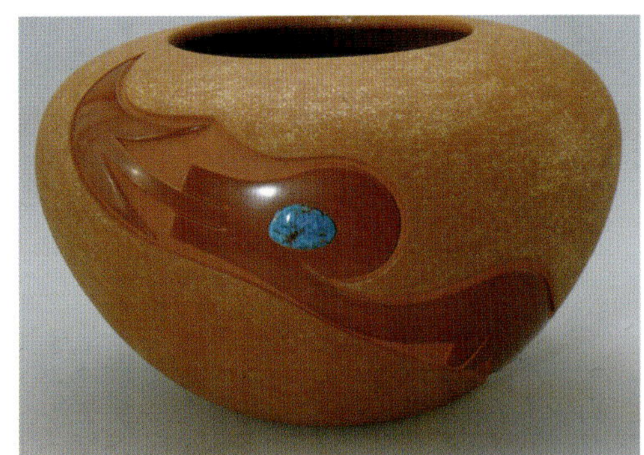

Artist: **Tse Pe, Dora** (1939 -)
Date: c. 1990s
Pueblo: San Ildefonso (originally Zia)
Family: Daughter-in-law of Rose Gonzales
Height: 6 inches
Diameter: 10 inches

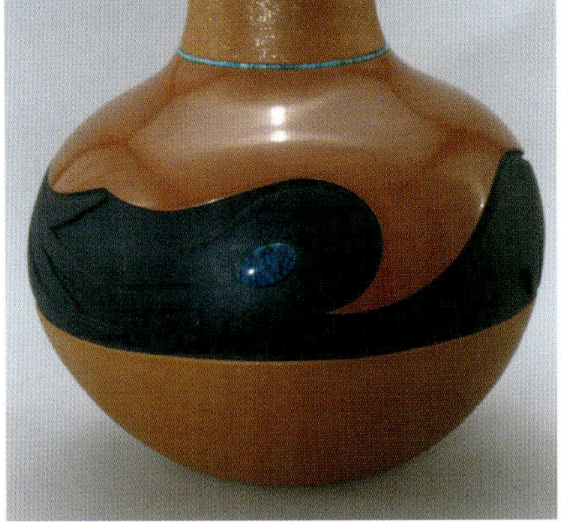

Artist: **Tse Pe, Dora** (1939 -)
Date: c. 1990s
Pueblo: San Ildefonso (originally Zia)
Family: Daughter-in-law of Rose Gonzales
Height: 9 inches
Diameter: 8 inches

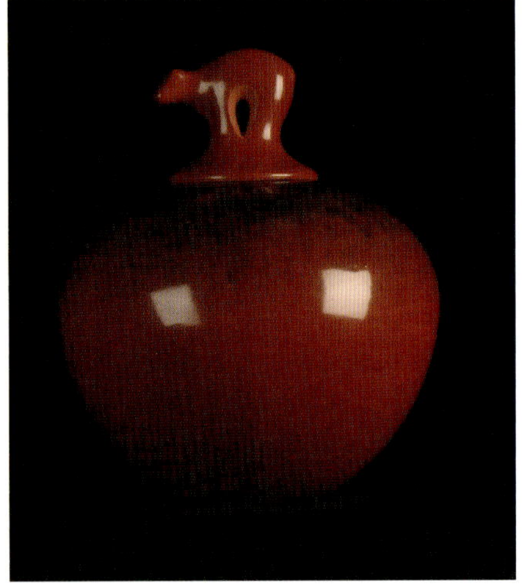

Artist: **Sanchez, Russell** (1966 -)
Date: 1995
Pueblo: San Ildefonso
Family: Nephew of Rose Gonzales
Height: 8.75 inches with lid
Diameter: 6.5 inches

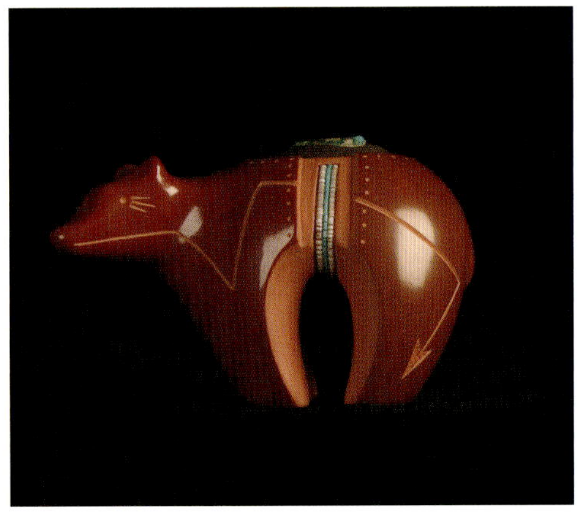

Artist: **Sanchez, Russell** (1966 -)
Date: c. 1995-2000
Pueblo: San Ildefonso
Family: Nephew of Rose Gonzales
Height: 3 inches
Diameter: 4 inches

San Ildefonso Pueblo

Artist: **Sanchez, Russell** (1966 -)
Date: c. 2006
Pueblo: San Ildefonso
Family: Nephew of Rose Gonzales
Height: 8.25 inches
Diameter: 6.5 inches

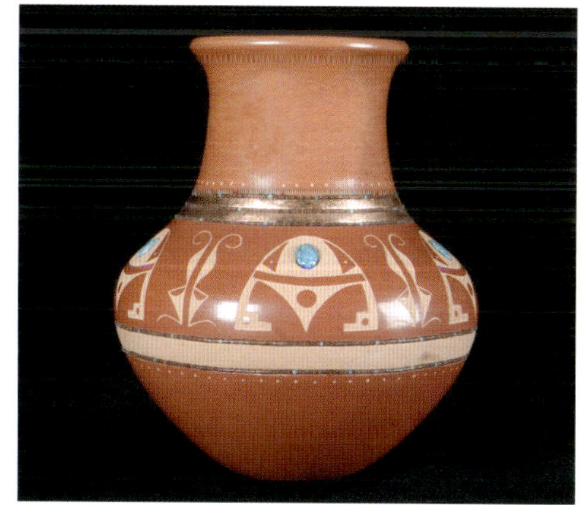

Other San Ildefonso Potters

Artist: **Blue Corn** (Crucita Gonzales, 1921-1999)
Date: n.d.
Pueblo: San Ildefonso
Height: 2.5 inches
Diameter: 3.5 inches

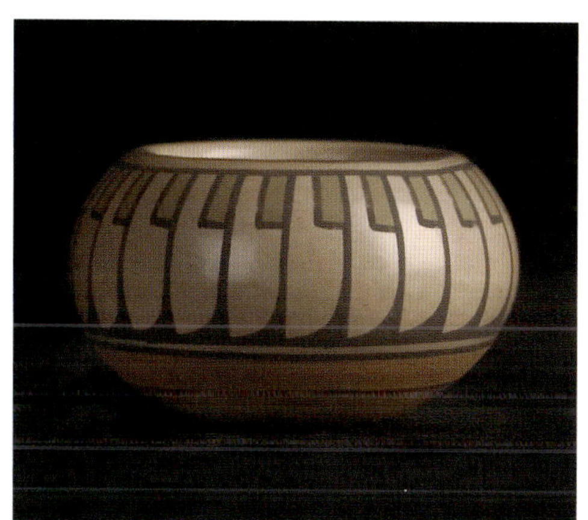

Artist: **Blue Corn** (Crucita Gonzales, 1921-1999)
Date: c. 1965
Pueblo: San Ildefonso
Height: 10 inches
Diameter: 8.5 inches

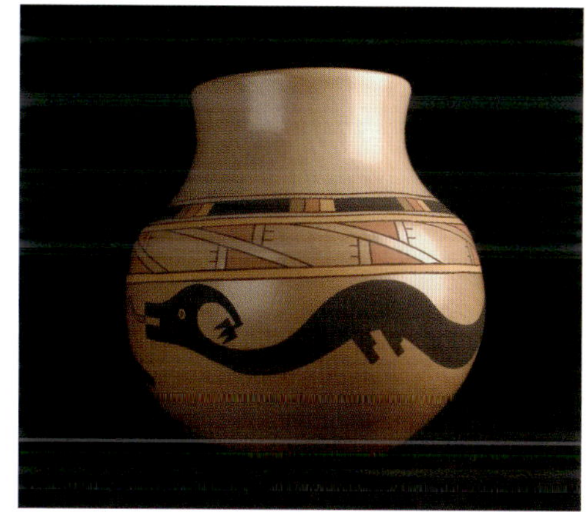

Artist: **Blue Corn** (Crucita Gonzales, 1921-1999)
Date: c. 1980
Pueblo: San Ildefonso
Diameter: 14 inches

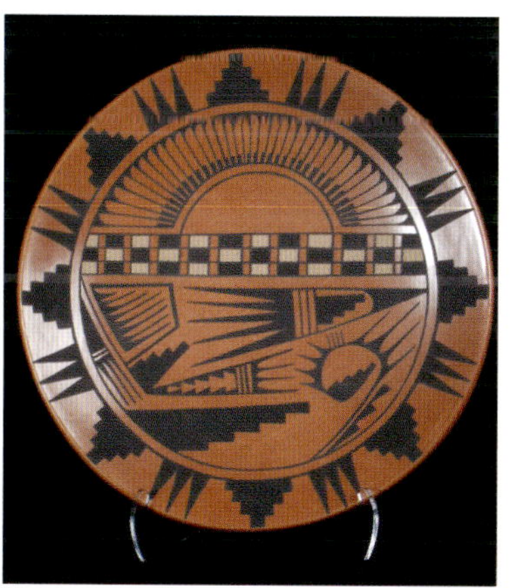

San Ildefonso Pueblo

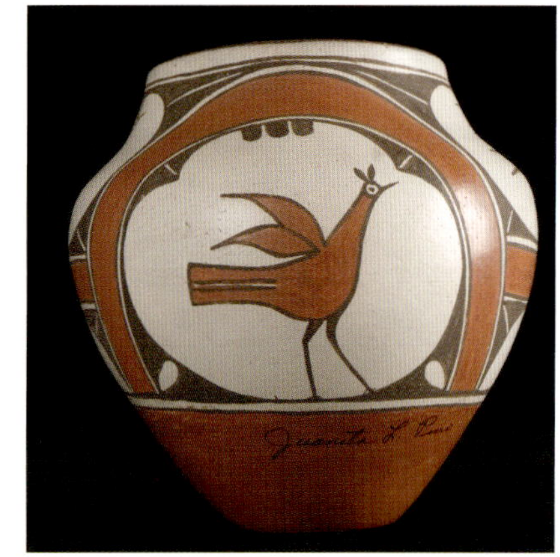

Artist: **Piño, Jaunita L.**
Date: n.d.
Pueblo: San Ildefonso
Height: 9 inches
Diameter: 8.25 inches

Santa Clara Pueblo

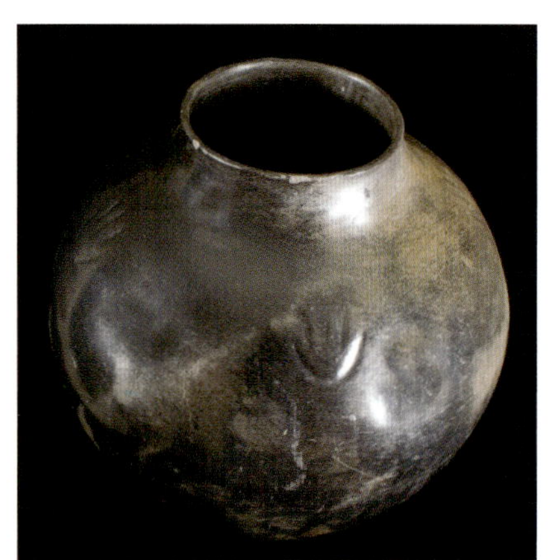

Artist: **Tafoya, Sara Fina** (1863 - 1949)
Date: c. 1920s
Pueblo: Santa Clara
Family: Tafoya (Matriarch)
Height: 22 inches
Diameter: 19 inches

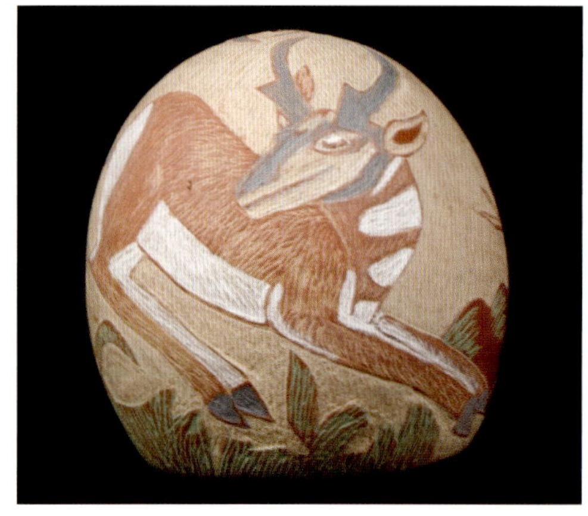

Artist: **Tafoya, Camilio "Sunflower"** (1902 - 1995)
Date: c. 1990
Pueblo: Santa Clara
Family: Son of Sara Fina Tafoya
Height: 1.75 inches
Diameter: 1.25 inches

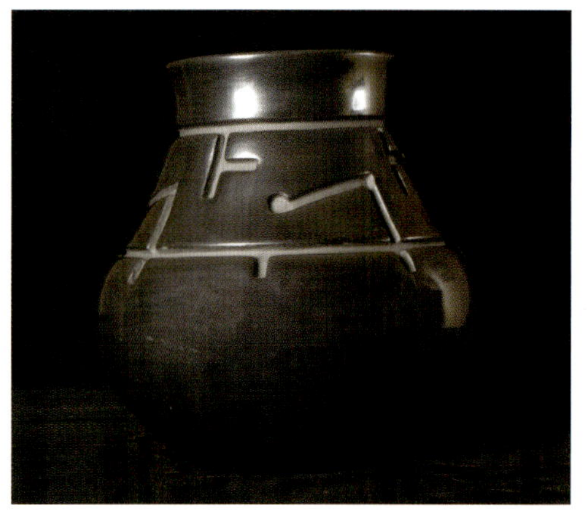

Artist: **Tafoya, Margaret** (1904 - 2001)
Date: c. 1970s
Pueblo: Santa Clara
Family: Daughter of Sara Fina Tafoya
Height: 9 inches
Diameter: 9 Inches

Santa Clara Pueblo

Artist: **Tafoya, Margaret** (1904 - 2001)
Date: c. 1980s
Pueblo: Santa Clara
Family: Daughter of Sara Fina Tafoya
Height: 5.75 inches
Diameter: 6 Inches

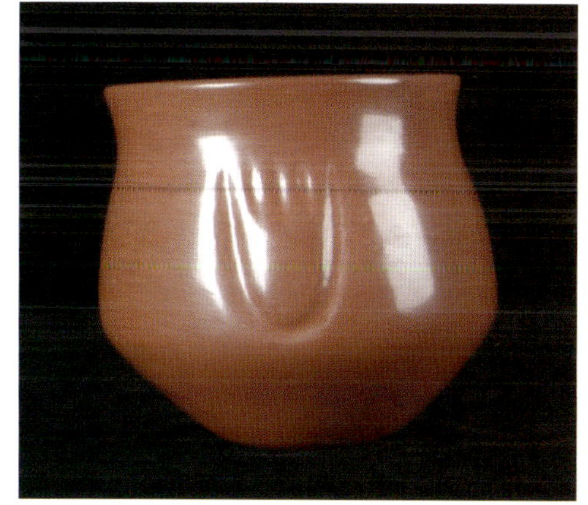

Artist: **Naranjo, Teresita** (1919 - 1999)
Date: c. 1980s
Pueblo: Santa Clara
Family: Granddaughter of Sara Fina Tafoya
Height: 6 inches
Diameter: 5.25 inches

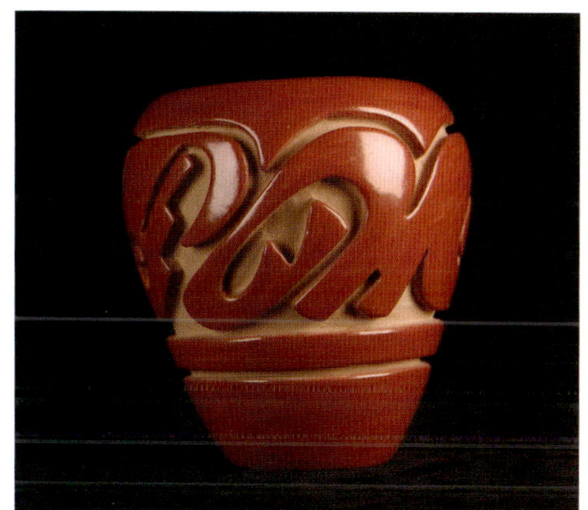

Artist: **Tafoya, Shirley "Cactus Blossom"** (1947 -)
Date: c. 1980
Pueblo: Santa Clara
Family: Granddaughter of Sara Fina Tafoya
Height: 2.5 inches
Diameter: 2.5 inches

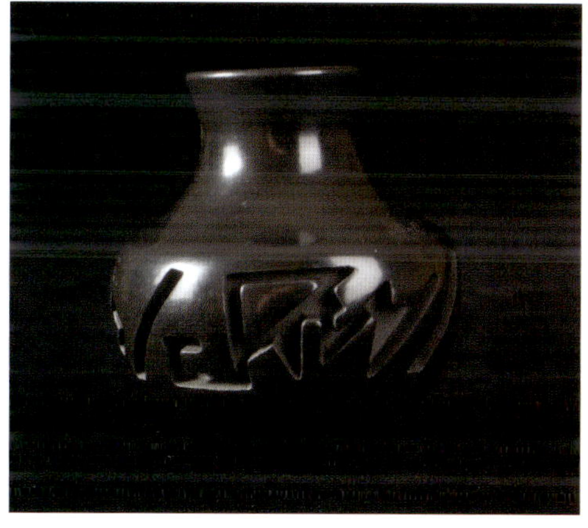

Artist: **Medicine Flower, Grace** (1938 -)
Date: c. 2000
Pueblo: Santa Clara
Family: Granddaughter of Sara Fina Tafoya
Height: 6 inches
Diameter: 7 inches

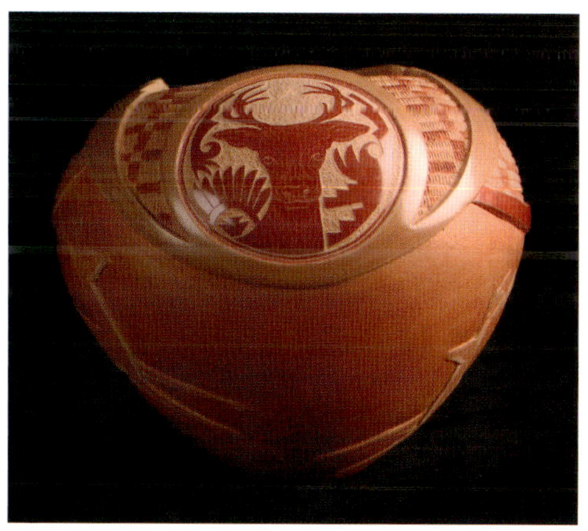

Santa Clara Pueblo

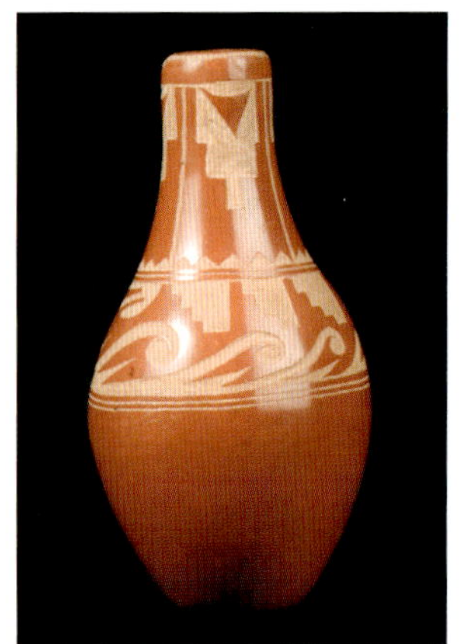

Artist: **Medicine Flower, Grace** (1938 -)
Date: 1994
Pueblo: Santa Clara
Family: Granddaughter of Sara Fina Tafoya
Height: 2 inches
Diameter: 1 inch

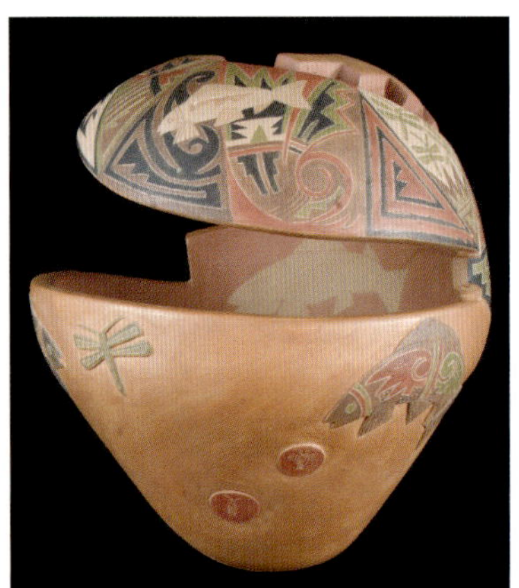

Artist: **Medicine Flower, Grace** (1938 -)
Date: 2005
Pueblo: Santa Clara
Family: Granddaughter of Sara Fina Tafoya
Height: 10 inches
Diameter: 8 inches

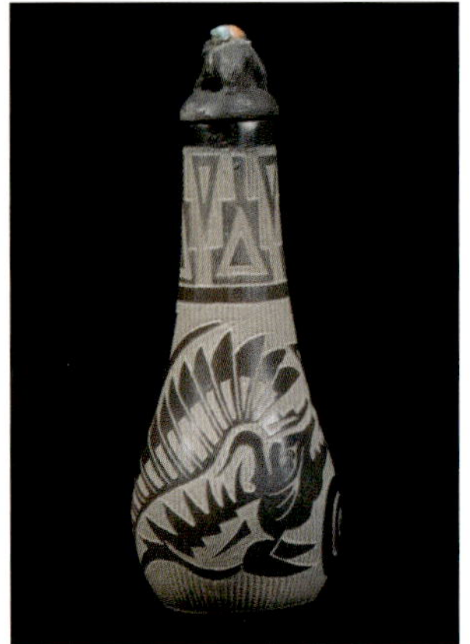

Artist: **Lonewolf, Joseph** (1932 -)
Date: 1976
Pueblo: Santa Clara
Family: Grandson of Sara Fina Tafoya
Height: 3.5 inches
Diameter: 1.5 inches

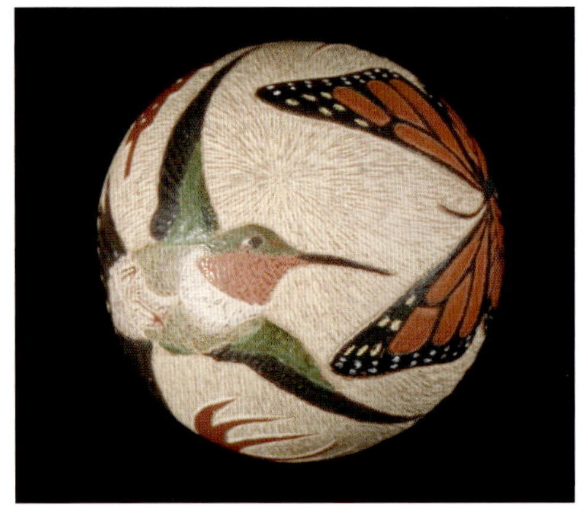

Artist: **Lonewolf, Joseph** (1932 -)
Date: n.d.
Pueblo: Santa Clara
Family: Grandson of Sara Fina Tafoya
Height: 1 inch
Diameter: 1 inch

Santa Clara Pueblo

Artist: **Lonewolf, Joseph** (1932 -)
Date: n.d.
Pueblo: Santa Clara
Family: Grandson of Sara Fina Tafoya
Height: 1.875 inches
Diameter: 1.5 inches

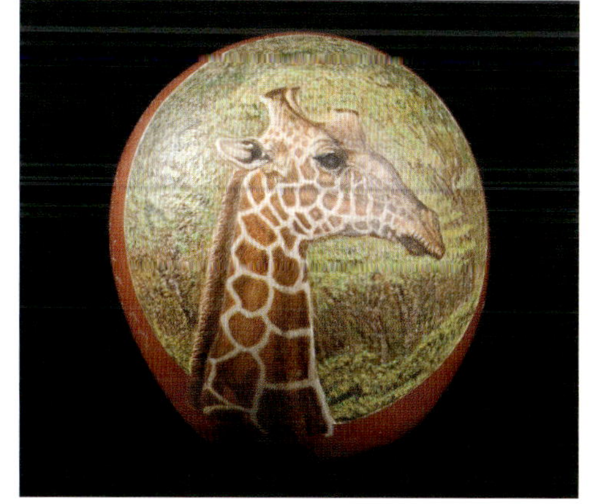

Artist: **Lonewolf, Joseph** (1932 -)
Date: 1986
Pueblo: Santa Clara
Family: Grandson of Sara Fina Tafoya
Height: 2.125 inches
Diameter: 2 inches

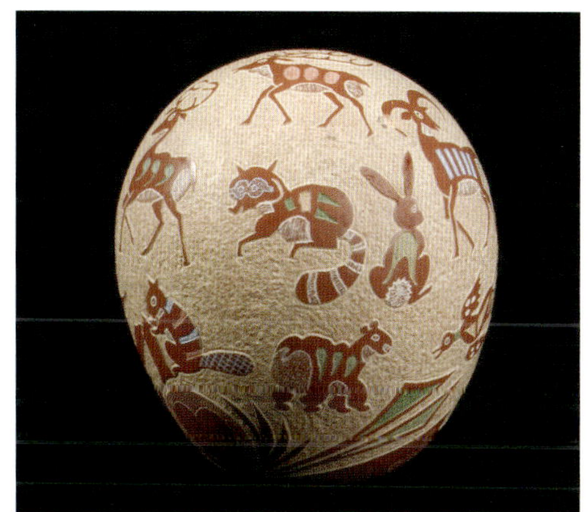

Artist: **Lonewolf, Joseph** (1932 -)
Date: c. 1997
Pueblo: Santa Clara
Family: Grandson of Sara Fina Tafoya
Height: 0.875 inch
Diameter: 0.75 inch

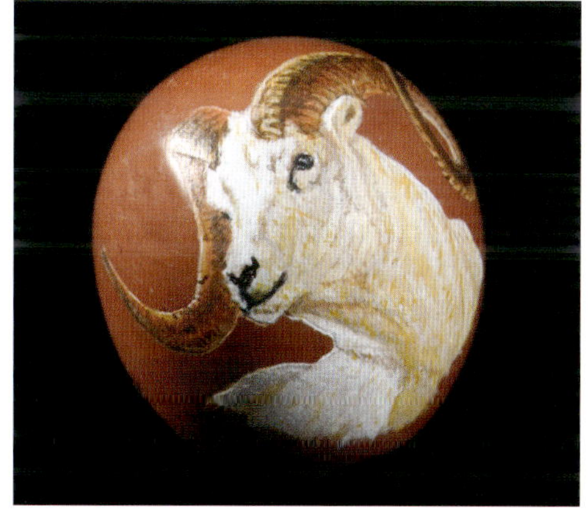

Artist: **Lonewolf, Joseph** (1932 -)
Date: 1977
Pueblo: Santa Clara
Family: Grandson of Sara Fina Tafoya
Height: 1.75 inches
Diameter: 1.5 inches

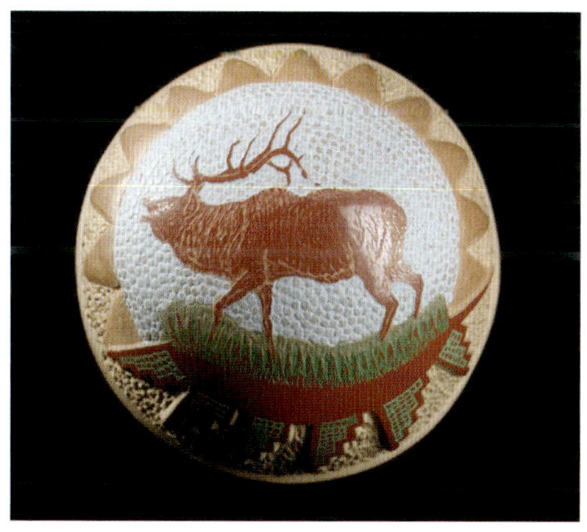

Santa Clara Pueblo

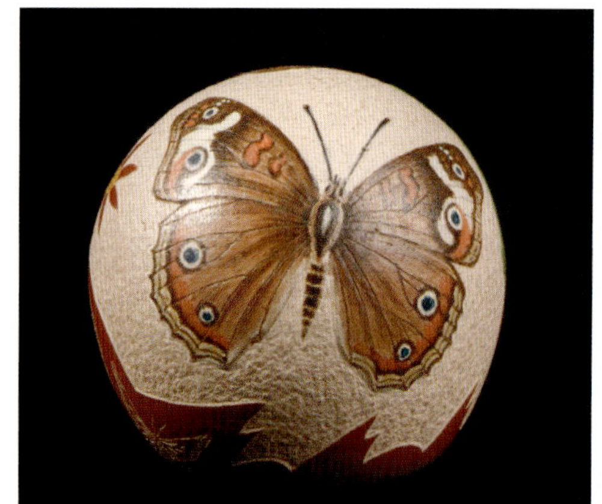

Artist: **Lonewolf, Joseph** (1932 -)
Date: n.d.
Pueblo: Santa Clara
Family: Grandson of Sara Fina Tafoya
Height: 1.25 inches
Diameter: 1.25 inches

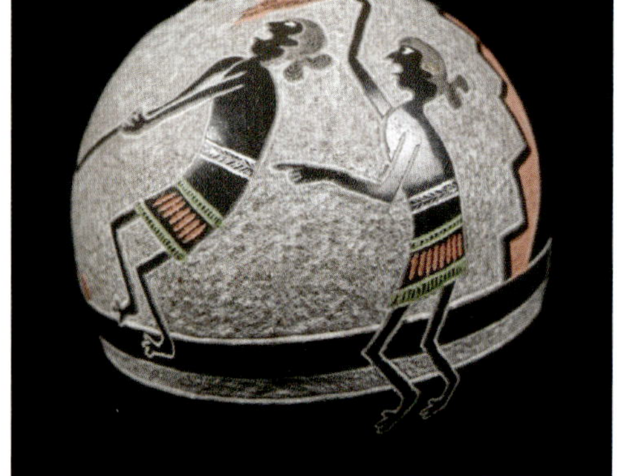

Artist: **Lonewolf, Joseph** (1932 -)
Date: n.d.
Pueblo: Santa Clara
Family: Grandson of Sara Fina Tafoya
Height: 1.25 inches
Diameter: 1.25 inches

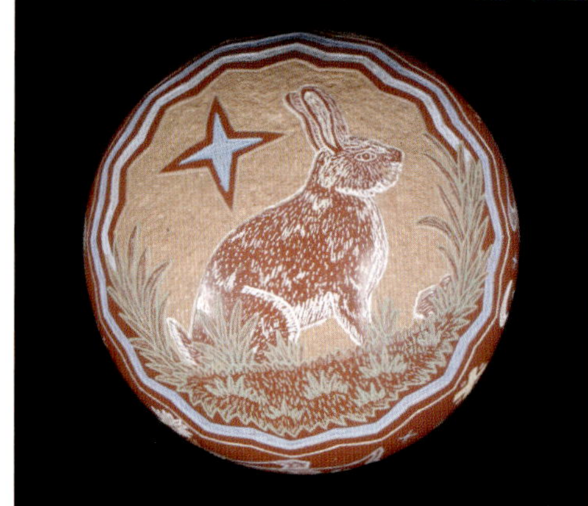

Artist: **Lonewolf, Greg** (1952 -)
Date: n.d.
Pueblo: Santa Clara
Family: Great-grandson of Sara Fina Tafoya
Height: 1.5 inches
Diameter: 1.5 inches

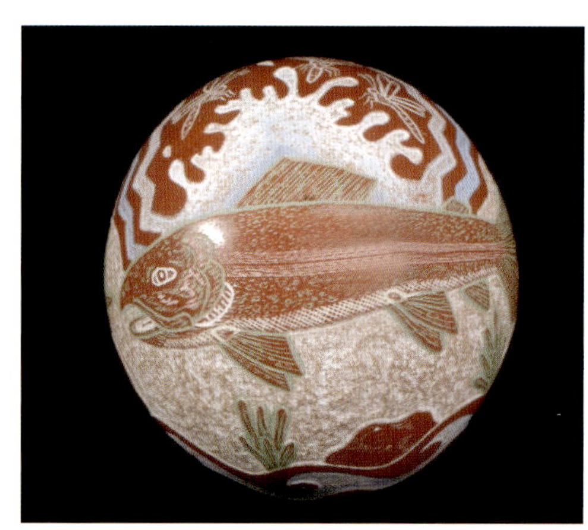

Artist: **Lonewolf, Greg** (1952 -)
Date: n.d.
Pueblo: Santa Clara
Family: Great-grandson of Sara Fina Tafoya
Height: 1.5 inches
Diameter: 1.25 inches

Santa Clara Pueblo

Artist: **Lonewolf, Greg** (1952 -)
Date: n.d.
Pueblo: Santa Clara
Family: Great-grandson of Sara Fina Tafoya
Height: 2 inches
Diameter: 1.5 inches

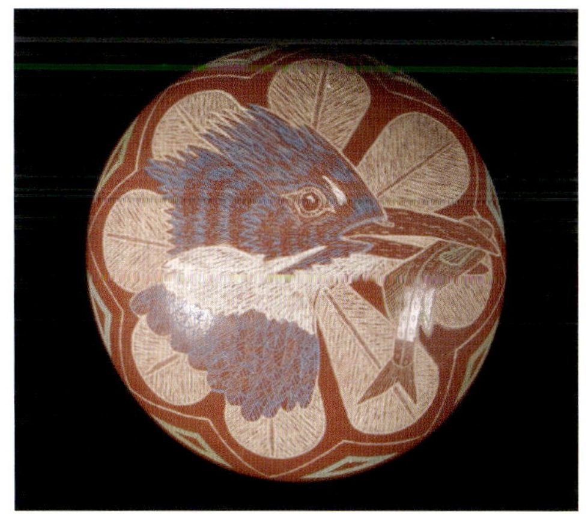

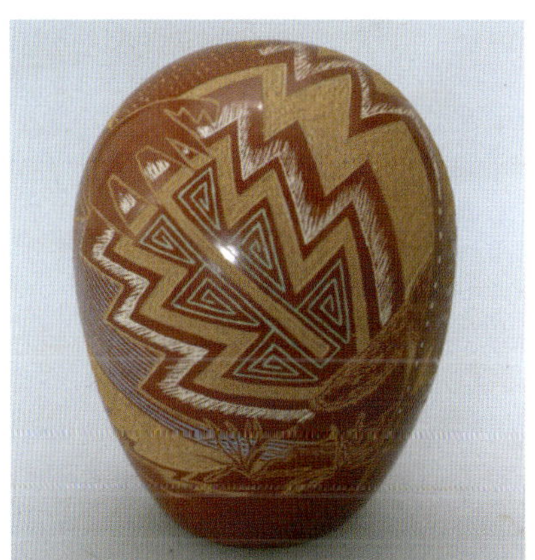

Artist: **Lonewolf, Rosemary "Apple Blossom"** (1953 -)
Date: 1996
Title: "What the Big Bad Wolf is Really Afraid of"
Pueblo: Santa Clara
Family: Great-granddaughter of Sara Fina Tafoya
Height: 4 inches
Diameter: 3 inches

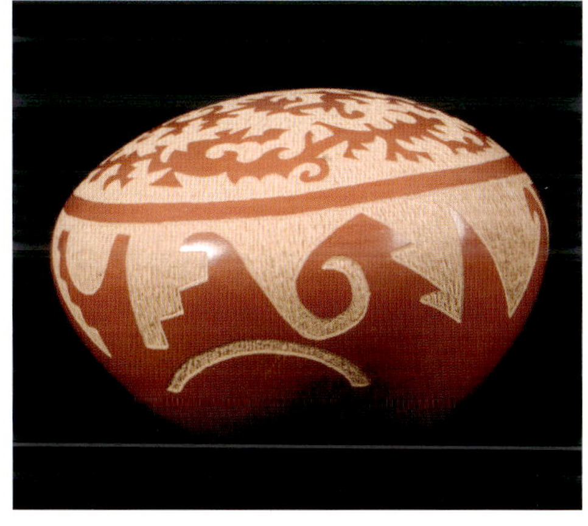

Artist: **Romero, Susan "Snowflake"** (1955 -)
Date: c. 1997
Pueblo: Santa Clara
Family: Great-granddaughter of Sara Fina Tafoya
Height: 1.5 inches
Diameter: 2 inches

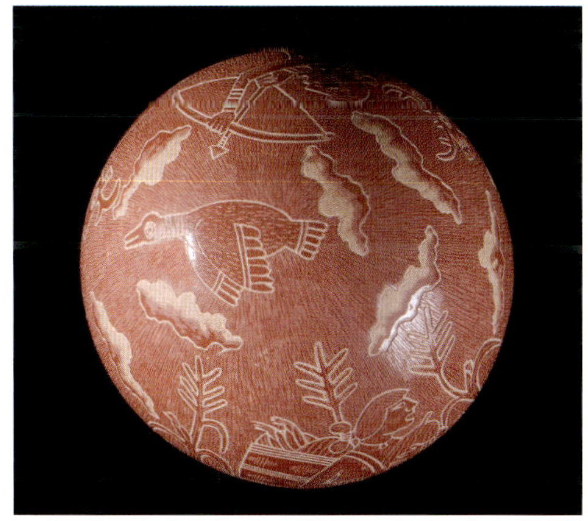

Artist: **Romero, Susan "Snowflake"** (1955 -)
Date: c. 1997
Pueblo: Santa Clara
Family: Great-granddaughter of Sara Fina Tafoya
Height: 2.5 inches
Diameter: 1.75 inches

Santa Clara Pueblo

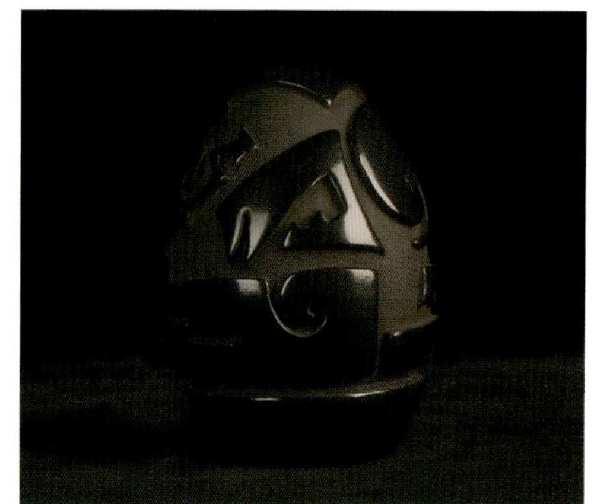

Artist: **Cain, Linda** (1949 -)
Date: c. 1985-90
Pueblo: Santa Clara
Family: Great-granddaughter of Sara Fina Tafoya
Height: 5.5 inches
Diameter: 3.5 inches

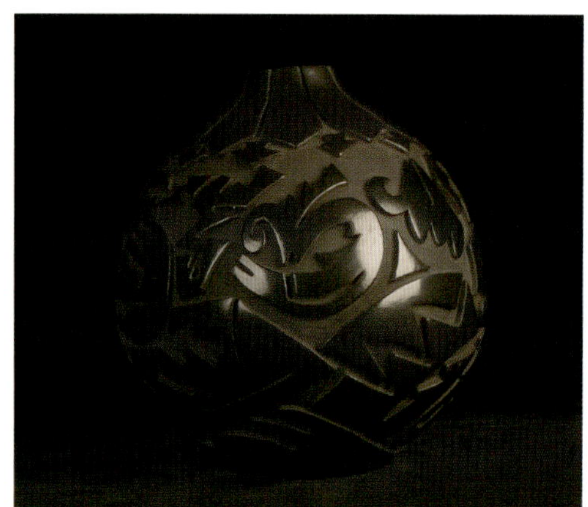

Artist: **Cain, Linda** (1949 -)
Date: 1992
Pueblo: Santa Clara
Family: Great-granddaughter of Sara Fina Tafoya
Height: 8 inches
Diameter: 5 inches

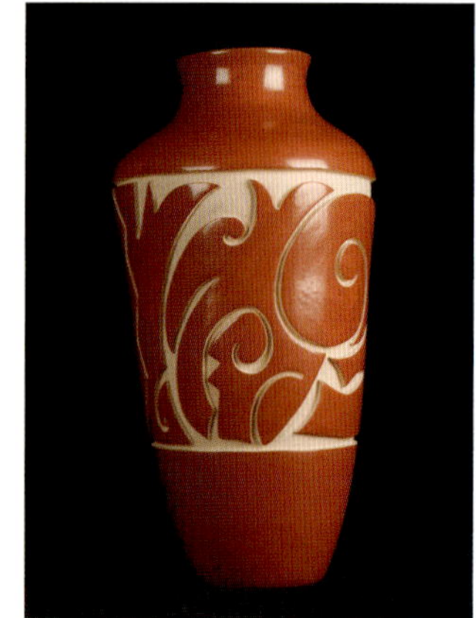

Artist: **Cain, Linda** (1949 -)
Date: 2002
Pueblo: Santa Clara
Family: Great-granddaughter of Sara Fina Tafoya
Height: 12.5 inches
Diameter: 6 inches

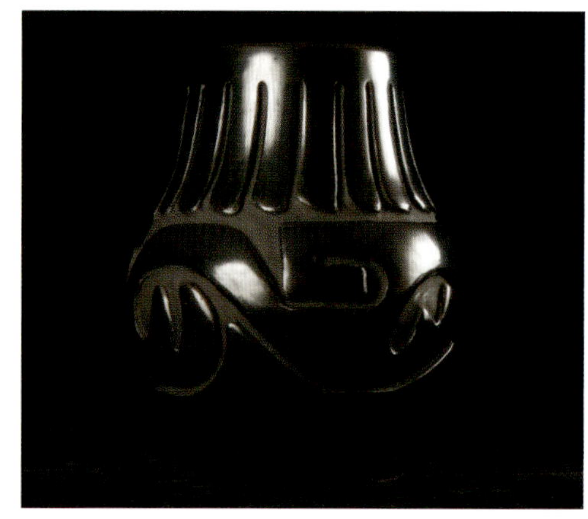

Artist: **Chevarria (also Chavarria), Stella** (1939 -)
Date: c. 1970s
Pueblo: Santa Clara
Family: Great-granddaughter of Sara Fina Tafoya
Height: 6.25 inches
Diameter: 5.25 inches

Santa Clara Pueblo

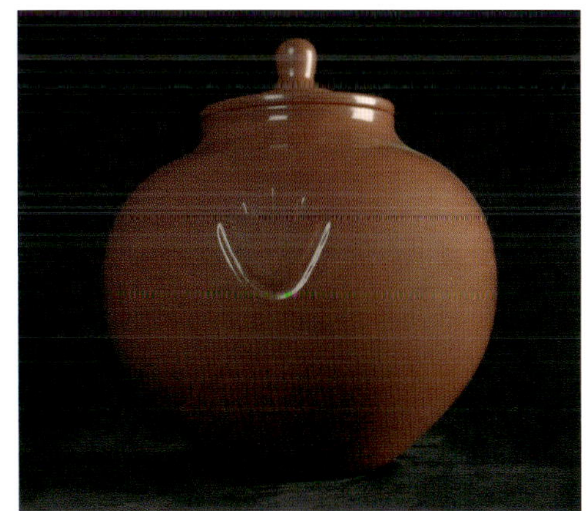

Artist: **Ebelacker, James** (1960 -)
Date: 2002
Pueblo: Santa Clara
Family: Great-grandson of Sara Fina Tafoya
Height: 11 inches
Diameter: 11.5 inches

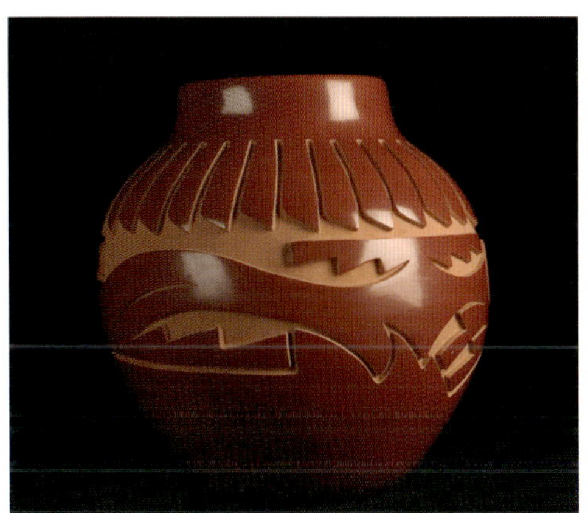

Artist: **Vigil, Ethel** (1950 -)
Date: c. 2004
Pueblo: Santa Clara
Family: Great-granddaughter of Sara Fina Tafoya
Height: 7 inches
Diameter: 7 inches

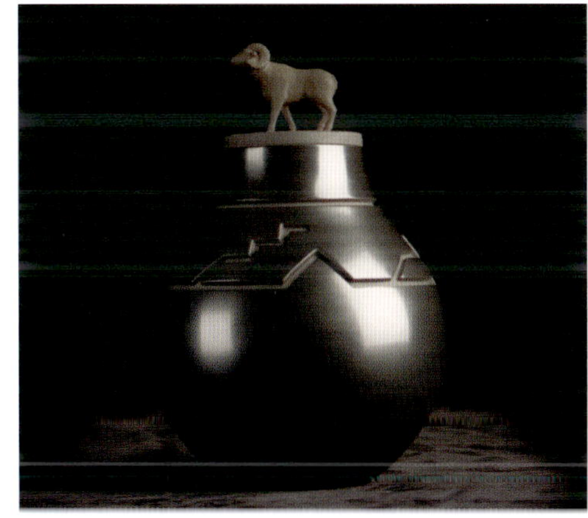

Artist: **Roller, Jeff** (1963 -)
Date: 1999
Pueblo: Santa Clara
Family: Great-grandson of Sara Fina Tafoya
Height: 8.5 inches with lid
Diameter: 4.75 inches

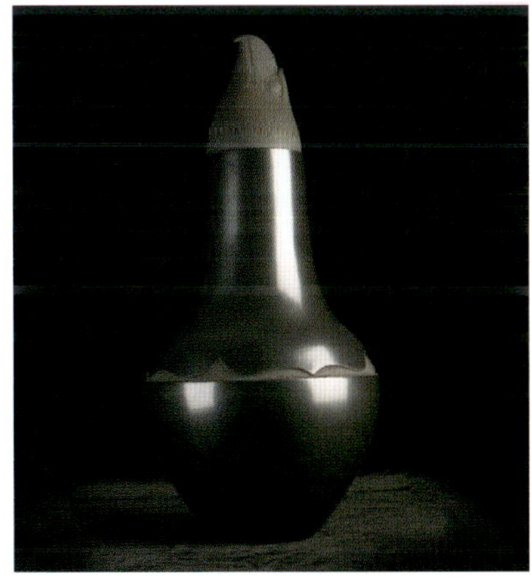

Artist: **Roller, Jeff** (1963 -)
Date: 2000
Pueblo: Santa Clara
Family: Great-grandson of Sara Fina Tafoya
Height: 15.5 inches with lid
Diameter: 7 inches

Santa Clara Pueblo

Artist: **Youngblood, Nancy** (1955 -)
Date: 1991
Pueblo: Santa Clara
Family: Great-granddaughter of Sara Fina Tafoya
Height: 6.25 inches with lid
Diameter: 4.25 inches

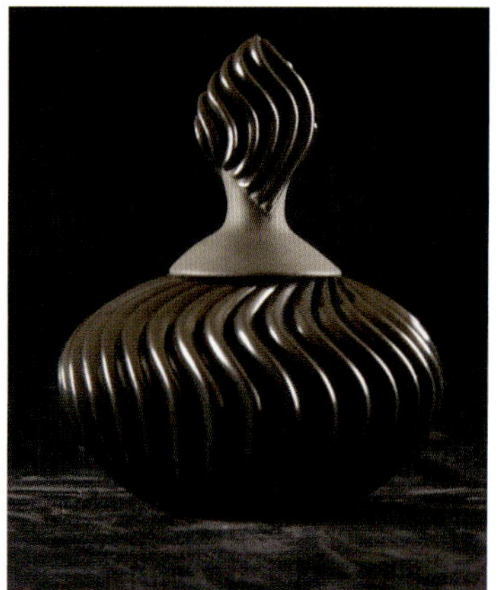

Artist: **Youngblood, Nancy** (1955 -)
Date: 2003
Pueblo: Santa Clara
Family: Great-granddaughter of Sara Fina Tafoya
Height: 10 inches with lid
Diameter: 6 inches

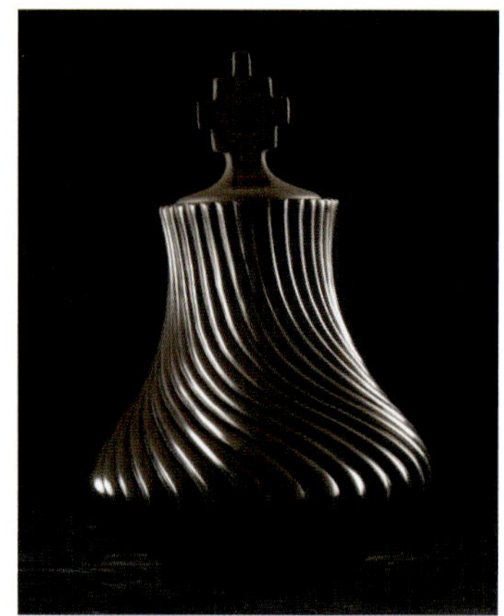

Artist: **Youngblood, Nancy** (1955 -
Date: 2003
Pueblo: Santa Clara
Family: Great-granddaughter of Sara Fina Tafoya
Height: 3.5 inches
Diameter: 6 inches

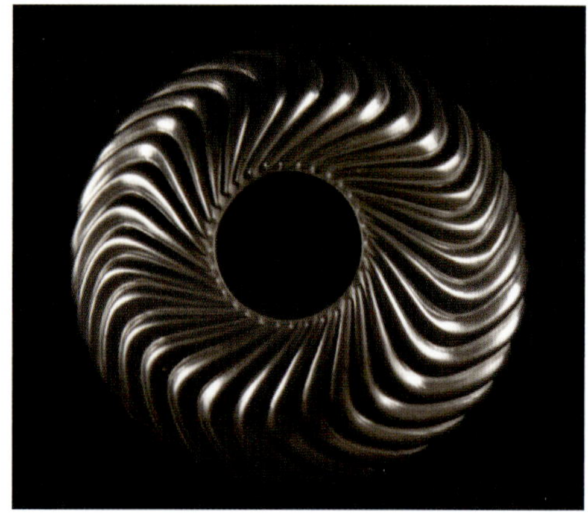

Artist: **Youngblood, Nancy** (1955 -)
Date: 1993
Pueblo: Santa Clara
Family: Great-granddaughter of Sara Fina Tafoya
Height: 6.5 inches
Diameter: 9 inches

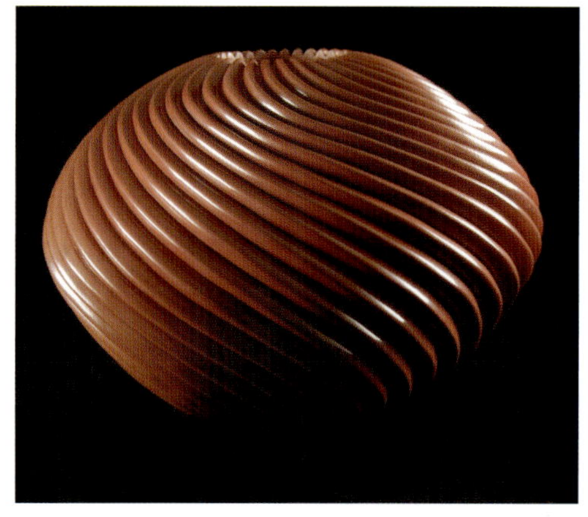

Santa Clara Pueblo

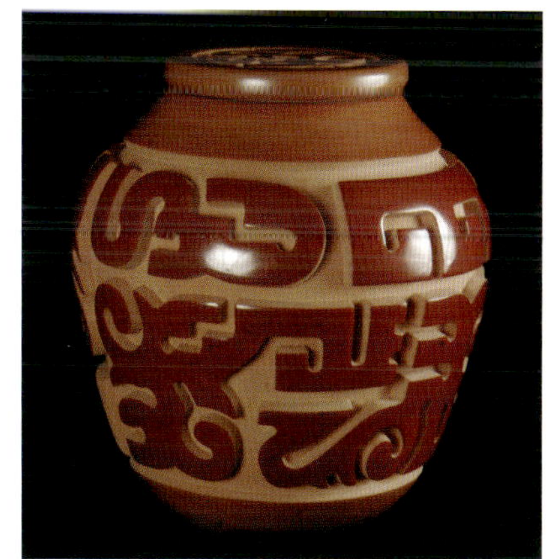

Artist: **Youngblood, Nathan** (1954 -)
Date: c. 1995
Pueblo: Santa Clara
Family: Great-grandson of Sara Fina Tafoya
Height: 6.75 inches
Diameter: 6 inches

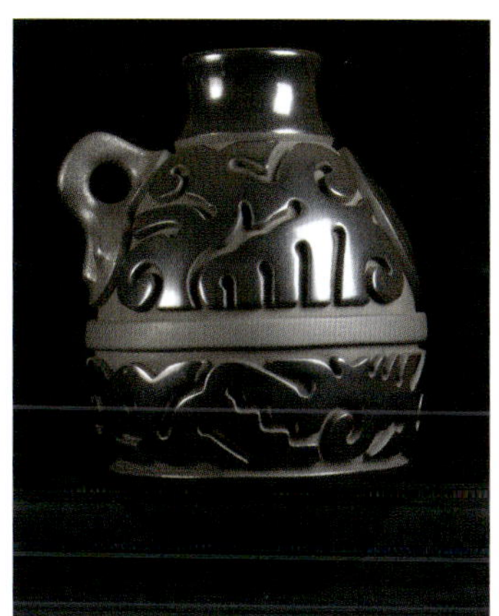

Artist: **Youngblood, Nathan** (1954 -)
Date: 2005
Pueblo: Santa Clara
Family: Great-grandson of Sara Fina Tafoya
Height: 10.5 inches
Diameter: 6.5 inches

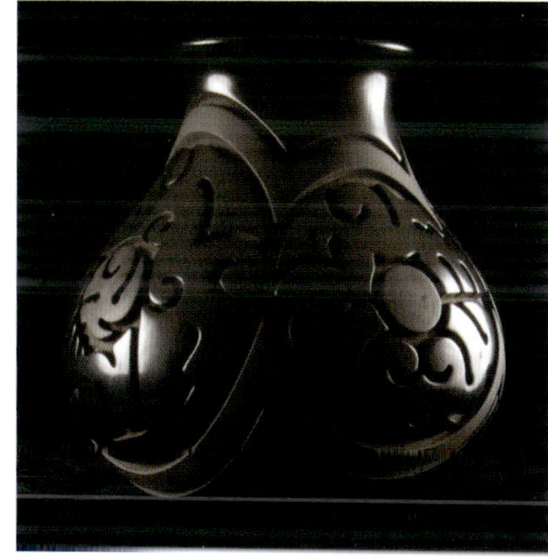

Artist: **Youngblood, Nathan** (1954 -)
Date: c. 1995-2000
Pueblo: Santa Clara
Family: Great-grandson of Sara Fina Tafoya
Height: 10.25 inches
Diameter: 8.5 inches

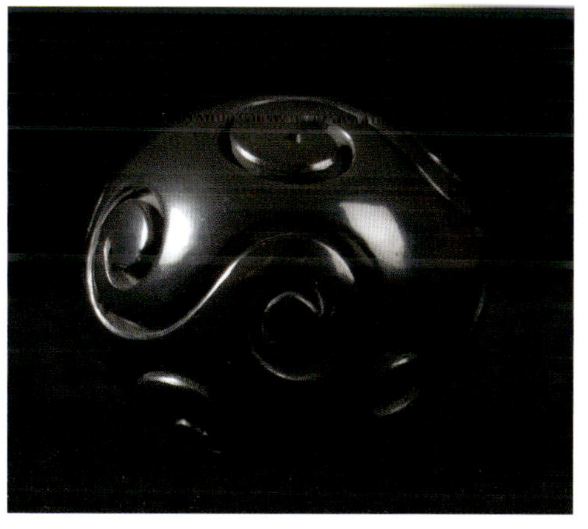

Artist: **Tafoya-Oyenque, Linda** (1962 -)
Date: 1988
Pueblo: Santa Clara
Family: Great-granddaughter of Sara Fina Tafoya
Height: 2.5 inches
Diameter: 2.5 inches

Santa Clara Pueblo

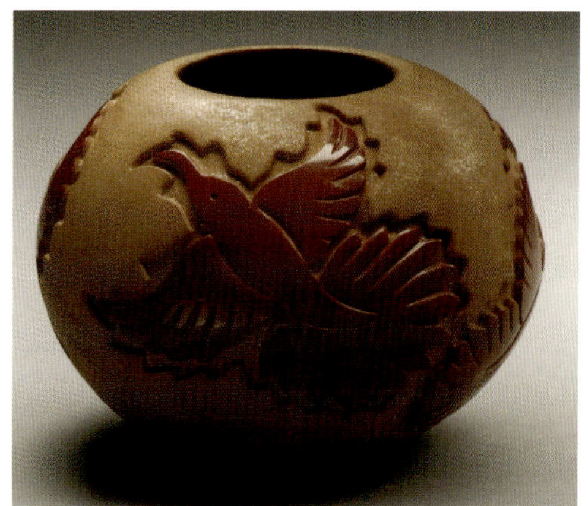

Artist: **Tafoya-Oyenque, Linda** (1962 -)
Date: c. 1997
Pueblo: Santa Clara
Family: Great-granddaughter of Sara Fina Tafoya
Height: 5 inches
Diameter: 6 inches

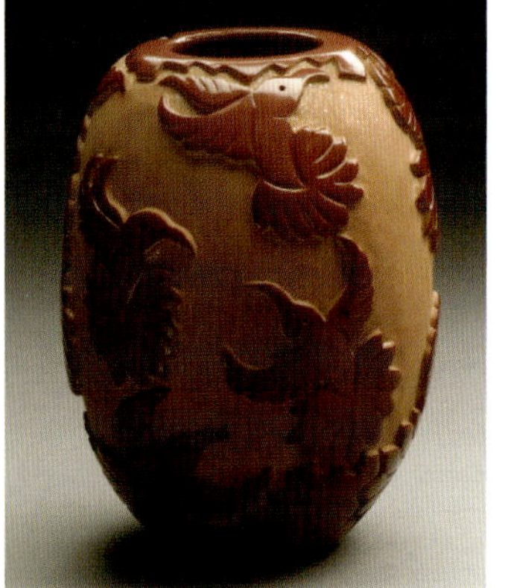

Artist: **Tafoya-Oyenque, Linda** (1962 -)
Date: 1997
Pueblo: Santa Clara
Family: Great-granddaughter of Sara Fina Tafoya
Height: 8.5 inches
Diameter: 6 inches

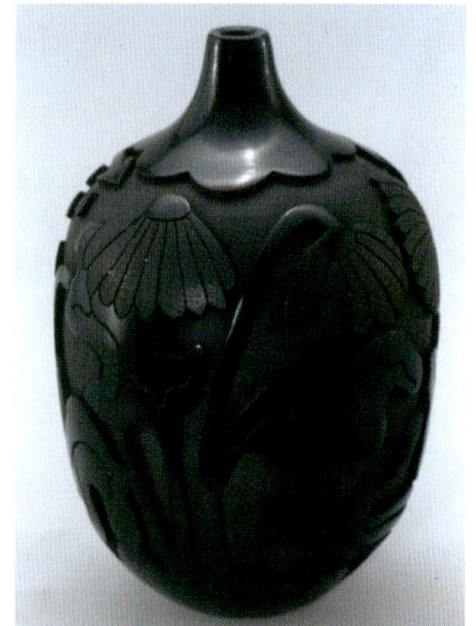

Artist: **Borts-Medlock, Autumn** (1967 -)
Date: 2005
Pueblo: Santa Clara
Family: Great-great-granddaughter of Sara Fina Tafoya
Height: 10.5 inches
Diameter: 7 inches

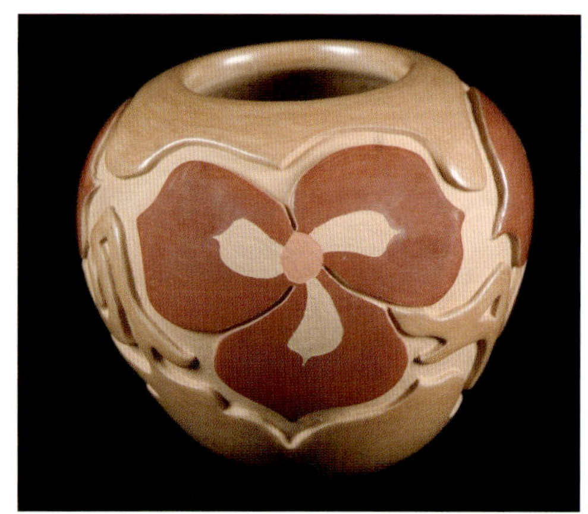

Artist: **Borts-Medlock, Autumn** (1967 -)
Date: 1995
Pueblo: Santa Clara
Family: Great-great-granddaughter of Sara Fina Tafoya
Height: 4 inches
Diameter: 4 inches

Santa Clara Pueblo

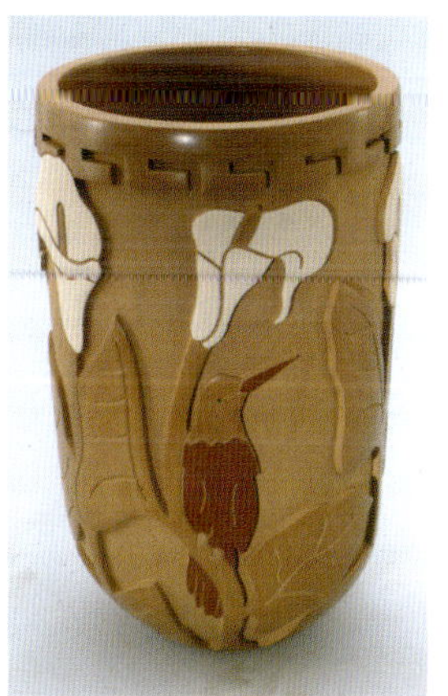

Artist: **Borts-Medlock, Autumn** (1967 -)
Date: 2001
Pueblo: Santa Clara
Family: Great-great-granddaughter of Sara Fina Tafoya
Height: 10 inches
Diameter: 6 inches

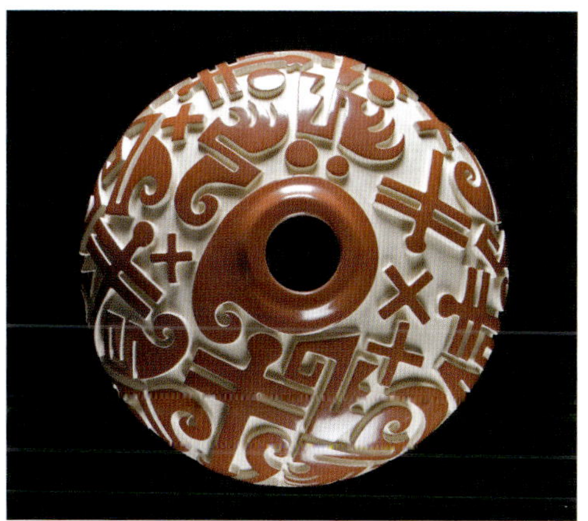

Artist: **Garcia, Tammy** (1969 -)
Date: 1994
Pueblo: Santa Clara
Family: Great-great-granddaughter of Sara Fina Tafoya
Height: 4.25 inches
Diameter: 7 inches

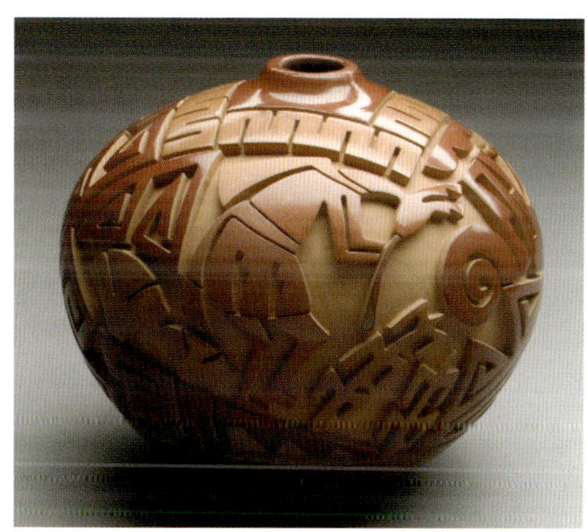

Artist: **Garcia, Tammy** (1969 -)
Date: 1996
Pueblo: Santa Clara
Family: Great-great-granddaughter of Sara Fina Tafoya
Height: 6.5 inches
Diameter: 7 inches

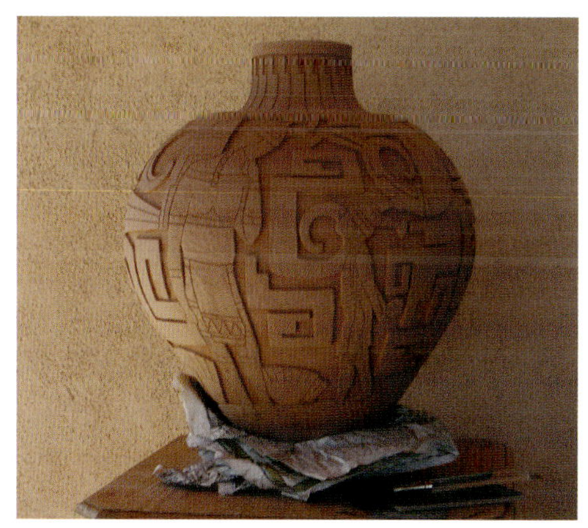

Artist: **Garcia, Tammy** (1969 -)
Date: 2007 (pictured in progress)
Pueblo: Santa Clara
Family: Great-great-granddaughter of Sara Fina Tafoya
Height: 18.5 inches
Diameter: 15.75 inches

The Tafoya Family

Santa Clara Pueblo

Artist: **Tafoya, Emily** (c. 1960 -)
Date: n.d.
Pueblo: Santa Clara (of Kiowa descent)
Family: Married to Ray Tafoya
Height: 2.25 inches
Diameter: 2.5 inches

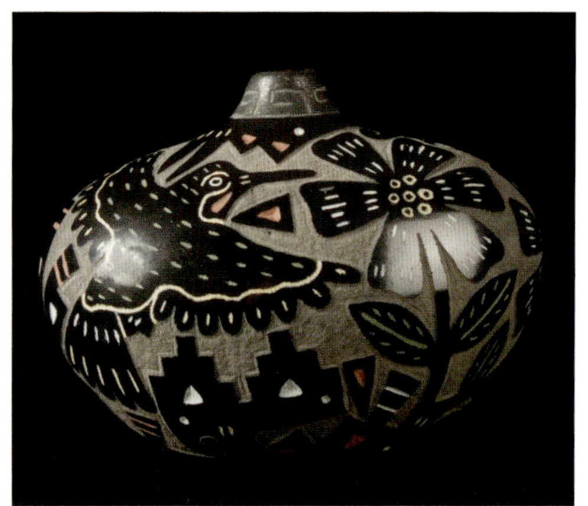

Artist: **Tafoya Moquino, Jennifer** (1977 -)
Date: c. 2002-04
Pueblo: Santa Clara
Family: Daughter of Emily and Ray Tafoya
Height: 9.5 inches
Diameter: 5 inches

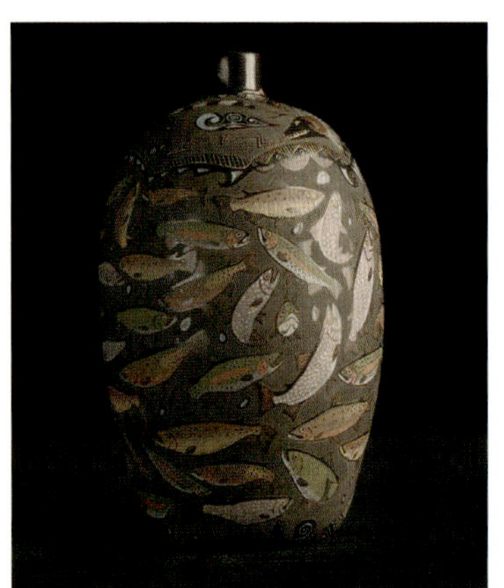

The Gutierrez Family

Artist: **Gutierrez, Margaret & Luther**
(1936 -) & (1911 - 1987)
Date: c. 1980s
Pueblo: Santa Clara
Family: Gutierrez
Height: 4 inches
Diameter: 5 inches

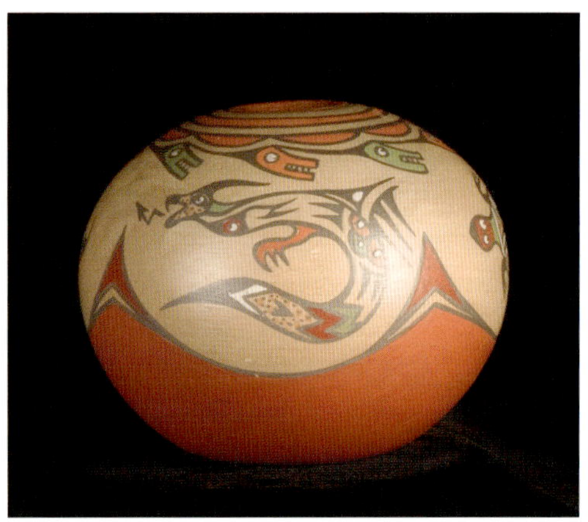

Artist: **Gutierrez, Margaret & Luther**
(1936 -) & (1911 - 1987)
Date: c. 1980s
Pueblo: Santa Clara
Family: Gutierrez
Height: 6 inches
Diameter: 5.5 inches

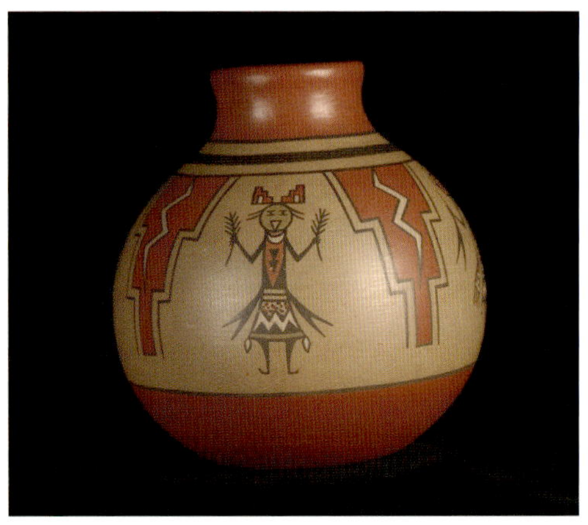

Santa Clara Pueblo

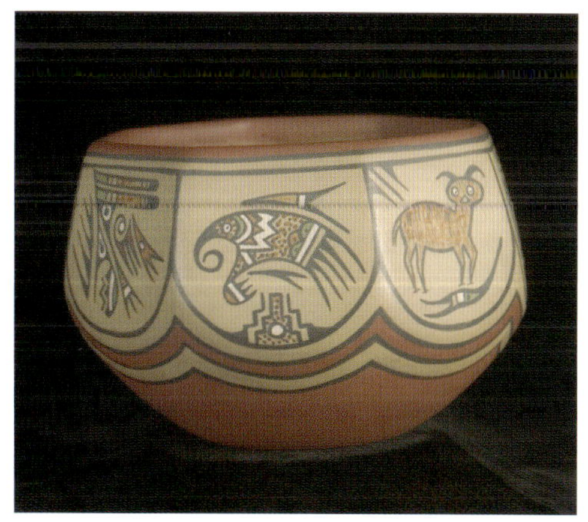

Artist: **Gutierrez, Margaret & Luther**
(1936 -) & (1911 - 1987)
Date: c. 1975
Pueblo: Santa Clara
Family: Gutierrez
Height: 4.5 inches
Diameter: 7 inches

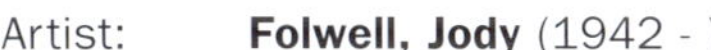

Other Santa Clara Potters

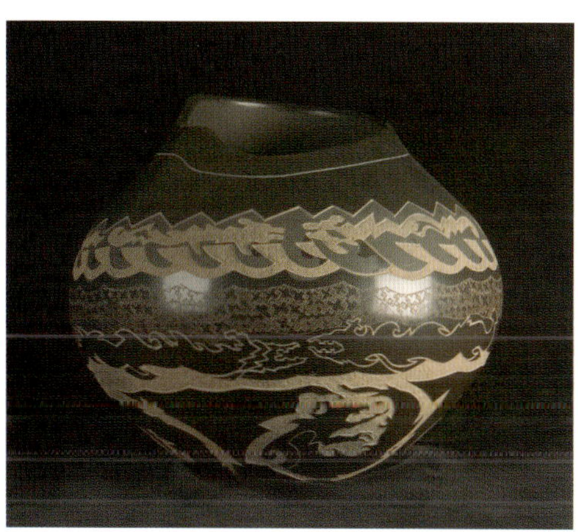

Artist: **Folwell, Jody** (1942 -)
Date: c. 1997
Pueblo: Santa Clara
Height: 9.5 inches
Diameter: 9.5 inches

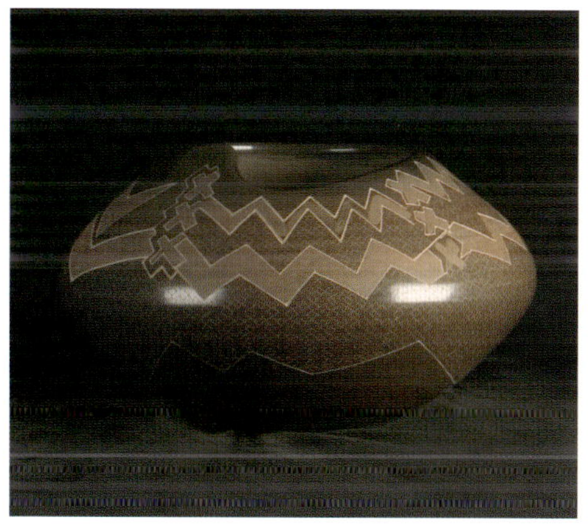

Artist: **Folwell, Jody** (1942 -)
Date: c. 1996
Pueblo: Santa Clara
Height: 5 inches
Diameter: 7.75 inches

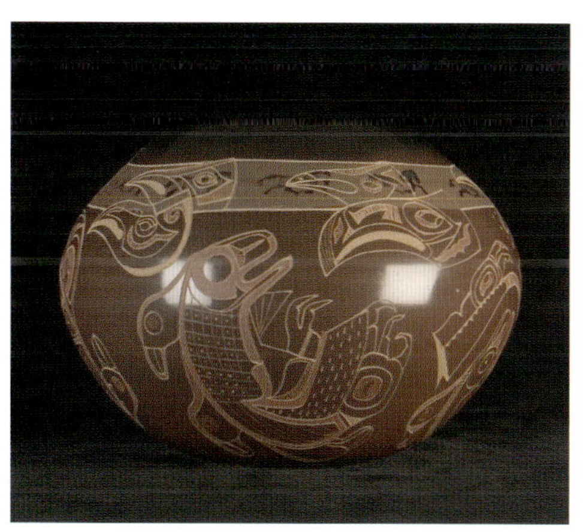

Artist: **Folwell, Jody** (1942 -)
Date: c. 1997
Pueblo: Santa Clara
Height: 6.5 inches
Diameter: 9 inches

Santa Clara Pueblo

Artist: **Folwell, Susan** (1970 -)
Title: "Slaughter of the Lambs"
Date: c. 2001
Pueblo: Santa Clara
Height: 11 inches
Diameter: 16 inches

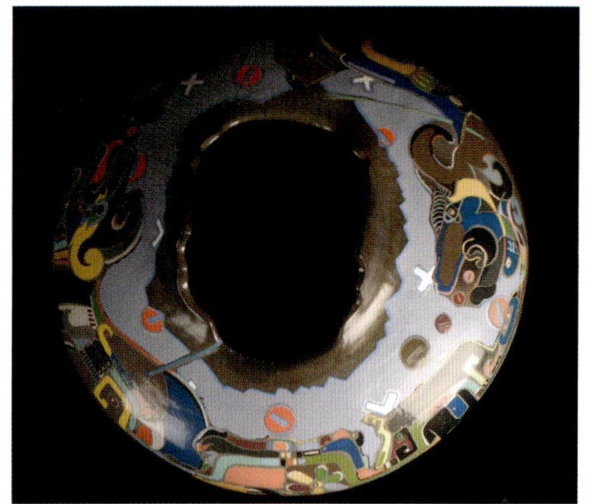

Artist: **Folwell, Susan** (1970 -)
Title: "Medicine Man"
Date: c. 2005
Pueblo: Santa Clara
Height: 14.5 inches
Diameter: 7 inches

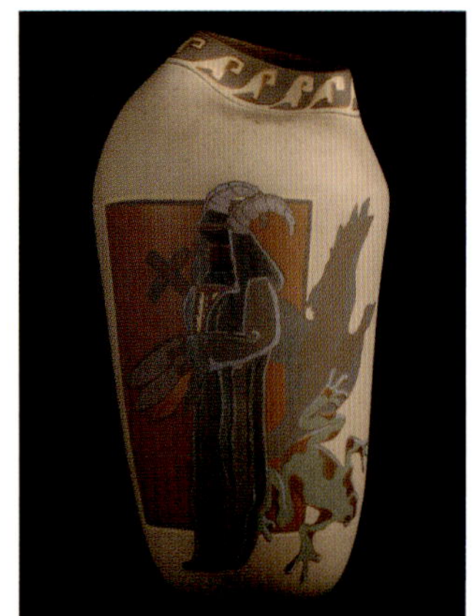

Artist: **Folwell, Susan** (1970 -)
Title: "Coyotes"
Date: c. 2004
Pueblo: Santa Clara
Height: 11 inches
Diameter: 10 inches

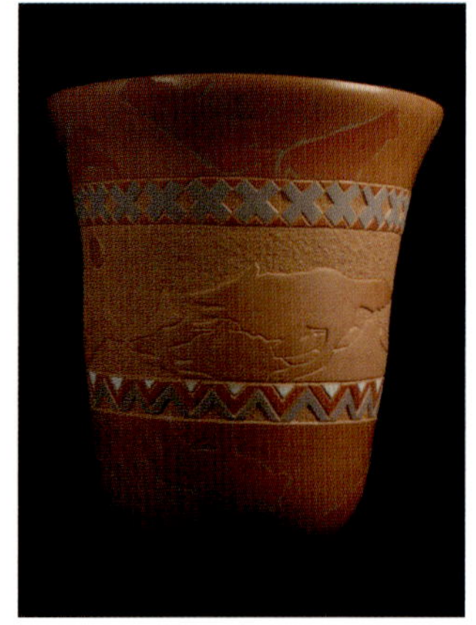

Artist: **Folwell, Susan** (1970 -)
Title: "Homage to the Pottery Gods"
Date: 2007
Pueblo: Santa Clara
Height: 12.5 inches
Diameter: 11 inches

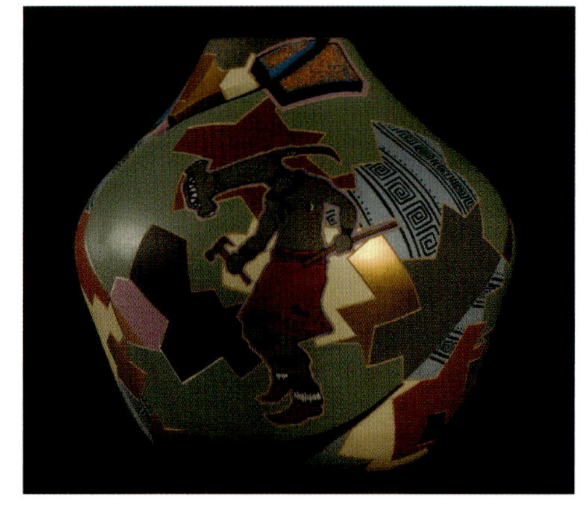

Santa Clara Pueblo

Artist: **Garcia, Effie** (c. 1953 -)
Date: c. 1980s
Pueblo: Santa Clara
Height: 3 inches
Diameter: 4 inches

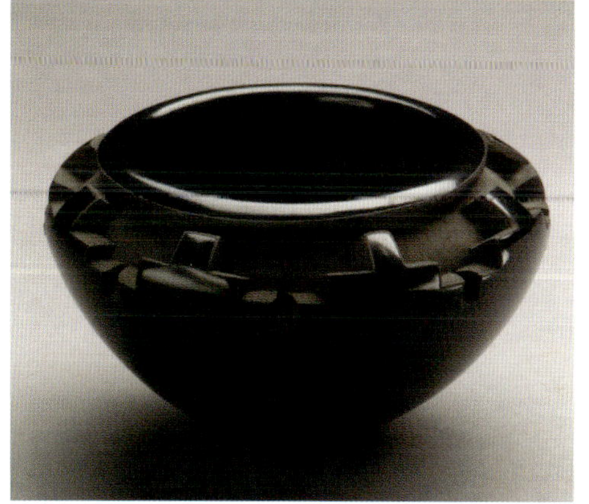

Artist: **Garcia, Gloria "Goldenrod"** (1942 -)
Date: c. 1998
Pueblo: Santa Clara
Height: 2.25 inches
Diameter: 2.75 inches

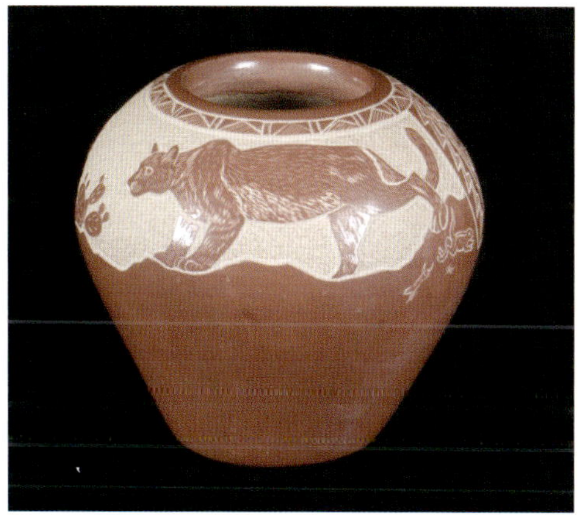

Artist: **Gutierrez, Lois** (active 1970 - 1993)
Date: 1998
Pueblo: Santa Clara
Height: 12 inches
Diameter: 11 inches

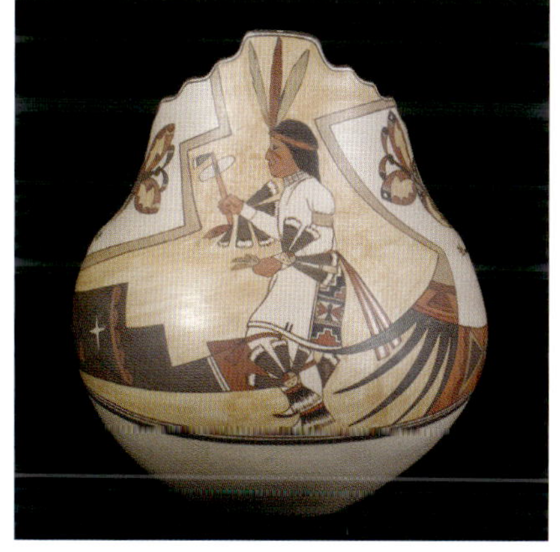

Artist: **Haungooah, Art Cody** (1943 - 1985)
Date: 1974
Pueblo: Santa Clara (of Kiowa descent)
Height: 2 inches
Diameter: 2 inches

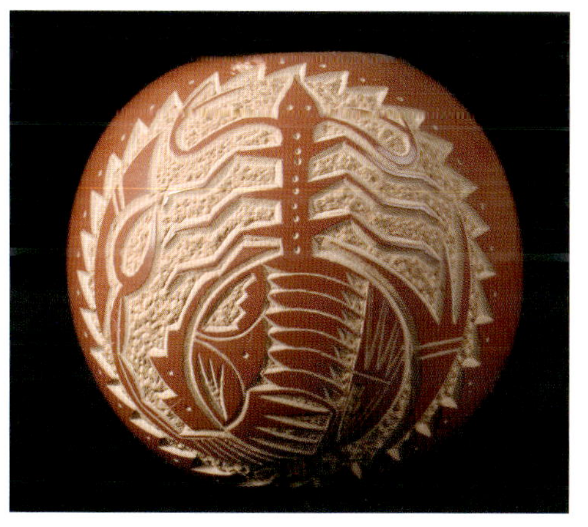

Santa Clara Pueblo

Artist: **Haungooah, Art Cody** (1943 - 1985)
Date: 1976
Pueblo: Santa Clara (of Kiowa descent)
Height: 0.875 inch
Diameter: 1.75 inches

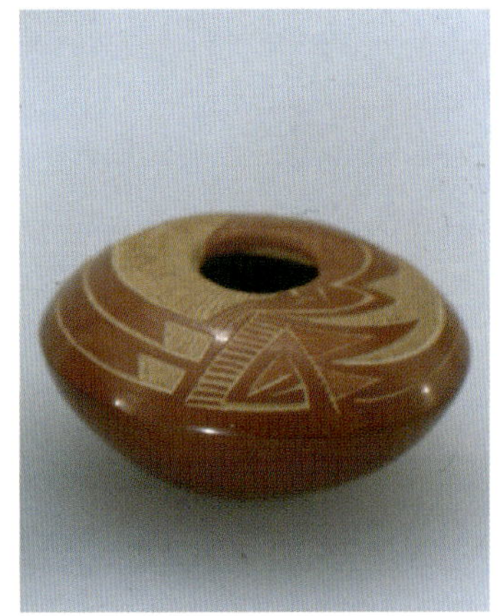

Artist: **Haungooah, Art Cody** (1943 - 1985)
Date: c. 1975-1980
Pueblo: Santa Clara (of Kiowa descent)
Height: 1 inch
Diameter: 0.75 inches

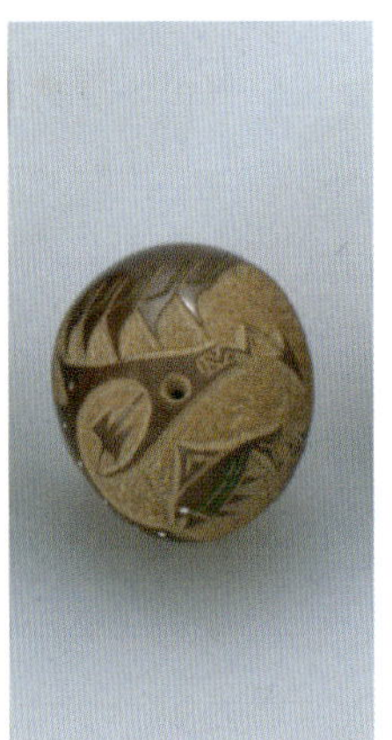

Artist: **Moquino, Corn** (active 1963 - present)
Date: 1992
Pueblo: Santa Clara (originally Zia)
Height: 12.25 inches with lid
Diameter: 6.75 inches

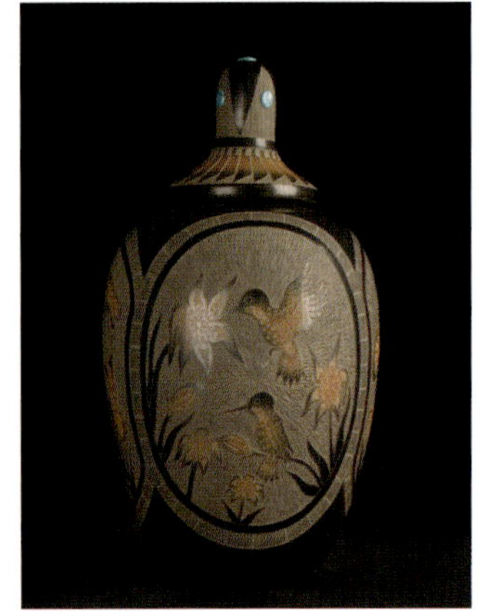

Artist: **Naranjo, Forrest** (1963 -)
Date: c. 2001
Pueblo: Santa Clara
Height: 4 inches
Diameter: 3.5 inches

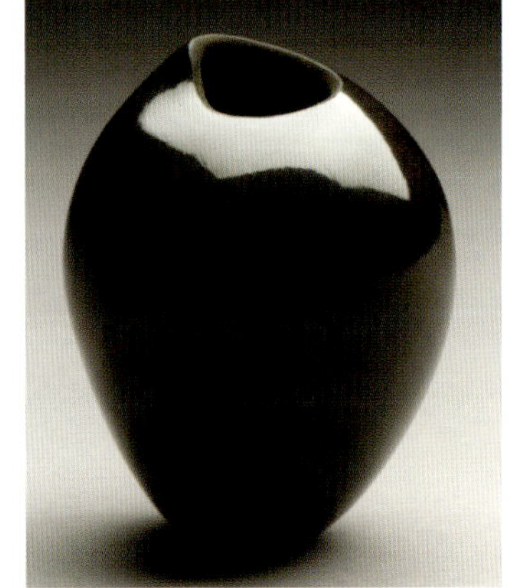

Santa Clara Pueblo

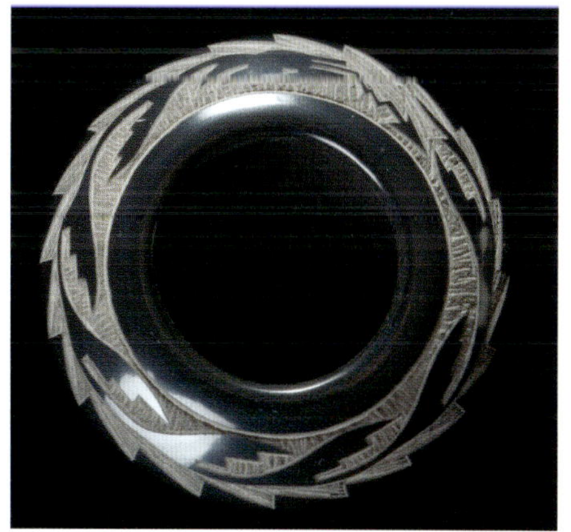

Artist: **Naranjo, Geraldine "Geri"** (active 1975 - present)
Date: c. 1990
Pueblo: Santa Clara
Height: 0.875 inch
Diameter: 1.5 inches

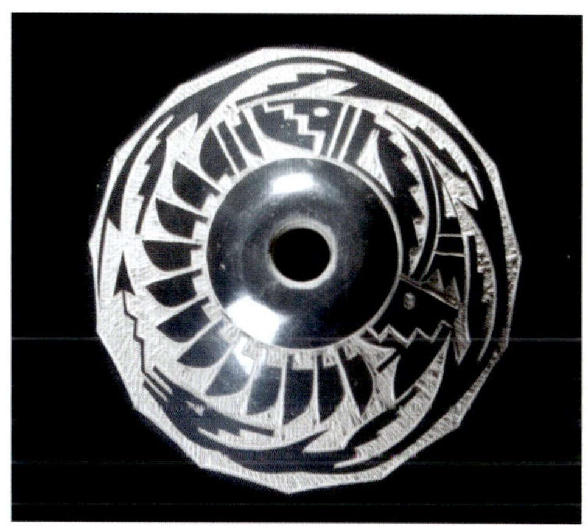

Artist: **Naranjo, Geraldine "Geri"** (active 1975 - present)
Date: c. 1995
Pueblo: Santa Clara
Height: 1.25 inches
Diameter: 1.25 inches

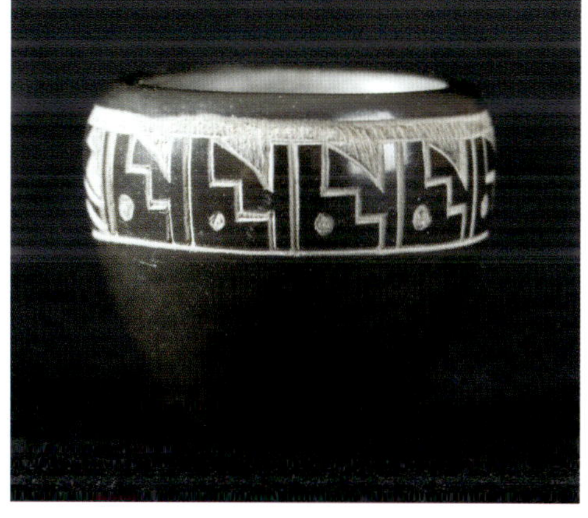

Artist: **Naranjo, Monica** (1976 -)
Date: c. 1995
Pueblo: Santa Clara
Height: 1.25 inches
Diameter: 1.25 inches

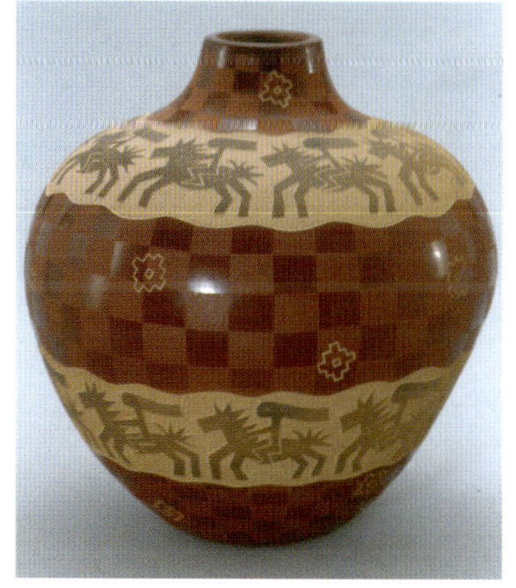

Artist: **Naranjo, Jody** (1969 -)
Date: 2006
Pueblo: Santa Clara
Height: 9 inches
Diameter: 8 inches

Santa Clara Pueblo

Artist: **Naranjo, Paul** (c. 1957 - 2002)
Date: c. 1990-95
Pueblo: Santa Clara
Height: 13.5 inches
Diameter: 11 inches

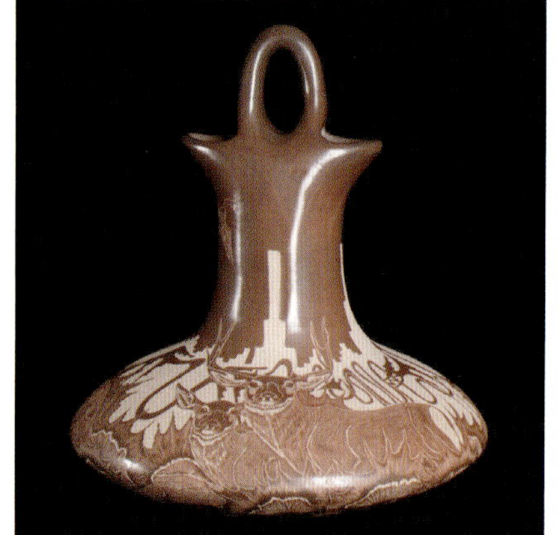

Artist: **Naranjo, Paul** (c. 1957 - 2002)
Date: c. 1990-95
Pueblo: Santa Clara
Height: 6 inches
Diameter: 13 inches

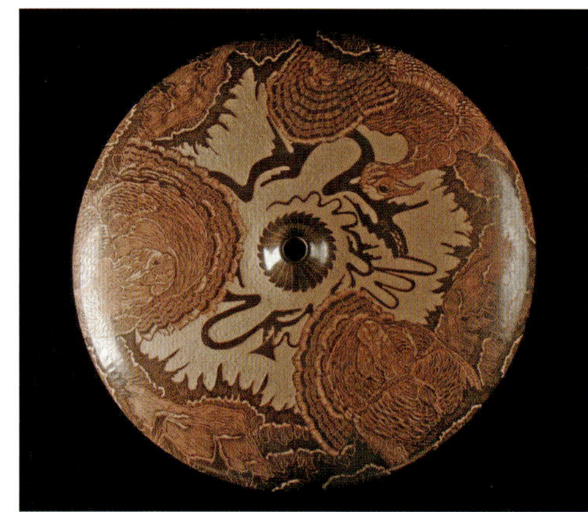

Artist: **Shupla, Helen** (1928 - 1985)
Date: c. 1970s
Pueblo: Santa Clara
Height: 9.5 inches
Diameter: 7 inches

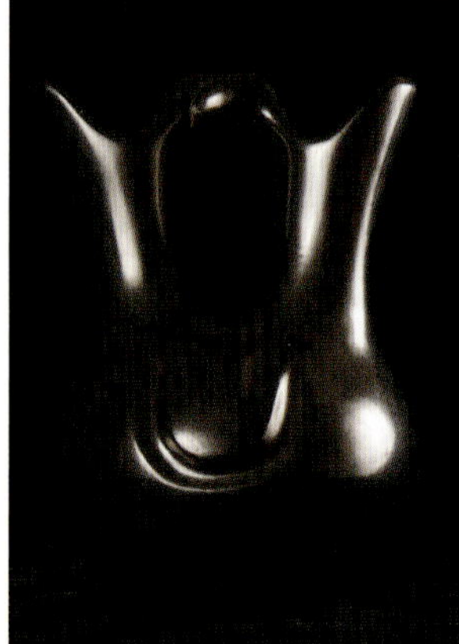

Artist: **Shupla, Helen** (1928 - 1985)
Date: c. 1970s
Pueblo: Santa Clara
Height: 7 inches
Diameter: 11 inches

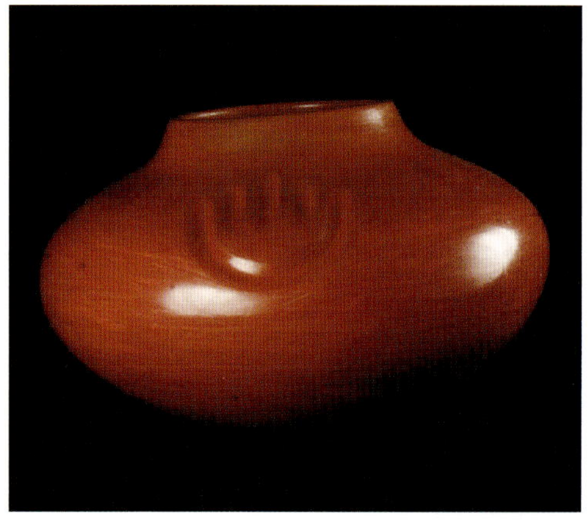

Santa Clara Pueblo

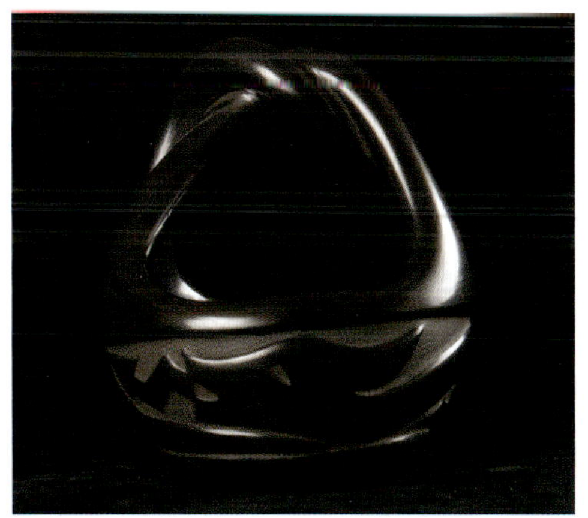

Artist: **Singer, Mary** (1936 -)
Date: c. 1980s
Pueblo: Santa Clara
Height: 7 inches
Diameter: 6 inches

Santo Domingo Pueblo

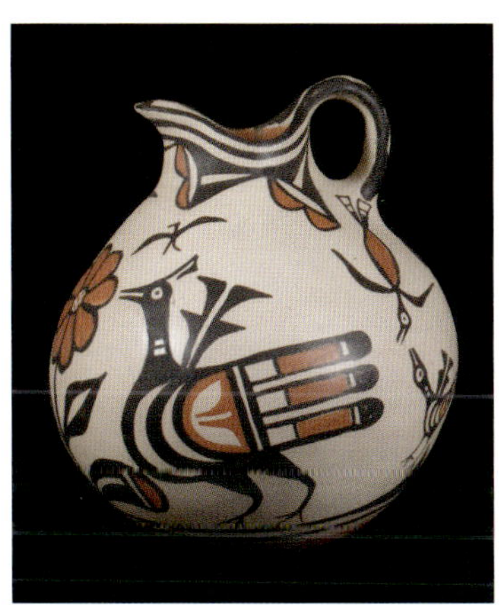

Artist: **Tenorio, Robert** (1950 -)
Date: 2000
Pueblo: Santo Domingo
Height: 10 inches
Diameter: 10 inches

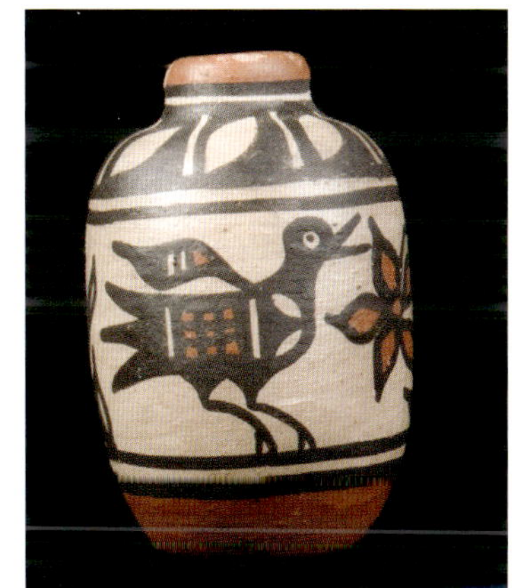

Artist: **Tenorio, Thomas** (1963 -)
Date: 1992
Pueblo: Santo Domingo
Height: 1.75 inches
Diameter: 1.25 inches

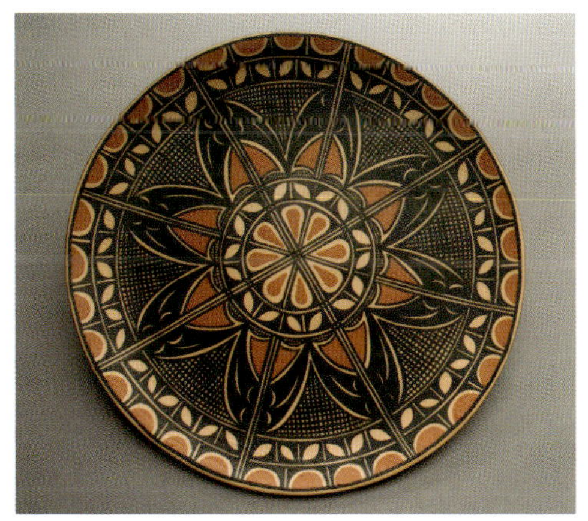

Artist: **Tenorio, Thomas** (1963 -)
Date: 2002
Pueblo: Santo Domingo
Diameter: 12 inches

Wyandot

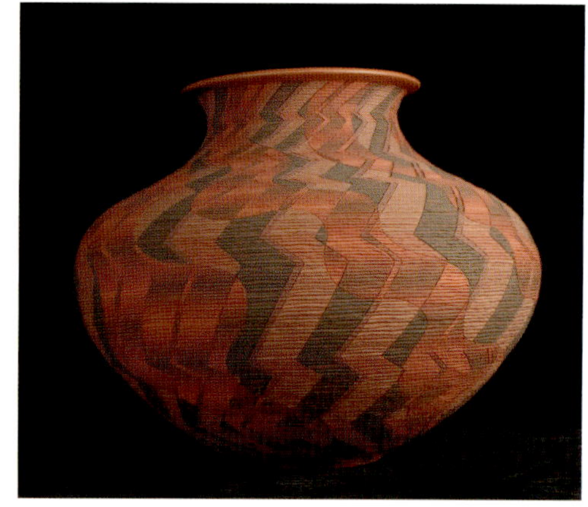

Artist: **Smith, Richard Zane** (1955 -)
Date: 2003
Tribe: Wyandot
Height: 10.25 inches
Diameter: 12 inches

Zuni Pueblo

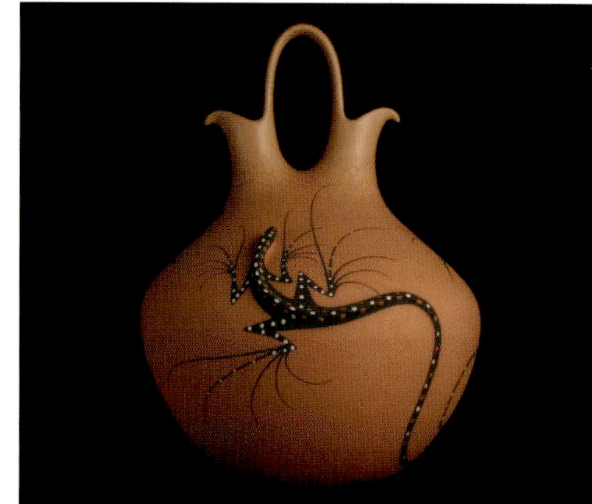

Artist: **Cellicion, Deldrick**
Date: c. 2004
Pueblo: Zuni
Height: 14 inches
Diameter: 9.25 inches

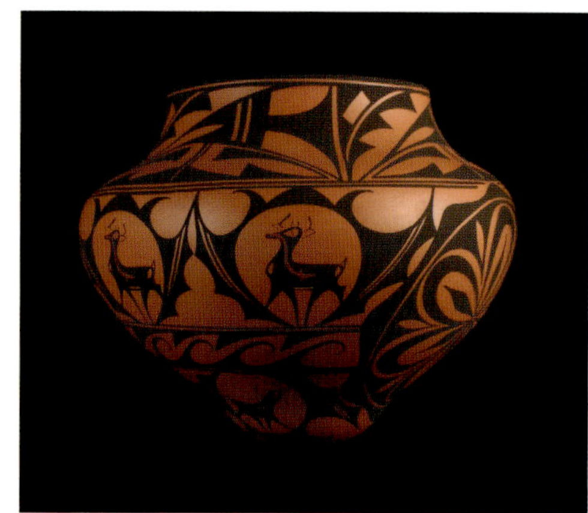

Artist: **Peynetsa, Anderson**
Date: 2001
Pueblo: Zuni
Height: 10 inches
Diameter: 12 inches

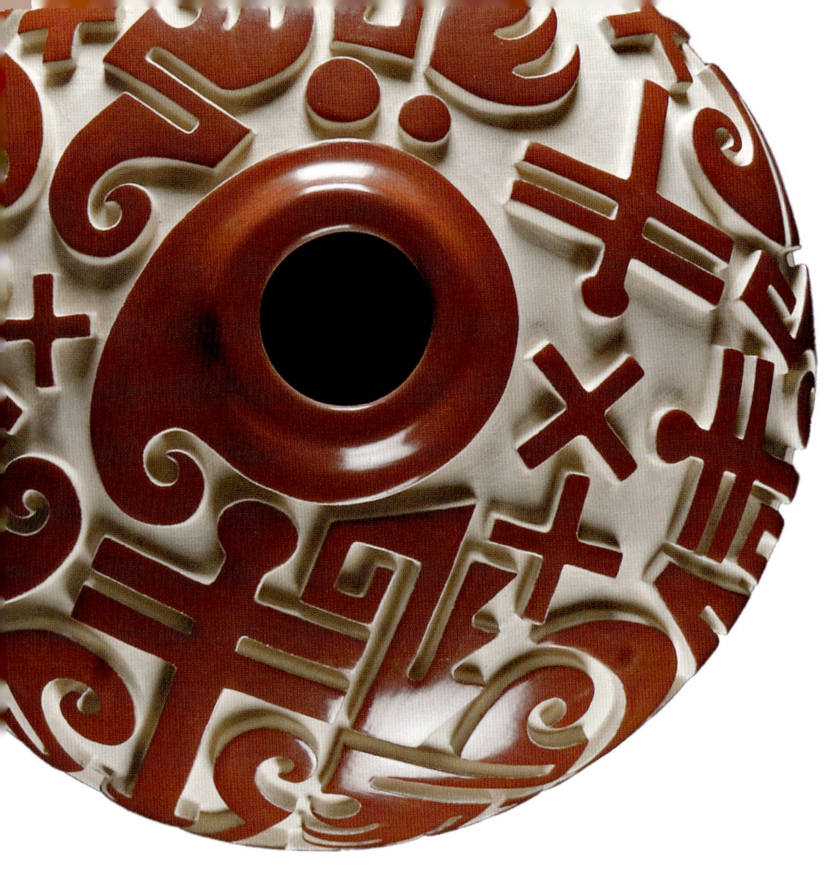

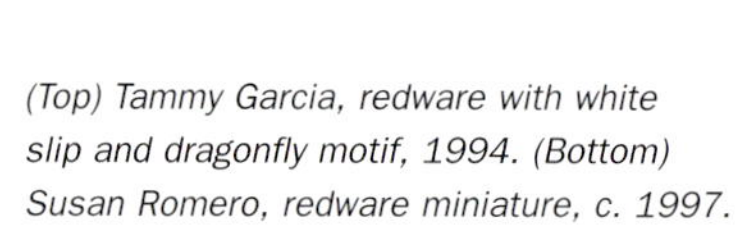

(Top) Tammy Garcia, redware with white slip and dragonfly motif, 1994. (Bottom) Susan Romero, redware miniature, c. 1997.

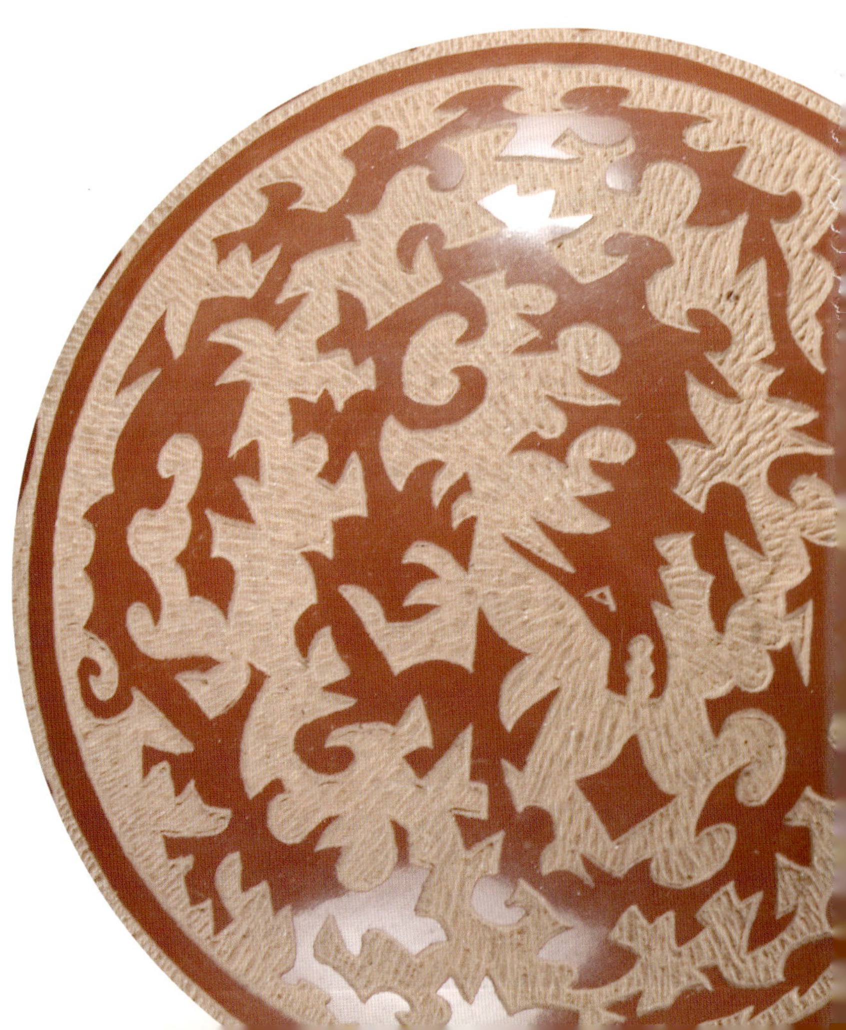

Bibliography

Anderson, Duane. "All That Glitters: The Emergence of Native American Micaceous Art Pottery in Northern New Mexico." Santa Fe: School of American Research Press, 1999.

Bassman, Theda. "Treasures of the Navajo." Flagstaff: Northland Publishing Co., 1997.

Blair, Mary Ellen. "The Legacy of a Master Potter: Nampeyo and Her Descendants." Tucson: Rio Nuevo Publishers, 1999.

Blair, Mary Ellen, & Blair, Laurence. "Margaret Tafoya: A Tewa Potter's Heritage and Legacy." Westchester, PA: Schiffer Publishing, Ltd. 1986.

Clark, Garth. "Free Spirit: The New Native American Potter." 's-Hertogenbosch, Netherlands: Stedelijk Museum, 2006.

Cohen, Lee M., ed. "Art of Clay: Timeless Pottery of the Southwest." Santa Fe: Clear Light Publishers, 1993.

Collins, John E. "Hopi Traditions in Pottery and Painting Honoring Grace Chapella, Potter (1874-)." Boston: NU Masters Gallery, 1977.

Collins, John E. "Nampeyo, Hopi Potter (Her Artistry and Her Legacy)" Northland Press: Flagstaff, 1974

Collins, John E. and Dockstader, Frederick J. "A Tribute to Lucy M. Lewis: Acoma Potter." Museum of North Orange County, 1975.

Desdera, Don. "Artistry in Clay." Flagstaff: Northland Publishing Co., 1985.

Dillingham, Rick. "Fourteen Families in Pueblo Pottery." Albuquerque: University of New Mexico Press, 1974.

Dillingham, Rick. "Seven Families in Pueblo Pottery." Albuquerque: University of New Mexico Press, 1974.

Fauntleroy, Gussie. "The Ones to Watch." Southwestern Art. August 2005, p. 175.

Fauntleroy, Gussie. "Swirling with Success." Indian Market, June 2006, pp. 92-8.

Fauntleroy, Gussie. "Translating Tradition: New Mexico's Russell Sanchez Blends Old and New Ideas," Southwest Art Magazine, May 2006.

Frisbie, Theodore R. "The Influence of J. Walter Fewkes on Nampeyo: Fact or Fancy?" In Shroeder, Albert H. ed. The Changing Ways of Southwestern Indians: A Historic Perspective. Glorieta, NM: Rio Grande Press, 1973, pp. 231-43.

Hayes, Allan & Blom, John. "Southwestern Pottery: Anasazi to Zuni." Flagstaff: Northland Publishing Co., 1996.

Hucko, Bruce. "Al Qöyawayma: Potter and Engineer Extraordinaire," Native Peoples Magazine, November/December, 2002.

Indyke, Dottie. "Lawrence Namoki." Southwest Art Magazine.

Jacka, Jerry & Gill, Spencer. "Pottery Treasures." Portland: Graphic Art Center Publishing Co., 1976.

Jacka, Jerry, & Jacka, Lois. "Beyond Tradition: Contemporary Indian Art and its Evolution." Flagstaff: Northland Press, 1988.

Jacka, Lois E. "Enduring Traditions." Flagstaff: Northland Publishing Co., 1994.

Johnson, Ken. "Art in Review: Virgil Ortiz." The New York Times, March 26, 2004, Leisure- Weekend.

Jung, Carl G. "Four archetypes: Mother/rebirth/spirit/trickster." Princeton, NJ: Princeton University Press, 1969.

Kramer, Barbara. "Nampeyo and Her Pottery." Tucson: University of Arizona Press, 2003.

Marriott, Alice. "Maria: The Potter of San Ildefonso." Norman: University of Oklahoma Press, 1948.

Martin, Douglas. "Margaret Tafoya, 96, Pueblo Potter Whose Work Found a Global Audience." The New York Times. March 5, 2001, Late Edition - Final, Section B, Page 6, Column 1.

Naranjo, Jose Ray. "Tewa Sae'Wa: Contemporary and Traditional Pottery." Espanola, NM: Naranjo Trading, 1986.

Peterson, Susan H. "Lucy M. Lewis: American Indian Potter." Tokyo: Kodansha International, 2nd Rev. Ed., 2004.

Peterson, Susan H. "Pottery of American Indian Women: The Legacy of Generations." Susan Ressler, ed., Abbeville Press and The National Museum of Women in the Arts, 1997.

Peterson, Susan H. "Maria Martinez: Five Generations of Potters." Washington D.c. : Smithsonian Institution Press, 1978.

Rose, Benjamin. "Tammy Garcia: Form Without Boundaries." Irving, Texas: Tapestry Press, 2003.

Schaaf, Gregory. "Hopi-Tewa Pottery: 500 Artist Biographies, Ca. 1800-Present." Santa Fe: Center for Indigenous Arts & Cultures, 1998.

Schaaf, Gregory. "Pueblo Indian Pottery: 750 Artist Biographies, Ca. 1800-Present." Santa Fe: Center for Indigenous Arts & Cultures, 2000.

Schaaf, Gregory. "Pueblo Indian Pottery: 2000 Artist Biographies, c. 1800-Present." Santa Fe: Center for Indigenous Arts & Cultures, 2002.

Servin, James. "Virgil Ortiz: The Art and Times of a Santa Fe Artist." Woman to Woman, Spring 2003.

Spivey, Richard L. "Maria." Flagstaff: Northland Publishing Co., 1979.

Struever, Martha H. "Painted Perfection: The Pottery of Dextra Quotskuyva." Santa Fe: Wheelwright Museum of the American Indian, 2001.

Toulouse, Betty. "Pueblo Pottery of the New Mexico Indians." Santa Fe: Museum of New Mexico Press, 1977.

Trimble, Stephen. "Talking with the Clay." Santa Fe: School of American Research Press, 1987.

Whittington, Susan Roller. Eulogy for Margaret Tafoya. Mass of the Resurrection celebrated: Tuesday, February 27, 2001 9:00 a.m.

_________."The Pottery Jewels of Joseph Lonewolf." Phoenix, Arizona. The Dandick Company, 1975.

_________. "Traditions and New Ideas", Southwest Art Magazine, May 2006.

Index of Artists